Streams
~in the~
DESERT

Mrs. Charles E. Cowman

ZondervanPublishingHouse

Grand Rapids, Michigan

A Division of HarperCollins*Publishers*

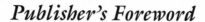

Publisher's Foreword

In 1925 the first edition of *Streams in the Desert* was released. In it were thoughts, quotations, and spiritual inspiration which had helped to sustain Mrs. Charles E. Cowman during her years of missionary work in Japan and China—particularly the six years she nursed her husband while he was dying. After two years and three thousand books in print it was suggested to Mrs. Cowman that since all her friends had copies, there was probably no need to print any more.

From this humble beginning *Streams in the Desert* has become a daily devotional classic, a leader in its field for more than forty years. At various times it has appeared in more than a dozen languages, and at present is in four foreign language editions. Its ministry is worldwide, unhindered by national, political, or geographic boundaries. From a royal palace in North Africa and a presidential mansion in Asia to wartime concentration camps . . . from primitive huts in remote corners of the world to elegantly furnished houses in cultural centers . . . to thousands of homes representing a cross section of the world today, *Streams in the Desert* continues to bring its spiritual refreshment, its words of encouragement and inspiration just suited for the moment's need.

For the readers of the millions of copies now in print, *Streams in the Desert* is more than a book—it is a living word of confidence and assurance, God's message for the day.

The Publisher

A Personal Word ...

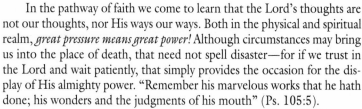

In the pathway of faith we come to learn that the Lord's thoughts are not our thoughts, nor His ways our ways. Both in the physical and spiritual realm, *great pressure means great power!* Although circumstances may bring us into the place of death, that need not spell disaster—for if we trust in the Lord and wait patiently, that simply provides the occasion for the display of His almighty power. "Remember his marvelous works that he hath done; his wonders and the judgments of his mouth" (Ps. 105:5).

Mrs. Charles E. Cowman

In the wilderness shall waters break out, and streams in the desert (Isa. 35:6).

January 1

The land whither ye go to possess it is a land of hills and valleys and drinketh water of the rain of heaven: a land which the Lord thy God careth for: the eyes of the Lord thy God are always upon it, from the beginning of the year even unto the end of the year (Deut. 11:11–12).

Today, dear friends, we stand upon the verge of the unknown. There lies before us the new year and we are going forth to possess it. Who can tell what we shall find? What new experiences, what changes shall come, what new needs shall arise? But here is the cheering, comforting, gladdening message from our heavenly Father, *"The Lord thy God careth for it." "His eyes are upon it away to the ending of the year."*

All our supply is to come from the Lord. Here are springs that shall never dry; here are fountains and streams that shall never be cut off. Here, anxious one, is the gracious pledge of the heavenly Father. If He be the source of our mercies they can never fail us. No heat, no drought can parch that river, "the streams whereof make glad the city of God."

The land is a land of *hills* and *valleys*. It is not all smooth nor all down-hill. If life were all one dead level of dull sameness it would oppress us; we want the hills and the valleys. The hills collect the rain for a hundred fruitful valleys. Ah, so it is with us! It is the hill difficulty that drives us to the throne of grace and brings down the shower of blessing; the hills, the bleak hills of life that we wonder at and perhaps grumble at, bring down the showers. How many have perished in the wilderness, buried under its golden sands, who would have lived and thriven in the hill country; how many would have been killed by the frost, blighted with winds, swept desolate of tree and fruit but for the hill—stern, hard, rugged, so steep to climb. God's hills are a gracious protection for His people against their foes!

We cannot tell what loss and sorrow and trial are doing. Trust only. The Father comes near to take our hand and lead us on our way today. It shall be a good, a blessed new year!

He leads us on by paths we did not know;
Upward He leads us, though our steps be slow,
Though oft we faint and falter on the way,
Though storms and darkness oft obscure the day;
Yet when the clouds are gone,
We know He leads us on.

He leads us on through all the unquiet years;
Past all our dreamland hopes, and doubts and fears,
He guides our steps, through all the tangled maze
Of losses, sorrows, and o'er clouded days;
We know His will is done;
And still He leads us on.

N. L. ZINZENDORF

January 2

And there was an enlarging, and a winding about still upward to the side chambers: for the winding about of the house went still upward round about the house: therefore the breadth of the house was still upward and so increased from the lowest chamber to the highest by the midst (Ezek. 41:7).

Still upward be thine onward course:
For this I pray today;
Still upward as the years go by,
And seasons pass away.

Still upward in this coming year,
Thy path is all untried;
Still upward may'st thou journey on,
Close by thy Savior's side.

Still upward e'en though sorrow come,
And trials crush thine heart;
Still upward may they draw thy soul,
With Christ to walk apart.

Still upward till the day shall break,
And shadows all have flown;
Still upward till in Heaven you wake,
And stand before the throne.

We ought not to rest content in the mists of the valley when the summit of Tabor awaits us. How pure are the dews of the hills, how fresh is the mountain air, how rich the fare of the dwellers aloft, whose windows look into the New Jerusalem! Many saints are content to live like men in coal mines, who see not the sun. Tears mar their faces when they might anoint them with celestial oil. Satisfied I am that many a believer pines in a dungeon when he might walk on the palace roof, and view the goodly land and Lebanon. Rouse thee, O believer, from thy low condition! Cast away thy sloth, thy lethargy, thy coldness, or whatever interferes with thy chaste and pure love to Christ. Make Him the source, the center, and the circumference of all thy soul's range of delight. Rest no longer satisfied with thy dwarfish attainments. Aspire to a higher, a nobler, a fuller life. Upward to heaven! Nearer to God! C. H. SPURGEON

> *I want to scale the utmost height,*
> *And catch a gleam of glory bright;*
> *But still I'll pray, till heaven I've found,*
> *Lord, lead me on to higher ground!*

Not many of us are living at our best. We linger in the lowlands because we are afraid to climb the mountains. The steepness and ruggedness dismay us, and so we stay in the misty valleys and do not learn the mystery of the hills. We do not know what we lose in our self-indulgence, what glory awaits us if only we had courage for the mountain climb, what blessing we should find if only we would move to the uplands of God. J. R. M.

> *Too low they build who build beneath the stars.*

January 3

I will lead on softly, according as the cattle that goeth before me and the children be able to endure (Gen. 33:14).

What a beautiful picture of Jacob's thoughtfulness for the cattle and the children! He would not allow them to be overdriven even for one day. He would not lead on according to what a strong man like Esau could do and expected them to do, but only according to what they were able to endure. He knew exactly how far they could go in a day; and he made that his only consideration in arranging the marches. He had gone the same wilderness journey years before, and knew all about its roughness and heat and length, by personal experience. And so he said, "I will lead on softly" (Gen. 33:14). "For ye have not passed this way heretofore" (Josh. 3:4).

We have not passed this way heretofore, but the Lord Jesus has. It is all untrodden and unknown ground to us, but He knows it all by personal experience. The steep bits that take away our breath, the stony bits that make our feet ache so, the hot shadeless stretches that make us feel so exhausted, the rushing rivers that we have to pass through—Jesus has gone through it all before us. "He was wearied with his journey."

Not some, but all the many waters went over Him, and yet did not quench His love. He was made a perfect leader by the things which He suffered. "He knoweth our frame; he *remembereth that we are dust.*" Think of that when you are tempted to question the gentleness of His leading. He is *remembering* all the time; and not one step will He make you take beyond what your foot is able to endure. Never mind if you think it will not be able for the step that seems to come next; either He will so strengthen it that it shall be able, or He will call a sudden halt, and you shall not have to take it at all. Frances Ridley Havergal 🐚

> *In "pastures green"? Not always; sometimes He*
> *Who knowest best, in kindness leadeth me*
> *In weary ways, where heavy shadows be.*
> *So, whether on the hill-tops high and fair*
> *I dwell, or in the sunless valleys, where*
> *The shadows lie, what matter? He is there.*
>
> Barry 🐚

January 4

Jesus saith unto him, Go thy way; thy son liveth. And the man believed the word that Jesus had spoken unto him, and he went his way (John 4:50).
When ye pray, believe (Mark 11:24).

When there is a matter that requires definite prayer, pray till you believe God, until with unfeigned lips you can thank Him for the answer. If the answer still tarries outwardly, do not pray for it in such a way that it is evident that you are not definitely believing for it. Such a prayer in place of being a help will be a hindrance; and when you are finished praying, you will find that your faith has weakened or has entirely gone. The urgency that you felt to offer this kind of prayer is clearly from self and Satan. It may not be wrong to mention the matter in question to the Lord again, if He is keeping you waiting, but be sure you do so in such a way that it implies faith. *Do not pray yourself out of faith.* You may tell Him that you are waiting and that you are still believing Him and therefore praise Him for the answer. There is nothing that so fully clinches faith as to be so sure of the answer that you can thank God for it. Prayers that pray us out of faith deny both God's promise in His Word and also His whisper "Yes," that He gave us in our hearts. Such prayers are but the expression of the unrest of one's heart, and unrest implies unbelief in reference to the answer to prayer. "For we which have believed do enter into rest" (Heb. 4:3). This prayer that prays ourselves out of faith frequently arises from centering our thoughts on the difficulty rather than on God's promise. Abraham "considered not his own body," "he staggered not at the promise of God" (Rom. 4:19–20). May we watch and pray that we enter not into temptation of praying ourselves out of faith. C. H. P. ☞

Faith is not a sense, nor sight, nor reason, but a taking God at His word. EVANS ☞

The beginning of anxiety is the end of faith, and the beginning of true faith is the end of anxiety. GEORGE MUELLER ☞

You will never learn faith in comfortable surroundings. God gives us the promises in a quiet hour; God seals our covenants with great and gracious words, then He steps back and waits to see how much we believe; then He lets the tempter come, and the test seems to contradict all that He has spoken. It is then that faith wins its crown. That is the time to look up through the storm, and among the trembling, frightened seamen cry, "I believe God that it shall be even as it was told me."

Believe and trust; through stars and suns,
Through life and death, through soul and sense,
His wise, paternal purpose runs;
The darkness of His Providence
Is starlit with Divine intents.

January 5

Lord, there is none beside thee to help (2 Chron. 14:11 RV).

⟨～⟩

Remind God of His entire responsibility. "There is none beside thee to help." The odds against Asa were enormous. There were a million men in arms against him, besides three hundred chariots. It seemed impossible to hold his own against that vast multitude. There were no allies who would come to his help; his only hope, therefore, was in God. It may be that your difficulties have been allowed to come to so alarming a pitch that you may be compelled to renounce all creature aid, to which in lesser trials you have had recourse, and cast yourself back on your almighty Friend.

Put God between yourself and the foe. To Asa's faith, Jehovah seemed to stand between the might of Zerah and himself, as one who had no strength.

Nor was he mistaken. We are told that the Ethiopians were destroyed before the Lord and *before His host,* as though celestial combatants flung themselves against the foe in Israel's behalf, and put the large host to rout, so that Israel had only to follow up and gather the spoil. Our God is Jehovah of hosts, who can summon unexpected reinforcements at any moment to aid His people. Believe that He is there between you and your difficulty, and what baffles you will flee before Him, as clouds before the gale. F. B. MEYER

> *When nothing whereon to lean remains,*
> *When strongholds crumble to dust;*
> *When nothing is sure but that God still reigns,*
> *That is just the time to trust.*
>
> *'Tis better to walk by faith than sight,*
> *In this path of yours and mine;*
> *And the pitch-black night, when there's no outer light*
> *Is the time for faith to shine.*

Abraham believed God, and said to sight, "Stand back!" and to the laws of nature, "Hold your peace!" and to a misgiving heart, "Silence, thou lying tempter!" He *believed* God. JOSEPH PARKER

January 6

When thou passest through the waters . . . they shall not overflow thee (Isa. 43:2).

God does not open paths for us in advance of our coming. He does not promise help before help is needed. He does not remove obstacles out of our way before we reach them. Yet when we are on the edge of our need, God's hand is stretched out.

Many people forget this, and are forever worrying about difficulties which they foresee in the future. They expect that God is going to make the way plain and open before them, miles and miles ahead; whereas He has promised to do it only step by step as they may need. You must get to the waters and into their floods before you can claim the promise. Many people dread death, and lament that they have not "dying grace." Of course, they will not have dying grace when they are in good health, in the midst of life's duties, with death far in advance. Why should they have it then? Grace for duty is what they need then, living grace; then dying grace when they come to die. J. R. M.

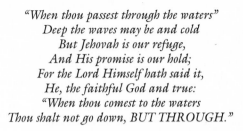

"When thou passest through the waters"
Deep the waves may be and cold
But Jehovah is our refuge,
And His promise is our hold;
For the Lord Himself hath said it,
He, the faithful God and true:
"When thou comest to the waters
Thou shalt not go down, BUT THROUGH."

Seas of sorrow, seas of trial,
Bitterest anguish, fiercest pain,
Rolling surges of temptation
Sweeping over heart and brain—
They shall never overflow us
For we know His word is true;
All His waves and all His billows
He will lead us safely THROUGH.

Threatening breakers of destruction,
Doubt's insidious undertow,
Shall not sink us, shall not drag us
Out to ocean depths of woe;
For His promise shall sustain us,
Praise the Lord, whose Word is true!
We shall not go down, or under,
For He saith, "Thou passest THROUGH."

ANNIE JOHNSON FLINT

January 7

I have learned, in whatsoever state I am, therewith to be content
(Phil. 4:11).

Paul, denied of every comfort, wrote the above words in his dungeon. A story is told of a king who went into his garden one morning, and found everything withered and dying. He asked the oak that stood near the gate what the trouble was. He found it was sick of life and determined to die because it was not tall and beautiful like the pine. The pine was all out of heart because it could not bear grapes, like the vine. The vine was going to throw its life away because it could not stand erect and have as fine a fruit as the peach tree. The geranium was fretting because it was not tall and fragrant like the lilac; and so on all through the garden. Coming to a heartsease, he found its bright face lifted as cheery as ever. "Well, heartsease, I'm glad, amidst all this discouragement, to find one brave little flower. You do not seem to be the least disheartened." "No, I am not of much account, but I thought that if you wanted an oak, or a pine, or a peach tree, or a lilac, you would have planted one; but as I knew you wanted a heartsease, I am determined to be the best little heartsease that I can."

Others may do a greater work,
But you have your part to do;
And no one in all God's heritage
Can do it so well as you.

They who are God's without reserve, are in every state content; for they will only what He wills, and desire to do for Him whatever He desires them to do; they strip themselves of everything, and in this nakedness find all things restored a hundredfold.

January 8

I will cause the shower to come down in his season; there shall be showers of blessing (Ezek. 34:26).

What is thy *season* this morning? Is it a season of drought? Then that is the season for showers. Is it a season of great heaviness and black clouds? Then that is the season for showers. "As thy day so shall thy strength be." "I will give thee *showers* of blessing." The word is in the plural. All kinds of blessings God will send. All God's blessings go together, like links in a golden chain. If He gives converting grace, He will also give comforting grace. He will send "showers of blessings." Look up today, O parched plant, and open thy leaves and flowers for a heavenly watering. C. H. SPURGEON 🍂

Let but thy heart become a valley low,
And God will rain on it till it will overflow.

Thou, O Lord, canst transform my thorn into a flower. And I want my thorn transformed into a flower. Job got the sunshine after the rain, but has the rain been all waste? Job wants to know, I want to know, if the shower had nothing to do with the shining. And Thou canst tell me—Thy cross can tell me. Thou hast crowned Thy sorrow. Be this my crown, O Lord. I only triumph in Thee when I have learned the radiance of the rain. GEORGE MATHESON 🍂

The fruitful life seeks showers as well as sunshine.

The landscape, brown and sere beneath the sun,
Needs but the cloud to lift it into life;
The dews may damp the leaves of tree and flower,
But it requires the cloud-distilled shower
To bring rich verdure to the lifeless life.

Ah, how like this, the landscape of a life:
Dews of trial fall like incense, rich and sweet;
But bearing little in the crystal tray—
Like nymphs of night, dews lift at break of day
And transient impress leave, like lips that meet.

But clouds of trials, bearing burdens rare,
Leave in the soul, a moisture settled deep:
Life kindles by the magic law of God;
And where before the thirsty camel trod,
There richest beauties to life's landscape leap.

Then read thou in each cloud that comes to thee
The words of Paul, in letters large and clear:
So shall those clouds thy soul with blessing feed,
And with a constant trust as thou dost read,
All things together work for good. Fret not, nor fear!

January 9

For I reckon that the sufferings of this present time are not worthy to be compared with the glory which shall be revealed in us (Rom. 8:18).

I kept for nearly a year the flask-shaped cocoon of an emperor moth. It is very peculiar in its construction. A narrow opening is left in the neck of the flask, through which the perfect insect forces its way, so that a forsaken cocoon is as entire as one still tenanted, no rupture of the interlacing fibers having taken place. The great disproportion between the means of egress and the size of the imprisoned insect makes one wonder how the exit is ever accomplished at all—and it never is without great labor and difficulty. It is supposed that the pressure to which the moth's body is subjected in passing through such a narrow opening is a provision of nature for forcing the juices into the vessels of the wings, these being less developed at the period of emerging from the chrysalis than they are in other insects.

I happened to witness the first efforts of my prisoned moth to escape from its long confinement. During a whole forenoon, from time to time, I watched it patiently striving and struggling to get out. It never seemed able to get beyond a certain point, and at last my patience was exhausted. Very probably the confining fibers were drier and less elastic than if the cocoon had been left all winter on its native heather, as nature meant it to be. At all events I thought I was wiser and more compassionate than its Maker, and I resolved to give it a helping hand. With the point of my scissors I snipped the confining threads to make the exit just a very little easier, and lo! immediately, and with perfect ease, out crawled my moth dragging a huge swollen body and little shriveled wings. In vain I watched to see that marvelous process of expansion in which these silently and swiftly develop before one's eyes; and as I traced the exquisite spots and markings of diverse colors which were all there in miniature, I longed to see these assume their due proportions and the creature to appear in all its perfect beauty, as it is, in truth, one of the loveliest of its kind. But I looked in vain. My false tenderness had proved its ruin. It never was anything but a stunted abortion, crawling painfully through that brief life which it should have spent flying through the air on rainbow wings. I have thought of it often, often, when watching with pitiful eyes those who were struggling with sorrow, suffering, and distress; and I would fain cut short the discipline and give deliverance. Short-sighted man! How know I that one of these pangs or groans could be spared? The farsighted, perfect love that seeks the perfection of its object does not weakly shrink from present, transient suffering. Our Father's love is too true to be weak. Because He loves His children, He chastises them that they may be partakers of His holiness. With this glorious end in view, He spares not for their crying. Made perfect through sufferings, as the Elder Brother was, the sons of God are trained up to obedience and brought to glory through much tribulation. FROM A TRACT

January 10

They were forbidden of the Holy Ghost to preach the word in Asia (Acts 16:6).

It is interesting to study the methods of His guidance as it was extended toward these early heralds of the cross. It consisted largely in prohibitions, when they attempted to take another course than the right. When they would turn to the left, to Asia, He stayed them. When they sought to turn to the right, to Bithynia, again He stayed them. In after years Paul would do some of the greatest work of his life in that very region; but just now the door was closed against him by the Holy Spirit. The time was not yet ripe for the attack on these apparently impregnable bastions of the kingdom of Satan. Apollos must come there for pioneer work. Paul and Barnabas are needed yet more urgently elsewhere, and must receive further training before undertaking this responsible task.

Beloved, whenever you are doubtful as to your course, submit your judgment absolutely to the Spirit of God, and ask Him to shut against you every door but the right one. Say, "Blessed Spirit, I cast on Thee the entire responsibility of closing against my steps any and every course which is not of God. Let me hear Thy voice behind me whenever I turn to the right hand or the left."

In the meanwhile, continue along the path which you have been already treading. Abide in the calling in which you are called, unless you are clearly told to do something else. The Spirit of Jesus waits to be to you, O pilgrim, what He was to Paul. Only be careful to obey His least prohibition; and where after believing prayer, there are no apparent hindrances, go forward with enlarged heart. Do not be surprised if the answer comes in closed doors. But when doors are shut right and left, an open road is sure to lead to Troas. There Luke awaits, and visions will point the way, where vast opportunities stand open, and faithful friends are waiting. FROM PAUL, BY MEYER

Is there some problem in your life to solve,
Some passage seeming full of mystery?
God knows, who brings the hidden things to light.
He keeps the key.

Is there some door closed by the Father's hand
Which widely opened you had hoped to see?
Trust God and wait—for when He shuts the door
He keeps the key.

Is there some earnest prayer unanswered yet,
Or answered NOT as you had thought 'twould be?
God will make clear His purpose by-and-by.
He keeps the key.

Have patience with your God, your patient God,
All wise, all knowing, no long tarrier He,
And of the door of all thy future life
He keeps the key.

Unfailing comfort, sweet and blessed rest,
To know of EVERY door He keeps the key.
That He at last when just HE sees 'tis best,
Will give it THEE.

ANONYMOUS

January 11

Comfort ye, comfort ye my people, saith your God (Isa. 40:1).

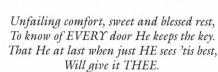

Store up comfort. This was the prophet's mission. The world is full of comfortless hearts, and ere thou are sufficient for this lofty ministry, thou must be trained. And thy training is costly in the extreme; for, to render it perfect, thou too must pass through the same afflictions as are wringing countless hearts of tears and blood. Thus thy own life becomes the hospital ward where thou art taught the divine art of comfort. Thou art wounded, that in the binding up of thy wounds by the Great Physician, thou mayest learn how to render first aid to the wounded everywhere. Dost thou wonder why thou art passing through some special sorrow? Wait till ten years are passed, and thou wilt find many others afflicted as thou art. Thou wilt tell them how thou hast suffered and hast been comforted; then as the tale is unfolded, and the anodynes applied which once thy God wrapped around thee, in the eager look and the gleam of hope that shall chase the shadow of despair across the soul, *thou shalt know why* thou wast afflicted, and bless God for the discipline that stored thy life with such a fund of experience and helpfulness. SELECTED

God does not comfort us to make us comfortable, but to make us *comforters.* DR. JOWETT

> *They tell me I must bruise*
> *The rose's leaf,*
> *Ere I can keep and use*
> *Its fragrance brief.*
>
> *They tell me I must break*
> *The skylark's heart,*
> *Ere her cage song will make*
> *The silence start.*
>
> *They tell me love must bleed,*
> *And friendship weep,*

Ere in my deepest need
I touch that deep.

Must it be always so
With precious things?
Must they be bruised and go
With beaten wings?

Ah, yes! by crushing days,
By caging nights, by scar
Of thorn and stony ways,
These blessings are!

January 12

Reckon it nothing but joy . . . whenever you find yourself hedged
in by the various trials, be assured that the testing of your faith
leads to power of endurance (James 1:2–3 WEYMOUTH).

God hedges in His own that He may preserve them, but oftentimes they only see the wrong side of the hedge, and so misunderstand His dealings. It was so with Job (Job 3:23). Ah, but Satan knew the value of that hedge! See his testimony in chapter 1:10. Through the leaves of every trial there are chinks of light to shine through. Thorns do not prick you unless you lean against them, and not one touches without His knowledge. The words that hurt you, the letter which gave you pain, the cruel wound of your dearest friend, shortness of money—are all known to Him, who sympathizes as none else can and watches to see if, through all, you will dare to trust Him wholly.

The hawthorn hedge that keeps us from intruding,
Looks very fierce and bare
When stripped by winter, every branch protruding
Its thorns that would wound and tear.

But spring-time comes; and like the rod that budded,
Each twig breaks out in green;
And cushions soft of tender leaves are studded,
Where spines alone were seen.

The sorrows, that to us seem so perplexing,
Are mercies kindly sent

21

To guard our wayward souls from sadder vexing,
And greater ills prevent.

To save us from the pit, no screen of roses
Would serve for our defense,
The hindrance that completely interposes
Stings back like thorny fence.

At first when smarting from the shock, complaining
Of wounds that freely bleed,
God's hedges of severity us paining,
May seem severe indeed.

But afterwards, God's blessed spring-time cometh,
And bitter murmurs cease;
The sharp severity that pierced us bloometh,
And yields the fruits of peace.

Then let us sing, our guarded way thus wending
Life's hidden snares among,
Of mercy and of judgment sweetly blending;
Earth's sad, but lovely song.

January 13

In all these things we are more than conquerors through him that loved us (Rom. 8:37).

This is more than victory. This is a triumph so complete that we have not only escaped defeat and destruction, but we have destroyed our enemies and won a spoil so rich and valuable that we can thank God that the battle ever came. How can we be "more than conquerors"? We can get out of the conflict a spiritual discipline that will greatly strengthen our faith and establish our spiritual character. Temptation is necessary to settle and confirm us in the spiritual life. It is like the fire which burns in the colors of mineral painting, or like winds that cause the mighty cedars of the mountain to strike more deeply into the soil. Our spiritual conflicts are among our choicest blessings, and our great adversary is used to train us for his ultimate defeat. The ancient Phrygians had a legend that every time they conquered an enemy the victor absorbed the physical strength of his victim and added so much more to his own strength and valor. So temptation victoriously met doubles our spiritual strength and equipment. It is possible thus not only to defeat our enemy, but to capture him and make him fight in our ranks. The prophet Isaiah speaks of flying on the shoulders of the Philistines (Isa. 11:14). These Philistines were their deadly foes, but the figure suggested that they would be enabled not only to conquer the Philistines, but to use them to carry the victors on their shoulders for further triumphs. Just as the wise sailor can use a head wind to carry him forward by tacking and taking advantage of its impelling force; so it is possible for us in our spiritual life through the victorious grace of God to turn to account the things that seem most unfriendly and unfavorable, and to be able to say continually, "The things that were against me have happened to the furtherance of the gospel." FROM *LIFE MORE ABUNDANTLY*

A noted scientist observing that "early voyagers fancied that the coral-building animals instinctively built up the great circles of the Atoll Islands to afford themselves protection in the inner parts," has disproved this fancy by showing that the insect builders can only live and thrive fronting the open ocean, and in a highly aerated foam of its resistless billows. So it has been commonly thought that protected ease is the most favorable condition of life, whereas all the noblest and strongest lives prove on the contrary that the endurance of hardship is the making of the men, and the factor that distinguishes between existence and vigorous vitality. Hardship makes character. SELECTED

Now thanks be unto God Who always leads us forth to triumph with the Anointed One, and Who diffuses by us the fragrance of the knowledge of Him in every place (2 Cor. 2:14—literal translation).

January 14

He putteth forth his own sheep (John 10:4).

Oh, this is bitter work for Him and us—bitter for us to go, but equally bitter for Him to cause us pain; yet it must be done. It would not be conducive to our true welfare to stay always in one happy and comfortable lot. He therefore puts us forth. The fold is deserted, that the sheep may wander over the bracing mountain slope. The laborers must be thrust out into the harvest, else the golden grain would spoil.

Take heart! It could not be better to stay when He determines otherwise; and if the loving hand of our Lord puts us forth, it must be well. On, in His name, to green pastures and still waters and mountain heights! *He goeth before thee.* Whatever awaits us is encountered first by Him. Faith's eye can always discern His majestic presence in front; and when that cannot be seen, it is dangerous to move forward. Bind this comfort to your heart, that the Savior has tried for Himself all the experiences through which He asks you to pass; and He would not ask you to pass through them unless He was sure that they were not too difficult for your feet or too trying for your strength.

This is the blessed life—not anxious to see far in front, nor careful about the next step, not eager to choose the path, nor weighted with the heavy responsibilities of the future, but quietly following behind the Shepherd, *one step at a time.*

> *Dark is the sky! and veiled the unknown morrow!*
> *Dark is life's way, for night is not yet o'er;*
> *The longed-for glimpse I may not meanwhile borrow;*
> *But, this I know, HE GOETH ON BEFORE.*
>
> *Dangers are nigh! and fears my mind are shaking;*
> *Heart seems to dread what life may hold in store;*
> *But I am His—He knows the way I'm taking,*
> *More blessed still—HE GOETH ON BEFORE.*
>
> *Doubts cast their weird, unwelcome shadows o'er me,*
> *Doubts that life's best—life's choicest things are o'er;*
> *What but His Word can strengthen, can restore me,*
> *And this blest fact; that still HE GOES BEFORE.*
>
> *HE GOES BEFORE! Be this my consolation!*
> *He goes before! On this my heart would dwell!*
> *He goes before! This guarantees salvation!*
> *HE GOES BEFORE! And therefore all is well.*
>
> J. Danson Smith

The Oriental shepherd was always *ahead* of his sheep. He was down *in front.* Any attack upon them had to take him into account. Now God is down in front. He is in the tomorrows. It is tomorrow that fills men with dread. *God is there already.* All the tomorrows of our life have to pass Him before they can get to us. F. B. M.

> *God is in every tomorrow,*
> *Therefore I live for today,*
> *Certain of finding at sunrise,*
> *Guidance and strength for the way;*

Power for each moment of weakness,
Hope for each moment of pain,
Comfort for every sorrow,
Sunshine and joy after rain.

January 15

And the Lord appeared unto Isaac the same night (Gen. 26:24).

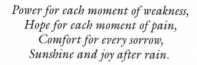

"Appeared the same night," the night on which he went to Beer-sheba. Do you think this revelation was an accident? Do you think the *time* of it was an accident? Do you think it could have happened on any other night as well as this? If so, you are grievously mistaken. Why did it come to Isaac in the night on which he reached Beer-sheba? Because that was the night on which he reached *rest*. In his old locality, he had been tormented. There had been a whole series of petty quarrels about the possession of paltry wells. There are no worries like *little* worries, particularly if there is an accumulation of them. Isaac felt this. Even after the strife was past, the place retained a disagreeable association. He determined to leave. He sought change of scene. He pitched his tent away from the place of former strife. That very night the revelation came. God spoke when there was no inward storm. He could not speak when the mind was fretted; His voice demands the silence of the soul. Only in the *hush* of the spirit could Isaac hear the garments of his God sweep by. His *still* night was his *starry* night.

My soul, hast thou pondered these words, "Be still, and know"? In the hour of perturbation, thou canst not hear the answer to thy prayers. How often has the answer seemed to come long after! The heart got no response in the moment of its crying—in its thunder, its earthquake, and its fire. But when the crying ceased, when the stillness fell, when thy hand desisted from knocking on the iron gate, when the interest of *other* lives broke the tragedy of thine own, then appeared the long-delayed reply. Thou must rest, O soul, if thou wouldst have thy heart's desire. Still the beating of thy pulse of personal care. Hide thy tempest of individual trouble behind the altar of a common tribulation and, that same night, the Lord shall appear to thee. The rainbow shall span the place of the subsiding flood, and in thy stillness thou shalt hear the everlasting music. GEORGE MATHESON

Tread in solitude thy pathway,
Quiet heart and undismayed.

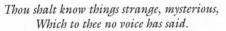

Thou shalt know things strange, mysterious,
Which to thee no voice has said.

While the crowd of petty hustlers
Grasps at vain and paltry things,
Thou wilt see a great world rising
Where soft mystic music rings.

Leave the dusty road to others,
Spotless keep thy soul and bright,
As the radiant ocean's surface
When the sun is taking flight.
FROM THE GERMAN OF V. SCHOFFEL—H. F.

January 16

And there arose a great storm (Mark 4:37).

Some of the storms of life come *suddenly:* a great sorrow, a bitter disappointment, a crushing defeat. Some come *slowly.* They appear upon the ragged edges of the horizon no larger than a man's hand, but, trouble that seems so insignificant spreads until it covers the sky and overwhelms us.

Yet it is in the storm that God equips us for service. When God wants an oak He plants it on the moor where the storms will shake it and the rains will beat down upon it, and it is in the midnight battle with elements that the oak wins its rugged fiber and becomes the king of the forest.

When God wants to make a man He puts him into some storm. The history of mankind is always rough and rugged. No man is made until he has been out into the surge of the storm and found the sublime fulfillment of the prayer: "O God, take me, break me, make me."

A Frenchman has painted a picture of universal genius. There stand orators, philosophers and martyrs, all who have achieved preeminence in any phase of life; the remarkable fact about the picture is this: Every man who is preeminent for his ability was first preeminent for suffering. In the foreground stands that figure of the man who was denied the promised land, Moses. Beside him is another, feeling his way—blind Homer. Milton is there, blind and heartbroken. Now comes the form of One who towers above them all. What is His characteristic? His face is marred more than any man's. The artist might have written under that great picture, "The Storm."

The beauties of nature come after the storm. The rugged beauty of the mountain is born in a storm, and the heroes of life are the storm-swept and battle-scarred.

You have been in the storms and swept by the blasts. Have they left you broken, weary, beaten in the valley, or have they lifted you to the sunlit summits of a richer, deeper, more abiding manhood and womanhood? Have they left you with more sympathy with the storm-swept and the battle-scarred? SELECTED

> *The wind that blows can never kill*
> *The tree God plants;*
> *It bloweth east, it bloweth west,*
> *The tender leaves have little rest,*
> *But any wind that blows is best.*
> *The tree that God plants*
> *Strikes deeper root, grows higher still,*
> *Spreads greater boughs, for God's good will*
> *Meets all its wants.*
>
> *There is no storm hath power to blast*
> *The tree God knows;*
> *No thunderbolt, nor beating rain,*
> *Nor lightning flash, nor hurricane;*
> *When they are spent, it doth remain,*
> *The tree God knows,*
> *Through every tempest standeth fast,*
> *And from its first day to its last*
> *Still fairer grows.*

SELECTED

January 17

O Daniel, servant of the living God, is thy God whom thou servest continually, able to deliver thee? (Dan. 6:20).

How many times we find this expression in the Scriptures, and yet it is just this very thing that we are so prone to lose sight of. We know it is written *"the living God"*; but in our daily life there is scarcely anything we practically so much lose sight of as the fact that God is *the living God*; that He is now whatever He was three or four thousand years since; that He has the same sovereign power, the same saving love toward those who love and serve Him as ever He had and that He will do for them now what He did for others two, three, four thousand years ago, simply because He is the living God, the unchanging One. Oh, how therefore we should confide in Him, and in our darkest moments never lose sight of the fact that He *is* still and ever will be *the living God!*

Be assured, if you walk with Him and look to Him and expect help from Him, He will never fail you. An older brother who has known the Lord for forty-four years, who writes this, says to you for your encouragement that He has never failed him. In the greatest difficulties, in the heaviest trials, in the deepest poverty and necessities, He has never failed me; but because I was enabled by His grace to trust Him, He has always appeared for my help. I delight in speaking well of His name. GEORGE MUELLER

Luther was once found at a moment of peril and fear, when he had need to grasp unseen strength, sitting in an abstracted mood tracing on the table with his finger the words, "Vivit! Vivit!" ("He lives! He lives!"). It is our hope for ourselves, and for His truth, and for mankind. Men come and go; leaders, teachers, thinkers speak and work for a season, and then fall silent and impotent. He abides. They die, but He lives. They are lights kindled, and, therefore, sooner or later quenched; but He is the true light from which they draw all their brightness, and He shines forevermore. ALEXANDER MACLAREN

"One day I came to know Dr. John Douglas Adam," writes C. G. Trumbull. "I learned from him that what he counted his greatest spiritual asset was his *unvarying consciousness of the actual presence of Jesus.* Nothing bore him up so, he said, as the realization that Jesus was *always* with him in actual presence; and that this was so independent of his own feelings, independent of his deserts, and independent of his own notions as to how Jesus would manifest His presence.

"Moreover, he said that Christ was the home of his thoughts. Whenever his mind was free from other matters it would turn to Christ; and he would talk aloud to Christ when he was alone—on the street, anywhere—as easily and naturally as to a human friend. So real to him was Jesus' *actual presence.*"

January 18

Now thanks be unto God, which always causeth us to triumph in Christ (2 Cor. 2:14).

God gets His greatest victories out of apparent defeats. Very often the enemy seems to triumph for a little, and God lets it be so; but then He comes in and upsets all the work of the enemy, overthrows the apparent victory, and as the Bible says, "turns the way of the wicked upside down." Thus He gives a great deal larger victory than we would have known if He had not allowed the enemy, seemingly, to triumph in the first place.

The story of the three Hebrew children being cast into the fiery furnace is a familiar one. Here was an apparent victory for the enemy. It *looked* as if the servants of the living God were going to have a terrible defeat. We have all been in places where it seemed as though we were defeated, and the enemy rejoiced. We can imagine what a complete defeat this looked to be. They fell down into the flames, and their enemies watched them to see them burn up in that awful fire, but were greatly astonished to see them walking around in the fire enjoying themselves. Nebuchadnezzar told them to "come forth out of the midst of the fire." Not even a hair was singed, nor was the smell of fire on their garments, "because there is no other god that can deliver after this sort."

This apparent defeat resulted in a marvelous victory.

Suppose that these three men had lost their faith and courage, and had complained, saying, *"Why* did not God keep us out of the furnace!" They would have been burned, and God would not have been glorified. If there is a great trial in your life today, do not own it as a *defeat,* but continue, by faith, to claim the victory through Him who is able to make you more than conqueror, and a glorious victory will soon be apparent. Let us learn that in all the hard places God brings us into, He is making opportunities for us to exercise such faith in Him as will bring about blessed results and greatly glorify His name. FROM LIFE OF PRAISE ☙

Defeat may serve as well as victory
To shake the soul and let the glory out.
When the great oak is straining in the wind,
The boughs drink in new beauty, and the trunk
Sends down a deeper root on the windward side.
Only the soul that knows the mighty grief
Can know the mighty rapture. Sorrows come
To stretch out spaces in the heart for joy.

January 19

Men ought always to pray and not to faint (Luke 18:1).

"Go to the ant." Tammerlane used to relate to his friends an anecdote of his early life. "I once," he said, "was forced to take shelter from my enemies in a ruined building, where I sat alone many hours. Desiring to divert my mind from my hopeless condition, I fixed my eyes on an ant that was carrying a grain of corn larger than itself up a high wall. I numbered the efforts it made to accomplish this object. The grain fell sixty-nine times to the ground; but the insect *persevered*, and the seventieth time it reached the top. This sight gave me courage at the moment, and I never forgot the lesson. FROM THE KING'S BUSINESS 🐚

Prayer which takes the fact that past prayers have not been answered as a reason for languor, has already ceased to be the prayer of faith. To the prayer of faith the fact that prayers remain unanswered is only evidence that the moment of the answer is *so much nearer.* From first to last, the lessons and examples of our Lord all tell us that prayer which cannot persevere and urge its plea importunately, and renew, and renew itself again, and gather strength from every past petition, is not the prayer that will prevail. WILLIAM ARTHUR 🐚

Rubenstein, the great musician, once said, "If I omit practice one day, I notice it; if two days, my friends notice it; if three days, the public notices it." It is the old doctrine, *"Practice makes perfect."* We must continue believing, continue praying, continue doing His will. Suppose along any line of art, one should cease practicing, we know what the result would be. If we would only use the same quality of common sense in our religion that we use in our everyday life, we should go on to perfection.

The motto of David Livingstone was in these words, "I determined never to stop until I had come to the end and achieved my purpose." By unfaltering persistence and faith in God he conquered.

January 20

Sorrow is better than laughter; for by the sadness of the countenance the heart is made better (Eccles. 7:3).

When sorrow comes under the power of divine grace, it works out a manifold ministry in our lives. Sorrow reveals unknown depths in the soul, and unknown capabilities of experience and service. Gay, trifling people are always shallow, and never suspect the little meannesses in their nature. Sorrow is God's plowshare that turns up and subsoils the depths of the soul, that it may yield richer harvests. If we had never fallen, or were in a glorified state, then the strong torrents of divine joy would be the normal force to open up all our souls' capacities; but in a fallen world, sorrow, with despair taken out of it, is the chosen power to reveal ourselves to ourselves. Hence it is sorrow that makes us think deeply, long, and soberly.

Sorrow makes us go slower and more considerately, and introspect our motives and dispositions. It is sorrow that opens up within us the capacities of the heavenly life, and it is sorrow that makes us willing to launch our capacities on a boundless sea of service for God and our fellows.

We may suppose a class of indolent people living at the base of a great mountain range, who had never ventured to explore the valleys and canyons back in the mountains; and someday, when a great thunderstorm goes careening through the mountains, it turns the hidden glens into echoing trumpets, and reveals the inner recesses of the valley, like the convolutions of a monster shell, and then the dwellers at the foot of the hills are astonished at the labyrinths and unexplored recesses of a region so near by, and yet so little known. So it is with many souls who indolently live on the outer edge of their own natures until great thunderstorms of sorrow reveal hidden depths within that were never hitherto suspected.

God never uses anybody to a large degree, until after He breaks that one all to pieces. Joseph had more sorrow than all the other sons of Jacob, and it led him out into a ministry of bread for all nations. For this reason, the Holy Spirit said of him, "Joseph is a fruitful bough . . . by a well, whose branches run over the wall" (Gen. 49:22). It takes sorrow to widen the soul. FROM THE HEAVENLY LIFE

The dark brown mould's upturned
By the sharp-pointed plow;
And I've a lesson learned.

My life is but a field,
Stretched out beneath God's sky,
Some harvest rich to yield.

Where grows the golden grain?
Where faith? Where sympathy?
In a furrow cut by pain.

MALTBIE D. BABCOCK

Every person and every nation must take lessons in God's school of adversity. "We can say, 'Blessed is night, for it reveals to us the stars.' In the same way we can say, 'Blessed is sorrow, for it reveals God's comfort.' The floods washed away home and mill, all the poor man had in the world. But as he stood on the scene of his loss, after the water had subsided, brokenhearted and discouraged, he saw something shining in the bank which the waters had washed bare. 'It looks like gold,' he said. It was gold. The flood which had beggared him made him rich. So it is ofttimes in life." H. C. Trumbull

January 21

None of these things move me (Acts 20:24).

We read in the Book of Samuel that the moment that David was crowned at Hebron, " All the Philistines came up to seek David." And the moment we get anything from the Lord worth contending for, then the Devil comes to seek us.

When the enemy meets us at the threshold of any great work for God, let us accept it as "a token of salvation," and claim double blessing, victory, and power. Power is developed by resistance. The cannon carries twice as far because the exploding power has to find its way through resistance. The way electricity is produced in the powerhouse yonder is by the sharp friction of the revolving wheels. And so we shall find some day that even Satan has been one of God's agencies of blessing. From Days of Heaven upon Earth

> *A hero is not fed on sweets,*
> *Daily his own heart he eats;*
> *Chambers of the great are jails,*
> *And head winds right for royal sails.*
>
> Emerson

Tribulation is the way to triumph. The valleyway opens into the highway. Tribulation's imprint is on all great things. *Crowns are cast in crucibles.* Chains of character that wind about the feet of God are forged in earthly flames. No man is greatest victor till he has trodden the winepress of woe. With seams of anguish deep in His brow, the "Man of Sorrows" said, "In the world ye shall have tribulation"—but after this sob comes the psalm of promise, "Be of good cheer, I have overcome the world." The footprints are traceable everywhere. Bloodmarks stain the steps that lead to thrones. Scars are the price of scepters. Our crowns will be wrested from the giants we conquer. Grief has always been the lot of greatness. It is an open secret.

> *The mark of rank in nature*
> *Is capacity for pain;*

And the anguish of the singer
Makes the sweetest of the strain.

Tribulation has always marked the trail of the true reformer. It is the story of Paul, Luther, Savonarola, Knox, Wesley, and all the rest of the mighty army. They came through great tribulation to their place of power.

Every great book has been written with the author's blood. "These are they that have come out of great tribulation." Who was the peerless poet of the Greeks? Homer. But that illustrious singer was blind. Who wrote the fadeless dream of *Pilgrim's Progress*? A prince in royal purple upon a couch of ease? Nay! The trailing splendor of that vision gilded the dingy walls of old Bedford jail while John Bunyan, a princely prisoner, a glorious genius, made a faithful transcript of the scene.

Great is the facile conqueror;
Yet haply, he, who, wounded sore,
Breathless, all covered o'er with blood and sweat,
Sinks fainting, but fighting evermore—
Is greater yet.

SELECTED

January 22

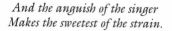

Into a desert place apart (Matt. 14:13).

"There is no music in a rest, but there is the making of music in it." In our whole life-melody the music is broken off here and there by "rests," and we foolishly think we have come to the end of the tune. God sends a time of forced leisure, sickness, disappointed plans, frustrated efforts, and makes a sudden pause in the choral hymn of our lives; and we lament that our voices must be silent, and our part missing in the music which ever goes up to the ear of the Creator. How does the musician read the "rest"? See him beat the time with unvarying count, and catch up the next note true and steady, as if no breaking place had come between.

Not without design does God write the music of our lives. Be it ours to learn the tune, and not be dismayed at the "rests." They are not to be slurred over, not to be omitted, not to destroy the melody, not to change the keynote. If we look up, God Himself will beat the time for us. With the eye on Him, we shall strike the next note full and clear. If we sadly say to ourselves, "There is no music in a 'rest,'" let us not forget "there is the making of music in it." The making of music is often a slow and painful process in this life. How patiently God works to teach us! How long He waits for us to learn the lesson! RUSKIN

Called aside—
From the glad working of thy busy life,
From the world's ceaseless stir of care and strife,
Into the shade and stillness by thy Heavenly Guide
For a brief space thou hast been called aside.

Called aside—
Perhaps into a desert garden dim;
And yet not alone, when thou hast been with Him,
And heard His voice in sweetest accents say:
"Child, wilt thou not with Me this still hour stay?"

Called aside—
In hidden paths with Christ thy Lord to tread,
Deeper to drink at the sweet Fountainhead,
Closer in fellowship with Him to roam,
Nearer, perchance, to feel thy Heavenly Home.

Called aside—
Oh, knowledge deeper grows with Him alone;
In secret oft His deeper love is shown,
And learnt in many an hour of dark distress
Some rare, sweet lesson of His tenderness.

Called aside—
We thank thee for the stillness and the shade;
We thank Thee for the hidden paths Thy love hath made,
And, so that we have wept and watched with Thee,
We thank Thee for our dark Gethsemane.

Called aside—
Oh, restful thought—He doeth all things well;
Oh, blessed sense, with Christ alone to dwell;
So in the shadow of Thy cross to hide,
We thank Thee, Lord, to have been called aside.

January 23

Why standest thou afar off, O Lord? (Ps. 10:1).

God is "a very present help in trouble." But He permits trouble to pursue us, as though He were indifferent to its overwhelming pressure, that we may be brought to the end of ourselves, and led to discover the treasure of darkness, the unmeasurable gains of tribulation. We may be sure that He who permits the suffering is with us in it. It may be that we shall see Him only when the trial is passing; but we must dare to believe that He never leaves the crucible. Our eyes are holden; and we cannot behold Him whom our soul loveth. It is dark—the bandages blind us so that we cannot see the form of our High Priest; but He is there, deeply touched. Let us not rely on feeling, but on faith in His unswerving fidelity; and though we see Him not, let us talk to Him. Directly we begin to speak to Jesus, as being literally present, though His presence is veiled, there comes an answering voice which shows that He is in the shadow, keeping watch upon His own. Your Father is as near when you journey through the dark tunnel as when under the open heaven! FROM DAILY DEVOTIONAL COMMENTARY 🖝

What though the path be all unknown?
What though the way be drear?
Its shades I traverse not alone
When steps of Thine are near.

January 24

But the dove found no rest for the sole of her foot, and she returned unto him. . . . And the dove came in to him in the evening; and, lo, in her mouth was an olive leaf (Gen. 8:9–11).

God knows just when to withhold from us any visible sign of encouragement, and when to grant us such a sign. How good it is that we may trust Him anyway! When all visible evidences that He is remembering us are withheld, that is best; He wants us to realize that His Word, His promise of remembrance, is more substantial and dependable than any evidence of our senses. When He sends the visible evidence, that is well also; we appreciate it all the more after we have trusted Him without it. Those who are readiest to trust God without other evidence than His Word always receive the greatest number of visible evidences of His love. C. G. TRUMBULL 🖝

Believing Him; if storm-clouds gather darkly 'round,
And even if the heavens seem brass, without a sound?
He hears each prayer and even notes the sparrow's fall.

And praising Him; when sorrow, grief, and pain are near,
And even when we lose the thing that seems most dear?
Our loss is gain. Praise Him; in Him we have our All.

Our hand in His; e'en though the path seems long and drear
We scarcely see a step ahead, and almost fear?
He guides aright. He has it thus to keep us near.

And satisfied; when every path is blocked and bare,
And worldly things are gone and dead which were so fair?
Believe and rest and trust in Him, He comes to stay.

Delays are not refusals; many a prayer is registered, and underneath it the words: "My time is not yet come." God has a set time as well as a set purpose, and He who orders the bounds of our habitation orders also the time of our deliverance. SELECTED

January 25

Thy rod and thy staff they comfort me (Ps. 23:4).

At my father's house in the country there is a little closet in the chimney corner where are kept the canes and walkingsticks of several generations of our family. In my visits to the old house, when my father and I are going out for a walk, we often go to the cane closet and pick out our sticks to suit the fancy of the occasion. In this I have frequently been reminded that the Word of God is a staff.

During the war, when the season of discouragement and impending danger was upon us, the verse, "He shall not be afraid of evil tidings; his heart is fixed, trusting in the Lord," was a staff to walk with on many dark days.

When death took away our child and left us almost heartbroken, I found another staff in the promise that "weeping may endure for the night, but joy cometh in the morning."

When in impaired health, I was exiled for a year, not knowing whether I should be permitted to return to my home and work again, I took with me this staff which never failed, "He knoweth the thoughts that he thinketh toward me, thoughts of peace and not of evil."

In times of special danger or doubt, when human judgment has seemed to be set at naught, I have found it easy to go forward with this staff, "In quietness and confidence shall be your strength." And in emergencies, when there has seemed to be no adequate time for deliberation or for action, I have never found that this staff has failed me, "He that believeth shall not make haste." BENJAMIN VAUGHAN ABBOTT, IN THE OUTLOOK 🍃

"I had never known," said Martin Luther's wife, "what such and such things meant, in such and such psalms, such complaints and workings of spirit; I had never understood the practice of Christian duties, had not God brought me under some affliction." It is very true that God's rod is as the schoolmaster's pointer to the child, pointing out the letter, that he may the better take notice of it; thus He pointeth out to us many good lessons which we should never otherwise have learned. SELECTED 🍃

God always sends His staff with His rod.

Thy shoes shall be iron and brass; and as thy days, so shall thy strength be (Deut. 33:25).

Each of us may be sure that if God sends us on stony paths He will provide us with strong shoes, and He will not send us out on any journey for which He does not equip us well. MACLAREN 🍃

January 26

I have begun to give; . . . begin to possess (Deut. 2:31).

A great deal is said in the Bible about waiting for God. The lesson cannot be too strongly enforced. We easily grow impatient of God's delays. Much of our trouble in life comes out of our restless, sometimes reckless, haste. We cannot *wait* for the fruit to ripen, but insist on plucking it while it is green. We cannot *wait* for the answers to our prayers, although the things we ask for may require long years in their preparation for us. We are exhorted to walk with God; but ofttimes God walks very slowly. But there is another phase of the lesson. *God often waits for us.*

We fail many times to receive the blessing He has ready for us, because we do not go forward with Him. While we miss much good through not waiting for God, we also miss much through *over-waiting*. There are times when our strength is to sit still, but there are also times when we are to go forward with a firm step.

There are many divine promises which are conditioned upon the beginning of some action on our part. When we begin to obey, God will begin to bless us. Great things were promised to Abraham, but not one of them could have been obtained by waiting in Chaldea. He must leave home, friends, and country, and go out into unknown paths and press on in unfaltering obedience in order to receive the promises. The ten lepers were told to show themselves to the priest, and *"as they went they were cleansed."* If they had waited to *see the cleansing* come in their flesh before they would start, they would never have seen it. God was waiting to cleanse them; and the moment their faith began to work, the blessing came.

When the Israelites were shut in by a pursuing army at the Red Sea, they were commanded to "Go forward." Their duty was no longer one of waiting, but of rising up from bended knees and going forward in the way of heroic faith. They were commanded to show their faith at another time by beginning their march over the Jordan while the river ran to its widest banks. The key to unlock the gate into the land of promise they held in their own hands, and the gate would not turn on its hinges until they had approached it and unlocked it. That key was faith. We are set to fight certain battles. We say we can never be victorious; that we never can conquer these enemies; but, as we enter the conflict, *One* comes and fights by our side, and through Him we are more than conquerors. If we had waited, trembling and fearing, for our Helper to come before we would join the battle, we should have waited in vain. This would have been the *over-waiting* of unbelief. God is waiting to pour richest blessings upon you. Press forward with bold confidence and take what is yours. "I have begun to give, begin to possess." J. R. MILLER

January 27

Stablish, strengthen, settle you (1 Peter 5:10).

In taking Christ in any new relationship, we must first have sufficient intellectual light to satisfy our mind that we are entitled to stand in this relationship. The shadow of a question here will wreck our confidence. Then, having seen this, we must make the venture, the committal, the choice, and take the place just as definitely as the tree is planted in the soil, or the bride gives herself away at the marriage altar. It must be once and for all, without reserve, without recall.

Then there is a season of establishing, settling, and testing, during which we must "stay put" until the new relationship gets so fixed as to become a permanent habit. It is just the same as when the surgeon sets the broken arm. He puts it in splints to keep it from vibration. So God has His spiritual splints that He wants to put upon His children and keep them quiet and unmoved until they pass the first stage of faith. It is not always easy work for us, "but the God of all grace, who hath called us unto his eternal glory by Jesus Christ, after that ye have suffered awhile, stablish, strengthen, settle you." A. B. SIMPSON ☞

There is a natural law in sin and sickness; and if we just let ourselves go and sink into the trend of circumstances, we shall go down and sink under the power of the tempter. But there is another law of spiritual life and of physical life in Christ Jesus to which we can rise, and through which we can counterpoise and overcome the other law that bears us down.

But to do this requires real spiritual energy and fixed purpose and a settled posture and habit of faith. It is just the same as when we use the power in our factory. We must turn on the belt and keep it on. The power is there, but we must keep the connection; and while we do so, the higher power will work and all the machinery will be in operation.

There is a spiritual law of choosing, believing, abiding, and holding steady in our walk with God, which is essential to the working of the Holy Ghost either in our sanctification or healing. FROM DAYS OF HEAVEN UPON EARTH ☞

January 28

I am jealous over you with God's own jealousy (2 Cor. 11:2 WEYMOUTH).

☜～☞

How an old harper dotes on his harp! How he fondles and caresses it, as a child resting on his bosom! His life is bound up in it. But, see him tuning it. He grasps it firmly, strikes a chord with a sharp, quick blow; and while it quivers as if in pain, he leans over intently to catch the first note that rises. The note, as he feared, is false and harsh. He strains the chord with the torturing thumbscrew; and though it seems ready to snap with the tension, he strikes it again, bending down to listen softly as before, till at length you see a smile on his face as the first true tone trembles upward.

So it may be that God is dealing with you. Loving you better than any harper loves his harp, He finds you a mass of jarring discords. He wrings your heartstrings with some torturing anguish; He bends over you tenderly, striking and listening; and, hearing only a harsh murmur, strikes you again, while His heart bleeds for you, anxiously waiting for that strain—"Not my will, but thine be done"—which is melody sweet to His ear as angels' songs. Nor will He cease to strike until your chastened soul shall blend with all the pure and infinite harmonies of His own being. SELECTED ☞

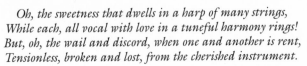

Oh, the sweetness that dwells in a harp of many strings,
While each, all vocal with love in a tuneful harmony rings!
But, oh, the wail and discord, when one and another is rent,
Tensionless, broken and lost, from the cherished instrument.

For rapture of love is linked with the pain or fear of loss,
And the hand that takes the crown, must ache with many a cross;
Yet he who hath never a conflict, hath never a victor's palm,
And only the toilers know the sweetness of rest and calm.

Only between the storms can the Alpine traveller know
Transcendent glory of clearness, marvels of gleam and glow;
Had he the brightness unbroken of cloudless summer days,
This had been dimmed by the dust and the veil of brooding haze.

Who would dare the choice, neither or both to know,
The finest quiver of joy or the agony thrill of woe!
Never the exquisite pain, then never the exquisite bliss,
For the heart that is dull to that can never be strung to this.

January 29

God is in the midst of her; she shall not be moved: God shall help her, and that right early (Ps. 46:5).

"Shall not be moved"—what an inspiring declaration! Can it be possible that we, who are so easily moved by the things of earth, can arrive at a place where nothing can upset us or disturb our calm? Yes, it is possible; and the apostle Paul knew it. When he was on his way to Jerusalem where he foresaw that "bonds and afflictions" awaited him, he could say triumphantly, "But none of these things move me." Everything in Paul's life and experience that could be shaken had been shaken, and he no longer counted his life, or any of life's possessions, dear to him. And we, if we will but let God have His way with us, may come to the same place, so that neither the fret and tear of little things of life, nor the great and heavy trials, can have power to move us from the peace that passeth understanding, which is declared to be the portion of those who have learned to rest only on God.

"Him that overcometh will I make a pillar in the temple of my God; and he shall go no more out." To be as immovable as a pillar in the house of our God, is an end for which one would gladly endure all the shakings that may be necessary to bring us there! HANNAH WHITALL SMITH

When God is in the midst of a kingdom or city He makes it as firm as Mount Zion, that cannot be removed. When He is in the midst of a soul, though calamities throng about it on all hands, and roar like the billows of the sea, yet there is a constant calm within, such a peace as the world can neither give nor take away. What is it but want of lodging God in the soul, and that in His stead the world is in men's hearts, that make them shake like leaves at every blast of danger? ARCHBISHOP LEIGHTON

"They that trust in the Lord shall be as Mount Zion, which cannot be removed, but abideth forever." There is a quaint old Scottish version that puts iron into our blood:

> *Who sticketh to God in stable trust*
> *As Zion's mount he stands full just,*
> *Which moveth no whit, nor yet doth reel,*
> *But standeth forever as stiff as steel!*

January 30

I will be as the dew unto Israel (Hos. 14:5).

The dew is a source of freshness. It is nature's provision for renewing the face of the earth. It falls at night, and without it the vegetation would die. It is this great value of the dew which is so often recognized in the Scriptures. It is used as the symbol of spiritual refreshing. Just as nature is bathed in dew, so the Lord renews His people. In Titus 3:5 the same thought of spiritual refreshing is connected with the ministry of the Holy Ghost—"renewing of the Holy Ghost."

Many Christian workers do not recognize the importance of the heavenly dew in their lives, and as a result they lack freshness and vigor. Their spirits are drooping for lack of dew.

Beloved fellow-worker, you recognize the folly of a laboring man attempting to do his day's work without eating. Do you recognize the folly of a servant of God attempting to minister without eating of the heavenly manna? Nor will it suffice to have spiritual nourishment occasionally. Every day you must receive the renewing of the Holy Ghost. You know when your whole being is pulsating with the vigor and freshness of divine life and when you feel jaded and worn. Quietness and absorption bring the dew. At night when the leaf and blade are still, the vegetable pores are open to receive the refreshing and invigorating bath; so spiritual dew comes from quiet lingering in the Master's presence. Get still before Him.

Haste will prevent your receiving the dew. Wait before God until you feel saturated with His presence; then go forth to your next duty with the conscious freshness and vigor of Christ. DR. PARDINGTON

Dew will never gather while there is either heat or wind. The temperature must fall, and the wind cease, and the air come to a point of coolness and rest—absolute rest, so to speak—before it can yield up its invisible particles of moisture to bedew either herb or flower. So the grace of God does not come forth to rest the soul of man until the *still point* is fairly and fully reached.

Drop Thy still dews of quietness,
Till all our strivings cease:
Take from our souls the strain and stress;
And let our ordered lives confess
The beauty of Thy peace.

Breathe through the pulses of desire
Thy coolness and Thy balm;
Let sense be dumb, its beats expire:
Speak through the earthquake, wind and fire,
O still small voice of calm!

January 31

He giveth quietness (Job 34:29).

Quietness amid the dash of the storm. We sail the lake with Him still; and as we reach its middle waters, far from land, under midnight skies, suddenly a great storm sweeps down. Earth and hell seem arrayed against us, and each billow threatens to overwhelm. Then He arises from His sleep, and rebukes the winds and the waves; His hand waves benediction and repose over the rage of the tempestuous elements. His voice is heard above the scream of the wind in the cordage and the conflict of the billows, "Peace, be still!" Can you not hear it? And there is instantly a great calm. "He giveth quietness." *Quietness amid the loss of inward consolations.* He sometimes withdraws these, because we make too much of them. We are tempted to look at our joy, our ecstasies, our transports, or our visions, with too great complacency. Then love for love's sake, withdraws them. But, by His grace, He leads us to distinguish between them and Himself. He draws nigh, and whispers the assurance of His presence. Thus an infinite calm comes to keep our heart and mind. "He giveth quietness."

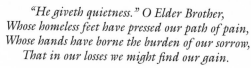

"He giveth quietness." O Elder Brother,
Whose homeless feet have pressed our path of pain,
Whose hands have borne the burden of our sorrow,
That in our losses we might find our gain.

Of all Thy gifts and infinite consolings,
I ask but this: in every troubled hour
To hear Thy voice through all the tumults stealing,
And rest serene beneath its tranquil power.

Cares cannot fret me if my soul be dwelling
In the still air of faith's untroubled day;
Grief cannot shake me if I walk beside thee,
My hand in Thine along the darkening way.

Content to know there comes a radiant morning
When from all shadows I shall find release;
Serene to wait the rapture of its dawning—
Who can make trouble when Thou sendest peace?

February 1

This thing is from me (1 Kings 12:24).

Life's disappointments are veiled love's appointments.
REV. C. A. FOX

My child, I have a message for you today; let me whisper it in your ear, that it may gild with glory any storm clouds which may arise, and smooth the rough places upon which you may have to tread. It is short, only five words, but let them sink into your inmost soul; use them as a pillow upon which to rest your weary head. *This thing is from ME.*

Have you ever thought of it, that all that concerns you concerns Me too? For, "he that toucheth you, toucheth the apple of mine eye" (Zech. 2:8). You are very precious in My sight (Isa. 43:4). Therefore, it is My special delight to educate you.

I would have you learn when temptations assail you, and the "enemy comes in like a flood," that this thing is from Me, that your weakness needs My might, and your safety lies in letting Me fight for you.

Are you in difficult circumstances, surrounded by people who do not understand you, who never consult your taste, who put you in the background? This thing is from Me. I am the God of circumstances.

Thou camest not to thy place by accident, it is the very place God meant for thee.

Have you not asked to be made humble? See then, I have placed you in the very school where this lesson is taught; your surroundings and companions are only working out My will.

Are you in money difficulties? Is it hard to make both ends meet? This thing is from Me, for I am your purse-bearer and would have you draw from and depend upon Me. My supplies are limitless (Phil. 4:19). I would have you prove my promises. Let it not be said of you, "In this thing ye did not believe the Lord your God" (Deut. 1:32).

Are you passing through a night of sorrow? This thing is from Me. I am the Man of Sorrows and acquainted with grief. I have let earthly comforters fail you, that by turning to Me you may obtain everlasting consolation (2 Thess. 2:16–17). Have you longed to do some great work for Me and instead have been laid aside on a bed of pain and weakness? This thing is from Me. I could not get your attention in your busy days and I want to teach you some of My deepest lessons. "They also serve who only stand and wait." Some of My greatest workers are those shut out from active service, that they may learn to wield the weapon of all-prayer.

This day I place in your hand this pot of holy oil. Make use of it free, My child. Let every circumstance that arises, every word that pains you, every interruption that would make you impatient, every revelation of your weakness be anointed with it. The sting will go as you learn to see Me in all things. LAURA A. BARTER SNOW ☙

"This is from Me," the Saviour said,
As bending low He kissed my brow,
"For One who loves you thus has led.
Just rest in Me, be patient now,
Your Father knows you have need of this,
Tho', why perchance you cannot see—
Grieve not for things you've seemed to miss.
The thing I send is best for thee."

Then, looking through my tears, I plead,
"Dear Lord, forgive, I did not know ,
'Twill not be hard since Thou dost tread,
Each path before me here below.
And for my good this thing must be,
His grace sufficient for each test.
So still I'll sing, 'Whatever be
God's way for me is always best.'"

February 2

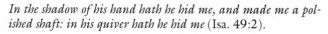

In the shadow of his hand hath he hid me, and made me a pol-
ished shaft: in his quiver hath he hid me (Isa. 49:2).

"In the shadow." We must all go there sometimes. The glare of the daylight is too brilliant; our eyes become injured, and unable to discern the delicate shades of color, or appreciate neutral tints—the shadowed chamber of sickness, the shadowed house of mourning, the shadowed life from which the sunlight has gone.

But fear not! It is the shadow of God's hand. He is leading thee. There are lessons that can be learned only there.

The photograph of His face can only be fixed in the dark chamber. But do not suppose that He has cast thee aside. Thou art still in His quiver; He has not flung thee away as a worthless thing.

He is only keeping thee close till the moment comes when He can send thee most swiftly and surely on some errand in which He will be glorified. Oh, shadowed, solitary ones, remember how closely the quiver is bound to the warrior, within easy reach of the hand, and guarded jealously. FROM CHRIST IN ISAIAH, *BY MEYER*

In some spheres the shadow condition is the condition of greatest growth. The beautiful Indian corn never grows more rapidly than in the shadow of a warm summer night. The sun curls the leaves in the sultry noon light, but they quickly unfold, if a cloud slips over the sky. There is a service in the shadow that is not in the shine. The world of stellar beauty is never seen at its best till the shadows of night slip over the sky. There are beauties that bloom in the shade that will not bloom in the sun. There is much greenery in lands of fog and clouds and shadow. The florist has "evening glories" now, as well as "morning glories." The "evening glory" will not shine in the noon's splendor, but comes to its best as the shadows of evening deepen.

> *If all of life were sunshine,*
> *Our faces would be fain*
> *To feel once more upon them*
> *The cooling splash of rain.*
>
> HENRY VAN DYKE

February 3

And immediately the spirit driveth him into the wilderness (Mark 1:12).

It seemed a strange proof of divine favor. "Immediately." Immediately after what? After the opened heavens and the dovelike peace and voice of the Father's blessing, "Thou art my beloved Son, in whom I am well pleased." It is no abnormal experience. Thou, too, hast passed through it, O my soul. Are not the times of thy deepest depression just the moments that follow thy loftiest flight? Yesterday thou wert soaring far in the firmament, and singing in the radiance of the morn; today thy wings are folded and thy song silent. At noon thou wert basking in the sunshine of a Father's smile; at eve thou art saying in the wilderness, "My way is hid from the Lord."

Nay, but, my soul, the very suddenness of the change is a proof that it is not revolutionary.

Hast thou weighed the comfort of that word "Immediately"? Why does it come so soon after the blessing? Just to show that it is the sequel to the blessing. God shines on thee to make thee fit for life's desert-places—for its Gethsemanes, for its Calvaries. He lifts thee up that He may give thee strength to go farther down; He illuminates thee that He may send thee into the night, that He may make thee a help to the helpless.

Not at all times art thou worthy of the wilderness; thou art only worthy of the wilderness after the splendors of Jordan. Nothing but the Son's vision can fit thee for the Spirit's burden; only the glory of the baptism can support the hunger of the desert. GEORGE MATHESON

After benediction comes battle.

The time of testing that marks and mightily enriches a soul's spiritual career is no ordinary one, but a period when all hell seems let loose, a period when we realize our souls are brought into a net, when we know that God is permitting us to be in the Devil's hand. But it is a period which always ends in certain triumph for those who have committed the keeping of their souls to Him, a period of marvelous "nevertheless afterward" of abundant usefulness, the sixty-fold that surely follows. APHRA WHITE

February 4

I will cause thee to ride upon the high places of the earth (Isa. 58: 14).

Those who fly through the air in airships tell us that one of the first rules they learn is to turn their ship toward the wind, and fly against it. The wind lifts the ship up to higher heights. Where did they learn that? They learned it from the birds. If a bird is flying for pleasure, it goes with the wind. But if the bird meets danger, it turns right around and faces the wind, in order that it may rise higher; and it flies away toward the very sun.

Sufferings are God's winds, His contrary winds, sometimes His strong winds. They are God's hurricanes, but they take human life and lift it to higher levels and toward God's heavens.

You have seen in the summertime a day when the atmosphere was so oppressive that you could hardly breathe? But a cloud appeared on the western horizon and that cloud grew larger and threw out rich blessing for the world. The storm rose, lightning flashed and thunder pealed. The storm covered the world, and the atmosphere was cleansed; new life was in the air, and the world was changed.

Human life is worked out according to exactly the same principle. When the storm breaks, the atmosphere is changed, clarified, filled with new life; and a part of heaven is brought down to earth. SELECTED

Obstacles ought to set us singing. The wind finds voice, not when rushing across the open sea, but when hindered by the outstretched arms of the pine trees, or broken by the fine strings of an aeolian harp. Then it has songs of power and beauty. Set your freed soul sweeping across the obstacles of life, through grim forests of pain, against even the tiny hindrances and frets that love uses, and it, too, will find its singing voice. SELECTED

> *Be like a bird that, halting in its flight,*
> *Rests on a bough too slight.*
> *And feeling it give way beneath him sings,*
> *Knowing he hath wings.*

February 5

Ye shall not go out with haste (Isa. 52:12).

I do not believe that we have begun to understand the marvelous power there is in stillness. We are in such a hurry—we must be doing—so that we are in danger of not giving God a chance to work. You may depend upon it; God never says to us, "Stand still," or "Sit still," or "Be still," unless *He* is going to do something.

This is our trouble in regard to our Christian life; *we* want to do something to be Christians when we need to let *Him* work in us. Do you know how still you have to be when your likeness is being taken?

Now God has one eternal purpose concerning us, and that is that we should be like His Son; and in order that this may be so, we must be passive. We hear so much about activity, maybe we need to know what it is to be quiet. FROM CRUMBS ᔕ

Sit still, my daughter! Just sit calmly still!
Nor deem these days—these waiting days—as ill!
The One who loves thee best, who plans thy way,
Hath not forgotten thy great need today!
And, if He waits, 'tis sure He waits to prove
To thee, His tender child, His heart's deep love.

Sit still, my daughter! Just sit calmly still!
Thou longest much to know thy dear Lord's will!
While anxious thoughts would almost steal their way
Corrodingly within, because of His delay—
Persuade thyself in simple faith to rest
That He, who knows and loves, will do the best.

Sit still, my daughter! Just sit calmly still!
Nor move one step, not even one, until
His way hath opened. Then, ah then, how sweet!
How glad thy heart, and then how swift thy feet
Thy inner being then, ah then, how strong!
And waiting days not counted then too long.

Sit still, my daughter! Just sit calmly still!
What higher service could'st thou for Him fill?
'Tis hard! ah yes! But choicest things must cost!
For lack of losing all how much is lost!
'Tis hard, 'tis true! But then—He giveth grace
To count the hardest spot the sweetest place.

J. DANSON SMITH ᔕ

48

February 6

He turned the sea into dry land; they went through the flood on foot: there did we rejoice in him (Ps. 66:6).

⌒⌒

It is a striking assertion, "through *the floods*" (the place where we might have expected nothing but trembling and terror, anguish and dismay), "there," says the psalmist, "did we rejoice in him!"

How many there are who can endorse this as their experience: that "there," in their very seasons of distress and sadness, they have been enabled, as they never did before, to triumph and rejoice.

How near their God in covenant is brought! How brightly shine His promises! In the day of our prosperity we cannot see the brilliancy of these. Like the sun at noon, hiding out the stars from sight, they are indiscernible; but when night overtakes, the deep, dark night of sorrow, out come these clustering stars—blessed constellations of Bible hope and promise of consolation.

Like Jacob at Jabbok, it is when our earthly sun goes down that the Divine Angel comes forth, and we wrestle with Him and prevail.

It was at night, "in the evening," Aaron lit the sanctuary lamps. It is in the night of trouble the brightest lamps of the believer are often kindled.

It was in his loneliness and exile John had the glorious vision of his Redeemer. There is many a Patmos still in the world, whose brightest remembrances are those of God's presence and upholding grace and love in solitude and sadness.

How many pilgrims, still passing through these Red Seas and Jordans of earthly affliction, will be enabled in the retrospect of eternity to say—full of the memories of God's great goodness—"We went through the flood on foot, *there*—there, in these dark experiences, with the surging waves on every side, deep calling to deep, Jordan, as when Israel crossed it, in 'the time of the overflowing' (flood), yet, *'there did* we rejoice in Him!'" DR. MACDUFF

And I will give her her vineyards from thence, and the valley of Achor for a door of hope: and she shall sing THERE (Hos. 2:15).

February 7

Why art thou cast down, O my soul? (Ps. 43:5).

⌒⌒

Is there ever any ground to be cast down? There are two reasons, but only two. If we are as yet unconverted, we have ground to be cast down; or if we have been converted and live in sin, then we are rightly cast down.

But except for these two things there is no ground to be cast down, for all else may be brought before God in prayer with supplication and thanksgiving. And regarding all our necessities, all our difficulties, all our trials, we may exercise faith in the power of God, and in the love of God.

"Hope thou in God." Oh, remember this: There is never a time when we may not hope in God. Whatever our necessities, however great our difficulties, and though to all appearance help is impossible, yet our business is to hope in God, and it will be found that it is not in vain. In the Lord's own time help will come.

Oh, the hundreds, yea, the thousands of times that I have found it thus within the past seventy years and four months!

When it seemed impossible that help could come, help did come; for God has His own resources. He is not confined. In ten thousand different ways, and at ten thousand different times God may help us.

Our business is to spread our cases before the Lord, in childlike simplicity to pour out all our heart before God, saying,

"I do not deserve that Thou shouldst hear me and answer my requests, but for the sake of my precious Lord Jesus; for His sake answer my prayer, and give me grace quietly to wait till it please Thee to answer my prayer. For I believe Thou wilt do it in Thine own time and way."

"For I shall yet praise him." More prayer, more exercise of faith, more patient waiting, and the result will be blessing, abundant blessing. Thus I have found it many hundreds of times, and therefore I continually say to myself, *"Hope thou in God."* GEORGE MUELLER

February 8

Lo, I am with you all the appointed days (Matt. 28:20, VARIORUM version).

Do not look forward to the changes and chances of this life in fear. Rather look at them with full hope that, as they arise, God, whose you are, will deliver you out of them. He has kept you hitherto; do you but hold fast to His dear hand, and He will lead you safely through all things; and when you cannot stand, He will bear you in His arms.

Do not look forward to what may happen tomorrow. The same everlasting Father who cares for you today will take care of you tomorrow, and every day. Either He will shield you from suffering, or He will give you unfailing strength to bear it. Be at peace, then, put aside all anxious thoughts and imaginations. FRANCES DE SALES 🖎

The Lord is my shepherd.

Not *was,* not *may be,* nor *will be.* "The Lord is my shepherd," *is* on Sunday, *is* on Monday, and *is* through every day of the week; *is* in January, *is* in December, and every month of the year; *is* at home, and *is* in China; *is* in peace, and *is* in war; in abundance, and in penury. J. HUDSON TAYLOR 🖎

> *HE will silently plan for thee,*
> *Object thou of omniscient care;*
> *God Himself undertakes to be*
> *Thy Pilot through each subtle snare.*
>
> *He WILL silently plan for thee,*
> *So certainly, He cannot fail!*
> *Rest on the faithfulness of God,*
> *In Him thou surely shalt prevail.*
>
> *He will SILENTLY plan for thee*
> *Some wonderful surprise of love.*
> *Eye hath not seen, nor ear hath heard,*
> *But it is kept for thee above.*
>
> *He will silently PLAN for thee,*
> *His purposes shall all unfold;*
> *The tangled skein shall shine at last,*
> *A masterpiece of skill untold.*
>
> *He will silently plan FOR THEE,*
> *Happy child of a Father's care,*
> *As though no other claimed His love,*
> *But thou alone to Him wert dear.*
>
> E. MARY GRIMES 🖎

Whatever our faith says God is, He will be.

February 9

He answered her not a word (Matt. 15:23).
He will rest in his love (Zeph. 3:17).

It may be a child of God is reading these words who has had some great crushing sorrow, some bitter disappointment, some heartbreaking blow from a totally unexpected quarter. You are longing for your Master's voice bidding you, "Be of good cheer," but only silence and a sense of mystery and misery meet you—"He answered her not a word."

God's tender heart must often ache listening to all the sad, complaining cries which arise from our weak, impatient hearts, because we do not see that for our own sakes He answers not at all or otherwise than seems best to our tear-blinded, shortsighted eyes.

The silences of Jesus are as eloquent as His speech and may be a sign, not of His disapproval, but of His approval and of a deep purpose of blessing for you.

"Why art thou cast down, O . . . soul?" Thou shalt yet praise Him, yes, even for His silence. Listen to an old and beautiful story of how one Christian dreamed that she saw three others at prayer. As they knelt the Master drew near to them.

As He approached the first of the three, He bent over her in tenderness and grace, with smiles full of radiant love and spoke to her in accents of purest, sweetest music.

Leaving her, He came to the next, but only placed His hand upon her bowed head, and gave her one look of loving approval.

The third woman He passed almost abruptly without stopping for a word or glance. The woman in her dream said to herself, "How greatly He must love the first one, to the second He gave His approval, but none of the special demonstrations of love He gave the first; and the third must have grieved Him deeply, for He gave her no word at all and not even a passing look.

"I wonder what she has done, and why He made so much difference between them?" As she tried to account for the action of her Lord, He Himself stood by her and said: "O woman! how wrongly hast thou interpreted Me. The first kneeling woman needs all the weight of My tenderness and care to keep her feet in My narrow way. She needs My love, thought, and help every moment of the day. Without it she would fail and fall.

"The second has stronger faith and deeper love, and I can trust her to trust Me however things may go and whatever people do.

"The third, whom I seemed not to notice, and even to neglect has faith and love of the finest quality, and her I am training by quick and drastic processes for the highest and holiest service.

"She knows Me so intimately, and trusts Me so utterly, that she is independent of words or looks or any outward intimation of My approval. She is not dismayed nor discouraged by any circumstances through which I arrange that she shall pass; she trusts Me when sense and reason and every finer instinct of the natural heart would rebel—because she knows that I am working in her for eternity, and that what I do, though she knows not the explanation now, she will understand hereafter.

"I am silent in My love because I love beyond the power of words to express, or of human hearts to understand, and also for your sakes that you may learn to love and trust Me in Spirit-taught, spontaneous response to My love, without the spur of anything outward to call it forth."

He "will do marvels" if you will learn the mystery of His silence, and praise Him, for every time He withdraws His gifts that you may better know and love the Giver. SELECTED ❧

February 10

Dearly beloved, avenge not yourselves (Rom. 12:19).

There are seasons when to be *still* demands immeasurably higher strength than to act. Composure is often the highest result of power. To the vilest and most deadly charges Jesus responded with deep, unbroken silence, such as excited the wonder of the judge and the spectators. To the grossest insults, the most violent ill-treatment and mockery that might well bring indignation into the feeblest heart, He responded with voiceless, complacent calmness. Those who are unjustly accused, and causelessly ill-treated know what tremendous strength is necessary to keep silence to God.

> *Men may misjudge thy aim,*
> *Think they have cause to blame,*
> *Say, thou art wrong;*
> *Keep on thy quiet way,*
> *Christ is the Judge, not they,*
> *Fear not, be strong.*

Saint Paul said, *"None of these things move me."*

He did not say, none of these things *hurt* me. It is one thing to be hurt, and quite another to be moved. Saint Paul had a very tender heart. We do not read of any apostle who cried as Saint Paul did. It takes a strong man to cry. Jesus wept, and He was the manliest Man that ever lived. So it does not say, none of these things hurt me. But the apostle had determined not to move from what he believed was right. He did not count as we are apt to count; he did not care for ease; he did not care for this mortal life. He cared for only one thing, and that was to be loyal to Christ, to have His smile. To Saint Paul, more than to any other man, His work was wages, His smile was heaven. MARGARET BOTTOME 🖎

February 11

As soon as the soles of the feet of the priests . . . shall rest in the waters . . . the waters . . . shall be cut off (Josh. 3:13).

The people were not to wait in their camps until the way was opened, they were to walk by faith. They were to break camp, pack up their goods, form in line to march, and move down to the very banks before the river would be opened.

If they had come down to the edge of the river and then had stopped for the stream to divide before they stepped into it, they would have waited in vain. They must take one step into the water before the river would be cut off.

We must learn to take God at His Word, and go straight on in duty, although we see no way in which we can go forward. The reason we are so often balked by difficulties is that we expect to see them removed before we try to pass through them.

If we would move straight on in faith, the path would be opened for us. We stand still, waiting for the obstacle to be removed, when we ought to go forward as if there were no obstacles. FROM EVENING THOUGHTS 🖎

What a lesson of perseverance Columbus gave to the world in the face of tremendous difficulties!

> *Behind him lay the gray Azores,*
> *Behind the gates of Hercules;*
> *Before him not the ghost of shores,*
> *Before him only shoreless seas,*
> *The good Mate said: "Now we must pray,*
> *For lo! the very stars are gone.*
> *Brave Admiral, speak, what shall I say?"*
> *"Why, say, 'Sail on! sail on! and on!'"*
>
> *"My men grow mutinous day by day;*
> *My men grow ghastly wan and weak!"*

The stout Mate thought of home; a spray
Of salt wave washed his swarthy cheek.
"What shall I say, brave Admiral, say,
If we sight naught but seas at dawn?"
"Why, you shall say at break of day,
'Sail on! sail on! sail on! and on!'"

They sailed. They sailed. Then spake the Mate:
"This mad sea shows its teeth tonight.
He curls his lip, he lies in wait,
With lifted teeth, as if to bite!
Brave Admiral, say but one good word;
What shall we do when hope is gone?"
The words leapt like a leaping sword:
"Sail on! sail on! sail on! and on!"

Then, pale and worn, he kept his deck
And peered through darkness. Ah! that night
Of all dark nights! And then a speck—
A light! A light! A light! A light!
It grew, a starlit flag unfurled!
It grew to be Time's burst of dawn.
He gained a world; he gave that world
Its grandest lesson: "On! sail on!"

JOAQUIN MILLER 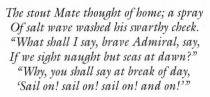

Faith that goes forward triumphs.

February 12

Your heavenly Father knoweth (Matt. 6:32).

A visitor at a school for the deaf and dumb was writing questions on the blackboard for the children. By and by he wrote this sentence: "Why has God made me to hear and speak, and made you deaf and dumb?"

The awful sentence fell upon the little ones like a fierce blow in the face. They sat palsied before that dreadful "Why?" And then a little girl arose.

Her lip was trembling. Her eyes were swimming with tears. Straight to the board she walked, and, picking up the crayon, wrote with firm hand these precious words: *"Even so, Father, for so it seemed good in thy sight!"* What a reply! It reaches up and lays hold of an eternal truth upon which the maturest believer as well as the youngest child of God may alike securely rest—the truth that God is your Father.

Do you mean that? Do you really and fully believe that? When you do, then your dove of faith will no longer wander in weary unrest, but will settle down forever in its eternal resting place of peace. "Your Father!"

I can still believe that a day comes for all of us, however far off it may be, when we shall understand; when these tragedies that now blacken and darken the very air of heaven for us, will sink into their places in a scheme so august, so magnificent, so joyful, that we shall laugh for wonder and delight. ARTHUR CHRISTOPHER BACON 🐝

No chance hath brought this ill to me;
'Tis God's own hand, so let it be,
He seeth what I cannot see.
There is a need-be for each pain,
And He one day will make it plain
That earthly loss is heavenly gain.
Like as a piece of tapestry
Viewed from the back appears to be
Naught but threads tangled hopelessly;
But in the front a picture fair
Rewards the worker for his care,
Proving his skill and patience rare.
Thou art the Workman, I the frame.
Lord, for the glory of Thy Name,
Perfect Thine image on the same.

SELECTED 🐝

February 13

The hill country shall be thine (Josh. 17:18 RV).

〰️

There is always room higher up. When the valleys are full of Canaanites, whose iron chariots withstand your progress, get up into the hills, occupy the upper spaces. If you can no longer work for God, pray for those who can. If you cannot move earth by your speech, you may move heaven. If the development of life on the lower slopes is impossible, through limitations of service, the necessity of maintaining others, and suchlike restrictions, let it break out toward the unseen, the eternal, the divine.

Faith can fell forests. Even if the tribes had realized what treasures lay above them, they would hardly have dared to suppose it possible to rid the hills of their dense forest growth. But as God indicated their task, He reminded them that they had power enough. The visions of things that seem impossible are presented to us, like these forest-covered steeps, not to mock us, but to incite us to spiritual exploits which would be impossible unless God had stored within us the great strength of His own indwelling.

Difficulty is sent to reveal to us what God can do in answer to the faith that prays and works. Are you straitened in the valleys? Get away to the hills, live there; get honey out of the rock, and wealth out of the terraced slopes now hidden by forest. FROM DAILY DEVOTIONAL COMMENTARY 🐦

> *Got any rivers they say are uncrossable,*
> *Got any mountains they say "can't tunnel through"?*
> *We specialize in the wholly impossible,*
> *Doing the things they say you can't do.*
> SONG OF THE PANAMA BUILDERS 🐦

February 14

And again I say, Rejoice (Phil. 4:4).

It is a good thing to rejoice in the Lord. Perhaps you have tried this, and the first time seemed to fail. Never mind, keep right on and when you cannot *feel* any joy, when there is no spring, and no seeming comfort and encouragement, still rejoice, and *count it all joy.* Even when you fall into diverse temptations, reckon it joy and delight and God will make your reckoning good. Do you suppose your Father will let you carry the banner of His victory and His gladness on to the front of the battle, and then coolly stand back and see you captured or beaten back by the enemy? NEVER! The Holy Spirit will sustain you in your bold advance, and fill your heart with gladness and praise, and you will find your heart all exhilarated and refreshed by the fullness within. Lord teach me to rejoice in Thee, and to "rejoice evermore." SELECTED 🐦

> *The weakest saint may Satan rout,*
> *Who meets him with a praiseful shout.*

> *Be filled with the Spirit, ... singing and making melody in your heart to the Lord* (Eph. 5:18–19).

Here the apostle urges the use of singing as one of the inspiring helps in the spiritual life. He counsels his readers not to seek their stimulus through the body, but through the spirit; not by the quickening of the flesh, but by the exaltation of the soul.

> *Sometimes a light surprises*
> *The Christian while he sings.*

Let us sing even when we do not feel like it, for thus we may give wings to leaden feet and turn weariness into strength. J. H. JOWETT 🕊

At midnight Paul and Silas prayed, and sang praises unto God: and the prisoners heard them (Acts 16:25).

Oh, Paul, thou wondrous example to the flock, who could thus glory, bearing in the body as thou didst "the marks of the Lord Jesus"! Marks from the stoning almost to the death, from thrice beating with rods, from those hundred and ninety-five stripes laid on thee by the Jews, and from stripes received in that Philippian jail, which had they not drawn blood would not have called for washing! Surely the grace which enabled thee to sing praises under such suffering is all-sufficient grace. J. ROACH 🕊

> *Oh, let us rejoice in the Lord, evermore,*
> *When darts of the tempter are flying,*
> *For Satan still dreads, as he oft did of yore,*
> *Our singing much more than our sighing.*

February 15

Fret not thyself (Ps. 37:1).

Do not get into a perilous heat about things. If ever heat were justified, it was surely justified in the circumstances outlined in the psalm. Evildoers were moving about clothed in purple and fine linen, and faring sumptuously every day. "Workers of iniquity" were climbing into the supreme places of power, and were tyrannizing their less fortunate brethren. Sinful men and women were stalking through the land in the pride of life and basking in the light and comfort of great prosperity, and good men were becoming heated and fretful.

"Fret not thyself." Do not get unduly heated! Keep cool! Even in a good cause, fretfulness is not a wise helpmeet. Fretting only heats the bearings; it does not generate the steam. It is no help to a train for the axles to get hot; their heat is only a hindrance. When the axles get heated, it is because of unnecessary friction; dry surfaces are grinding together, which ought to be kept in smooth cooperation by a delicate cushion of oil.

And is it not a suggestive fact that this word "fret" is closely akin to the word "friction," and is an indication of absence of the anointing oil of the grace of God?

In fretfulness, a little bit of grit gets into the bearings—some slight disappointment, some ingratitude, some discourtesy—and the smooth working of the life is checked. Friction begets heat; and with the heat, most dangerous conditions are created.

Do not let thy bearing get hot. Let the oil of the Lord keep thee cool, lest by reason of an unholy heat thou be reckoned among the evildoers. FROM THE SILVER LINING ☞

> *Dear restless heart, be still; don't fret and worry so;*
> *God has a thousand ways His love and help to show;*
> *Just trust, and trust, and trust, until His will you know.*
>
> *Dear restless heart, be still, for peace is God's own smile,*
> *His love can every wrong and sorrow reconcile;*
> *Just love, and love, and love, and calmly wait awhile.*
>
> *Dear restless heart, be brave; don't moan and sorrow so,*
> *He hath a meaning kind in chilly winds that blow;*
> *Just hope, and hope, and hope, until you braver grow.*
>
> *Dear restless heart, repose upon His breast this hour,*
> *His grace is strength and life, His love is bloom and flower;*
> *Just rest, and rest, and rest, within His tender power.*
>
> *Dear restless heart, be still! Don't struggle to be free;*
> *God's life is in your life, from Him you may not flee;*
> *Just pray, and pray, and pray, till you have faith to see.*
>
> EDITH WILLIS LINN ☞

February 16

Though I have afflicted thee, I will afflict thee no more (Nah. 1:12).

❦

There is a limit to affliction. God sends it, and removes it. Do you sigh and say, "When will the end be?" Let us quietly wait and patiently endure the will of the Lord till He cometh. Our Father takes away the rod when His design in using it is fully served.

If the affliction is sent for testing us, that our graces may glorify God, it will end when the Lord has made us bear witness to His praise.

We would not wish the affliction to depart until God has gotten out of us all the honor which we can possibly yield Him. There may be today "a great calm." Who knows how soon those raging billows will give place to a sea of glass, and the sea birds sit on the gentle waves?

After long tribulation, the flail is hung up, and the wheat rests in the garner. We may, before many hours are past, be just as happy as now we are sorrowful.

It is not hard for the Lord to turn night into day. He that sends the clouds can as easily clear the skies. Let us be of good cheer. It is better farther on. *Let us sing Hallelujah by anticipation.* C. H. SPURGEON

The great Husbandman is not always threshing. Trial is only for a season. The showers soon pass. Weeping may tarry only for the few hours of the short summer night; it must be gone at daybreak. Our light affliction is but for a moment. Trial is for a purpose, *"If needs be."*

The very fact of trial proves that there is something in us very precious to our Lord; else He would not spend so much pains and time on us. Christ would not test us if He did not see the precious ore of faith mingled in the rocky matrix of our nature; and it is to bring this out into purity and beauty that He forces us through the fiery ordeal.

Be patient, O sufferer! The result will more than compensate for all our trials, when we see how they wrought out the far more exceeding and eternal weight of glory. To have one word of God's commendation; to be honored before the holy angels; to be glorified in Christ, so as to be better able to flash His glory on Himself—ah! that will more than repay for all. FROM TRIED BY FIRE

As the weights of the clock, or the ballast in the vessel, are necessary for their right ordering, so is trouble in the soul-life. The sweetest scents are only obtained by tremendous pressure; the fairest flowers grow amid alpine snow-solitudes; the fairest gems have suffered longest from the lapidary's wheel; the noblest statues have borne most blows of the chisel. All, however, are under law. Nothing happens that has not been *appointed* with consummate care and foresight. FROM DAILY DEVOTIONAL COMMENTARY

February 17

The land which I do give to them, even to the children of Israel
(Josh. 1:2).

God here speaks in the immediate present. It is not something He is going to do, but something He does do, this moment. So faith ever speaks. So God ever gives. So He is meeting you today, in the present moment. This is the test of faith. So long as you are waiting for a thing, hoping for it, looking for it, you are not believing. It may be hope, it may be earnest desire, but it is not faith; for "faith is the substance of things hoped for, the evidence of things not seen." The command in regard to believing prayer is the present tense. "When ye pray, believe that ye receive the things that ye desire, and ye shall have them." Have we come to that moment? Have we met God in His everlasting NOW? FROM JOSHUA, BY SIMPSON

True faith counts on God, and believes before it sees. Naturally, we want some evidence that our petition is granted before we believe; but when we walk by faith we need no other evidence than God's Word. He has spoken, and according to our faith it shall be done unto us. We shall see because we have believed, and this faith sustains us in the most trying places, when everything around us seems to contradict God's Word.

The psalmist says, "I had fainted, unless I had *believed to see* the goodness of the Lord in the land of the living" (Ps. 27:13). He did not see as yet the Lord's answer to his prayers, but he *believed to see;* and this kept him from fainting.

If we have the faith that believes to see, it will keep us from growing discouraged. We shall "laugh at impossibilities," we shall watch with delight to see how God is going to open up a path through the Red Sea when there is no human way out of our difficulty. It is just in such places of severe testing that our faith grows and strengthens.

Have you been waiting upon God, dear troubled one, during long nights and weary days, and have feared that you were forgotten? Nay, lift up your head, and begin to praise Him even now for the deliverance which is on its way to you. FROM LIFE OF PRAISE

February 18

Have faith that whatever you ask for in prayer is already granted you, and you will find that it will be (Mark 11:24).

When my little son was about ten years of age, his grandmother promised him a stamp album for Christmas. Christmas came, but no stamp album, and no word from Grandmother. The matter, however, was not mentioned; but when his playmates came to see his Christmas presents, I was astonished, after he had named over this and that as gifts received, to hear him add, "And a stamp album from Grandmother."

I had heard it several times, when I called him to me, and said, "But, Georgie, you did not get an album from your grandmother. Why do you say so?"

There was a wondering look on his face, as if he thought it strange that I should ask such a question, and he replied, "Well, Mamma, Grandma *said*, so it is the same *as*." I could not say a word to check his faith.

A month went by, and nothing was heard about the album. Finally, one day, I said, to test his faith, and really wondering in my heart why the album had not been sent, "Well, Georgie, I think Grandma has forgotten her promise."

"Oh, no, Mamma," he quickly and firmly said, "she hasn't."

I watched the dear, trusting face, which, for a while, looked very sober, as if debating the possibilities I had suggested. Finally a bright light passed over it, and he said, "Mamma, do you think it would do any good if I should write to her *thanking* her for the album?"

"I do not know," I said, "but you might try it."

A rich spiritual truth began to dawn upon me. In a few minutes a letter was prepared and committed to the mail, and he went off whistling his confidence in his grandma. In just a short time a letter came, saying:

"My dear Georgie: I have not forgotten my promise to you, of an album. I tried to get such a book as you desired, but could not get the sort you wanted; so I sent on to New York. It did not get there till after Christmas, and it was still not right, so I sent for another, and as it has not come as yet, I send you three dollars to get one in Chicago. Your loving grandma."

As he read the letter, his face was the face of a victor. "Now, Mamma, didn't I tell you?" came from the depths of a heart that never doubted, that, "against hope, believed in hope" that the stamp album would come. While he was trusting, Grandma was working, and in due season faith became sight.

It is so human to want sight when we step out on the promises of God, but our Savior said to Thomas, and to the long roll of doubters who have ever since followed him: "Blessed are they who have not seen, and yet have believed." Mrs. Rounds

February 19

And every branch that beareth fruit he purgeth it, that it may bring forth more fruit (John 15:2).

A child of God was dazed by the variety of afflictions which seemed to make her their target. Walking past a vineyard in the rich autumnal glow she noticed the untrimmed appearance and the luxuriant wealth of leaves on the vines, that the ground was given over to a tangle of weeds and grass, and that the whole place looked utterly uncared for; and as she pondered, the heavenly Gardener whispered so precious a message that she would fain pass it on:

"My dear child, are you wondering at the sequence of trials in your life? Behold that vineyard and learn of it. The gardener ceases to prune, to trim, to harrow, or to pluck the ripe fruit only when he expects nothing more from the vine during that season. It is left to itself, because the season of fruit is past and further effort for the present would yield no profit. Comparative uselessness is the condition of freedom from suffering. Do you then wish me to cease pruning your life? Shall I leave you alone?" And the comforted heart cried, "No!" HOMERA HOMER-DIXON

> *It is the branch that bears the fruit,*
> *That feels the knife,*
> *To prune it for a larger growth,*
> *A fuller life.*
>
> *Though every budding twig be lopped,*
> *And every grace*
> *Of swaying tendril, springing leaf,*
> *Be lost a space.*
>
> *O thou whose life of joy seems reft,*
> *Of beauty shorn;*
> *Whose aspirations lie in dust,*
> *All bruised and torn,*
>
> *Rejoice, tho' each desire, each dream,*
> *Each hope of thine*
> *Shall fall and fade; it is the hand*
> *Of Love Divine*
>
> *That holds the knife, that cuts and breaks*
> *With tenderest touch,*
> *That thou, whose life has borne some fruit*
> *May'st now bear much.*

ANNIE JOHNSON FLINT

February 20

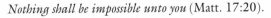

Nothing shall be impossible unto you (Matt. 17:20).

It is possible, for those who really are willing to reckon on the power of the Lord for keeping and victory, to lead a life in which His promises are taken as they stand and are found to be true.

It is possible to cast all our care upon Him daily and to enjoy deep peace in doing it.

It is possible to have the thoughts and imaginations of our hearts purified, in the deepest meaning of the word.

It is possible to see the will of God in everything, and to receive it, not with sighing, but with singing.

It is possible by taking complete refuge in divine power to become strong through and through; and, where previously our greatest weakness lay, to find that things which formerly upset all our resolves to be patient, or pure, or humble, furnish today an opportunity—through Him who loved us, and works in us as an agreement with His will and a blessed sense of His presence and His power—to make sin powerless over us.

These things are DIVINE POSSIBILITIES, and because they are His work, the true experience of them will always cause us to bow lower at His feet and to learn to thirst and long for more.

We cannot possibly be satisfied with anything less—each day, each hour, each moment, in Christ, through the power of the Holy Spirit—than to WALK WITH GOD. H. C. G. MOULE

We may have as much of God as we will. Christ puts the key of the treasure chamber into our hand, and bids us take all that we want. If a man is admitted into the bullion vault of a bank, and told to help himself, and comes out with one cent, whose fault is it that he is poor? Whose fault is it that Christian people generally have such scanty portions of the free riches of God? MCLAREN

February 21

Rest in the Lord, and wait patiently for him (Ps. 37:7).

Have you prayed and prayed and waited and waited, and still there is no manifestation?

Are you tired of seeing nothing move? Are you just at the point of giving it all up? Perhaps you have not waited in the right way? This would take you out of the right place—the place where He can meet you.

"*With patience wait*" (Rom. 8:25). Patience takes away *worry*. He said He would come, and His promise is equal to His presence. Patience takes away your *weeping*. Why feel sad and despondent? He knows your need better than you do, and His purpose in waiting is to bring more glory out of it all. Patience takes away self-*works*. The work He desires is that you "believe" (John 6:29), and when you believe, you may then know that all is well. Patience takes away all *want*. Your desire for the thing you wish is perhaps stronger than your desire for the will of God to be fulfilled in its arrival.

Patience takes away all *weakening*. Instead of having the delaying time, a time of letting go, know that God is getting a larger supply ready and must get you ready too. Patience takes away all *wobbling*. "Make me stand upon my standing" (Dan. 8:18, margin). God's foundations are steady; and when His patience is within, we are steady while we wait. Patience gives *worship*. A praiseful patience sometimes "longsuffering with joyfulness" (Col. 1:11) is the best part of it all. "Let [all these phases of] patience have her perfect work" (James 1:4), while you wait, and you will find great enrichment. C. H. P. ✸

> Hold steady when the fires burn,
> When inner lessons come to learn,
> And from this path there seems no turn—
> "Let patience have her perfect work."
>
> L. S. P. ✸

February 22

If thou canst believe, all things are possible to him that believeth (Mark 9:23).

✤

Seldom have we heard a better definition of faith than was given once in one of our meetings, by a dear old colored woman, as she answered the question of a young man *how to take the Lord for needed help*.

In her characteristic way, pointing her finger toward him, she said with great emphasis: "You've just got to believe that He's done it and it's done." The great danger with most of us is that, after we ask Him to do it, we do not believe that it is done, but we keep on helping Him, and getting others to help Him; and waiting to see how He is going to do it.

Faith adds its "Amen" to God's "Yea," and then takes its hands off, and leaves God to finish His work. Its language is, "Commit thy way unto the Lord, trust also in him; and he worketh." FROM DAYS OF HEAVEN UPON EARTH 🖉

> *I simply take Him at His word,*
> *I praise Him that my prayer is heard,*
> *And claim my answer from the Lord;*
> *I take, He undertakes.*

An active faith can give thanks for a promise, though it be not as yet performed; knowing that God's bonds are as good as ready money. MATTHEW HENRY 🖉

> *Passive faith accepts the word as true—*
> *But never moves.*
> *Active faith begins the work to do,*
> *And thereby proves.*

> *Passive faith says, "I believe it! every word of God is true.*
> *Well I know He hath not spoken what He cannot, will not, do.*
> *He hath bidden me, 'Go forward!' but a closed-up way I see,*
> *When the waters are divided, soon in Canaan's land I'll be.*
> *Lo! I hear His voice commanding, 'Rise and walk: take up thy bed';*
> *And, 'Stretch forth thy withered member!' which for so long has been dead.*
> *When I am a little stronger, then, I know I'll surely stand:*
> *When there comes a thrill of healing, I will use with ease my other hand.*
> *Yes, I know that 'God is able' and full willing all to do:*
> *I believe that every promise, sometime, will to me come true."*

> *Active faith says, "I believe it! and the promise now I take,*
> *Knowing well, as I receive it, God, each promise, real will make.*
> *So I step into the waters, finding there an open way;*
> *Onward press, the land possessing; nothing can my progress stay.*
> *Yea, I rise at His commanding, walk straightway, and joyfully:*
> *This, my hand so sadly shrivelled, as I reach, restored shall be.*
> *What beyond His faithful promise, would I wish or do I need?*
> *Looking not for 'signs or wonders,' I'll no contradiction heed.*
> *Well I know that 'God is able,' and full willing all to do:*
> *I believe that every promise, at this moment can come true."*

> *Passive faith but praises in the light,*
> *When sun doth shine.*
> *Active faith will praise in darkest night—*
> *Which faith is thine?*

SELECTED 🖉

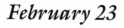

February 23

And there came a lion (1 Sam. 17:34).

It is a source of inspiration and strength to come in touch with the youthful David, trusting God. Through faith in God he conquered a lion and a bear, and afterward overthrew the mighty Goliath. When that lion came to despoil that flock, it came as a wondrous *opportunity* to David. If he had failed or faltered he would have missed God's opportunity for him and probably would never have come to be God's chosen king of Israel. *"And there came a lion."*

One would not think that a lion was a special blessing from God; one would think that only an occasion of alarm. The lion was *God's opportunity in disguise*. Every difficulty that presents itself to us, if we receive it in the right way, is God's opportunity. Every temptation that comes is God's opportunity.

When the "lion" comes, recognize it as God's opportunity no matter how rough the exterior. The very tabernacle of God was covered with badgers' skins and goats' hair; one would not think there would be any glory there. The Shekinah of God was manifest under that kind of covering. May God open our eyes to see Him, whether in temptations, trials, dangers, or misfortunes. C. H. P.

February 24

John did no miracle: but all things that John spake of this man were true (John 10:41).

You may be very discontented with yourself. You are no genius, have no brilliant gifts, and are inconspicuous for any special faculty. Mediocrity is the law of your existence. Your days are remarkable for nothing but sameness and insipidity. Yet you may live a great life.

John did no miracle, but Jesus said that among those born of women there had not appeared a greater than he.

John's main business was to bear witness to the Light, and this may be yours and mine. John was content to be only a voice, if men would think of Christ.

Be willing to be only a voice, heard but not seen; a mirror whose surface is lost to view, because it reflects the dazzling glory of the sun; a breeze that springs up just before daylight, and says, "The dawn! the dawn!" and then dies away.

Do the commonest and smallest things as beneath His eye. If you must live with uncongenial people, set to the conquest by love. If you have made a great mistake in your life, do not let it becloud all of it; but, locking the secret in your breast, compel it to yield strength and sweetness.

We are doing more good than we know, sowing seed, starting streamlets, giving men true thoughts of Christ, to which they will refer one day as the first things that started them thinking of Him; and, of my part, I shall be satisfied if no great mausoleum is raised over my grave, but that simple souls shall gather there when I am gone, and say, "He was a good man; he wrought no miracles, but he spake words about Christ, which led me to know Him for myself." GEORGE MATHESON

Thy Hidden Ones (Ps. 83:3)

Thick green leaves from the soft brown earth,
Happy springtime hath called them forth;
First faint promise of summer bloom
Breathes from the fragrant, sweet perfume,
Under the leaves.

Lift them! what marvelous beauty lies
Hidden beneath, from our thoughtless eyes!
Mayflowers, rosy or purest white,
Lift their cups to the sudden light,
Under the leaves.

Are there no lives whose holy deeds—
Seen by no eye save His who reads
Motive and action—in silence grow
Into rare beauty, and bud and blow
Under the leaves?
Fair white flowers of faith and trust,

Springing from spirits bruised and crushed;
Blossoms of love, rose-tinted and bright,
Touched and painted with Heaven's own light
Under the leaves.

Full fresh clusters of duty borne,
Fairest of all in that shadow grown;
Wondrous the fragrance that sweet and rare
Come from the flower-cups hidden there
Under the leaves.

Though unseen by our vision dim,
Bud and blossom are known to Him;
Wait we content for His heavenly ray—
Wait till our Master Himself one day
Lifteth the leaves.

God calls many of His most valued workers from the unknown
multitude (Luke 14:23).

February 25

Every place that the sole of your foot shall tread upon, that have
I given unto you (Josh. 1:3).

Beside the literal ground, unoccupied for Christ, there is the unclaimed, untrodden territory of *divine promises.* What did God say to Joshua? *"Every place* that the sole of your foot shall tread upon, that *have I given* unto you."* And then He draws the outlines of the land of promise—all theirs on one condition: *that they shall march through the length and breadth of it,* and measure it off with their own feet.

They never did that to more than one-third of the property, and consequently they never *had* more than one-third; they had just what they measured off, and no more.

In 2 Peter, we read of the "land of promise" that is opened up to us, and it is God's will that we should, as it were, measure off that territory by the feet of obedient faith and believing obedience, thus claiming and appropriating it for our own.

How many of us have ever taken possession of the promises of God in the name of Christ?

Here is a magnificent territory for faith to lay hold on and march through the length and breadth of, and faith has never done it yet.

Let us enter into all our inheritance. Let us lift up our eyes to the north and to the south, to the east and to the west, and hear Him say, "All the land that thou seest will I give to thee." A. T. Pierson

Wherever Judah should set his foot that should be his; wherever Benjamin should set his foot, that should be his. Each should get his inheritance by setting his foot upon it. Now, think you not, when either had set his foot upon a given territory, he did not instantly and instinctively feel, "This is mine"?

An old colored man, who had a marvelous experience in grace, was asked: "Daniel, why is it that you have so much peace and joy in religion?" "O Massa!" he replied, "I just fall flat on the exceeding great and precious promises, and I have all that is in them. Glory! Glory!" He who falls flat on the promises feels that all the riches embraced in them are his. FROM FAITH PAPERS

The Marquis of Salisbury was criticized for his Colonial policies and replied: "Gentlemen, get larger maps."

February 26

My grace is sufficient for thee (2 Cor. 12:9).

The other evening I was riding home after a heavy day's work. I felt very wearied, and sore depressed, when swiftly, and suddenly as a lightning flash, that text came to me, "My grace is sufficient for thee." I reached home and looked it up in the original, and at last it came to me in this way, *"MY grace is sufficient for thee"*; and I said, "I should think it is, Lord," and burst out laughing. I never fully understood what the holy laughter of Abraham was until then. It seemed to make unbelief so absurd. It was as though some little fish, being very thirsty, was troubled about drinking the river dry, and Father Thames said, "Drink away, little fish, my stream is sufficient for thee." Or, it seemed after the seven years of plenty, a mouse feared it might die of famine; and Joseph might say, "Cheer up, little mouse, my granaries are sufficient for thee." Again, I imagined a man away up yonder, in a lofty mountain, saying to himself, "I breathe so many cubic feet of air every year, I fear I shall exhaust the oxygen in the atmosphere," but the earth might say, "Breathe away, O man, and fill the lungs ever, my atmosphere is sufficient for thee." Oh, brethren, be great believers! Little faith will bring your souls to heaven, but great faith will bring heaven to your souls. C. H. SPURGEON

> *His grace is great enough to meet the great things—*
> *The crashing waves that overwhelm the soul,*
> *The roaring winds that leave us stunned and breathless,*
> *The sudden storms beyond our life's control.*
>
> *His grace is great enough to meet the small things—*
> *The little pin-prick troubles that annoy,*
> *The insect worries, buzzing and persistent,*
> *The squeaking wheels that grate upon our joy.*
>
> ANNIE JOHNSON FLINT

There is always a large balance to our credit in the bank of heaven waiting for our exercise of faith in drawing it. Draw heavily upon His resources.

February 27

And Jacob was left alone; and there wrestled a man with him until the breaking of the day (Gen. 32:24).

Left alone! What different sensations those words conjure up to each of us. To some they spell loneliness and desolation, to others rest and quiet. To be left alone *without* God would be too awful for words, but to be left alone *with* Him is a foretaste of heaven! If His followers spent more time alone with Him, we should have spiritual giants again.

The Master set us an example. Note how often He went to be *alone with God;* and He had a mighty purpose behind the command, "When thou prayest, enter into thy closet and *when thou hast shut thy door, pray.*"

The greatest miracles of Elijah and Elisha took place when they were alone with God. It was alone with God that Jacob became a prince; and just there that we, too, may become princes—"men [aye, and women too!] wondered at" (Zech. 3:8). Joshua was alone when the Lord came to him. (Josh. 1:1). Gideon and Jephthah were by themselves when commissioned to save Israel (Judg. 6:11 and 11:29). Moses was by himself at the wilderness bush (Exod. 3:1–5). Cornelius was praying by himself when the angel came to him (Acts 10:2). No one was with Peter on the housetop when he was instructed to go to the Gentiles (Acts 10:9). John the Baptist was alone in the wilderness (Luke 1:80), and John the Beloved alone in Patmos, when nearest to God (Rev. 1:9).

Covet to get alone with God. If we neglect it, we not only rob ourselves, but others, too, of blessing, since when we are blessed we are able to pass on blessing to others. It may mean less outside work; it must mean more depth and power, and the consequence, too, will be "they saw no man save Jesus only."

To be alone with God in prayer cannot be overemphasized.

> *If chosen men had never been alone,*
> *In deepest silence open-doored to God,*
> *No greatness would ever have been dreamed or done.*

February 28

Let us offer the sacrifice of praise to God continually (Heb. 13:15).

A city missionary, stumbling through the dirt of a dark entry, heard a voice say, "Who's there, Honey?" Striking a match, he caught a vision of earthly want and suffering, of saintly trust and peace, "cut in ebony"— calm, appealing eyes set amid the wrinkles of a pinched, black face that lay on a tattered bed. It was a bitter night in February, and she had no fire, no fuel, no light. She had had no supper, no dinner, no breakfast. She seemed to have nothing at all but rheumatism and faith in God. One could not well be more completely exiled from all pleasantness of circumstances, yet the favorite song of this old creature ran:

> *Nobody knows de trouble I see,*
> *Nobody knows but Jesus;*
> *Nobody knows de trouble I see—*
> *Sing Glory Hallelu!*

> *Sometimes I'm up, sometimes I'm down,*
> *Sometimes I'm level on the groun',*
> *Sometimes the glory shines aroun'—*
> *Sing Glory Hallelu!*

And so it went on: "Nobody knows de work I does, Nobody knows de griefs I has," the constant refrain being the *"Glory Hallelu!"* until the last verse rose:

> *Nobody knows de joys I has,*
> *Nobody knows but Jesus!*

"Troubled on every side, yet not distressed; perplexed, but not in despair; persecuted, but not forsaken; cast down, but not destroyed." It takes great Bible words to tell the cheer of the old negro auntie.

Remember Luther on his sickbed. Between his groans he managed to preach on this wise: "These pains and trouble here are like the type which the printers set; as they look now, we have to read them backwards, and they seem to have no sense or meaning in them; but up yonder, when the Lord God prints us off in the life to come, we shall find they make brave reading." Only we do not need to wait till then. Remember Paul walking the hurricane deck amid a boiling sea, bidding the frightened crew "Be of good cheer," Luther, the old negro auntie—all of them human sunflowers. WM. C. GARNETT

February 29

Launch out into the deep (Luke 5:4).

How deep He does not say. The depth into which we launch will depend upon how perfectly we have given up the shore, and the greatness of our need, and the apprehension of our possibilities. The fish were to be found in the deep, not in the shallow water.

So with us; our needs are to be met in the deep things of God. We are to launch out into the deep of God's Word, which the Spirit can open up to us in such crystal fathomless meaning that the same words we have accepted in times past will have an ocean meaning in them, which renders their first meaning to us very shallow.

Into the deep of the atonement, until Christ's precious blood is so illuminated by the Spirit that it becomes an omnipotent balm, and food and medicine for the soul and body.

Into the deep of the Father's will, until we apprehend it in its infinite minuteness and goodness, and its far-sweeping provision and care for us.

Into the deep of the Holy Spirit, until He becomes a bright, dazzling, sweet, fathomless summer sea, in which we bathe and bask and breathe, and lose ourselves and our sorrows in the calmness and peace of His everlasting presence.

Into the deep of the Holy Spirit, until He becomes a bright, marvelous answer to prayer, the most careful and tender guidance, the most thoughtful anticipation of our needs, the most accurate and supernatural shaping of our events.

Into the deep of God's purposes and coming kingdom, until the Lord's coming and His millennial reign are opened up to us; and beyond these the bright entrancing ages on ages unfold themselves, until the mental eye is dazed with light, and the heart flutters with inexpressible anticipations of its joy with Jesus and the glory to be revealed.

Into all these things, Jesus bids us launch. He made us and He made the deep, and to its fathomless depths He has fitted our longings and capabilities. FROM SOUL FOOD

> *Its streams the whole creation reach,*
> *So plenteous is the store;*
> *Enough for all, enough for each;*
> *Enough forevermore.*

The deep waters of the Holy Spirit are always accessible, because they are always *proceeding.* Will you not this day claim afresh to be immersed and drenched in these waters of life? The waters in Ezekiel's vision first of all oozed from under the doors of the temple. Then the man with the measuring line measured and found the waters to the ankles. Still further measurement, and they were waters to the knees. Once again they were measured and the waters were to the loins. Then they became waters to swim in—a river that could not be passed over (read Ezek. 47). How far have we advanced into this river of life? The Holy Spirit would have a complete self-effacement. Not merely ankle-deep, knee-deep, loin-deep, but self-deep. We ourselves hidden out of sight and bathed in this life-giving stream. Let go the shorelines and launch out into the deep. Never forget, the Man with the measuring line is with us today. J. G. M. ✵

March 1

Consider the work of God: for who can make that straight, which he hath made crooked? (Eccles. 7:13).

⌒

Often God seems to place His children in positions of profound difficulty, leading them into a wedge from which there is no escape; contriving a situation which no human judgment would have permitted, had it been previously consulted. The very cloud conducts them thither. You may be thus involved at this very hour.

It does seem perplexing and very serious to that degree, but it is perfectly right. The issue will more than justify Him who has brought you hither. It is a platform for the display of His almighty grace and power.

He will not only deliver you; but in doing so, He will give you a lesson that you will never forget, and to which, in many a psalm and song, in after days, you will revert. You will never be able to thank God enough for having done just as He has. SELECTED ✵

We may wait till He explains,
Because we know that Jesus reigns.

It puzzles me; but, Lord, Thou understandest,
And wilt one day explain this crooked thing.
Meanwhile, I know that it has worked out Thy best—
Its very crookedness taught me to cling.

Thou has fenced up my ways, made my paths crooked,
To keep my wand'ring eyes fixed on Thee,
To make me what I was not, humble, patient;
To draw my heart from earthly love to Thee.

So I will thank and praise Thee for this puzzle,
And trust where I cannot understand.
Rejoicing Thou dost hold me worth such testing,
I cling the closer to Thy guiding hand.

F. E. M. I. 🖋

March 2

Be ready in the morning, and come up . . . present thyself there to
me in the top of the mount. And no man shall come up with thee
(Exod. 34:2–3).

The morning watch is essential. You must not face the day until you have faced God, nor look into the face of others until you have looked into His.

You cannot expect to be victorious, if the day begins only in your own strength. Face the work of every day with the influence of a few thoughtful, quiet moments with your heart and God. Do not meet other people, even those of your own home, until you have first met the great Guest and honored Companion of your life—Jesus Christ.

Meet Him alone. Meet Him regularly. Meet Him with His open Book of counsel before you; and face the regular and the irregular duties of each day with the influence of His personality definitely controlling your every act.

> *Begin the day with God!*
> *He is thy Sun and Day!*
> *His is the radiance of thy dawn;*
> *To Him address thy day.*
>
> *Sing a new song at morn!*
> *Join the glad woods and hills:*
> *Join the fresh winds and seas and plains,*
> *Join the bright flowers and rills.*
>
> *Sing thy first song to God!*
> *Not to thy fellow men;*
> *Not to the creatures of His hand,*
> *But to the glorious One.*

Take thy first walk with God!
Let Him go forth with thee;
By stream, or sea, or mountain path,
Seek still His company.

Thy first transaction be
With God Himself above;
So shall thy business prosper well,
All the day be love.

HORATIUS BONAR

The men who have done the most for God in this world have been early upon their knees.

Matthew Henry used to be in his study at four, and remain there till eight; then, after breakfast and family prayer, he used to be there again till noon; after dinner, he resumed his book or pen till four, and spent the rest of the day in visiting friends.

Doddridge himself alludes to his "Family Expositor" as an example of the difference of rising between five and seven, which, in forty years, is nearly equivalent to ten years more of life.

Dr. Adam Clark's "Commentary" was chiefly prepared very early in the morning.

Barnes's popular and useful "Commentary" has been also the fruit of "early morning hours."

Simeon's "Sketches" were chiefly worked out between four and eight.

March 3

And the spirit cried, and rent him sore, and came out of him (Mark 9:26).

Evil never surrenders its hold without a sore fight. We never pass into any spiritual inheritance through the delightful exercises of a picnic, but always through the grim contentions of the battlefield. It is so in the secret realm of the soul. Every faculty which wins its spiritual freedom does so at the price of blood. Apollyon is not put to flight by a courteous request; he straddles across the full breadth of the way, and our progress has to be registered in blood and tears. This we must remember or we shall add to all the other burdens of life the gall of misinterpretation. We are not "born again" into soft and protected nurseries, but in the open country where we suck strength from the very terror of the tempest. "We must through much tribulation enter into the kingdom of God." DR. J. H. JOWETT

Faith of our Fathers! living still,
In spite of dungeon, fire and sword:
O how our hearts beat high with joy
Whene'er we hear that glorious word.
Faith of our Fathers! Holy Faith!
We will be true to Thee till death!

Our fathers, chained in prisons dark,
Were still in heart of conscience free;
How sweet would be their children's fate,
If they, like them, could die for Thee!

March 4

Followers of them who through faith and patience inherit the promises (Heb. 6:12).

They (heroes of faith) are calling to us from the heights that they have won, and telling us that what man once did man can do again. Not only do they remind us of the necessity of faith, but also of that patience by which faith has its perfect work. Let us fear to take ourselves out of the hands of our heavenly Guide or to miss a single lesson of His loving discipline by discouragement or doubt.

"There is only one thing," said a village blacksmith, "that I fear, and that is to be thrown on the scrap heap.

"When I am tempering a piece of steel, I first heat it, hammer it, and then suddenly plunge it into the bucket of cold water. I very soon find whether it will take temper or go to pieces in the process. When I discover after one or two tests that it is not going to allow itself to be tempered, I throw it on the scrap heap and sell it for a cent a pound when the junkman comes around.

"So I find the Lord tests me, too, by fire and water and heavy blows of His heavy hammer, and if I am willing to stand the test, or am not going to prove a fit subject for His tempering process, I am afraid He may throw me on the scrap heap."

When the fire is hottest, hold still, for there will be a blessed "afterward"; and with Job we may be able to say, "When he hath tried me I shall come forth as gold." SELECTED

Sainthood springs out of suffering. It takes eleven tons of pressure on a piano to tune it. God will tune you to harmonize with heaven's keynote if you can stand the strain.

> *Things that hurt and things that mar*
> *Shape the man for perfect praise;*
> *Shock and strain and ruin are*
> *Friendlier than the smiling days.*

March 5

We are made partakers of Christ, if we hold the beginning of our confidence steadfast unto the end (Heb. 3:14).

It is the last step that wins; and there is no place in the pilgrim's progress where so many dangers lurk as the region that lies hard by the portals of the Celestial City. It was there that Doubting Castle stood. It was there that the enchanted ground lured the tired traveler to fatal slumber. It is when heaven's heights are full in view that hell's gate is most persistent and full of deadly peril. "Let us not be weary in well-doing, for in due season we shall reap, *if we faint not.*" "So run, that ye may obtain."

> *In the bitter waves of woe*
> *Beaten and tossed about*
> *By the sullen winds that blow*
> *From the desolate shores of doubt,*
> *Where the anchors that faith has cast*
> *Are dragging in the gale,*
> *I am quietly holding fast*
> *To the things that cannot fail.*
>
> *And fierce though the fiends may fight,*
> *And long though the angels hide,*
> *I know that truth and right*
> *Have the universe on their side;*
> *And that somewhere beyond the stars*
> *Is a love that is better than fate.*
> *When the night unlocks her bars,*
> *I shall see Him—and I will wait.*

WASHINGTON GLADDEN

The problem of getting great things from God is being able to hold on for the last half hour. SELECTED

March 6

We trusted (Luke 24:21).

I have always felt so sorry that in that walk to Emmaus the disciples had not said to Jesus, "We *still* trust"; instead of *"We trusted."* That is so sad—something that is all over.

If they had only said, "Everything is against our hope; it looks as if our trust was vain, but we do not give up; we believe we shall see Him again." But no, they walked by His side declaring their lost faith, and He had to say to them, "O fools, and slow of heart to believe!"

Are we not in the same danger of having these words said to us? We can afford to lose anything and everything if we do not lose our faith in the God of truth and love.

Let us never put our faith, as these disciples did, in a past tense— *"We trusted."* But let us ever say, *"I am trusting."* FROM CRUMBS

> *The soft, sweet summer was warm and glowing,*
> *Bright were the blossoms on every bough:*
> *I trusted Him when the roses were blooming;*
> *I trust Him now....*
>
> *Small were my faith should it weakly falter*
> *Now that the roses have ceased to blow;*
> *Frail were the trust that now should alter,*
> *Doubting His love when storm clouds grow.*
> THE SONG OF A BIRD IN A WINTER STORM

March 7

We were troubled on every side (2 Cor. 7:5).

Why should God have to lead us thus, and allow the pressure to be so hard and constant? Well, in the first place, it shows His all-sufficient strength and grace much better than if we were exempt from pressure and trial. "The treasure is in earthen vessels, that the excellency of the power may be of God, and not of us."

It makes us more conscious of our dependence upon Him. God is constantly trying to teach us our dependence, and to hold us absolutely in His hand and hanging upon His care.

This was the place where Jesus Himself stood and where He wants us to stand, not with self-constituted strength, but with a hand ever leaning upon His, and a trust that dare not take one step alone. It teaches us trust.

There is no way of learning faith except by trial. It is God's school of faith, and it is far better for us to learn to trust God than to enjoy life.

The lesson of faith once learned, is an everlasting acquisition and an eternal fortune made; and without trust even riches will leave us poor. FROM DAYS OF HEAVEN UPON EARTH

Why must I weep when others sing?
"To test the deeps of suffering."
Why must I work while others rest?
"To spend my strength at God's request."
Why must I lose while others gain?
"To understand defeat's sharp pain."
Why must this lot of life be mine
When that which fairer seems is thine?
"Because God knows what plans for me
Shall blossom in eternity."

March 8

Do as thou hast said . . . that thy name may be magnified forever (1 Chron. 17:23–24).

This is a most blessed phase of true prayer. Many a time we ask for things which are not absolutely promised. We are not sure therefore until we have persevered for some time whether our petitions are in the line of God's purpose or no. There are other occasions, and in the life of David this was one, when we are fully persuaded that what we ask is according to God's will. We feel led to take up and plead some promise from the page of Scripture, under the special impression that it contains a message for us. At such times, in confident faith, we say, "Do as Thou hast said." There is hardly any position more utterly beautiful, strong, or safe, than to put the finger upon some promise of the divine word, and claim it. There need be no anguish, or struggle, or wrestling; we simply present the check and ask for cash, produce the promise, and claim its fulfillment; nor can there be any doubt as to the issue. It would give much interest to prayer, if we were more definite. It is far better to claim a few things specifically than a score vaguely. F. B. MEYER

Every promise of Scripture is a writing of God, which may be pleaded before Him with this reasonable request: *"Do as Thou hast said."* The Creator will not cheat His creature who depends upon His truth; and far more, the heavenly Father will not break His word to His own child.

"Remember the word unto thy servant, on which thou hast caused me to hope," is most prevalent pleading. It is a double argument: it is Thy *Word.* Wilt Thou not keep it? Why hast Thou spoken of it, if Thou wilt not make it good? Thou hast caused me to hope in it; wilt Thou disappoint the hope which Thou hast Thyself begotten in me? C. H. SPURGEON

Being absolutely certain that whatever promise he is bound by, he is able also to make good (Rom. 4:21 WEYMOUTH).

It is the everlasting faithfulness of God that makes a Bible promise "exceeding great and precious." Human promises are often worthless. Many a broken promise has left a broken heart. But since the world was made, God has never broken a single promise made to one of His trusting children.

Oh, it is sad for a poor Christian to stand at the door of the promise, in the dark night of affliction, afraid to draw the latch, whereas he should then come boldly for shelter as a child into his father's house. GURNAL

Every promise is built upon four pillars: God's justice and holiness, which will not suffer Him to deceive; His grace or goodness, which will not suffer Him to forget; His truth, which will not suffer Him to change, which makes Him able to accomplish. SELECTED

March 9

Look from the top (Song of Sol. 4:8).

Crushing weights give the Christian wings. It seems like a contradiction in terms, but it is a blessed truth. David out of some bitter experience cried: "Oh, that I had wings like a dove! for then would I fly away, and be at rest" (Ps. 55:6). But before he finished this meditation he seems to have realized that his wish for wings was a realizable one. For he says, "Cast thy burden upon the Lord, and he shall sustain thee."

The word "burden" is translated in the Bible margin, "what he (Jehovah) hath given thee." The saints' burdens are God-given; they lead him to "wait upon Jehovah," and when that is done, in the magic of trust, the "burden" is metamorphosed into a pair of wings, and the weighted one "mounts up with wings as eagles." FROM SUNDAY SCHOOL TIMES

One day when walking down the street,
On business bent, while thinking hard
About the "hundred cares" which seemed
Like thunder clouds about to break
In torrents, Self-pity said to me:
"You poor, poor thing, you have too much
To do. Your life is far too hard.
This heavy load will crush you soon."
A swift response of sympathy
Welled up within. The burning sun
Seemed more intense. The dust and noise
Of puffing motors flying past
With rasping blast of blowing horn
Incensed still more the whining nerves,
The fabled last back-breaking straw
To weary, troubled, fretting mind.

"Ah, yes, 'twill break and crush my life;
I cannot bear this constant strain
Of endless, aggravating cares;
They are too great for such as I."
So thus my heart condoled itself,
"Enjoying misery," when lo!
A "still small voice" distinctly said,
" 'Twas sent to lift you—not to crush."
I saw at once my great mistake.
My place was not beneath the load
But on the top! God meant it not
That I should carry it. He sent
It here to carry me. Full well
He knew my incapacity
Before the plan was made. He saw
A child of His in need of grace
And power to serve; a puny twig
Requiring sun and rain to grow;
An undeveloped chrysalis;
A weak soul lacking faith in God.
He could not help but see all this
And more. And then, with tender thought
He placed it where it had to grow—
Or die. To lie and cringe beneath
One's load means death, but life and power

Await all those who dare to rise above.
Our burdens are our wings; on them
We soar to higher realms of grace;
Without them we must roam for aye
On plains of undeveloped faith,
(For faith grows but by exercise
In circumstance impossible).

Oh, paradox of Heaven. The load
We think will crush was sent to lift us
Up to God! Then, soul of mine,
Climb up! for naught can e'er be crushed
Save what is underneath the weight.
How may we climb! By what ascent
Shall we surmount the carping cares
Of life! Within His word is found
The key which opens His secret stairs;
Alone with Christ, secluded there,
We mount our loads, and rest in Him.

MISS MARY BUTTERFIELD

March 10

The just shall live by faith (Heb. 10:38).

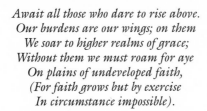

Seemings and feelings are often substituted for faith. Pleasurable emotions and deep satisfying experiences are part of the Christian life, but they are not all of it. Trials, conflicts, battles and testings lie along the way, and are not to be counted as misfortunes, but rather as part of our necessary discipline.

In all these varying experiences we are to reckon on Christ as dwelling in the heart, regardless of our feelings if we are walking obediently before Him. Here is where many get into trouble; they try to walk by feeling rather than faith.

One of the saints tells us that it seemed as though God had withdrawn Himself from her. His mercy *seemed* clean gone. For six weeks her desolation lasted, and then the heavenly Lover seemed to say: "Catherine, thou hast looked for Me without in the world of sense, but all the while I have been within waiting for thee; meet Me in the inner chamber of thy spirit, *for I am there.*"

Distinguish between the fact of God's presence, and the *emotion* of the fact. It is a happy thing when the soul seems desolate and deserted, if our faith can say, "I see Thee not. I feel Thee not, but Thou art certainly and graciously here, where I am as I am." Say it again and again: "Thou are here: though the bush does not seem to burn with fire, it *does* burn. I will take the shoes from off my feet, for the place on which I stand is holy ground." LONDON CHRISTIAN ☜

Believe God's Word and power more than you believe your own feelings and experiences. Your Rock is Christ, and it is not the Rock which ebbs and flows, but your sea. SAMUEL RUTHERFORD ☜

Keep your eye steadily fixed on the infinite grandeur of Christ's finished work and righteousness. Look to Jesus and believe, look to Jesus and live! Nay, more; as you look to him, hoist your sails and buffet manfully the sea of life. Do not remain in the haven of distrust, or sleeping on your shadows in inactive repose, or suffering your frames and feelings to pitch and toss on one another like vessels idly moored in a harbor. The religious life is not a brooding over emotions, grazing the keel of faith in the shallows, of dragging the anchor of hope through the oozy tide mud as if afraid of encountering the healthy breeze. Away! With your canvas spread to the gale, trusting in Him, who rules the raging of the waters. The safety of the tinted bird is to be on the wing. If its haunt be near the ground—if it fly low—it exposes itself to the fowler's net or snare. If we remain groveling on the low ground of feeling and emotion, we shall find ourselves entangled in a thousand meshes of doubt and despondency, temptation and unbelief. "But surely in vain the net is spread in the sight of THAT WHICH HATH A WING" (marginal reading Prov. 1:17). Hope thou in God. J. R. MACDUFF ☜

When I cannot enjoy the faith of assurance, I live by the faith of adherence.

MATTHEW HENRY ☜

March 11

Now after the death of Moses, the servant of the Lord, it came to pass that the Lord spake unto Joshua, the son of Nun, Moses' minister, saying, Moses my servant is dead; now, therefore arise, go over this Jordan, thou and all this people (Josh. 1:1–2).

Sorrow came to you yesterday, and emptied your home. Your first impulse now is to give up, and sit down in despair amid the wrecks of your hopes. But you dare not do it. You are in the line of battle, and the crisis is at hand. To falter a moment would be to imperil some holy interest. Other lives would be harmed by your pausing, holy interests would suffer, should your hands be folded. You must not linger even to indulge your grief.

A distinguished general related this pathetic incident of his own experience in time of war. The general's son was a lieutenant of battery. An assault was in progress. The father was leading his division in a charge; as he pressed on in the field, suddenly his eye was caught by the sight of a dead battery-officer lying just before him. One glance showed him it was his own son. His fatherly impulse was to stop beside the loved form and give vent to his grief, but the duty of the moment demanded that he should press on in the charge; so, quickly snatching one hot kiss from the dead lips, he hastened away, leading his command in the assault.

Weeping inconsolably beside a grave can never give back love's banished treasure, nor can any blessing come out of such sadness. Sorrow makes deep scars; it writes its record ineffaceably on the heart which suffers. We really never get over our great griefs; we are never altogether the same after we have passed through them as we were before. Yet there is a humanizing and fertilizing influence in sorrow which has been rightly accepted and cheerfully borne. Indeed, they are poor who have never suffered, and have none of sorrow's marks upon them. The joy set before us should shine upon our griefs as the sun shines through the clouds, glorifying them. God has so ordered, that in pressing on in duty we shall find the truest, richest comfort for ourselves. Sitting down to brood over our sorrows, the darkness deepens about us and creeps into our heart, and our strength changes to weakness. But, if we turn away from the gloom, and take up the tasks and duties to which God calls us, the light will come again, and we shall grow stronger. J. R. MILLER

Thou knowest that through our tears
Of hasty, selfish weeping
Comes surer sin, and for our petty fears
Of loss thou hast in keeping
A greater gain than all of which we dreamed;
Thou knowest that in grasping
The bright possessions which so precious seemed
We lose them; but if, clasping
Thy faithful hand, we tread with steadfast feet

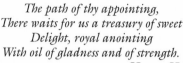

The path of thy appointing,
There waits for us a treasury of sweet
Delight, royal anointing
With oil of gladness and of strength.

HELEN HUNT JACKSON

March 12

The Lord brought an east wind upon the land all that day, and all that night; and when it was morning, the east wind brought the locusts.... Then Pharaoh called for Moses and Aaron in haste.... And the Lord turned a mighty strong west wind, which took away the locusts, and cast them into the Red sea; there remained not one locust in all the coasts of Egypt (Exod. 10:13, 16, 19).

See how in the olden times, when the Lord fought for Israel against the cruel Pharaoh, the *stormy winds* wrought out their deliverance; and yet again, in that grandest display of power—the last blow that God struck at the proud defiance of Egypt. A strange, almost cruel thing it must have seemed to Israel to be hemmed in by such a host of dangers—in front the wild sea defying them, on either hand the rocky heights cutting off all hope of escape, the night of hurricane gathering over them. It was as if that first deliverance had come only to hand them over to more certain death. Completing the terror there rang out the cry: *"The Egyptians are upon us!"*

When it seemed they were trapped for the foe, then came the glorious triumph. Forth swept the *stormy wind* and beat back the waves, and the hosts of Israel marched forward, down into the path of the great deep—a way arched over with God's protecting love.

On either hand were the crystal walls glowing in the light of the glory of the Lord; and high above them swept the thunder of the storm. So on through all that night; and when, at dawn the next day, the last of Israel's host set foot upon the other shore, the work of the *stormy wind* was done.

Then sang Israel unto the Lord the song of the *"stormy wind fulfilling his word."*

"The enemy said, I will pursue, I will overtake, I will divide the spoil.... Thou didst blow with thy wind, the sea covered them: they sank as lead in the mighty waters."

One day, by God's great mercy, we, too, shall stand upon the sea of glass, having the harps of God. Then we shall sing the song of Moses, the servant of God, and the song of the Lamb: "Just and true are thy ways, thou King of saints." We shall know then how the *stormy winds* have wrought out our deliverance.

Now you see only the mystery of this great sorrow; then you shall see how the threatening enemy was swept away in the wild night of fear and grief.

Now you look only at the loss; then you shall see how it struck at the evil that had begun to rivet its fetters upon you.

Now you shrink from the howling winds and muttering thunders; then you shall see how they beat back the waters of destruction, and opened up your way to the goodly land of promise. MARK GUY PEARSE

Though winds are wild,
And the gale unleashed,
My trusting heart still sings:
I know that they mean
No harm to me,
He rideth on their wings.

March 13

Just and true are thy ways, thou King of saints (Rev. 15:3).

The following incident is related by Mrs. Charles Spurgeon, who was a great sufferer for more than a quarter of a century:

"At the close of a dark and gloomy day, I lay resting on my couch as the deeper night drew on; and though all was bright within my cozy room, some of the external darkness seemed to have entered into my soul and obscured its spiritual vision. Vainly I tried to see the hand which I knew held mine, and guided my fog-enveloped feet along a steep and slippery path of suffering. In sorrow of heart I asked,

"'Why does my Lord thus deal with His child? Why does He so often send sharp and bitter pain to visit me? Why does He permit lingering weakness to hinder the sweet service I long to render to His poor servants?'

"These fretful questions were quickly answered, and through a strange language; no interpreter was needed save the conscious whisper of my heart.

"For a while silence reigned in the little room, broken only by the crackling of the oak log burning in the fireplace. Suddenly I heard a sweet, soft sound, a little, clear, musical note, like the tender trill of a robin beneath my window.

"'What can it be? Surely no bird can be singing out there at this time of the year and night.'

"Again came the faint, plaintive notes, so sweet, so melodious, yet mysterious enough to provoke our wonder. My friend exclaimed,

"'It comes from the log on the fire!' The fire was letting loose the imprisoned music from the old oak's inmost heart!

"Perchance he had garnered up this song in the days when all was well with him, when birds twittered merrily on his branches, and the soft sunlight flecked his tender leaves with gold. But he had grown old since then, and hardened; ring after ring of knotty growth had sealed up the long-forgotten melody, until the fierce tongues of the flames came to consume his callousness, and the vehement heart of the fire wrung from him at once a song and a sacrifice. 'Ah,' thought I, 'when the fire of affliction draws songs of praise from us, then indeed we are purified, and our God is glorified!'

"Perhaps some of us are like this old oak log, cold, hard, insensible; we should give forth no melodious sounds, were it not for the fire which kindles around us, and releases notes of trust in Him, and cheerful compliance with His will.

"As I mused the fire burned, and my soul found sweet comfort in the parable so strangely set forth before me.

"Singing in the fire! Yes, God helping us, if that is the only way to get harmony out of these hard apathetic hearts, let the furnace be heated seven times hotter than before."

March 14

Moses drew near unto the thick darkness where God was (Exod. 20:21).

God has still His hidden secrets, hidden from the wise and prudent. Do not fear them; be content to accept things that you cannot understand; wait patiently. Presently He will reveal to you the treasures of darkness, the riches of the glory of the mystery. Mystery is only the veil of God's face.

Do not be afraid to enter the cloud that is settling down on your life. God is in it. The other side is radiant with His glory. "Think it not strange concerning the fiery trial which is to try you, as though some strange thing happened unto you; but rejoice, inasmuch as ye are partakers of Christ's sufferings." When you seem loneliest and most forsaken, God is nigh. He is in the dark cloud. Plunge into the blackness of its darkness without flinching; under the shrouding curtain of His pavilion you will find God awaiting you. SELECTED 🖎

Hast thou a cloud?
Something that is dark and full of dread?
A messenger of tempest overhead?
A something that is darkening the sky;
A something growing darker bye and bye;
A something that thou fear'st will burst at last;
A cloud that doth a deep, long shadow cast,
God cometh in that cloud.

Hast thou a cloud?
It is Jehovah's triumph car: in this
He rideth to thee, o'er the wide abyss
It is the robe in which He wraps His form;
For He doth gird Him with the flashing storm.
It is the veil in which He hides the light
Of His fair face, too dazzling for thy sight.
God cometh in that cloud.

Hast thou a cloud?
A trial that is terrible to thee?
A black temptation threatening to see?
A loss of some dear one long thine own?
A mist, a veiling, bringing the unknown?
A mystery that unsubstantial seems:
A cloud between thee and the sun's bright beams?
God cometh in that cloud.

Hast thou a cloud?
A sickness—weak old age—distress and death?
These clouds will scatter at thy last faint breath.
Fear not the clouds that hover o'er thy barque,
Making the harbour's entrance dire and dark;
The cloud of death, though misty, chill and cold,
Will yet grow radiant with a fringe of gold.
GOD cometh in that cloud.

As Dr. C. stood on a high peak of the Rocky Mountains watching a storm raging below him, an eagle came up through the clouds and soared away toward the sun, and the water upon him glistened in the sunlight like diamonds. Had it not been for the storm he might have remained in the valley. The sorrows of life cause us to rise toward God.

March 15

Fear not, thou worm Jacob. . . . I will make thee a new sharp threshing instrument having teeth (Isa. 41:14, 15).

Could any two things be in greater contrast than a worm and an instrument with teeth? The worm is delicate, bruised by a stone, crushed beneath the passing wheel; an instrument with teeth can break and not be broken; it can grave its mark upon the rock. And the mighty God can convert the one into the other. He can take a man or a nation, who has all the impotence of the worm, and by the invigoration of His own Spirit, He can endow with strength by which a noble mark is left upon the history of the time.

And so the "worm" may take heart. The mighty God can make us stronger than our circumstances. He can bend them all to our good. In God's strength we can make them all pay tribute to our souls. We can even take hold of a black disappointment, break it open, and extract some jewel of grace. When God gives us will like iron, we can drive through difficulties as the iron share cuts through the toughest soil. "I will make thee," and shall He not do it? Dr. Jowett

Christ is building His kingdom with earth's broken things. Men want only the strong, the successful, the victorious, the unbroken, in building their kingdoms; but God is the God of the unsuccessful, of those who have failed. Heaven is filling with earth's broken lives, and there is no bruised reed that Christ cannot take and restore to glorious blessedness and beauty. He can take the life crushed by pain or sorrow and make it into a harp whose music shall be all praise. He can lift earth's saddest failure up to heaven's glory. J. R. Miller

Follow Me, and I will make you . . .
Make you speak My words with power,
Make you channels of My mercy,
Make you helpful every hour.

Follow Me, and I will make you . . .
Make you what you cannot be—
Make you loving, trustful, godly,
Make you even like to Me.

L. S. P.

March 16

In one of Ralph Conner's books he tells a story of Gwen. Gwen was a wild, willful lassie and one who had always been accustomed to having her own way. Then one day she met with a terrible accident which crippled her for life. She became very rebellious and in the murmuring state she was visited by the sky pilot, as the missionary among the mountaineers was termed.

He told her the parable of the canyon. "At first there were no canyons, but only the broad, open prairie. One day the Master of the prairie, walking over his great lawns, where were only grasses, asked the prairie, 'Where are your flowers?' and the prairie said, 'Master, I have no seeds.'

"Then he spoke to the birds, and they carried seeds of every kind of flower and strewed them far and wide, and soon the prairie bloomed with crocuses and roses and buffalo beans and the yellow crowfoot and the wild sunflowers and the red lilies all summer long. Then the Master came and was well pleased; but he missed the flowers he loved best of all, and he said to the prairie: 'Where are the clematis and the columbine, the sweet violets and wildflowers, and all the ferns and flowering shrubs?'

"And again he spoke to the birds, and again they carried all the seeds and scattered them far and wide. But, again, when the Master came he could not find the flowers he loved best of all, and he said:

"'Where are those my sweetest flowers?' and the prairie cried sorrowfully:

"'Oh, Master, I cannot keep the flowers, for the winds sweep fiercely, and the sun beats upon my breast, and they wither up and fly away.'

"Then the Master spoke to the lightning, and with one swift blow the lightning cleft the prairie to the heart. And the prairie rocked and groaned in agony, and for many a day moaned bitterly over the black, jagged, gaping wound.

"But the river poured its waters through the cleft, and carried down deep black mold, and once more the birds carried seeds and strewed them in the canyon. And after a long time the rough rocks were decked out with soft mosses and trailing vine, and all the nooks were hung with clematis and columbine, and great elms lifted their huge tops high up into the sunlight, and down about their feet clustered the low cedars and balsams, and everywhere the violets and windflower and maidenhair grew and bloomed, till the canyon became the Master's favorite place for rest and peace and joy."

Then the sky pilot read to her: "The fruit—I'll read 'flowers'—of the Spirit are love, joy, peace, longsuffering, gentleness—and some of these grow only in the canyon."

"Which are the canyon flowers?" asked Gwen softly, and the pilot answered: "Gentleness, meekness, longsuffering; but though the others, love, joy, peace, bloom in the open, yet never with so rich a bloom and so sweet a perfume as in the canyon."

For a long time Gwen lay quite still, and then said wistfully, while her lips trembled: "There are no flowers in my canyon but only ragged rocks."

"Some day they will bloom, Gwen dear; the Master will find them, and we, too, shall see them."

Beloved, when *you* come to your canyon, remember!

March 17

Be thou there till I bring thee word (Matt. 2:13).

I'll stay where You've put me; I will, dear Lord,
Though I wanted so badly to go;
I was eager to march with the "rank and file,"
Yes, I wanted to lead them, You know.
I planned to keep step to the music loud,
To cheer when the banner unfurled,
To stand in the midst of the fight straight and proud,
But I'll stay where You've put me.

I'll stay where You've put me; I'll work, dear Lord,
Though the field be narrow and small,
And the ground be fallow, and the stones lie thick,
And there seems to be no life at all.
The field is thine own, only give me the seed,
I'll sow it with never a fear;
I'll till the dry soil while I wait for the rain,
And rejoice when the green blades appear;
I'll work where You've put me.

I'll stay where You've put me; I will, dear Lord;
I'll bear the day's burden and heat,
Always trusting Thee fully; when even has come
I'll lay heavy sheaves at Thy feet.

And then, when my earth work is ended and done,
In the light of eternity's glow,
Life's record all closed, I surely shall find
It was better to stay than to go;
I'll stay where You've put me.

"Oh, restless heart, that beat against your prison bars of circumstances, yearning for a wider sphere of usefulness, leave God to order all your days. Patience and trust, in the dullness of the routine of life, will be the best preparation for a courageous bearing of the tug and strain of the larger opportunity which God may sometime send you."

March 18

He answered no thing (Mark 15:3).

There is no spectacle in all the Bible so sublime as the silent Savior answering not a word to the men who were maligning Him, and whom He could have laid prostrate at His feet by one look of divine power, or one word of fiery rebuke. But He let them say and do their worst, and He stood in THE POWER OF STILLNESS—God's holy silent Lamb.

There is a stillness that lets God work for us, and holds our peace; the stillness that ceases from its contriving and its self-vindication, and its expedients of wisdom and forethought, and lets God provide and answer the cruel blow, in His own unfailing, faithful love.

How often we lose God's interposition by taking up our own cause, and striking for our defense. God give to us this silent power, this conquered spirit! And after the heat and strife of earth are over, men will remember us as we remember the morning dew, the gentle light and sunshine, the evening breeze, the Lamb of Calvary, and the gentle, holy heavenly Dove. A. B. SIMPSON

The day when Jesus stood alone
And felt the hearts of men like stone,
And knew He came but to atone—
That day "He held His peace."

They witnessed falsely to His word,
They bound Him with a cruel cord,
And mockingly proclaimed Him Lord;
"But Jesus held His peace."

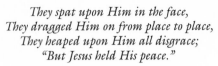

They spat upon Him in the face,
They dragged Him on from place to place,
They heaped upon Him all disgrace;
"But Jesus held His peace."

My friend, have you for far much less,
With rage, which you called righteousness,
Resented slights with great distress?
Your Saviour "held His peace."

L. S. P. 🐦

I remember once hearing Bishop Whipple, of Minnesota, so well known as "The Apostle of the Indians," utter these beautiful words: "For thirty years I have tried to see the face of Christ in those with whom I differed." When this spirit actuates us we shall be preserved at once from a narrow bigotry and an easygoing tolerance, from passionate vindictiveness and everything that would mar or injure our testimony for Him who came not to destroy men's lives, but to save them. W. H. GRIFFITH THOMAS 🐦

March 19

Beloved, do not be surprised at the ordeal that has come to test you . . . you are sharing what Christ suffered; so rejoice in it (1 Peter 4:12).

Many a waiting hour was needful to enrich the harp of David, and many a waiting hour in the wilderness will gather for us a psalm of "thanksgiving, and the voice of melody," to cheer the hearts of fainting ones here below, and to make glad our Father's house on high.

What was the preparation of the son of Jesse for the songs like unto which none others have ever sounded on this earth?

The outrage of the wicked, which brought forth cries for God's help; then, the faint hope in God's goodness blossomed into a song of rejoicing for His mighty deliverances and manifold mercies. Every sorrow was another string to his harp; every deliverance another theme for praise.

One thrill of anguish spared, one blessing unmarked or unprized, one difficulty or danger evaded, how great would have been our loss in that thrilling psalmody in which God's people today find the expression of their grief or praise!

To wait for God, and to suffer His will, is to know Him in the fellowship of His sufferings, and to be conformed to the likeness of His Son.

So now, if the vessel is to be enlarged for spiritual under-standing, be not affrighted at the wider sphere of suffering that awaits you. The divine capacity of sympathy will have a more extended sphere, for the breathing of the Holy Ghost in the new creation never made a stoic, but left the heart's affection tender and true. ANNA SHIPTON

"He tested me ere He entrusted me" (1 Tim. 1:12, WAY'S translation).

March 20

As sorrowful, yet always rejoicing (2 Cor. 6:10).

The stoic scorns to shed a tear; the Christian is not forbidden to weep. The soul may be dumb with excessive grief, as the shearer's scissors pass over the quivering flesh; or, when the heart is on the point of breaking beneath the meeting surges of trial, the sufferer may seek relief by crying out with a loud voice. *But there is something even better.*

They say that springs of sweet fresh water well up amid the brine of salt seas; that the fairest alpine flowers bloom in the wildest and most rugged mountain passes; that the noblest psalms were the outcome of the profoundest agony of soul.

Be it so. And thus amid manifold trials, souls which love God will find reasons for bounding, leaping joy. Though deep call to deep, yet the Lord's song will be heard in silver cadence through the night. And *it is possible in the darkest hour* that ever swept a human life to bless the God and Father of our Lord Jesus Christ. Have you learned this lesson yet? Not simply to endure God's will, nor only to choose it; but to rejoice in it with joy unspeakable and full of glory. FROM TRIED AS BY FIRE

> *I will be still, my bruised heart faintly murmured,*
> *As o'er me rolled a crushing load of woe;*
> *Then cry, the call, e'en the low moan was stifled;*
> *I pressed my lips; I barred the tear drop's flow.*
>
> *I will be still, although I cannot see it,*
> *The love that bares a soul and fans pain's fire;*
> *That takes away the last sweet drop of solace,*
> *Breaks the lone harp string, hides Thy precious lyre.*
>
> *But God is love, so I will bide me, bide me—*
> *We'll doubt not, Soul, we will be very still;*

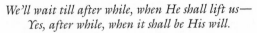

We'll wait till after while, when He shall lift us—
Yes, after while, when it shall be His will.

And I did listen to my heart's brave promise;
And I did quiver, struggling to be still;
And I did lift my tearless eyes to Heaven,
Repeating ever, "Yea, Christ, have Thy will."

But soon my heart upspake from 'neath our burden,
Reproved my tight-drawn lips, my visage sad:
"We can do more than this, O Soul," it whispered.
"We can be more than still, we can be glad!"

And now my heart and I are sweetly singing—
Singing without the sound of tuneful strings;
Drinking abundant waters in the desert;
Crushed, and yet soaring as on eagle's wings.

S. P. W.

March 21

According to your faith be it unto you (Matt. 9:29).

"Praying through" might be defined as *praying one's way into full faith,* emerging while yet praying into the assurance that one has been accepted and heard, so that one becomes actually aware of receiving, by firmest anticipation and in advance of the event, the thing for which he asks.

Let us remember that no earthly circumstances can hinder the fulfillment of His Word if we look steadfastly at the immutability of that Word and not at the uncertainty of this ever-changing world. God would have us believe His Word without other confirmation, *and then* He is ready to give us "according to our faith."

> *When once His Word is past,*
> *When He hath said, "I will," (Heb. 13:5)*
> *The thing shall come at last;*
> *God keeps His promise still (2 Cor. 1:20).*

The prayer of the Pentecostal age was like a cheque to be paid in coin over the counter. SIR R. ANDERSON

And God said ... and it was so (Gen. 1:9).

March 22

And when forty years were expired, there appeared to him in the wilderness of Mount Sinai an angel of the Lord in a flame of fire in a bush ... saying ... I have seen the affliction of my people which is in Egypt, and I have heard their groaning, and am come down to deliver them. And now come, I will send thee into Egypt (Acts 7:30, 32, 34).

That was a long wait in preparation for a great mission. When God delays, He is not inactive. He is getting ready His instruments, He is ripening our powers; and at the appointed moment we shall arise equal to our task. Even Jesus of Nazareth was thirty years in privacy, growing in wisdom before He began His work. Dr. Jowett

God is never in a hurry but spends years with those He expects to greatly use. He never thinks the days of preparation too long or too dull.

The hardest ingredient in suffering is often *time*. A short, sharp pang is easily borne, but when a sorrow drags its weary way through long, monotonous years, and day after day returns with the same dull routine of hopeless agony, the heart loses its strength, and without the grace of God, is sure to sink into the very sullenness of despair. Joseph's was a long trial, and God often has to burn His lessons into the depths of our being by the fires of protracted pain. "He shall sit as a refiner and purifier of silver," but He knows how long, and like a true goldsmith He stops the fires the moment He sees His image in the glowing metal. We may not see now the outcome of the beautiful plan which God is hiding in the shadow of His hand; it yet may be long concealed; but faith may be sure that He is sitting on the throne, calmly waiting the hour when, with adoring rapture, we shall say, "All things have worked together for good." Like Joseph, let us be more careful to learn all the lessons in the school of sorrow than we are anxious for the hour of deliverance. There is a "need-be" for every lesson, and when we are ready, our deliverance will surely come, and we shall find that we could not have stood in our place of higher service without the very things that were taught us in the ordeal. God is educating us for the future, for higher service and nobler blessings; and if we have the qualities that fit us for a throne, nothing can keep us from it when God's time has come. Don't steal tomorrow out of God's hands. Give God time to speak to you and reveal His will. He is never too late; learn to wait. Selected

He never comes too late; He knoweth what is best;
Vex not thyself in vain; until He cometh—REST.

Do not run impetuously before the Lord; learn to wait His time: the minute hand as well as the hour hand must point the exact moment for action.

March 23

Out of the spoils won in battles did they dedicate to maintain the house of the Lord (1 Chron. 26:27).

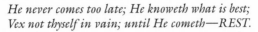

Physical force is stored in the bowels of the earth, in the coal mines, which came from the fiery heat that burned up great forests in ancient ages; and so spiritual force is stored in the depths of our being, through the very pain which we cannot understand.

Someday we shall find that the spoils we have won from our trials were just preparing us to become true "Great Hearts" in the *Pilgrim's Progress,* and to lead our fellow pilgrims triumphantly through trial to the city of the King.

But let us never forget that the source of helping other people must be victorious suffering. The whining, murmuring pang never does anybody any good.

Paul did not carry a cemetery with him, but a chorus of victorious praise; and the harder the trial, the more he trusted and rejoiced, shouting from the very altar of sacrifice. He said, "Yea, and if I be offered upon the service and sacrifice of your faith, I joy and rejoice with you all." Lord, help me this day to draw strength from all that comes to me! FROM DAYS OF HEAVEN UPON EARTH

He placed me in a little cage,
Away from gardens fair;
But I must sing the sweetest songs
Because He placed me there.
Not beat my wings against the cage
If it's my Maker's will,
But raise my voice to heaven's gate
And sing the louder still!

March 24

And Jacob said, O God of my father Abraham, and God of my father Isaac, the Lord which saidst unto me, Return unto thy country, and to thy kindred, and I will deal well with thee: Deliver me, I pray thee (Gen. 32:9, 11).

There are many healthy symptoms in that prayer. In some respects it may serve as a mold into which our own spirits may pour themselves, when melted in the fiery furnace of sorrow.

He began by quoting God's promise: "Thou saidst." He did so twice (9 and 12). Ah, he has got God in his power then! God puts Himself within our reach in His promises; and when we can say to Him, "Thou saidst," He cannot say nay. He must do as He has said. If Herod was so particular for his oath's sake, what will not our God be? Be sure in prayer, to get your feet well on a promise; it will give you purchase enough to force open the gates of heaven, and to take it by force. FROM PRACTICAL PORTIONS FOR THE PRAYER-LIFE 🐦

Jesus desires that we shall be definite in our requests, and that we shall ask for some special thing. "What will ye that I shall do unto you?" is the question that He asks of every one who in affliction and trial comes to Him. Make your requests with definite earnestness if you would have definite answers. Aimlessness in prayer accounts for so many seemingly unanswered prayers. Be definite in your petition. Fill out your check for something definite, and it will be cashed at the bank of heaven when presented in Jesus' name. *Dare to be definite with God.* SELECTED 🐦

Miss Havergal has said: "Every year, I might almost say every day, that I live, I seem to see more clearly how all the rest and gladness and power of our Christian life hinges on one thing; and that is, taking God at His word, believing that He really means exactly what He says, and accepting the very words in which He reveals His goodness and grace, without substituting others or altering the precise modes and tenses which He has seen fit to use."

Bring Christ's Word—Christ's promise, and Christ's sacrifice—His blood, with thee, and not one of heaven's blessings can be denied thee. ADAM CLARKE 🐦

March 25

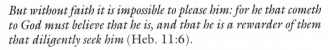

But without faith it is impossible to please him: for he that cometh to God must believe that he is, and that he is a rewarder of them that diligently seek him (Heb. 11:6).

The faith for desperate days.

The Bible is full of such days. Its record is made up of them, its songs are inspired by them, its prophecy is concerned with them, and its revelation has come through them.

The desperate days are the stepping-stones in the path of light. They seem to have been God's opportunity and man's school of wisdom.

There is a story of an Old Testament love feast in Psalm 107, and in every story of deliverance the point of desperation gave God His chance. The "wit's end" of desperation was the beginning of God's power. Recall the promise of seed as the stars of heaven, and as the sands of the sea, to a couple as good as dead. Read again the story of the Red Sea and its deliverance, and of Jordan with its ark standing midstream. Study once more the prayers of Asa, Jehoshaphat, and Hezekiah, when they were sore pressed and knew not what to do. Go over the history of Nehemiah, Daniel, Hosea, and Habakkuk. Stand with awe in the darkness of Gethsemane, and linger by the grave in Joseph's garden through those terrible days. Call the witnesses of the early church, and ask the apostles the story of their desperate days.

Desperation is better than despair.

Faith did not make our desperate days. Its work is to sustain and solve them. The only alternative to a desperate faith is despair, and faith holds on and prevails.

There is no more heroic example of desperate faith than that of the three Hebrew children. The situation was desperate, but they answered bravely, "Our God whom we serve is able to deliver us from the burning, fiery furnace; and he will deliver us out of thine hand, O king. But if not, be it known unto thee, O king, that we will not serve thy gods, nor worship the golden image which thou hast set up." I like that, "but if not!"

I have only space to mention Gethsemane. Ponder deeply its "Nevertheless." "If it is possible . . . nevertheless!" Deep darkness had settled upon the soul of our Lord. Trust meant anguish unto blood and darkness to the descent of hell—Nevertheless! Nevertheless!!

Now get your hymn book and sing your favorite hymn of desperate faith. REV. S. CHADWICK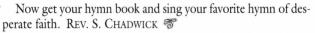

When obstacles and trials seem
Like prison walls to be,
I do the little I can do
And leave the rest to Thee.

And when there seems no chance, no change,
From grief can set me free,
Hope finds its strength in helplessness,
And calmly waits for Thee.

March 26

Look from the place where thou art, northward, and southward,
and eastward, and westward: for all the land which thou seest,
to thee will I give it (Gen. 13:14–15).

No instinct can be put in you by the Holy Ghost but He purposes to fulfill. Let your faith then rise and soar away and claim all the land you can discover. S. A. KEEN

All you can apprehend in the vision of faith is your own. Look as far as you can, for it is all yours. All that you long to be as a Christian, all that you long to do for God, are within the possibilities of faith. Then come, still closer, and with your Bible before you, and your soul open to all the influences of the Spirit, let your whole being receive the baptism of His presence; and as He opens your understanding to see all His fullness, believe He has it all for you. Accept for yourself all the promises of His Word, all the desires He awakens within you, all the possibilities of what you may be as a follower of Jesus. All the land you see is given to you.

The actual provisions of His grace come from the inner vision. He who puts the instinct in the bosom of yonder bird to cross the continent in search of summer sunshine in the southern clime is too good to deceive it, and just as surely as He has put the instinct in its breast, so has He also put the balmy breezes and the vernal sunshine yonder to meet it when it arrives.

He who breathes into our hearts the heavenly hope, will not deceive or fail us when we press forward to its realization. SELECTED

And found as he had said unto them (Luke 22:13).

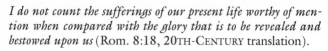

I do not count the sufferings of our present life worthy of mention when compared with the glory that is to be revealed and bestowed upon us (Rom. 8:18, 20TH-CENTURY translation).

A remarkable incident occurred recently at a wedding in England. A young man of large wealth and high social position, who had been blinded by an accident when he was ten years old, and who won university honors in spite of his blindness, had won a beautiful bride, though he had never looked upon her face. A little while before his marriage he submitted to a course of treatment by experts, and the climax came on the day of his wedding.

The day came, and the presents, and guests. There were present cabinet ministers and generals and bishops and learned men and women. The bridegroom, dressed for the wedding, his eyes still shrouded in linen, drove to the church with his father, and the famous oculist met them in the vestry.

The bride entered the church on the arm of her white-haired father. So moved was she that she could hardly speak. Was her lover at last to see her face that others admired, but which he knew only through his delicate fingertips?

As she neared the altar, while the soft strains of the wedding march floated through the church, her eyes fell on a strange group.

The father stood there with his son. Before the latter was the great oculist in the act of cutting away the last bandage. The bridegroom took a step forward, with the spasmodic uncertainty of one who cannot believe that he is awake. A beam of rose-colored light from a pane in the chancel window fell across his face, but he did not seem to see it.

Did he see anything? Yes! Recovering in an instant his steadiness of mien, and with a dignity and joy never before seen in his face, he went forward to meet his bride. They looked into each other's eyes, and one would have thought that his eyes would never wander from her face.

"At last!" she said. "At last," he echoed solemnly, bowing his head. That was a scene of great dramatic power, and no doubt of great joy, and is but a mere suggestion of what will actually take place in heaven when the Christian who has been walking through this world of trial and sorrow, shall see HIM face-to-face. SELECTED

Just a-wearying for you,
Jesus, Lord, beloved and true;
Wishing for you, wondering when

You'll be coming back again,
Under all I say and do,
Just a-wearying for you.

Some glad day, all watching past,
You will come for me at last;
Then I'll see you, hear your voice,
Be with you, with you rejoice;
How the sweet hope thrills me through,
Sets me a-wearying for you.

March 28

And it shall come to pass, as soon as the soles of the feet of the priests that bear the ark of the Lord, the Lord of all the earth, shall rest in the waters of Jordan, that the waters of Jordan shall be cut off from the waters that come down from above; and they shall stand upon an heap (Josh. 3:13).

Brave Levites! Who can help admiring them, to carry the ark right into the stream; for the waters were not divided till their feet dipped in the water (v. 15). God had not promised aught else. God honors faith. "Obstinate faith," that the PROMISE sees and "looks to that alone." You can fancy how the people would watch these holy men march on, and some of the bystanders would be saying, "You would not catch me running that risk! Why, man, the ark will be carried away!" Not so; "the priests stood firm on dry ground." We must not overlook the fact that faith on our part helps God to carry out His plans. "Come up to the help of the Lord."

The ark had staves for the shoulders. Even the ark did not move itself; it was carried. When God is the architect, men are the masons and laborers. Faith assists God. It can stop the mouth of the lions and quench the violence of fire. It yet honors God, and God honors it. Oh, for this faith that will go on, leaving God to fulfill His promise when He sees fit! Fellow Levites, let us shoulder our load, and do not let us look as if we were carrying God's coffin. It is the ark of the living God! Sing as you march toward the flood! THOMAS CHAMPNESS

One of the special marks of the Holy Ghost in the apostolic church was the spirit of boldness. One of the most essential qualities of the faith that is to attempt great things for God, and expect great things from God, is holy audacity. Where we are dealing with a supernatural Being, and taking from

Him things that are humanly impossible, it is easier to take much than little; it is easier to stand in a place of audacious trust than in a place of cautious, timid clinging to the shore.

Like wise seamen in the life of faith, let us launch out into the deep, and find that all things are possible with God, and all things are possible unto him that believeth.

Let us, today, attempt great things for God; take His faith and believe for them and His strength to accomplish them. FROM DAYS OF HEAVEN UPON EARTH 🐟

March 29

Consider the lilies . . . how they grow (Matt. 6:28).

"I need oil," said an ancient monk; so he planted an olive sapling. "Lord," he prayed, "it needs rain that its tender roots may drink and swell. Send gentle showers." And the Lord sent gentle showers. "Lord," prayed the monk, "my tree needs sun. Send sun, I pray Thee." And the sun shone, gilding the dripping clouds. "Now frost, my Lord, to brace its tissues," cried the monk. And behold, the little tree stood sparkling with frost, but at evening it died.

Then the monk sought the cell of a brother monk, and told his strange experience. "I, too, planted a little tree," he said, "and see! it thrives well. But I entrust my tree to its God. He who made it knows better what it needs than a man like me. I laid no condition. I fixed not ways or means. 'Lord, send what it needs,' I prayed, 'storm or sunshine, wind, rain, or frost. Thou hast made it and Thou dost know.'"

> *Yes, leave it with Him,*
> *The lilies all do,*
> *And they grow—*
> *They grow in the rain,*
> *And they grow in the dew—*
> *Yes, they grow:*
> *They grow in the darkness, all hid in the night—*
> *They grow in the sunshine, revealed by the light—*
> *Still they grow.*
>
> *Yes, leave it with Him,*
> *'Tis more dear to His heart,*
> *You will know,*
> *Than the lilies that bloom,*

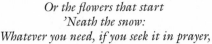

Or the flowers that start
'Neath the snow:
Whatever you need, if you seek it in prayer,
You can leave it with Him—for you are His care.
You, you know.

SELECTED 🍃

March 30

Behold, all ye that kindle a fire, that compass yourselves about with sparks: walk in the light of your fire, and in the sparks that ye have kindled. This shall ye have of mine hand; ye shall lie down in sorrow (Isa. 50:11).

What a solemn warning to those who walk in darkness and yet who try to help themselves out into the light. They are represented as kindling a fire, and compassing themselves with sparks. What does this mean?

Why, it means that when we are in darkness the temptation is to find a way without trusting in the Lord and relying upon Him. Instead of letting Him help us out, we try to help ourselves out. We seek the light of nature, and get the advice of our friends. We try the conclusions of our reason, and might almost be tempted to accept a way of deliverance which would not be of God at all.

All these are fires of our own kindling; rushlights that will surely lead us onto the shoals. And God will let us walk in the light of those sparks, but the end will be sorrow.

Beloved, do not try to get out of a dark place, except in God's time and in God's way. The time of trouble is meant to teach you lessons that you sorely need.

Premature deliverance may frustrate God's work of grace in your life. Just commit the whole situation to Him. Be willing to abide in darkness so long as you have His presence. Remember that it is better to walk in the dark with God than to walk alone in the light. FROM THE STILL SMALL VOICE 🍃

Cease meddling with God's plans and will. You touch anything of His, and you mar the work. You may move the hands of a clock to suit you, but you do not change the time; so you may hurry the unfolding of God's will, but you harm and do not help the work. You can open a rosebud but you spoil the flower. Leave all to Him. Hands down. Thy will, not mine. STEPHEN MERRITT 🍃

His Way

God bade me go when I would stay
('Twas cool within the wood);
I did not know the reason why.
I heard a boulder crashing by
Across the path where I stood.

He bade me stay when I would go;
"Thy will be done," I said.
They found one day at early dawn,
Across the way I would have gone,
A serpent with a mangled head.

No more I ask the reason why,
Although I may not see
The path ahead, His way I go;
For though I know not, He doth know,
And He will choose safe paths for me.

FROM THE SUNDAY SCHOOL TIMES

March 31

The wind was contrary (Matt. 14:24).

Rude and blustering the winds of March often are. Do they not typify the tempestuous seasons of my life? But, indeed, I ought to be glad that I make acquaintance with these seasons. Better it is that the rains descend and the floods come than that I should stay perpetually in the Lotus Land where it seems always afternoon, or in that deep meadowed Valley of Avilion where never wind blows loudly. Storms of temptation appear cruel, but do they not give intenser earnestness to prayer? Do they not compel me to seize the promises with a tighter hand grip? Do they not leave me with a character refined?

Storms of bereavement are keen; but, then, they are one of the Father's ways of driving me to Himself, that in the secret of His presence His voice may speak to my heart, soft and low. There is a glory of the Master which can be seen only when the wind is contrary and the ship tossed with waves.

"Jesus Christ is no security *against* storms, but He is perfect security *in* storms. He has never promised you an easy passage, only a safe landing."

Oh, set your sail to the heavenly gale,
And then, no matter what winds prevail,
No reef can wreck you, no calm delay;
No mist shall hinder, no storm shall stay;
Though far you wander and long you roam
Through salt sea sprays and o'er white sea foam,
No wind that can blow but shall speed you Home.

ANNIE JOHNSON FLINT

April 1

Though he slay me, yet will I trust in him (Job 13:15).
For I know whom I have believed (2 Tim. 1:12).

I will not doubt, though all my ships at sea
Come drifting home with broken masts and sails;
I will believe the Hand which never fails,
From seeming evil worketh good for me.
And though I weep because those sails are tattered,
Still will I cry, while my best hopes lie shattered:
"I trust in Thee."

I will not doubt, though all my prayers return
Unanswered from the still, white realm above;
I will believe it is an all-wise love
Which has refused these things for which I yearn;
And though at times I cannot keep from grieving,
Yet the pure ardor of my fixed believing
Undimmed shall burn.

I will not doubt, though sorrows fall like rain,
And troubles swarm like bees about a hive.
I will believe the heights for which I strive
Are only reached by anguish and by pain;
And though I groan and writhe beneath my crosses,
I yet shall see through my severest losses
The greater gain.

I will not doubt. Well anchored in this faith,
Like some staunch ship, my soul braves every gale;
So strong its courage that it will not quail

To breast the mighty unknown sea of death.
Oh, may I cry, though body parts with spirit,
"I do not doubt," so listening worlds may hear it,
With my last breath.

"In fierce storms," said an old seaman, "we must do one thing; there is only one way: we must put the ship in a certain position and keep her there."

This, Christian, is what you must do. Sometimes, like Paul, you can see neither sun nor stars, and no small tempest lies on you; and then you can do but one thing; there is only one way.

Reason cannot help you; past experiences give you no light. Even prayer fetches no consolation. Only a single course is left. You must put your soul in one position and keep it there.

You must stay upon the Lord; and come what may—winds, waves, cross-seas, thunder, lightning, frowning rocks, roaring breakers—no matter what, you must lash yourself to the helm, and hold fast your confidence in God's faithfulness, His covenant engagement, His everlasting love in Christ Jesus. RICHARD FULLER 🖋

April 2

They looked . . . and behold, the glory of the Lord appeared in the cloud (Exod. 16:10).

Get into the habit of looking for the silver lining of the cloud, and when you have found it, continue to look at it rather than at the leaden gray in the middle.

Do not yield to discouragement no matter how sorely pressed or beset you may be. A discouraged soul is helpless. He can neither resist the wiles of the enemy himself, while in this state, nor can he prevail in prayer for others.

Flee from every symptom of this deadly foe as you would flee from a viper. And be not slow in turning your back on it, unless you want to bite the dust in bitter defeat.

Search out God's promises and say aloud of each one: "This promise is *mine*." If you still experience a feeling of doubt and discouragement, pour out your heart to God and ask Him to rebuke the adversary who is so mercilessly nagging you.

The very instant you wholeheartedly turn away from every symptom of distrust and discouragement, the blessed Holy Spirit will quicken your faith and inbreathe divine strength into your soul.

At first you may not be conscious of this; still as you resolutely and uncompromisingly *"snub"* every tendency toward doubt and depression that assails you, you will soon be made aware that the powers of darkness are falling back.

Oh, if our eyes could only behold the solid phalanx of strength, of power, that is ever behind every turning away from the hosts of darkness, God-ward, what scant heed would be given to the effort of the wily foe to distress, depress, discourage us!

All the marvelous attributes of the Godhead are on the side of the weakest believer, who in the name of Christ, and in simple, childlike trust, yields himself to God and turns to Him for help and guidance. SELECTED

On a day in the autumn, I saw a prairie eagle mortally wounded by a rifle shot. His eyes still gleamed like a circle of light. Then he slowly turned his head, and gave one more searching and longing look at the sky. He had often swept those starry spaces with his wonderful wings. The beautiful sky was the home of his heart. It was the eagle's domain. A thousand times he had exploited there his splendid strength. In those faraway heights he had played with the lightnings, and raced with the winds, and now, so far away from home, the eagle lay dying, done to the death, because for once he forgot and flew too low. The soul is that eagle. This is not its home. It must not lose the skyward look. We must keep faith, we must keep hope, we must keep courage, we must keep Christ. We would better creep away from the battlefield at once if we are not going to be brave. There is no time for the soul to stampede. Keep the skyward look, my soul; keep the skyward look!

> *Keep looking up—*
> *The waves that roar around thy feet,*
> *Jehovah-Jireh will defeat*
> *When looking up.*
>
> *Keep looking up—*
> *Though darkness seems to wrap thy soul;*
> *The Light of Light shall fill thy soul*
> *When looking up.*
>
> *Keep looking up—*
> *When worn, distracted with the fight;*
> *Your Captain gives you conquering might*
> *When you look up.*

We can never see the sun rise by looking into the west. JAPANESE PROVERB

April 3

Glorify ye the Lord in the fires (Isa. 24:15).

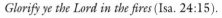

Mark the little word "*in*"! We are to honor Him in the trial—in that which is an affliction indeed and though there have been cases where God did not let His saints feel the fire, yet, ordinarily, fire hurts.

But just here we are to glorify Him by our perfect faith in His goodness and love that has permitted all this to come upon us.

And more than that, we are to believe that out of this is coming something more for His praise than could have come but for this fiery trial.

We can only go through some fires with a large faith; little faith will fail. We must have the victory *in* the furnace. MARGARET BOTTOME

A man has as much religion as he can show in times of trouble. The men who were cast into the fiery furnace came out as they went in—except their *bonds*.

How often in some furnace of affliction God strikes *them* off! Their bodies were unhurt—their skin not even blistered. Their hair was unsinged, their garments not scorched, and even the smell of fire had not passed upon them. And that is the way Christians should come out of furnace trials—liberated from their bonds, but untouched by the flames.

Triumphing over them in it (Col. 2:15).

That is the real triumph—triumphing over sickness, *in it;* triumphing over death, *dying;* triumphing over adverse circumstances, *in them.* Oh, believe me, there is a power that can make us victors in the strife. There are heights to be reached where we can look down and over the way we have come, and sing our song of triumph on this side of heaven. We can make others regard us as rich, while we are poor, and make many rich in our poverty. Our triumph is to be *in it.* Christ's triumph was *in* His humiliation. Possibly our triumph, also, is to be made manifest in what seems to others humiliation. MARGARET BOTTOME

Is there not something captivating in the sight of a man or a woman burdened with many tribulations and yet carrying a heart as sound as a bell? Is there not something contagiously valorous in the vision of one who is greatly tempted, but is more than conqueror? Is it not heartening to see some pilgrim who is broken in body, but who retains the splendor of an unbroken patience? What a witness all this offers to the enduement of His grace! J. H. JOWETT

When each earthly prop gives under,
And life seems a restless sea,
Are you then a God-kept wonder,
Satisfied and calm and free?

April 4

Elisha prayed, and said, Lord, I pray thee, open his eyes, that he may see (2 Kings 6:17).

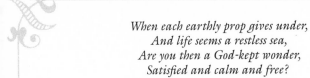

This is the prayer we need to pray for ourselves and for one another, "Lord, open our eyes that we may see"; for the world all around us, as well as around the prophet, is full of God's horses and chariots, waiting to carry us to places of glorious victory. And when our eyes are thus opened, we shall see in all events of life, whether great or small, whether joyful or sad, a "chariot" for our souls.

Everything that comes to us becomes a chariot the moment we treat it as such; and, on the other hand, even the smallest trial may be a juggernaut car to crush us into misery or despair if we consider it.

It lies with each of us to choose which they shall be. It all depends, not upon what these events are, but upon how we take them. If we lie down under them, and let them roll over us and crush us, they become juggernaut cars, but if we climb up into them, as into a car of victory, and make them carry us triumphantly onward and upward, they become the chariots of God. HANNAH WHITALL SMITH

The Lord cannot do much with a crushed soul, hence the adversary's attempt to push the Lord's people into despair and hopelessness over the condition of themselves, or of the church. It has often been said that a dispirited army goes forth to battle with the certainty of being beaten. We heard a missionary say recently that she had been invalided home purely because her spirit had fainted, with the consequence that her body sunk also. We need to understand more of these attacks of the enemy upon our spirits and how to resist them. If the enemy can dislodge us from our position, then he seeks to "wear us out" (Dan. 7:25) by a prolonged siege, so that at last we, out of sheer weakness, let go the cry of victory.

April 5

Thou shalt shut the door upon thee and upon thy sons (2 Kings 4:4).

They were to be alone with God, for they were not dealing with the laws of nature, nor human government, nor the church, nor the priesthood, nor even with the great prophet of God, but they must needs be isolated from all creatures, from all leaning circumstance, from all props of human reason, and swung off, as it were, into the vast blue interstellar space, hanging on God alone, in touch with the fountain of miracles.

Here is a part in the program of God's dealings, a secret chamber of isolation in prayer and faith which every soul must enter that is very fruitful.

There are times and places where God will form a mysterious wall around us, and cut away all props, and all the ordinary ways of doing things, and shut us up to something divine, which is utterly new and unexpected, something that old circumstances do not fit into, where we do not know just what will happen, where God is cutting the cloth of our lives on a new pattern, where He makes us look to Himself.

Most religious people live in a sort of treadmill life, where they can calculate almost everything that will happen, but the souls that God leads out into immediate and special dealings, He shuts in where all they know is that God has hold of them, and is dealing with them, and their expectation is from Him alone.

Like this widow, we must be detached from *outward* things and *attached inwardly to the Lord alone* in order to see His wonders. FROM SOUL FOOD 🍃

In the sorest trials God often makes the sweetest discoveries of Himself.
FROM GEMS 🍃

God sometimes shuts the door and shuts us in,
That He may speak, perchance through grief or pain,
And softly, heart to heart, above the din,
May tell some precious thought to us again.

April 6

I will stand upon my watch, and set me upon the tower, and will watch to see what he will say unto me (Hab. 2:1).

There is no waiting on God for help, and there is no help from God, without watchful expectation on our part. If we ever fail to receive strength and defense from Him, it is because we are not on the outlook for it. Many a proffered succor from heaven goes past us, because we are not standing on our watchtower to catch the far-off indications of its approach, and to fling open the gates of our heart for its entrance. He whose expectation does not lead him to be on the alert for its coming will get but little. Watch for God in the events of your life.

The old homely proverb says: "They that watch for providence will never want a providence to watch for," and you may turn it the other way and say, "They that do not watch for providences will never have a providence to watch for." Unless you put out your water jars when it rains you will catch no water.

We want to be more businesslike and use common sense with God in pleading promises. If you were to go to one of the banks, and see a man go in and out and lay a piece of paper on the table, and take it up again and nothing more—if he did that several times a day, I think there would soon be orders to keep the man out.

Those men who come to the bank in earnest present their checks, they wait until they receive their gold, and then they go; but not without having transacted real business.

They do not put the paper down, speak about the excellent signature, and discuss the excellent document; but they want their money for it, and they are not content without it. These are the people who are always welcome at the bank, and not triflers. Alas, a great many people play at praying. They do not expect God to give them an answer, and thus they are mere triflers. Our heavenly Father would have us do real business with Him in our praying. C. H. SPURGEON ☞

Thine expectation shall not be cut off.

April 7

Their strength is to sit still (Isa. 30:7).

In order really to know God, *inward stillness* is absolutely necessary. I remember when I first learned this. A time of great emergency had risen in my life, when every part of my being seemed to throb with anxiety, and when the necessity for immediate and vigorous action seemed overpowering; and yet circumstances were such that I could do nothing, and the person who could, would not stir.

For a little while it seemed as if I must fly to pieces with the inward turmoil, when suddenly the still small voice whispered in the depths of my soul, "Be still, and know that I am God." The word was with power, and

I hearkened. I composed my body to perfect stillness, and I constrained my troubled spirit into quietness, and looked up and waited; and then I did "know" that it was God, God even in the very emergency and in my helplessness to meet it; and I rested in Him. It was an experience that I would not have missed for worlds; and I may add also, that out of this stillness seemed to arise a power to deal with the emergency, that very soon brought it to a successful issue. I learned then effectually that my "strength was to sit still." HANNAH WHITALL SMITH

There is a perfect passivity which is not indolence. It is a living stillness born of trust. Quiet tension is not trust. It is simply *compressed anxiety*.

> *Not in the tumult of the rending storm,*
> *Not in the earthquake or devouring flame;*
> *But in the hush that could all fear transform,*
> *The still, small whisper to the prophet came.*
>
> *O Soul, keep silence on the mount of God,*
> *Though cares and needs throb around thee like a sea;*
> *From supplications and desires unshod,*
> *Be still, and hear what God shall say to thee.*
>
> *All fellowship hath interludes of rest,*
> *New strength maturing in each poise of power;*
> *The sweetest Alleluias of the blest*
> *Are silent, for the space of half an hour.*
>
> *O rest, in utter quietude of soul,*
> *Abandon words, leave prayer and praise awhile;*
> *Let thy whole being, hushed in His control,*
> *Learn the full meaning of His voice and smile.*
>
> *Not as an athlete wrestling for a crown,*
> *Not taking Heaven by violence of will;*
> *But with thy Father as a child sit down,*
> *And know the bliss that follows His "Be Still!"*
>
> MARY ROWLES JARVIS

April 8

Therefore I take pleasure in infirmities, in reproaches, in necessities, in persecutions, in distresses for Christ's sake: for when I am weak, then am I strong (2 Cor. 12:10).

The literal translation of this verse gives a startling emphasis to it, and makes it speak for itself with a force that we have probably never realized. Here it is: "Therefore I take pleasure in being without strength, in insults, in being pinched, in being chased about, in being cooped up in a corner for Christ's sake; for when I am without strength, then am I *dynamite.*"

Here is the secret of divine all-sufficiency, to come to the end of everything in ourselves and in our circumstances. When we reach this place, we will stop asking for sympathy because of our hard situation or bad treatment, for we will recognize these things as the very conditions of our blessing, and we will turn from them to God and find in them a claim upon Him. A. B. SIMPSON 🐝

George Matheson, the well-known blind preacher of Scotland, who recently went to be with the Lord, said: "My God, I have never thanked Thee for my thorn. I have thanked Thee a thousand times for my roses, but not once for my thorn. I have been looking forward to a world where I shall get compensation for my cross; but I have never thought of my cross as itself a present glory.

"Teach me the glory of my cross; teach me the value of my thorn. Show me that I have climbed to Thee by the path of pain. Show me that my tears have made my rainbows."

> *Alas for him who never sees*
> *The stars shine through the cypress trees.*

April 9

All these things are against me (Gen. 42:36).
All things work together for good to them that love God (Rom. 8:28).

Many people are wanting power. Now how is power produced? The other day we passed the great works where the trolley engines are supplied with electricity. We heard the hum and roar of the countless wheels, and we asked our friend, "How do they make the power?"

"Why," he said, "just by the revolution of those wheels and the friction they produce. The rubbing creates the electric current."

And so, when God wants to bring more power into your life, He brings more pressure. He is generating spiritual force by hard rubbing. Some do not like it and try to run away from the pressure, instead of getting the power and using it to rise above the painful causes.

Opposition is essential to a true equilibrium of forces. The centripetal and centrifugal forces acting in opposition to each other keep our planet in her orbit. The one propelling, and the other repelling, so act and react, that instead of sweeping off into space in a pathway of desolation, she pursues her even orbit around her solar center.

So God guides our lives. It is not enough to have an impelling force—we need just as much a repelling force, and so He holds us back by the testing ordeals of life, by the pressure of temptation and trial, by the things that seem against us, but really are furthering our way and establishing our goings.

Let us thank Him for both, let us take the weights as well as the wings, and thus divinely impelled, let us press on with faith and patience in our high and heavenly calling. A. B. SIMPSON

In a factory building there are wheels and gearings,
There are cranks and pulleys, beltings tight or slack—
Some are whirling swiftly, some are turning slowly,
Some are thrusting forward, some are pulling back;
Some are smooth and silent, some are rough and noisy,
Pounding, rattling, clanking, moving with a jerk;

In a wild confusion in a seeming chaos,
Lifting, pushing, driving—but they do their work.
From the mightiest lever to the tiniest pinion,
All things move together for the purpose planned;
And behind the working is a mind controlling,
And a force directing, and a guiding hand.

So all things are working for the Lord's beloved;
Some things might be hurtful if alone they stood;
Some might seem to hinder; some might draw us backward;
But they work together, and they work for good,
All the thwarted longings, all the stern denials,
All the contradictions, hard to understand.
And the force that holds them, speeds them and retards them,
Stops and starts and guides them—is our Father's hand.

ANNIE JOHNSON FLINT

April 10

Show me wherefore thou contendest with me (Job 10:2).

Perhaps, O tried soul, the Lord is doing this to develop thy graces. There are some of thy graces which would never have been *discovered* if it were not for the trials. Dost thou not know that thy faith never looks so grand in summer weather as it does in winter? Love is too oft like a glow-worm, showing but little light except it be in the midst of surrounding darkness. Hope itself is like a star—not to be seen in the sunshine of prosperity, and only to be discovered in the night of adversity. Afflictions are often the black folds in which God doth set the jewels of His children's graces, to make them shine the better.

It was but a little while ago that, on thy knees, thou wast saying, "Lord, I fear I have no faith: let me know that I have faith."

Was not this really, though perhaps unconsciously, praying for trials?— for how canst thou know that thou hast faith until thy faith is exercised? Depend upon it. God often sends us trials that our graces may be discovered, and that we may be certified of their existence. Besides, it is not merely discovery; *real growth in grace* is the result of sanctified trials.

God trains His soldiers, not in tents of ease and luxury, but by turning them out and using them to forced marches and hard service. He makes them ford through streams, and swim through rivers and climb mountains, and walk many a weary mile with heavy knapsacks on their backs. Well, Christian, may not this account for the troubles through which you are passing? Is not this the reason why He is contending with you? C. H. SPURGEON

To be left unmolested by Satan is no evidence of blessing.

April 11

What I tell you in darkness, that speak ye in light (Matt. 10:27).

Our Lord is constantly taking us into the dark, that He may tell us things. Into the dark of the shadowed home, where bereavement has drawn the blinds; into the dark of the lonely, desolate life, where some infirmity closes us in from the light and stir of life; into the dark of some crushing sorrow and disappointment.

Then He tells us His secrets, great and wonderful, eternal and infinite; He causes the eye which has become dazzled by the glare of the earth to behold the heavenly constellations; and the ear to detect the undertones of His voice, which is often drowned amid the tumult of earth's strident cries.

But such revelations always imply a corresponding responsibility—"that *speak ye* in the light—that *proclaim* upon the housetops."

We are not meant to always linger in the dark, or stay in the closet; presently we shall be summoned to take our place in the rush and storm of life; and when that moment comes, we are to speak and proclaim what we have learned.

This gives new meaning to suffering, the saddest element in which is often its apparent aimlessness. "How useless I am!" "What am I doing for the betterment of men?" "Wherefore this waste of the precious spikenard of my soul?"

Such are the desperate laments of the sufferer. But God has a purpose in it all. He has withdrawn His child to the higher altitudes of fellowship, that he may hear God speaking face-to-face, and bear the message to his fellows at the mountain foot.

Were the forty days wasted that Moses spent on the mount or the period spent at Horeb by Elijah, or the years spent in Arabia by Paul?

There is no shortcut to the life of faith, which is the all-vital condition of a holy and victorious life. We must have periods of lonely meditation and fellowship with God. That our souls should have their mountains of fellowship, their valley of quiet rest beneath the shadow of the great rock, their nights beneath the stars, when darkness has veiled the material and silenced the stir of human life, and has opened the view of the infinite and eternal, is as indispensable as that our bodies should have food.

Thus alone can the sense of God's presence become the fixed possession of the soul, enabling it to say repeatedly, with the psalmist, "Thou art near, O God." F. B. MEYER

Some hearts, like evening primroses, open more beautifully in the shadows of life.

April 12

And Jesus being full of the Holy Ghost returned from Jordan, and was led by the Spirit into the wilderness, being forty days tempted of the devil (Luke 4:1–2).

Jesus was full of the Holy Ghost, and yet He was tempted. Temptation often comes upon a man with its strongest power when he is nearest to God. As someone has said, "The Devil aims high." He got one apostle to say he did not even know Christ.

Very few men have such conflicts with the Devil as Martin Luther had. Why? Because Martin Luther was going to shake the very kingdom of hell. Oh, what conflicts John Bunyan had!

If a man has much of the Spirit of God, he will have great conflicts with the tempter. God permits temptation because it does for us what the storms do for the oaks—it roots us; and what the fire does for the paintings on the porcelain—it makes them permanent.

You never know that you have a grip on Christ, or that He has a grip on you, as well as when the Devil is using all his force to attract you from Him; then you feel the pull of Christ's right hand. SELECTED

Extraordinary afflictions are not always the punishment of extraordinary sins, but sometimes the trial of extraordinary graces. God hath many sharp-cutting instruments, and rough files for the polishing of His jewels; and those He especially loves, and means to make the most resplendent, He hath oftenest His tools upon. ARCHBISHOP LEIGHTON

I bear my willing witness that I owe more to the fire, and the hammer, and the file, than to anything else in my Lord's workshop. I sometimes question whether I have ever learned anything except through the rod. When my schoolroom is darkened, I see most. C. H. SPURGEON

April 13

And the hand of the Lord was there upon me; and he said unto me, Arise, go forth into the plain, and I will there talk with thee (Ezek. 3:22).

Did you ever hear of anyone being much used for Christ who did not have some *special* waiting time, some complete *upset* of all his or her plans first; from Saint Paul's being sent off into the desert of Arabia for three years, when he must have been boiling over with the glad tidings, down to the present day?

You were looking forward to telling about trusting Jesus in Syria; now He says, "I want you to *show* what it is to trust Me, without waiting for Syria."

My own case is far less severe, but the same in principle, that when I thought the door was flung open for me to go with a bound into literary work, it is opposed, and doctor steps in and says, simply, "Never! She must choose between writing and living; she can't do both."

That was in 1860. Then I came out of the shell with *Ministry of Song* in 1869, and saw the evident wisdom of being kept waiting nine years in

the shade. God's love being unchangeable, He is just as loving when we do not see or feel His love. Also His love and His sovereignty are co-equal and universal; so He withholds the enjoyment and
conscious progress because He knows best what will really ripen and further His work in us. MEMORIALS OF FRANCES RIDLEY HAVERGAL

I laid it down in silence,
This work of mine,
And took what had been sent me—
A resting time.
The Master's voice had called me
To rest apart;
"Apart with Jesus only,"
Echoed my heart.

I took the rest and stillness
From His own Hand,
And felt this present illness
Was what He planned.
How often we choose labor,
When He says "Rest"—
Our ways are blind and crooked;
His way is best.

The work Himself has given,
He will complete.
There may be other errands
For tired feet;
There may be other duties
For tired hands,
The present, is obedience
To His commands.

There is a blessed resting
In lying still,
In letting His hand mould us,
Just as He will.
His work must be completed.
His lesson set;
He is the higher Workman:
Do not forget!

It is not only "working."
We must be trained;

And Jesus "learnt" obedience,
Through suffering gained.
For us, His yoke is easy,
His burden light.
His discipline most needful,
And all is right.

We are but under-workmen;
They never choose
If this tool or if that one
Their hands shall use.
In working or in waiting
May we fulfill
Not ours at all, but only
The Master's will!

Selected

God provides resting places as well as working places. Rest, then, and be thankful when He brings you, wearied to a wayside well.

April 14

For the Lord himself shall descend from heaven with a shout, with the voice of the archangel, and with the trump of God: and the dead in Christ shall rise first: then we which are alive and remain shall be caught up together with them in the clouds, to meet the Lord in the air: and so shall we ever be with the Lord (1 Thess. 4:16, 17).

It was "very early in the morning" while "it was yet dark," that Jesus rose from the dead. Not the sun, but only the morning star shone upon His opening tomb. The shadows had not fled, the citizens of Jerusalem had not awaked. It was still night—the hour of sleep and darkness, when He arose. Nor did His rising break the slumbers of the city. So shall it be "very early in the morning while it is yet dark," and when nought but the morning star is shining, that Christ's body, the church, shall arise. Like Him, His saints shall awake when the children of the night and darkness are still sleeping their sleep of death. In their arising they disturb no one. The world hears not the voice that summons them. As Jesus laid them quietly to rest, each in his own still tomb, like children in the arms of their mother, so, as quietly, as gently, shall He awake them when the hour arrives. To them come the quickening words, "Awake and sing, ye that dwell in dust" (Isa. 26:19). Into their tomb the earliest ray of glory finds its way. They drink in the first gleams of morning, while as yet the eastern clouds give but the faintest signs of the uprising. Its genial fragrance, its soothing stillness, its bracing freshness, its sweet loneliness, its quiet purity, all so solemn and yet so full of hope, these are theirs.

Oh, the contrast between these things and the dark night through which they have passed! Oh, the contrast between these things and the grave from which they have sprung! And as they shake off the encumbering turf, flinging mortality aside and rising, in glorified bodies, to meet their Lord in the air they are lighted and guided upward, along the untrodden pathway, by the beams of that Star of the morning, which, like the Star of Bethlehem, conducts them to the presence of the King. "Weeping may endure for a night, but joy cometh in the morning." HORATIUS BONAR

> *While the hosts cry Hosanna, from heaven descending,*
> *With glorified saints and the angels attending,*
> *With grace on His brow, like a halo of glory,*
> *Will Jesus receive His own.*

> *Even so, come quickly.*

A soldier said, "When I die do not sound taps over my grave, but reveille, the morning call, the summons to rise."

April 15

I trust in thy word (Ps. 119:42).

Just in proportion in which we believe that God will do just what He has said, is our faith strong or weak. Faith has nothing to do with feelings, or with impressions, with improbabilities, or with outward appearances. If we desire to couple them with faith, then we are no longer resting on the Word of God because faith needs nothing of the kind. *Faith rests on the naked Word of God.* When we take Him at His Word the heart is at peace.

God delights to exercise faith, first for blessing in our own souls, then for blessing in the church at large, and also for those without. But this exercise we shrink from instead of welcoming. When trials come, we should say: "My heavenly Father puts this cup of trial into my hands, that I may have something sweet afterwards."

Trials are the food of faith. Oh, let us leave ourselves in the hands of our heavenly Father! It is the joy of His heart to do good to all His children.

But trials and difficulties are not the only means by which faith is exercised and thereby increased. *There is the reading of the Scriptures, that we may by them acquaint ourselves with God as He has revealed Himself in His Word.*

Are you able to say, from the acquaintance you have made with God, that He is a lovely Being? If not, let me affectionately entreat you to ask God to bring you to this, that you may admire His gentleness and kindness, that you may be able to say how good He is, and what a delight it is to the heart of God to do good to His children.

Now the nearer we come to this in our inmost souls, the more ready we are to leave ourselves in His hands, satisfied with all His dealings with us. And when trial comes, we shall say:

"I will wait and see what good God will do to me by it, assured He will do it." Thus we shall bear an honorable testimony before the world, and thus we shall strengthen the hands of others. GEORGE MUELLER

April 16

By faith Abraham, when he was called to go out into a place which he should after receive for an inheritance, obeyed (Heb. 11:8).

Whither he went, he knew not; it was enough for him to know that he went with God. He leant not so much upon the promises as upon the Promiser. He looked not on the difficulties of his lot, but on the King, eternal, immortal, invisible, the only wise God, who had deigned to appoint his course, and would certainly vindicate Himself. O glorious faith! This is thy work, these are thy possibilities; contentment to sail with sealed orders, because of unwavering confidence in the wisdom of the Lord High Admiral; willinghood to rise up, leave all, and follow Christ, because of the glad assurance that earth's best cannot bear comparison with heaven's least. F. B. M.

It is by no means enough to set out cheerfully with your God on any venture of faith. Tear into smallest pieces any itinerary for the journey which your imagination may have drawn up.

Nothing will fall out as you expect.

Your guide will keep to no beaten path. He will lead you by a way such as you never dreamed your eyes would look upon. He knows no fear, and He expects you to fear nothing while He is with you.

The day had gone; alone and weak
I groped my way within a bleak
And sunless land.
The path that led into the light
I could not find! In that dark night
God took my hand.
He led me that I might not stray,
And brought me by a new, safe way
I had not known.
By waters still, through pastures green
I followed Him—the path was clean
Of briar and stone.
The heavy darkness lost its strength,
My waiting eyes beheld at length
The streaking dawn.
On, safely on, through sunrise glow
I walked, my hand in His, and lo,
The night had gone.

ANNIE PORTER JOHNSON

April 17

The hand of the Lord hath wrought this (Job 12:9).

Several years ago there was found in an African mine the most magnificent diamond in the world's history. It was presented to the king of England to blaze in his crown of state. The king sent it to Amsterdam to be cut. It was put into the hands of an expert lapidary. And what do you suppose he did with it?

He took the gem of priceless value, and cut a notch in it. Then he struck it a hard blow with his instrument, and lo! the superb jewel lay in his hand cleft in twain. What recklessness! what wastefulness! what criminal carelessness!

Not so. For days and weeks that blow had been studied and planned. Drawings and models had been made of the gem. Its quality, its defects, its lines of cleavage had all been studied with minutest care. The man to whom it was committed was one of the most skillful lapidaries in the world.

Do you say that blow was a mistake? Nay. It was the climax of the lapidary's skill. When he struck that blow, he did the one thing which would bring that gem to its most perfect shapeliness, radiance, and jewelled splendor. That blow which seemed to ruin the superb precious stone was, in fact, its perfect redemption. For, from those two halves were wrought the two magnificent gems which the skilled eye of the lapidary saw hidden in the rough, uncut stone as it came from the mine.

So, sometimes, God lets a stinging blow fall upon your life. The blood spurts. The nerves wince. The soul cries out in agony. The blow seems to you an appalling mistake. But it is not, for you are the most priceless jewel in the world to God. And He is the most skilled lapidary in the universe.

Someday you are to blaze in the diadem of the King. As you lie in His hand now He knows just how to deal with you. Not a blow will be permitted to fall upon your shrinking soul but that the love of God permits it, and works out from its depths, blessing and spiritual enrichment unseen, and unthought of by you. J. H. McC.

In one of George MacDonald's books occurs this fragment of conversation: "I wonder why God made me," said Mrs. Faber bitterly. "I'm sure I don't know what was the use of making me!"

"Perhaps not much yet," said Dorothy, "but then He hasn't done with you yet. He is making you now, and you are quarreling with the process."

If men would but believe that they are in process of creation, and consent to be made—let the Maker handle them as the potter the clay, yielding themselves in resplendent motion and submissive, hopeful action with the turning of His wheel—they would ere long find themselves able to welcome every pressure of that hand on them, even when it was felt in pain; and sometimes not only to believe but to recognize the divine end in view, the bringing of a son unto glory.

Not a single shaft can hit,
Till the God of love sees fit.

April 18

And he shall bring it to pass (Ps. 37:5).

I once thought that after I prayed that it was my duty to do everything that I could do to bring the answer to pass. He taught me a better way, and showed that my self-effort always hindered His working, and that when I prayed and definitely believed Him for anything, He wanted me to wait in the spirit of praise, and only do what He bade me. It seems so unsafe to just sit still, and do nothing but trust the Lord; and the temptation to take the battle into our own hands is often tremendous.

We all know how impossible it is to rescue a drowning man who tries to help his rescuer, and it is equally impossible for the Lord to fight our battles for us when we insist upon trying to fight them ourselves. It is not that He will not, but He cannot. Our interference hinders His working. C. H. P.

Spiritual forces cannot work while earthly forces are active.

It takes God time to answer prayer. We often fail to give God a chance in that respect. It takes time for God to paint a rose. It takes time for God to grow an oak. It takes time for God to make bread from wheat fields. He takes the earth. He pulverizes. He softens. He enriches. He wets with showers and dews. He warms with life. He gives the blade, the stock, the amber grain, and then at last the bread for the hungry.

All this takes time. Therefore we sow, and till, and wait, and trust, until all God's purpose has been wrought out. We give God a chance in this matter of time. We need to learn this same lesson in our prayer life. It takes God time to answer prayer. J. H. M.

April 19

Stand still, and see the salvation of the Lord (Exod. 14:13).

These words contain God's command to the believer when he is reduced to great straits and brought into extraordinary difficulties. He cannot retreat; he cannot go forward; he is shut upon the right hand and on the left. What is he now to do?

The Master's word to him is "stand still." It will be well for him if, at such times, he listens only to his Master's word, for other and evil advisers come with their suggestions. *Despair* whispers, "Lie down and die; give it all up." But God would have us put on a cheerful courage, and even in our worst times, rejoice in His love and faithfulness.

Cowardice says, "Retreat; go back to the worldling's way of action; you cannot play the Christian's part; it is too difficult. Relinquish your principles."

But, however much Satan may urge this course upon you, you cannot follow it, if you are a child of God. His divine fiat has bid thee go from strength to strength, and so thou shalt, and neither death nor hell shall turn thee from thy course. What if for a while thou art called to stand still; yet this is but to renew thy strength for some greater advance in due time.

Precipitancy cries, "Do something; stir yourself; to stand still and wait is sheer idleness." We *must* be doing something at once—*we* must do it, so we think—instead of looking to the Lord, who will not only do something, but will do everything.

Presumption boasts, "If the sea be before you, march into it, and expect a miracle." But faith listens neither to presumption, nor to despair, nor to cowardice, nor to precipitancy, but it hears God say, "Stand still," and immovable as a rock it stands.

"*Stand still*"—keep the posture of an upright man, ready for action, expecting further orders, cheerfully and patiently awaiting the directing voice; and it will not be long ere God shall say to you, as distinctly as Moses said it to the people of Israel, "Go forward." C. H. Spurgeon

> *Be quiet! why this anxious heed*
> *About thy tangled ways?*
> *God knows them all. He giveth speed*
> *And He allows delays.*
> *'Tis good for thee to walk by faith*
> *And not by sight.*
> *Take it on trust a little while.*
> *Soon shalt thou read the mystery aright*
> *In the full sunshine of His smile.*

In times of uncertainty, wait. Always, if you have any doubt, *wait.* Do not force yourself to any action. If you have a restraint in your spirit, wait until all is clear, and do not go against it.

April 20

Not by might, nor by power, but by my spirit, saith the Lord of hosts (Zech. 4:6).

My way led up a hill, and right at the foot I saw a boy on a bicycle. He was pedaling uphill against the wind, and evidently found it a tremendously hard work. Just as he was working most strenuously and doing his best painfully, there came a trolley car going in the same direction—up the hill.

It was not going too fast for the boy to get behind it, and with one hand to lay hold of the bar at the back. Then you know what happened. He went up the hill like a bird. Then it flashed upon me: "Why, I am like that boy on the bicycle in my weariness and weakness. I am pedaling uphill against all kinds of opposition, and am almost worn out with the task. But here at hand is a great available power, the strength of the Lord Jesus.

"I have only to get in touch with Him and to maintain communication with Him, though it may be only one little finger of faith, and that will be enough to make His power mine for the doing of this bit of service that just now seems too much for me." And I was helped to dismiss my weariness and to realize this truth. FROM THE LIFE OF FULLER PURPOSE ❧

Abandoned

Utterly abandoned to the Holy Ghost!
Seeking all His fulness at whatever cost;
Cutting all the shore-lines, launching in the deep
Of His mighty power—strong to save and keep.

Utterly abandoned to the Holy Ghost!
Oh! the sinking, sinking, until self is lost!
Until the emptied vessel lies broken at His feet;
Waiting till His filling shall make the work complete.

Utterly abandoned to the will of God;
Seeking for no other path than my Master trod;
Leaving ease and pleasure, making Him my choice,
Waiting for His guidance, listening for His voice.

Utterly abandoned! no will of my own;
For time and for eternity, His, and His alone;
All my plans and purposes lost in His sweet will,
Having nothing, yet in Him all things possessing still.

Utterly abandoned! 'tis so sweet to be
Captive in His bonds of love, yet so wondrous free;
Free from sin's entanglements, free from doubt and fear,
Free from every worry, burden, grief or care.

Utterly abandoned! oh, the rest is sweet,
As I tarry, waiting, at His blessed feet;
Waiting for the coming of the Guest divine,
Who my inmost being shall perfectly refine.

Lo! He comes and fills me, Holy Spirit sweet!
I, in Him, am satisfied! I, in Him, complete!
And the light within my soul shall nevermore grow dim
While I keep my covenant—abandoned unto Him!

AUTHOR UNKNOWN ❧

April 21

And being absolutely certain that whatever promise He is bound by, He is able to make good (Rom. 4:21).

We are told that Abraham could look at his own body and consider it as good as dead without being discouraged, because he was not looking at himself but at the almighty One.

He did not *stagger* at the promise, but stood straight up unbending beneath his mighty load of blessing. Instead of growing weak he waxed strong in the faith and grew more robust; the more difficulties became apparent, glorifying God through His very sufficiency and being "fully persuaded" (as the Greek expresses it) "that he who had promised was," not merely able, but—as it literally means "abundantly able"—munificently able, able with an infinite surplus of resources, infinitely able "to perform."

He is the God of boundless resources. The only limit is in us. Our asking, our thinking, our praying are too small; our expectations are too limited. He is trying to lift us up to a higher conception, and lure us on to a mightier expectation and appropriation. Oh, shall we put Him in derision? There is no limit to what we may ask and expect of our glorious El-Shaddai; and there is but one measure here given for His blessing, and that is "according to the power that worketh in us." A. B. SIMPSON

Climb to the treasure house of blessing on the ladder made of divine promises. By a promise as by a key open the door to the riches of God's grace and favor.

April 22

He knoweth the way that I take (Job 23:10).

Believer! What a glorious assurance! This way of thine—this, it may be, a crooked, mysterious, tangled way—this way of trial and tears. "He knoweth it." The furnace seven times heated—He lighted it. There is an almighty Guide knowing and directing our footsteps, whether it be to the bitter Marah pool, or to the joy and refreshment of Elim.

That way, dark to the Egyptians, has its pillar of cloud and fire for His own Israel. The furnace is hot; but not only can we trust the hand that kindles it, but we have the assurance that the fires are lighted not to consume, but to refine; and that when the refining process is completed (no sooner—no later) He brings His people forth as gold.

When they think Him least near, He is often nearest. "*When my* spirit was overwhelmed, *then* thou knewest my path."

Do we know of One brighter than the brightest radiance of the visible sun, visiting our chamber with the first waking beam of the morning; an eye of infinite tenderness and compassion following us throughout the day, knowing the way that we take?

The world, in its cold vocabulary in the hour of adversity, speaks of "*Providence*"—"the will of *Providence*"—"the strokes of *Providence.*" *Providence!* What is that?

Why dethrone a living, directing God from the sovereignty of His own earth? Why substitute an inanimate, deathlike abstraction, in place of an acting, controlling, personal Jehovah?

How it would take the sting from many a goading trial, to see what Job saw (in his hour of aggravated woe, when every earthly hope lay prostrate at his feet)—no hand but the divine. He saw that hand behind the gleaming swords of the Sabeans—he saw it behind the lightning flash—he saw it giving wings to the careening tempest—he saw it in the awful silence of his rifled home.

"*The Lord* gave, and *the Lord* hath taken away; blessed be the name of *the Lord!*"

Thus, seeing God in everything, his faith reached its climax when this once powerful prince of the desert, seated on his bed of ashes, could say, "Though he slay me, yet will I trust him." MACDUFF

April 23

Though I walk in the midst of trouble, thou wilt revive me (Ps. 138:7).

The Hebrew rendering of the above is "go on in the center of trouble." What descriptive words! We *have* called on God in the day of trouble; we have pleaded His promise of deliverance but no deliverance has been given; the enemy has continued oppressing until we were in the very thick of the fight, in the center of trouble. Why then trouble the Master any further?

When Martha said, "Lord, if thou hadst been here my brother had not died," our Lord met her lack of hope with His further promise, "Thy brother shall rise again." And when we walk "in the center of trouble" and are tempted to think like Martha that the time of deliverance is past, He meets us too with a promise from His Word. "Though I walk in the midst of trouble, *thou wilt revive me.*"

Though His answer has so long delayed, though we may still continue to "go on" in the midst of trouble, *"the center of trouble" is the place where He revives, not the place where He fails us.*

When in the hopeless place, the continued hopeless place, is the very time when He will stretch forth His hand against the wrath of our enemies and perfect that which concerneth us, the very time when He will make the attack to cease and fail and come to an end. What occasion is there then for fainting? APHRA WHITE 🦋

The Eye of the Storm

Fear not that the whirlwind shall carry thee hence,
Nor wait for its onslaught in breathless suspense,
Nor shrink from the whips of the terrible hail,
But pass through the edge to the heart of the tale,
For there is a shelter, sunlighted and warm,
And Faith sees her God through the eye of the storm.

The passionate tempest with rush and wild roar
And threatenings of evil may beat on the shore,
The waves may be mountains, the fields battle plains,
And the earth be immersed in a deluge of rains,
Yet, the soul, stayed on God, may sing bravely its psalm,
For the heart of the storm is the center of calm.

Let hope be not quenched in the blackness of night,
Though the cyclone awhile may have blotted the light,
For behind the great darkness the stars ever shine,
And the light of God's heavens, His love shall make thine,
Let no gloom dim thine eyes, but uplift them on high
To the face of thy God and the blue of His sky.

The storm is thy shelter from danger and sin,
And God Himself takes thee for safety within;
The tempest with Him passeth into deep calm,
And the roar of the winds is the sound of a psalm.
Be glad and serene when the tempest clouds form;
God smiles on His child in the eye of the storm.

April 24

Faith is . . . the evidence of things not seen (Heb. 11:1).

True faith drops its letter in the post office box, and lets it go. Distrust holds on to a corner of it, and wonders that the answer never comes. I have some letters in my desk that have been written for weeks, but there was some slight uncertainty about the address or the contents, so they are yet unmailed. They have not done either me or anybody else any good yet. They will never accomplish anything until I let them go out of my hands and trust them to the postman and the mail.

This is the way with true faith. It hands its case over to God, and then He works. That is a fine verse in the Thirty-seventh Psalm: "Commit thy way unto the Lord, trust also in him, and he shall bring it to pass." But He never worketh till we commit. Faith is a receiving or, still better, a taking of God's proffered gifts. We may believe, and come, and commit, and rest; but we will not fully realize all our blessings until we begin to receive and come into the attitude of abiding and taking. FROM DAYS OF HEAVEN UPON EARTH

Dr. Payson, when a young man, wrote as follows, to an aged mother, burdened with intense anxiety on account of the condition of her son: "You give yourself too much trouble about him. After you have prayed for him, as you have done, and committed him to God, should you not cease to feel anxious respecting him? The command, 'Be careful for nothing,' is unlimited; and so is the expression, 'Casting *all* your care on him.' If we cast our burdens upon another, can they continue to press upon us? If we bring them away with us from the throne of grace, it is evident we do not leave them there. With respect to myself, I have made this one test of my prayers: if after committing anything to God, I can, like Hannah, come away and have my mind no more sad, my heart no more pained or anxious, I look upon it as one proof that I have prayed in faith; but, if I bring away my burden, I conclude that faith was not in exercise."

April 25

And there was Mary Magdalene and the other Mary, sitting over against the sepulchre (Matt. 27:61).

How strangely stupid is grief. It neither learns nor knows nor wishes to learn or know. When the sorrowing sisters sat over against the door of God's sepulchre, did they see the two thousand years that have passed triumphing away? Did they see anything but this: "Our Christ is gone!"

Your Christ and my Christ came from their loss. Myriad mourning hearts have had resurrection in the midst of their grief; and yet the sorrowing watchers looked at the seed-form of this result, and saw nothing. What they regarded as the end of life was the very preparation for coronation; for Christ was silent that He might live again in tenfold power.

They saw it not. They mourned, they wept, and went away, and came again, driven by their hearts to the sepulchre. Still it was a sepulchre, unprophetic, voiceless, lusterless.

So with us. Every man sits over against the sepulchre in his garden, in the first instance, and says, "This woe is irremediable. I see no benefit in it. I will take no comfort in it." And yet, right in our deepest and worst mishaps, often, our Christ is lying, waiting for resurrection.

Where our death seems to be, there our Savior is. Where the end of hope is, there is the brightest beginning of fruition. Where the darkness is thickest, there the bright beaming light that never is set is about to emerge. When the whole experience is consummated, then we find that a garden is not disfigured by a sepulchre. Our joys are made better if there be sorrow in the midst of them. And our sorrows are made bright by the joys that God has planted around about them. The flowers may not be pleasing to us, they may not be such as we are fond of plucking, but they are heart flowers, love, hope, faith, joy, peace—these are flowers which are planted around about every grave that is sunk in the Christian heart.

> *'Twas by a path of sorrows drear*
> *Christ entered into rest;*
> *And shall I look for roses here,*
> *Or think that earth is blessed?*
> *Heaven's whitest lilies blow*
> *From earth's sharp crown of woe:*
> *Who here his cross can meekly bear,*
> *Shall wear the kingly purple there.*

April 26

I even reckon all things as pure loss because of the priceless privilege of knowing Christ Jesus my Lord (Phil. 3:8 WEYMOUTH).

Shining is always costly. Light comes only at the cost of that which produces it. An unlit candle does no shining. Burning must come before shining. We cannot be of great use to others without cost to ourselves. Burning suggests suffering. We shrink from pain.

We are apt to feel that we are doing the greatest good in the world when we are strong, and able for active duty, and when the heart and hands are full of kindly service.

When we are called aside and can only suffer; when we are sick; when we are consumed with pain; when all our activities have been dropped, we feel that we are no longer of use, that we are not doing anything.

But, if we are patient and submissive, it is almost certain that we are a greater blessing to the world in our time of suffering and pain than we were in the days when we thought we were doing the most of our work. We are burning now, and shining because we are burning. FROM EVENING THOUGHTS ☞

"The glory of tomorrow is rooted in the drudgery of today."

Many want the glory without the cross, the shining without the burning, but crucifixion comes before coronation.

> Have you heard the tale of the aloe plant,
> Away in the sunny clime?
> By humble growth of a hundred years
> It reaches its blooming time;
> And then a wondrous bud at its crown
> Breaks into a thousand flowers;
> This floral queen, in its blooming seen,
> Is the pride of the tropical bowers,
> But the plant to the flower is sacrifice,
> For it blooms but once, and it dies.
>
> Have you further heard of the aloe plant,
> That grows in the sunny clime;
> How every one of its thousand flowers,
> As they drop in the blooming time,
> Is an infant plant that fastens its roots
> In the place where it falls on the ground,
> And as fast as they drop from the dying stem,
> Grow lively and lovely around?
> By dying, it liveth a thousand-fold
> In the young that spring from the death of the old.

Have you heard the tale of the pelican,
The Arabs' Gimel el Bahr,
That lives in the African solitudes,
Where the birds that live lonely are?
Have you heard how it loves its tender young,
And cares and toils for their good,
It brings them water from mountains far,
And fishes the seas for their food.
In famine it feeds them—what love can devise!
The blood of its bosom—and, feeding them, dies.

Have you heard this tale—the best of them all—
The tale of the Holy and True,
He dies, but His life, in untold souls
Lives on in the world anew;
His seed prevails, and is filling the earth,
As the stars fill the sky above.
He taught us to yield up the love of life,
For the sake of the life of love.
His death is our life, His loss is our gain;
The joy for the tear, the peace for the pain.

Selected

April 27

I am he that liveth, and was dead; and, behold, I am alive for evermore (Rev. 1:18).

Flowers! Easter lilies! speak to me this morning the same dear old lesson of immortality which you have been speaking to so many sorrowing souls.

Wise old Book! let me read again in your pages of firm assurance that to die is gain.

Poets! recite to me your verses which repeat in every line the gospel of eternal life.

Singers! break forth once more into songs of joy; let me hear again the well-known resurrection psalms.

Tree and blossom and bird and sea and sky and wind whisper it, sound it afresh, warble it, echo it, let it throb and pulsate through every atom and particle; let the air be filled with it.

Let it be told and retold and still retold until hope rises to conviction, and conviction to certitude of knowledge; until we, like Paul, even though going to our death, go with triumphant mien, with assured faith, and with serene and shining face.

O sad-faced mourners, who each day are wending
Through churchyard paths of cypress and of yew,
Leave for today the low graves you are tending,
And lift your eyes to God's eternal blue!

It is no time for bitterness or sadness;
Twine Easter lilies, not pale asphodels;
Let your souls thrill to the caress of gladness,
And answer the sweet chime of Easter bells.

If Christ were still within the grave's low prison,
A captive of the enemy we dread;
If from that moldering cell He had not risen,
Who then could chide the gloomy tears you shed?

If Christ were dead there would be need to sorrow,
But He has risen and vanquished death for aye;
Hush, then you sighs, if only till the morrow,
At Easter give your grief a holiday.

MAY RILEY SMITH ❧

A well-known minister was in his study writing an Easter sermon when the thought gripped him that his Lord was *living*. He jumped up excitedly and paced the floor repeating to himself, "Why Christ is alive, His ashes are warm, He is not the great 'I was,' He is the great 'I am.'" He is not only a fact, but a *living* fact. Glorious truth of Easter Day!

We believe that out of every grave there blooms an Easter lily, and in every tomb there sits an angel. We believe in a risen Lord. Turn not your faces to the past that we may worship only at His grave, but above and within that we may worship the Christ that lives. And because He lives, we shall live also. ABBOTT ❧

April 28

And when the children of Israel cried unto the Lord, the Lord raised up a deliverer ... who delivered them, even Othniel ... Caleb's younger brother. And the Spirit of the Lord came upon him (Judg. 3:9–10).

God is preparing His heroes; and when opportunity comes,
He can fit them into their place in a moment, and the world will
wonder where they came from.

Let the Holy Ghost prepare you, dear friend, by the discipline of life;
and when the last finishing touch has been given to the marble, it will be
easy for God to put it on the pedestal, and fit it into its niche.

There is a day coming when, like Othniel, we, too, shall judge the
nations, and rule and reign with Christ on the millennial earth. But ere that
glorious day can be we must let God prepare us, as He did Othniel at Kir-
jath-sepher, amid the trials of our present life, and the little victories, the
significance of which, perhaps, we little dream. At least, let us be sure of
this, and if the Holy Ghost has an Othniel ready, the Lord of heaven and
earth has a throne prepared for him. A. B. SIMPSON

> *Human strength and human greatness*
> *Spring not from life's sunny side,*
> *Heroes must be more than driftwood*
> *Floating on a waveless tide.*

"Every highway of human life dips in the dale now and then. Every
man must go through the tunnel of tribulation before he can travel on the
elevated road of triumph."

April 29

Elias was a man subject to like passions as we are (James 5:17).

Thank God for that! He got under a juniper tree, as you and I have
often done; he complained and murmured, as we have often done; was
unbelieving, as we have often been. But that was not the case when he really
got into touch with God. Though "a man subject to like passions as we
are," "he prayed praying." It is sublime in the original—not "earnestly,"
but "he prayed in prayer." He kept on praying. What is the lesson here?
You must *keep praying.*

Come up on the top of Carmel, and see that remarkable parable of faith
and sight. It was not the descent of the fire that now was necessary, but the
descent of the flood; and the man that can command the fire can command
the flood by the same means and methods. We are told that he bowed himself to the ground with his face between his knees; that is, shutting out all
sights and sounds. He was putting himself in a position where, beneath
his mantle, he could neither see nor hear what was going forward.

He said to his servant, "Go and take an observation." He went and came back, and said—how sublimely brief! one word—"Nothing!" What do we do under such circumstances?

We say, "It is just as I expected!" and we give up praying. Did Elijah? No, he said, "Go again." His servant again came back and said, "Nothing!" "Go again." "Nothing!"

By and by he came back, and said, "There is a little cloud like a man's hand." A man's hand had been raised in supplication, and presently down came the rain; and Ahab had not time to get back to the gate of Samaria with all his fast steeds. This is a parable of faith and sight—faith shutting itself up with God; sight taking observations and seeing nothing; faith going right on, and "praying in prayer," with utterly hopeless reports from sight.

Do you know how to pray that way, how to pray prevailingly? Let sight give as discouraging reports as it may, but pay no attention to these. The living God is still in the heavens and even to delay is part of His goodness. Arthur T. Pierson 🖎

Each of three boys gave a definition of faith which is an illustration of the tenacity of faith. The first boy said, "It is taking hold of Christ"; the second, "Keeping hold"; and the third, "Not letting go."

April 30

And the ill-favored and lean-fleshed kine did eat up the seven well favored and fat kine ... and the seven thin ears devoured the seven rank and full ears (Gen. 41:4, 7).

There is a warning for us in that dream, just as it stands: It *is* possible for the best years of our life, the best experiences, the best victories won, the best service rendered, to be swallowed up by times of failure, defeat, dishonor, uselessness in the kingdom. Some men's lives of rare promise and rare achievement have ended so. It is awful to think of, but it is true. *Yet it is never necessary.*

S. D. Gordon has said that the only assurance of safety against this tragedy is "fresh touch with God," daily, hourly. The blessed, fruitful, victorious experiences of yesterday are not only of no value to me today, but they will actually be eaten up or reversed by today's failures, *unless* they serve as incentives to still better, richer experiences today.

"Fresh touch with God," by abiding in Christ, alone will keep the lean kine and the ill-favored grain out of my life. From Messages for the Morning Watch 🖎

May 1

God that cannot lie promised (Titus 1:2).

Faith is not working up by willpower a sort of certainty that something is coming to pass, but it is seeing as an actual fact that God has said that this thing shall come to pass, and that it is true, and then rejoicing to know that it is true, and just resting because God has said it.

Faith turns the promise into a prophecy. While it is merely a promise it is contingent upon our cooperation. But when faith claims it, it becomes a prophecy, and we go forth feeling that it is something that must be done because God cannot lie. FROM DAYS OF HEAVEN UPON EARTH

I hear men praying everywhere for more faith, but when I listen to them carefully, and get at the real heart of their prayer, very often it is not more faith at all that they are wanting, but a change from faith to sight.

Faith says not, "I see that it is good for me, so God must have sent it," but, "God sent it, and so it must be good for me."

Faith, walking in the dark with God, only prays Him to clasp its hand more closely. PHILLIPS BROOKS

> *The Shepherd does not ask of thee*
> *Faith in thy faith, but only faith in Him;*
> *And this He meant in saying, "Come to me."*
> *In light or darkness seek to do His will,*
> *And leave the work of faith to Jesus still.*

May 2

The Lord hath prepared his throne in the heavens; and his kingdom ruleth over all (Ps. 103:19).

Some time since, in the early spring, I was going out at my door when round the corner came a blast of east wind—defiant and pitiless, fierce and withering—sending a cloud of dust before it.

I was just taking the latchkey from the door as I said, half impatiently, "I wish the wind would—" I was going to say change; but the word was checked, and the sentence was never finished.

As I went on my way, the incident became a parable to me.

There came an angel holding out a key, and he said: "My Master sends thee His love, and bids me give you this."

"What is it?" I asked wondering. "The key of the winds," said the angel, and disappeared.

Now indeed should I be happy. I hurried away up into the heights whence the winds came, and stood amongst the caves. "I will have done with the east wind at any rate—and that shall plague us no more," I cried; and calling in that friendless wind, I closed the door, and heard the echoes ringing in the hollow places. I turned the key triumphantly. "There," I said, "now we have done with that."

"What shall I choose in its place?" I asked myself, looking about me. "The south wind is pleasant"; and I thought of the lambs, and the young life on every hand, and the flowers that had begun to deck the hedgerows. But as I set the key within the door, it began to burn my hand.

"What am I doing?" I cried; "who knows what mischief I may bring about? How do I know what the fields want! Ten thousand things of ill may come of this foolish wish of mine."

Bewildered and ashamed, I looked up and prayed that the Lord would send His angel yet again to take the key; and for my part I promised that I would never want to have it anymore.

But lo, the Lord Himself stood by me. He reached His hand to take the key; and as I laid it down, I saw that it rested against the sacred wound-print.

It hurt me indeed that I could ever have murmured against anything wrought by Him who bear such sacred tokens of His love. Then He took the key and hung it on His girdle.

"Dost Thou keep the key of the winds?" I asked.

"I do, my child," He answered graciously.

And lo, I looked again and there hung all the keys of all my life. He saw my look of amazement, and asked, "Didst thou not know, my child, that my kingdom ruleth over all?"

"Over all, my Lord?" I answered; "then it is not safe for me to murmur at anything?" Then did He lay His hand upon me tenderly. "My child," He said, "thy only safety is, in everything, to love and trust and praise." MARK GUY PEARSE

May 3

And it shall come to pass that whosoever shall call on the name of the Lord shall be delivered (Joel 2:32).

Why do not I call on His name? Why do I run to this neighbor and that when God is so near and will hear my faintest call? Why do I sit down and devise schemes and invent plans? Why not at once roll myself and my burden upon the Lord?

Straightforward is the best runner—why do not I run at once to the living God? In vain shall I look for deliverance anywhere else; but with God I shall find it; for here I have His royal *shall* to make it sure.

I need not ask whether I may call on Him or not, for that word "Whosoever" is a very wide and comprehensive one. Whosoever means me, for it means anybody and everybody who calls upon God. I will therefore follow the leading of the text, and at once call upon the glorious Lord who has made so large a promise.

My case is urgent, and I do not see how I am to be delivered; but this is no business of mine. He who makes the promise will find ways and means of keeping it. It is mine to obey His commands; it is not mine to direct His counsels. I am His servant, not His solicitor. I call upon Him, and He will deliver. C. H. SPURGEON

May 4

He maketh sore, and bindeth up: he woundeth and his hands make whole (Job 5:18).

The ministry of a great sorrow

As we pass beneath the hills which have been shaken by the earthquake and torn by convulsion, we find that periods of perfect repose succeed those of destruction. The pools of calm water lie clear beneath their fallen rocks, the water lilies gleam, and the reeds whisper among the shadows; the village rises again over the forgotten graves, and its church tower, white through the storm twilight, proclaims a renewed appeal to His protection "in whose hand are all the corners of the earth, and the strength of the hills is his also." RUSKIN

God ploughed one day with an earthquake,
And drove His furrows deep!
The huddling plains upstarted,
The hills were all aleap!

But that is the mountains' secret,
Age-hidden in their breast;
"God's peace is everlasting,"
Are the dream-words of their rest.

He made them the haunts of beauty,
The home elect of His grace;
He spreadeth His mornings upon them,
His sunsets light their face.

His winds bring messages to them—
Wild storm-news from the main;
They sing it down the valleys
In the love-song of the rain.

They are nurseries for young rivers,
Nests for His flying cloud,
Homesteads for new-born races,
Masterful, free, and proud.

The people of tired cities
Come up to their shrines and pray;
God freshens again within them,
As He passes by all day.

And lo, I have caught their secret!
The beauty deeper than all!
This faith—that life's hard moments,
When the jarring sorrows befall,

Are but God ploughing His mountains;
And those mountains yet shall be
The source of His grace and freshness,
And His peace everlasting to me.

WILLIAM C. GANNETT

May 5

When they began to sing and praise, the Lord set ambushments
. . . and they were smitten (2 Chron. 20:22).

Oh, that we could reason less about our troubles, and sing and praise more! There are thousands of things that we wear as shackles which we might use as instruments with music in them, if we only knew how.

Those men that ponder, and meditate, and weigh the affairs of life, and study the mysterious developments of God's providence, and wonder why they should be burdened and thwarted and hampered—how different and how much more joyful would be their lives, if, instead of forever indulging in self-revolving and inward thinking, they would take their experiences, day by day, and lift them up, and praise God for them.

We can sing our cares away easier than we can reason them away. Sing in the morning. The birds are the earliest to sing, and birds are more without care than anything else that I know of.

Sing at evening. Singing is the last thing that robins do. When they have done their daily work; when they have flown their last flight, and picked up their last morsel of food, then on a topmost twig, they sing one song of praise.

Oh, that we might sing morning and evening, and let song touch song all the way through. SELECTED ❧

> *Don't let the song go out of your life*
> *Though it chance sometimes to flow*
> *In a minor strain; it will blend again*
> *With the major tone you know.*
>
> *What though shadows rise to obscure life's skies,*
> *And hide for a time the sun,*
> *The sooner they'll lift and reveal the rift,*
> *If you let the melody run.*
>
> *Don't let the song go out of your life;*
> *Though the voice may have lost its trill,*
> *Though the tremulous note may die in your throat,*
> *Let it sing in your spirit still.*
>
> *Don't let the song go out of your life;*
> *Let it ring in the soul while here;*
> *And when you go hence, 'twill follow you thence,*
> *And live on in another sphere.*

May 6

The secret of the Lord is with them that fear him (Ps. 25:14).

There are secrets of providence which God's dear children may learn. His dealings with them often seem, to the outward eye, dark and terrible. Faith looks deeper and says, "This is God's secret. You look only on the outside; I can look deeper and see the hidden meaning."

Sometimes diamonds are done up in rough packages, so that their value cannot be seen. When the tabernacle was built in the wilderness there was nothing rich in its outside appearance. The costly things were all within, and its outward covering of rough badger skin gave no hint of the valuable things which it contained.

God may send you, dear friends, some costly packages. Do not worry if they are done up in rough wrappings. You may be sure there are treasures of love, and kindness, and wisdom hidden within. If we take what He sends, *and trust Him* for the goodness in it, even in the dark, we shall learn the meaning of the secrets of providence. A. B. SIMPSON

> *Not until each loom is silent,*
> *And the shuttles cease to fly,*
> *Will God unroll the pattern*
> *And explain the reason why*
> *The dark threads are as needful*
> *In the Weaver's skillful hand,*
> *As the threads of gold and silver*
> *For the pattern which He planned.*

He that is mastered by Christ is the master of every circumstance. Does the circumstance press hard against you? Do not push it away. It is the Potter's hand. Your mastery will come, not by arresting its progress, but by enduring its discipline, for it is not only shaping you into a vessel of beauty and honor, but it is making your resources available.

May 7

He spake a parable unto them . . . that men ought always to pray, and not to faint (Luke 18:1).

No temptation in the life of intercession is more common than this of failure to *persevere*. We begin to pray for a certain thing; we put up our petitions for a day, a week, a month; and then, receiving as yet no definite answer, straightway we faint, and cease altogether from prayer concerning it.

This is a deadly fault. It is simply the snare of many beginnings with no completions. It is ruinous in all spheres of life.

The man who forms the habit of beginning without finishing has simply formed the habit of failure. The man who begins to pray about a thing and does not pray it through to a successful issue of answer has formed the same habit in prayer.

To faint is to fail; then defeat begets disheartenment, and unfaith in the reality of prayer, which is fatal to all success.

But someone says, "How long shall we pray? Do we not come to a place where we may cease from our petitions and rest the matter in God's hands?"

There is but one answer. *Pray until the thing you pray for has actually been granted, or until you have the assurance in your heart that it will be.*

Only at one of these two places dare we stay our importunity, for prayer is not only a calling upon God, but also a conflict with Satan. And inasmuch as God is using our intercession as a mighty factor of victory in that conflict, He alone, and not we, must decide when we dare cease from our petitioning. So we dare not stay our prayer until the answer itself *has* come, or until we receive the assurance that it *will* come.

In the first case, we stop because we see. In the other, we stop because we believe, and the faith of our hearts is just as sure as the sight of our eyes; for it is faith *from,* yes, the faith *of* God, within us.

More and more, as we live the prayer life, shall we come to experience and recognize this God-given assurance and know when to rest quietly in it, or when to continue our petitioning until we receive it. FROM THE PRACTICE OF PRAYER ☙

> *Tarry at the promise till God meets you there.*
> *He always returns by way of His promises.*
>
> SELECTED ☙

May 8

Walking in the midst of the fire (Dan. 3:25).

∼☙∽

The fire did not arrest their motion; they walked in the midst of it. It was one of the streets through which they moved to their destiny. The comfort of Christ's revelation is not that it teaches emancipation *from* sorrow, but emancipation *through* sorrow.

O my God, teach me, when the shadows have gathered, that I am only in a tunnel. It is enough for me to know that it will be all right some day.

They tell me that I shall stand upon the peaks of Olivet, the heights of resurrection glory. But I want more, O my Father; I want Calvary to lead up to it. I want to know that the shadows of this world are the shades of an avenue—the avenue to the house of my Father. Tell me I am only forced to climb because Thy house is on the hill! I shall receive *no* hurt from sorrow if I shall *walk* in the midst of the fire. GEORGE MATHESON

> *"The road is too rough," I said;*
> *"It is uphill all the way;*
> *No flowers, but thorns instead;*
> *And the skies over head are grey."*
> *But One took my hand at the entrance dim,*
> *And sweet is the road that I walk with Him.*
>
> *"The cross is too great," I cried—*
> *"More than the back can bear,*
> *So rough and heavy and wide,*
> *And nobody by to care."*
> *And One stooped softly and touched my hand:*
> *"I know. I care. And I understand."*
>
> *Then why do we fret and sigh;*
> *Cross-bearers all we go:*
> *But the road ends by-and-by*
> *In the dearest place we know,*
> *And every step in the journey we*
> *May take in the Lord's own company.*

May 9

Abraham stood yet before the Lord (Gen. 18:22).

The friend of God can plead with Him for others. Perhaps Abraham's height of faith and friendship seems beyond our little possibilities. Do not be discouraged, Abraham grew; so may we. He went step by step, not by great leaps.

The man whose faith has been deeply tested and who has come off victorious, is the man to whom supreme tests must come.

The finest jewels are most carefully cut and polished; the hottest fires try the most precious metal. Abraham would never have been called the father of the faithful if he had not been proved to the uttermost. Read Genesis, twenty-second chapter: "Take thy son, thine only son, whom thou lovest." See him going with a chastened, wistful, yet humbly obedient heart up Moriah's height, with the idol of his heart beside him about to be sacrificed at the command of God whom he had faithfully loved and served!

What a rebuke to our questionings of God's dealings with us! Away with all doubting explanations of this stupendous scene! It was an object lesson for the ages. Angels were looking.

Shall this man's faith stand forever for the strength and help of all God's people? Shall it be known through him that unfaltering faith will always prove the faithfulness of God?

Yes; and when faith has borne victoriously its uttermost test, the angel of the Lord—who? The Lord Jesus, Jehovah, He in whom "all the promises of God are yea and amen"—spoke to him, saying, "Now I know that thou fearest God." Thou hast trusted me to the uttermost. I will also trust thee; thou shalt ever be My friend, and I will bless thee, and make thee a blessing.

It is always so, and always will be. *"They that are of faith are blessed with faithful Abraham."* SELECTED

It is no small thing to be on terms of friendship with God.

May 10

I had fainted unless . . . (Ps. 27:13).

FAINT NOT!

How great is the temptation at this point! How the soul sinks, the heart grows sick, and the faith staggers under the keen trials and testings which come into our lives in times of special bereavement and suffering.

"I cannot bear up any longer, I am fainting under this providence. What shall I do? God tells me not to faint. But what can one do when he is fainting?"

What do you do when you are about to faint physically? You cannot *do* anything. You *cease* from your own doings. In your faintness, you fall

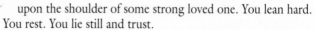

upon the shoulder of some strong loved one. You lean hard. You rest. You lie still and trust.

It is so when we are tempted to faint under affliction. God's message to us is not, "Be strong and of good courage," for He knows our strength and courage have fled away. But it is that sweet word, "Be still, and know that I am God."

Hudson Taylor was so feeble in the closing months of his life that he wrote a dear friend: "I am so weak I cannot write; I cannot read my Bible; I cannot even pray. I can only lie still in God's arms like a little child, and trust."

This wondrous man of God with all his spiritual power came to a place of physical suffering and weakness where he could only lie still and trust.

And that is all God asks of you, His dear child, when you grow faint in the fierce fires of affliction. Do not try *to be strong.* Just be *still* and *know that He is God,* and will sustain you, and bring you through.

God keeps His choicest cordials for our deepest faintings.

Stay firm and let thine heart take courage (Ps. 27:14, AFTER OSTERWALD).

> *Stay firm, He has not failed thee*
> *In all the past,*
> *And will He go and leave thee*
> *To sink at last?*
> *Nay, He said He will hide thee*
> *Beneath His wing;*
> *And sweetly there in safety*
> *Thou mayest sing.*

SELECTED

May 11

We went through fire and through water: But thou broughtest us out into a wealthy place (Ps. 66:12).

Paradoxical though it be, only that man is at rest who attains it through conflict. This peace, born of conflict, is not like the deadly hush preceding the tempest, but the serene and pure-aired quiet that follows it.

It is not generally the prosperous one, who has never sorrowed, who is strong and at rest. His quality has never been tried, and he knows not how he can stand even a gentle shock. He is not the safest sailor who never saw a tempest; he will do for fair-weather service, but when the storm is rising, place at the important post the man who has fought out a gale, who has tested the ship, who knows her hulk sound, her rigging strong, and her anchor-flukes able to grasp and hold by the ribs of the world.

When first affliction comes upon us, how everything gives way! Our clinging, tendril hopes are snapped, and our heart lies prostrate like a vine that the storm has torn from its trellis; but when the first shock is past, and we are able to look up, and say, "It is the Lord," faith lifts the shattered hopes once more, and binds them fast to the feet of God. Thus the end is confidence, safety, and peace. SELECTED

The adverse winds blew against my life;
My little ship with grief was tossed;
My plans were gone—heart full of strife,
And all my hope seemed to be lost—
"Then He arose"—one word of peace.
"There was a calm"—a sweet release.

A tempest great of doubt and fear
Possessed my mind; no light was there
To guide, or make my vision clear.
Dark night! 'twas more than I could bear—
"Then He arose," I saw His face—
"There was a calm" filled with His grace.

My heart was sinking 'neath the wave
Of deepening test and raging grief;
All seemed as lost, and none could save,
And nothing could bring me relief—
"Then He arose"—and spoke one word,
"There was a calm!" IT IS THE LORD.

L.S.P.

May 12

All things are possible to him that believeth (Mark 9:23).

The "all things" do not always come simply for the asking, for the reason that God is ever seeking to teach us the way of faith, and in our training in the faith-life there must be room for the trial of faith, the discipline of faith, the patience of faith, the courage of faith, and often many stages are passed before we really realize what is the end of faith, namely, the victory of faith.

Real moral fiber is developed through discipline of faith. You have made your request of God, but the answer does not come. What are you to do?

Keep on believing God's Word; never be moved away from it by what you see or feel, and thus as you stand steady, enlarged power and experience is being developed. The fact of looking at the apparent contradiction as to God's Word and being unmoved from your position of faith make you stronger on every other line.

Often God delays purposely, and the delay is just as much an answer to your prayer as is the fulfillment when it comes.

In the lives of all the great Bible characters, God worked thus. Abraham, Moses, and Elijah were not great in the beginning, but were made great through the discipline of their faith, and only thus were they fitted for the positions to which God had called them.

For example, in the case of Joseph whom the Lord was training for the throne of Egypt, we read in the Psalms: *"The word of the Lord tried him."* It was not the prison life with its hard beds or poor food that tried him, but it was the word God had spoken into his heart in the early years concerning elevation and honor which were greater than his brethren were to receive; it was this which was ever before him, when every step in his career made it seem more and more impossible of fulfillment, until he was there imprisoned, and all in innocency, while others who were perhaps justly incarcerated, were released, and he was left to languish alone.

These were hours that tried his soul, but hours of spiritual growth and development, that, "when his word came" (the word of release), found him fitted for the delicate task of dealing with his wayward brethren, with a love and patience only surpassed by God Himself.

No amount of persecution tries like such experiences as these. When God has spoken of His purpose to do, and yet the days go on and He does not do it, that is truly hard; but it is a discipline of faith that will bring us into a knowledge of God which would otherwise be impossible.

May 13

We know not what we should pray for as we ought (Rom. 8:26).

Much that perplexes us in our Christian experience is but the answer to our prayers. We pray for patience, and our Father sends those who tax us to the utmost; for *"tribulation worketh patience."*

We pray for submission, and God sends sufferings; for *"we learn obedience by the things we suffer."*

We pray for unselfishness, and God gives us opportunities to sacrifice ourselves by thinking on the things of others, and by laying down our lives for the brethren.

We pray for strength and humility, and some messenger of Satan torments us until we lie in the dust crying for its removal.

We pray, "Lord, increase our faith," and money takes wings; or the children are alarmingly ill; or a servant comes who is careless, extravagant, untidy or slow, or some hitherto unknown trial calls for an increase of faith along a line where we have not needed to exercise much faith before.

We pray for the Lamb-life, and are given a portion of lowly service, or we are injured and must seek no redress; for "he was led as a lamb to the slaughter and . . . opened not his mouth."

We pray for gentleness, and there comes a perfect storm of temptation to harshness and irritability. We pray for quietness, and every nerve is strung to the utmost tension, so that looking to Him we may learn that when He giveth quietness, no one can make trouble.

We pray for love, and God sends peculiar suffering and puts us with apparently unlovely people, and lets them say things which rasp the nerves and lacerate the heart; for love suffereth long and is kind, love is not impolite, love is not provoked. LOVE BEARETH ALL THINGS, believeth, hopeth and endureth, love never faileth. We pray for likeness to Jesus, and the answer is, "I have chosen thee in the furnace of affliction." "Can thine heart endure, or can thine hands be strong?" "Are ye able?"

The way to peace and victory is to accept every circumstance, every trial, straight from the hand of a loving Father; and to live up in the heavenly places, above the clouds, in the very presence of the throne, and to look down from the glory upon our environment as lovingly and divinely appointed. SELECTED

> *I prayed for strength, and then I lost awhile*
> *All sense of nearness, human and divine;*
> *The love I leaned on failed and pierced my heart,*
> *The hands I clung to loosed themselves from mine;*
> *But while I swayed, weak, trembling, and alone,*
> *The everlasting arms upheld my own.*
>
> *I prayed for light; the sun went down in clouds,*
> *The moon was darkened by a misty doubt,*
> *The stars of heaven were dimmed by earthly fears,*

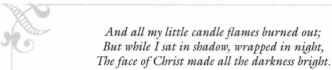

And all my little candle flames burned out;
But while I sat in shadow, wrapped in night,
The face of Christ made all the darkness bright.

I prayed for peace, and dreamed of restful ease,
A slumber drugged from pain, a hushed repose;
Above my head the skies were black with storm,
And fiercer grew the onslaught of my foes;
But while the battle raged, and wild winds blew,
I heard His voice and perfect peace I knew.

I thank Thee, Lord, Thou wert too wise to heed
My feeble prayers, and answer as I sought,
Since these rich gifts Thy bounty has bestowed
Have brought me more than all I asked or thought;
Giver of good, so answer each request
With Thine own giving, better than my best.

ANNIE JOHNSON FLINT

May 14

In the selfsame day, as God had said unto him (Gen. 17:23).

Instant obedience is the only kind of obedience there is; *delayed* obedience is disobedience. Every time God calls us to any duty, He is offering to make a covenant with us; doing the duty is our part, and He will do His part in special blessing.

The only way we can obey is to obey *"in the selfsame day,"* as Abraham did. To be sure, we often postpone a duty and then later on do it as fully as we can. It is better to do this than not to do it at all. But it is then, at best, only a crippled, disfigured, halfway sort of duty-doing; and a *postponed duty never can bring the full blessing that God intended, and that it would have brought if done at the earliest possible moment.*

It is a pity to rob ourselves, along with robbing God and others, by procrastination. *"In the selfsame day"* is the Genesis way of saying, "Do it now." FROM MESSAGES FOR THE MORNING WATCH

Luther says that a "true believer will crucify the question, 'Why?' He will obey without questioning." I will not be one of those who, except they see signs and wonders, will in no wise believe. I will obey without questioning.

Ours not to make reply,
Ours not to reason why,
Ours but to do and die.

Obedience is the fruit of faith; patience, the bloom on the fruit.
CHRISTINA ROSSETTI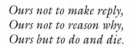

May 15

Men see not the bright light which is in the clouds (Job 37:21).

The world owes much of its beauty to cloudland. The unchanging blue of the Italian sky hardly compensates for the changefulness and glory of the clouds. Earth would become a wilderness apart from their ministry. There are clouds in human life, shadowing, refreshing, and sometimes draping it in blackness of night; but there is never a cloud without its bright light. "I do set my bow in the cloud!"

If we could see the clouds from the other side where they lie in billowy glory, bathed in the light they intercept, like heaped ranges of Alps, we should be amazed at their splendid magnificence.

We look at their underside; but who shall describe the bright light that bathes their summits and searches their valleys and is reflected from every pinnacle of their expanse? Is not every drop drinking in health-giving qualities, which it will carry to earth?

O child of God! If you could see your sorrows and troubles from the other side; if instead of looking up at them from earth, you would look down on them from the heavenly places where you sit with Christ; if you knew how they are reflecting in prismatic beauty before the gaze of heaven, the bright light of Christ's face, you would be content that they should cast their deep shadows over the mountain slopes of existence. Only remember that clouds are always moving and passing before God's cleansing wind. SELECTED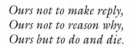

I cannot know why suddenly the storm
Should rage so fiercely round me in its wrath;
But this I know—God watches all my path,
And I can trust.

I may not draw aside the mystic veil
That hides the unknown future from my sight,
Nor know if for me waits the dark or light;
But I can trust.

I have no power to look across the tide,
To see while here the land beyond the river;
But this I know—I shall be God's forever;
So I can trust.

May 16

Fear not, Daniel: for from the first day that thou didst set thine heart to understand, and to chasten thyself before thy God, thy words were heard, and I am come for thy words. But the prince of the kingdom of Persia withstood me one and twenty days (Dan. 10:12–13).

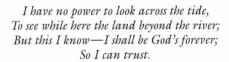

We have wonderful teaching here on prayer, and we are shown the direct hindrance from Satan.

Daniel had fasted and prayed twenty-one days, and had a very hard time in prayer. As far as we read the narrative, it was not because Daniel was not a good man, nor because his prayer was not right; but it was because of a special attack of Satan.

The Lord started a messenger to tell Daniel that his prayer was answered the moment Daniel began to pray; but an evil angel met the good angel and wrestled with him, hindering him. There was a conflict in the heavens; and Daniel seemed to go through an agony on earth the same as that which was going on in the heavens.

We wrestle not against flesh and blood, but against principalities, against powers ... against wicked spirits in high places (Eph. 6:12, margin).

Satan delayed the answer three full weeks. Daniel nearly succumbed, and Satan would have been glad to kill him; but God will not suffer anything to come above that we "are able to bear."

Many a Christian's prayer is hindered by Satan; but you need not fear when your prayers and faith pile up; for after a while they will be like a flood, and will not only sweep the answer through, but will also bring some new accompanying blessing. FROM A SERMON

Hell does its worst with the saints. The rarest souls have been tested with high pressures and temperatures, but heaven will not desert them. W. L. WATKINSON

May 17

And when forty years were expired, there appeared to him in the wilderness . . . an angel of the Lord . . . saying, . . . now come, I will send thee into Egypt (Acts 7:30–34).

Often the Lord calls us aside from our work for a season, and bids us be still and learn ere we go forth again to minister. There is no time lost in such waiting hours.

Fleeing from his enemies, the ancient knight found that his horse needed to be reshod. Prudence seemed to urge him on without delay, but higher wisdom taught him to halt a few minutes at the blacksmith's forge by the way, to have the shoe replaced; and although he heard the feet of his pursuers galloping hard behind, yet he waited those minutes until his charger was refitted for his flight. And then, leaping into his saddle just as they appeared a hundred yards away, he dashed away from them with the fleetness of the wind, and knew that his halting had hastened his escape.

So often God bids us tarry ere we go, and fully recover ourselves for the next stage of the journey and work. FROM DAYS OF HEAVEN UPON EARTH

Waiting! Yes, patiently waiting!
Till next steps made plain shall be;
To hear, with the inner hearing,
The Voice that will call for me.

Waiting! Yes, hopefully waiting!
With hope that need not grow dim;
The Master is pledged to guide me,
And my eyes are unto Him.

Waiting! Expectantly waiting!
Perhaps it may be today
The Master will quickly open
The gate to my future way.

Waiting! Yes, waiting! still waiting!
I know, though I've waited long,
That, while He withholds His purpose,
His waiting cannot be wrong.

Waiting! Yes, waiting! still waiting!
The Master will not be late:

He knoweth that I am waiting
For Him to unlatch the gate.

J. DANSON SMITH

May 18

I was crushed ... so much so that I despaired even of life, but that was to make me rely not on myself, but on the God who raises the dead (2 Cor. 1:8–9).

> Pressed out of measure and pressed to all length;
> Pressed so intensely it seems, beyond strength;
> Pressed in the body and pressed in the soul,
> Pressed in the mind till the dark surges roll.
> Pressure by foes, and a pressure from friends.
> Pressure on pressure, till life nearly ends.
>
> Pressed into knowing no helper but God;
> Pressed into loving the staff and the rod.
> Pressed into liberty where nothing clings;
> Pressed into faith for impossible things.
> Pressed into living a life in the Lord,
> Pressed into living a Christ-life outpoured.

The pressure of hard places makes us value life. Every time our life is given back to us from such a trial, it is like a new beginning, and we learn better how much it is worth, and make more of it for God and man. The pressure helps us to understand the trials of others, and fits us to help and sympathize with them.

There is a shallow, superficial nature, that gets hold of a theory or a promise lightly, and talks very glibly about the distrust of those who shrink from every trial; but the man or woman who has suffered much never does this, but is very tender and gentle, and knows what suffering really means. This is what Paul meant when he said, "Death worketh in you."

Trials and hard places are needed to press us forward, even as the furnace fires in the hold of that mighty ship give force that moves the piston, drives the engine, and propels that great vessel across the sea in the face of the winds and waves. A. B. SIMPSON

Out of the presses of pain,
Cometh the soul's best wine;
And the eyes that have shed no rain,
Can shed but little shine.

May 19

And it came to pass, before he had done speaking . . . and he said,
Blessed be Jehovah . . . who hath not forsaken his loving kindness
and his truth (Gen. 24:15, 27).

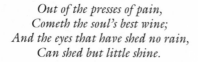

Every right prayer is answered before the prayer itself is finished—
before we have "done speaking." This is because God has pledged His
Word to us that whatsoever we ask in Christ's name (that is, in oneness with
Christ and His will) and in faith, shall be done.

As God's Word cannot fail, whenever we meet those simple conditions
in prayer, the answer to our prayer has been granted and completed in
heaven *as we pray,* even though its showing forth on earth may not occur
until long afterward.

So it is well to close every prayer with *praise* to God for the answer
that He has already granted; He who never forsakes His lovingkindness
and His truth. (See Dan. 9:20–27 and 10:12.) FROM MESSAGES FOR THE
MORNING WATCH 🖝

When we believe for a blessing, we must take the attitude of faith; and
begin to act and pray as if we had the blessing. We must treat God as if He
had given us our request. We must lean our weight over upon Him for the
thing that we have claimed, and just take it for granted that He gives it, and
is going to continue to give it. This is the attitude of trust.

When the wife is married, she at once falls into a new attitude, and acts
in accordance with the fact; and so when we take Christ as our Savior, as
our Sanctifier, as our Healer, or as our Deliverer, He expects us to fall into
the attitude of recognizing Him in the capacity that we have claimed, and
expect Him to be to us all that we have trusted Him for. SELECTED 🖝

The thing I ask when God doth bid me pray,
Begins in that same act to come my way.

Shall I refuse to drink the cup of sorrow which the Father has given me to drink? (John 18:11 WEYMOUTH).

God takes a thousand times more pains with us than the artist with his picture, by many touches of sorrow, and by many colors of circumstance, to bring us into the form which is the highest and noblest in His sight, if only we receive His gifts of myrrh in the right spirit.

But when the cup is put away, and these feelings are stifled or unheeded, a greater injury is done to the soul than can ever be amended. For no heart can conceive in what surpassing love God giveth us this myrrh; yet this which we ought to receive to our souls' good we suffer to pass by us in our sleepy indifference, and nothing comes of it.

Then we come and complain: "Alas, Lord! I am so dry, and it is so dark within me!" I tell thee, dear child, open thy heart to the pain, and it will do thee more good than if thou wert full of feeling and devoutness. TAULER

The cry of man's anguish went up to God,
"Lord take away pain:
The shadow that darkens the world Thou hast made,
The close-coiling chain
That strangles the heart, the burden that weighs
On the wings that would soar,
Lord, take away pain from the world Thou hast made,
That it love Thee the more."

Then answered the Lord to the cry of His world:
"Shall I take away pain,
And with it the power of the soul to endure,
Made strong by the strain?
Shall I take away pity, that knits heart to heart
And sacrifice high?
Will ye lose all your heroes that lift from the fire
White brows to the sky?
Shall I take away love that redeems with a price
And smiles at its loss?
Can ye spare from your lives that would climb unto Me
The Christ on His cross?"

May 21

I call to remembrance my song in the night (Ps. 77:6).

I have read somewhere of a little bird that will never sing the melody his master wishes while his cage is full of light. He learns a snatch of this, a bar of that, but never an entire song of its own until the cage is covered and the morning beams shut out.

A good many people never learn to sing until the darkling shadows fall. The fabled nightingale carols with his breast against a thorn. It was in the night that the song of the angels was heard. It was at midnight that the cry came, "Behold, the bridegroom cometh; go ye out to meet him."

Indeed it is extremely doubtful if a soul can really know the love of God in its richness and in its comforting, satisfying completeness until the skies are black and lowering.

Light comes out of darkness, morning out of the womb of the night.

James Creelman, in one of his letters, describes his trip through the Balkan states in search of Natalie, the exiled queen of Serbia.

"In that memorable journey," he says, "I learned for the first time that the world's supply of attar of roses comes from the Balkan Mountains. And the thing that interested me most," he goes on, "is that the roses must be gathered in the darkest hours. The pickers start out at one o'clock and finish picking them at two.

"At first it seemed to me a relic of superstition; but I investigated the picturesque mystery, and learned that actual scientific tests had proven that fully forty percent of the fragrance of roses disappeared in the light of day."

And in human life and human culture that is not a playful, fanciful conceit; it is a real veritable fact. MALCOLM J. MCLEOD 🐝

May 22

He worketh (Ps. 37:5).

The translation that we find in Young of "Commit thy way unto the Lord; trust also in him; and he shall bring it to pass," reads: *"Roll* upon *Jehovah* thy way; trust upon him: and he *worketh."*

It calls our attention to the *immediate* action of God when we truly commit, or roll out of our hands into His, the burden of whatever kind it may be; a way of sorrow, of difficulty, of physical need, or of anxiety for the conversion of some dear one.

"He worketh." When? *Now.* We are so in danger of postponing our expectation of His *acceptance of the trust,* and His undertaking to accomplish what we ask Him to do, instead of saying *as we commit, "He worketh."* "He worketh" *even now;* and praise Him that it is so.

The very expectancy enables the Holy Spirit to do the very thing we have *rolled upon Him.* It is out of *our* reach. We are not *trying* to do it anymore. *"He worketh!"*

Let us take the comfort out of it and not put our hands on it again. Oh, what a relief it brings! *He is* really working on the difficulty.

But someone may say, "I see no results." Never mind. *"He worketh,"* if you have *rolled it over* and are looking to Jesus to do it. Faith may be tested, but *"He worketh";* the *Word is sure!* V. H. F. 🦋

I will cry unto God most high; unto God that performeth all things for me (Ps. 57:2).

The beautiful old translation says, "He shall perform the cause which I have in hand." Does not that make it very real to us today? Just the very thing that "I have in hand"—my own particular bit of work today, this cause that I cannot manage, this thing that I undertook in miscalculation of my own powers—*this* is what I may ask Him to do "for me," and rest assured that He will perform it. "The wise and their works are in the hands of God." HAVERGAL 🦋

The Lord will go through with His covenant engagements. Whatever He takes in hand He will accomplish; hence past mercies are guarantees for the future and admirable reasons for continuing to cry unto Him. C. H. SPURGEON 🦋

May 23

At their wit's end, then they cry unto the Lord in their trouble, and he bringeth them out (Ps. 107:27–28).

Are you standing at "Wit's End Corner,"
Christian, with troubled brow?
Are you thinking of what is before you,
And all you are bearing now?
Does all the world seem against you,
And you in the battle alone?

Remember—at "Wit's End Corner"
Is just where God's power is shown.

Are you standing at "Wit's End Corner,"
Blinded with wearying pain,
Feeling you cannot endure it,
You cannot bear the strain,
Bruised through the constant suffering,
Dizzy, and dazed, and numb?
Remember—at "Wit's End Corner"
Is where Jesus loves to come.

Are you standing at "Wit's End Corner"?
Your work before you spread,
All lying begun, unfinished,
And pressing on heart and head,
Longing for strength to do it,
Stretching out trembling hands?
Remember—at "Wit's End Corner"
The Burden-bearer stands.

Are you standing at "Wit's End Corner"?
Then you're just in the very spot
To learn the wondrous resources
Of Him who faileth not;
No doubt to a brighter pathway
Your footsteps will soon be moved,
But only at "Wit's End Corner"
Is the "God who is able" proved.

ANTOINETTE WILSON

Do not get discouraged; it may be the last key in the bunch that opens the door. STANSIFER

May 24

For Sarah conceived and bare Abraham a son in his old age, at the set time of which God had spoken to him (Gen. 21:2).

"The counsel of the Lord standeth for ever, the thoughts of His heart to all generations" (Ps. 33:11). But we must be prepared to wait God's time. God has His *set times.* It is not for us to know them; indeed, we cannot know them; we must wait for them.

If God had told Abraham in Haran that he must wait for thirty years until he pressed the promised child to his bosom, his heart would have failed him. So, in gracious love, the length of the weary years was hidden, and only as they were nearly spent, and there were only a few more months to wait, God told him that "according to the time of life, Sarah shall have a son" (Gen. 18:14).

The *set time* came at last; and then the laughter that filled the patriarch's home made the aged pair forget the long and weary vigil.

Take heart, waiting one, thou waitest for One who cannot disappoint thee; and who will not be five minutes behind the appointed moment: ere long "your sorrow shall be turned into joy."

Ah, happy soul, when God makes thee laugh! Then sorrow and crying shall flee away forever, as darkness before the dawn. SELECTED

It is not for us who are passengers, to meddle with the chart and with the compass. Let that all-skilled Pilot alone with His own work. HALL

Some things cannot be done in a day. God does not make a sunset glory in a moment, but for days may be massing the mist out of which He builds His palaces beautiful in the west.

> *Some glorious morn—but when? Ah, who shall say?*
> *The steepest mountain will become a plain,*
> *And the parched land be satisfied with rain.*
> *The gates of brass all broken; iron bars,*
> *Transfigured, form a ladder to the stars.*
> *Rough places plain, and crooked ways all straight,*
> *For him who with a patient heart can wait.*
> *These things shall be on God's appointed day:*
> *It may not be tomorrow—yet it may.*

May 25

I endure all things for the sake of God's own people; so that they also may obtain salvation . . . and with it eternal glory (2 Tim. 2:10 WEYMOUTH).

If Job could have known as he sat there in the ashes, bruising his heart on this problem of providence—that in the trouble that had come upon him he was doing what one man may do to work out the problem for the world, he might again have taken courage. No man lives to himself. Job's life is but your life and mine written in larger text. . . . So, then, though we may not know what trials wait on any of us, we can believe that, as the days in which Job wrestled with his dark maladies are the only days that make him worth remembrance, and but for which his name had never been written in the Book of Life, so the days through which we struggle, finding no way, but never losing the light, will be the most significant we are called to live. ROBERT COLLYER 🍃

Who does not know that our most sorrowful days have been amongst our best? When the face is wreathed in smiles and we trip lightly over meadows bespangled with spring flowers, the heart is often running to waste.

The soul which is always blithe and gay misses the deepest life. It has its reward, and it is satisfied to its measure, though that measure is a very scanty one. But the heart is dwarfed; and the nature, which is capable of the highest heights, the deepest depths, is undeveloped; and life presently burns down to its socket without having known the resonance of the deepest chords of joy.

"Blessed are they that mourn." Stars shine brightest in the long dark night of winter. The gentians show their fairest bloom amid almost inaccessible heights of snow and ice.

God's promises seem to wait for the pressure of pain to trample out their richest juice as in a winepress. Only those who have sorrowed know how tender is the "Man of Sorrows." SELECTED 🍃

Thou hast but little sunshine, but thy long glooms are wisely appointed thee; for perhaps a stretch of summer weather would have made thee as a parched land and barren wilderness. Thy Lord knows best, and He has the clouds and the sun at His disposal. SELECTED 🍃

"It is a gray day." "Yes, but dinna ye see the patch of blue?" SCOTCH SHOEMAKER 🍃

May 26

Spring up, O well; sing ye unto it (Num. 21:17).

This was a strange song and a strange well. They had been traveling over the desert's barren sands, no water was in sight and they were famishing with thirst. Then God spake to Moses and said: "Gather the people together, and I will give them water," and this is how it came.

They gathered in circles on the sands. They took their staves and dug deep down into the burning earth and as they dug, they sang, *"Spring up, O well, sing ye unto it,"* and lo, there came a gurgling sound, a rush of

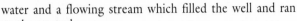

water and a flowing stream which filled the well and ran along the ground.

When they dug this well in the desert, they touched the stream that was running beneath, and reached the flowing tides that had long been out of sight.

How beautiful the picture given, telling us of the river of blessing that flows all through our lives, and we have only to reach by *faith* and *praise* to find our wants supplied in the most barren desert.

How did they reach the waters of this well? It was by *praise*. They sang upon the sand their song of faith, while with their staff of promise they dug the well.

Our *praise* will still open fountains in the desert, when murmuring will only bring us judgment, and even prayer may fail to reach the fountains of blessing.

There is nothing that pleases the Lord so much as *praise*. There is no test of faith so true as the grace of thanksgiving. *Are you praising God enough?* Are you thanking Him for your actual blessings that are more than can be numbered, and are you daring to praise Him even for those trials which are but blessings in disguise? Have you learned to praise Him in advance for the things that have not yet come? SELECTED

Thou waitest for deliverance!
O soul, thou waitest long!
Believe that now deliverance
Doth wait for thee in song!

Sigh not until deliverance
Thy fettered feet doth free:
With songs of glad deliverance
God now doth compass thee.

May 27

Bring them hither to me (Matt. 14:18).

Are you encompassed with needs at this very moment, and almost overwhelmed with difficulties, trials, and emergencies? These are all divinely provided vessels for the Holy Spirit to fill, and if you but rightly understood their meaning, they would become opportunities for receiving new blessings and deliverances which you can get in no other way.

Bring these vessels to God. Hold them steadily before Him in faith and prayer. Keep still, and stop your own restless working until He begins to work. Do nothing that He does not Himself command you to do. Give Him a chance to work, and He will surely do so; and the very trials that threatened to overcome you with discouragement and disaster, will become God's opportunity for the revelation of His grace and glory in your life, as you have never known Him before. "Bring them *[all needs]* to me." A. B. SIMPSON

My God shall supply all your need according to his riches in glory by Christ Jesus (Phil. 4:19).

What a source—"God!" What a supply—"His riches in glory!" What a channel—"Christ Jesus!" It is your sweet privilege to place *all your need* over against *His riches,* and lose sight of the former in the presence of the latter. His exhaustless treasury is thrown open to you, in all the love of His heart; go and draw upon it, in the artless simplicity of faith, and you will never have occasion to look to a creature-stream, or lean on a creature-prop. C. H. M.

My Cup Runneth Over

There is always something over,
When we trust our gracious Lord;
Every cup He fills o'erfloweth,
His great rivers all are broad.
Nothing narrow, nothing stinted,
Ever issues from His store;
To His own He gives full measure,
Running over, evermore.

There is always something over,
When we, from the Father's hand,
Take our portion with thanksgiving,
Praising for the path He planned.
Satisfaction, full and deepening,
Fills the soul, and lights the eye,
When the heart has trusted Jesus
All its need to satisfy.

There is always something over,
When we tell of all His love;
Unplumbed depths still lie beneath us,
Unscaled heights rise far above;
Human lips can never utter
All His wondrous tenderness,

We can only praise and wonder,
And His name forever bless.

MARGARET E. BARBER

How can He but, in giving Him, lavish on us all things (Rom. 8:32).

May 28

I will not let thee go, except thou bless me . . . and he blessed him there (Gen. 32:26, 29).

Jacob got the victory and the blessing not by wrestling, *but by clinging*. His limb was out of joint and he could struggle no longer, but he would not let go. Unable to wrestle, he wound his arms around the neck of his mysterious antagonist and hung all his helpless weight upon him, until at last he conquered.

We will not get victory in prayer until we too cease our struggling, giving up our own will, and throw our arms about our Father's neck in clinging faith.

What can puny human strength take by force out of the hand of omnipotence? Can we wrest blessing by force from God? It is never the violence of willfulness that prevails with God. It is the might of clinging faith that gets the blessing and the victories. It is not when we press and urge our own will, but when humility and trust unite in saying, "Not my will, but Thine." We are strong with God only in the degree that self is conquered and is dead. Not by wrestling, but by clinging can we get the blessing. J. R. MILLER

An incident from the prayer life of Charles H. Usher (illustrating *"soul-cling"* as a hindrance to prevailing prayer): "My little boy was very ill. The doctors held out little hope of his recovery. I had used all the knowledge of prayer which I possessed on his behalf, but he got worse and worse. This went on for several weeks.

"One day I stood watching him as he lay in his cot, and I saw that he could not live long unless he had a turn for the better. I said to God, 'O God, I have given much time in prayer for my boy and he gets no better; I must now leave him to Thee, and I will give myself to prayer for others. If it is Thy will to take him, I choose Thy will—I surrender him entirely to Thee.'

"I called in my dear wife and told her what I had done. She shed some tears but handed him over to God. Two days afterward a man of God came to see us. He had been very interested in our boy Frank and had been much in prayer for him.

"He said, 'God has given me faith to believe that he will recover—have you faith?'

"I said, 'I have surrendered him to God, but I will go again to God regarding him.' I did; and in prayer I discovered that I had faith for his recovery. From that time he began to get better. It was the *'soul-cling'* in my prayers which had hindered God answering; and if I had continued to cling and had been unwilling to surrender him, I doubt if my boy would be with me today.

"Child of God! If you want God to answer your prayers, you must be prepared to follow the footsteps of 'our father Abraham,' even to the Mount of Sacrifice." (See Rom. 4:12.)

May 29

I have called you friends (John 15:15).

Years ago there was an old German professor whose beautiful life was a marvel to his students. Some of them resolved to know the secret of it; so one of their number hid in the study where the old professor spent his evenings.

It was late when the teacher came in. He was very tired, but he sat down and spent an hour with his Bible. Then he bowed his head in secret prayer; and finally closing the Book of books, he said, "Well, Lord Jesus, we're on the same old terms."

To *know Him* is life's highest attainment; and at all costs, every Christian should strive to be "on the same old terms with Him."

The reality of Jesus comes as a result of secret prayer and a personal study of the Bible that is devotional and sympathetic. Christ becomes more real to the one who persists in the cultivation of His presence.

> *Speak thou to Him for He heareth,*
> *And spirit with spirit will meet!*
> *Nearer is He than breathing,*
> *Nearer than hands and feet.*
>
> MALTBIE D. BABCOCK

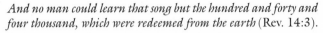

And no man could learn that song but the hundred and forty and four thousand, which were redeemed from the earth (Rev. 14:3).

There are songs which can only be learned in the valley. No art can teach them; no rules of voice can make them perfectly sung. Their music is in the heart. They are songs of memory, of personal experience. They bring out their burden from the shadow of the past; they mount on the wings of yesterday.

Saint John says that even in heaven there will be a song that can only be fully sung by the sons of earth—the strain of redemption. Doubtless it is a song of triumph, a hymn of victory to the Christ who made us free. But the sense of triumph must come from the memory of the chain.

No angel, no archangel can sing it so sweetly as I can. To sing it as I sing it, they must pass through my exile, and this they cannot do. None can learn it but the children of the cross.

And so, my soul, thou art receiving a music lesson from thy Father. Thou art being educated for the choir invisible. There are parts of the symphony that none can take but thee.

There are chords too minor for the angels. There may be heights in the symphony which are beyond the scale—heights which angels alone can reach; but there are depths which belong to *thee*, and can only be touched by thee.

Thy Father is training thee for the part the angels cannot sing; and the school is sorrow. I have heard many say that He sends sorrow to *prove* thee; nay, He sends sorrow to *educate* thee, to train thee for the choir invisible.

In the night He is preparing thy song. In the valley He is tuning thy voice. In the cloud He is deepening thy chords. In the rain He is sweetening thy melody. In the cold He is moulding thy expression. In the transition from hope to fear He is perfecting thy lights.

Despise not thy school of sorrow, O my soul; it will give thee a unique part in the universal song. GEORGE MATHESON

> *Is the midnight closing round you?*
> *Are the shadows dark and long?*
> *Ask Him to come close beside you,*
> *And He'll give you a new, sweet song.*
> *He'll give it and sing it with you;*
> *And when weakness lets it down,*
> *He'll take up the broken cadence,*
> *And blend it with His own.*

And many a rapturous minstrel
Among those sons of light,
Will say of His sweetest music
"I learned it in the night."
And many a rolling anthem,
That fills the Father's home,
Sobbed out its first rehearsal,
In the shade of a darkened room.

May 31

Like a shock of corn fully ripe (Job 5:26).

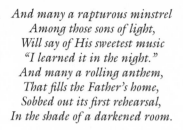

A gentleman, writing about the breaking up of old ships, recently said that it is not the age alone which improves the quality of the fiber in the wood of an old vessel, but the straining and wrenching of the vessel by the sea, the chemical action of the bilge water, and of many kinds of cargoes.

Some planks and veneers made from an oak beam which had been part of a ship eighty years old were exhibited a few years ago at a fashionable furniture store on Broadway, New York, and attracted general notice for the exquisite coloring and beautiful grain.

Equally striking were some beams of mahogany taken from a bark which sailed the seas sixty years ago. The years and the traffic had contracted the pores and deepened the color until it looked as superb in its chromatic intensity as an antique Chinese vase. It was made into a cabinet and has today a place of honor in the drawing-room of a wealthy New York family.

So there is a vast difference between the quality of old people who have lived flabby, self-indulgent, useless lives, and the fiber of those who have sailed all seas and carried all cargoes as the servants of God and the helpers of their fellow men.

Not only the wrenching and straining of life, but also something of the sweetness of the cargoes carried get into the very pores and fiber of character. LOUIS ALBERT BANKS

When the sun goes below the horizon he is not set; the heavens glow for a full hour after his departure. And when a great and good man sets, the sky of this world is luminous long after he is out of sight. Such a man cannot die out of this world. When he goes he leaves behind him much of himself. Being dead, he speaks. BEECHER

When Victor Hugo was past eighty years of age he gave expression to his religious faith in these sublime sentences: "I feel in myself the future life. I am like a forest which has been more than once cut down. The new shoots are livelier than ever. I am rising toward the sky. The sunshine is on my head. The earth gives me its generous sap, but Heaven lights me with its unknown worlds.

"You say the soul is nothing but the resultant of the bodily powers. Why, then, is my soul more luminous when my bodily powers begin to fail? Winter is on my head, but eternal spring is in my heart. I breathe at this hour the fragrance of the lilacs, the violets, and the roses as at twenty years. The nearer I approach the end the plainer I hear around me the immortal symphonies of the worlds which invite me. It is marvelous, yet simple."

June 1

This is the rest wherewith ye may cause the weary to rest; and this is the refreshing (Isa. 28:12).

Why dost thou worry thyself? What use can thy fretting serve? Thou art on board a vessel which thou couldst not steer even if the great Captain put thee at the helm, of which thou couldst not so much as reef a sail, yet thou worriest as if thou wert captain and helmsman. Oh, be quiet; God is Master!

Dost thou think that all this din and hurly-burly that is abroad betokens that God has left His throne?

No, man, His coursers rush furiously on, and His chariot is the storm; but there is a bit between their jaws, and He holds the reins, and guides them as He wills! Jehovah is Master yet; believe it; peace be unto thee! be not afraid. C. H. SPURGEON

> *Tonight, my soul, be still and sleep;*
> *The storms are raging on God's deep—*
> *God's deep, not thine; be still and sleep.*
>
> *Tonight, my soul, be still and sleep;*
> *God's hands shall still the tempter's sweep—*
> *God's hands, not thine; be still and sleep.*
>
> *Tonight, my soul, be still and sleep;*
> *God's love is strong while night hours creep—*
> *God's love, not thine; be still and sleep.*
>
> *Tonight, my soul, be still and sleep;*
> *God's heaven will comfort those who weep—*
> *God's heaven, not thine; be still and sleep.*

I entreat you, give no place to despondency. This is a dangerous temptation—a refined, not a gross temptation of the adversary. Melancholy contracts and withers the heart, and renders it unfit to receive the impressions of grace. It magnifies and gives a false coloring to objects, and thus renders your burdens too heavy to bear. God's designs regarding you, and His methods of bringing about these designs, are infinitely wise. MADAME GUYON ☞

June 2

For Abraham, when hope was gone, hoped on in faith. His faith never quailed (Rom. 4:18, 19).

We shall never forget a remark that George Mueller once made to a gentleman who had asked him the best way to have strong faith.

"The *only* way," replied the patriarch of faith, "to learn strong faith is to endure great trials. I have learned my faith by standing firm amid severe testings." This is very true. *The time to trust is when all else fails.*

Dear one, you scarcely realize the value of your present opportunity; if you are passing through great afflictions you are in the very soul of the strongest faith, and if you will only let go, He will teach you in these hours the mightiest hold upon His throne which you can ever know.

"Be not afraid, only believe." And if you are afraid, just look up and say, "What time I am afraid I will trust in thee," and you will yet thank God for the school of sorrow which was to you the school of faith. A. B. SIMPSON ☞

Great faith must have great trials.

God's greatest gifts come through travail. Whether we look into the spiritual or temporal sphere, can we discover anything, any great reform, any beneficent discovery, any soul-awakening revival, which did not come through the toils and tears, the vigils and blood-shedding of men and women whose sufferings were the pangs of its birth? If the temple of God is raised, David must bear sore afflictions; if the gospel of the grace of God is to be disentangled from Jewish tradition, Paul's life must be one long agony.

Take heart, O weary, burdened one, bowed down
Beneath thy cross;
Remember that thy greatest gain may come
Through greatest loss.
Thy life is nobler for a sacrifice,

And more divine.
Acres of bloom are crushed to make a drop
Of perfume fine.

Because of storms that lash the ocean waves,
The waters there
Keep purer than if the heavens o'erhead
Were always fair.
The brightest banner of the skies floats not
At noonday warm;
The rainbow traileth after thunder-clouds,
And after storm.

June 3

Let us pass over unto the other side (Mark 4:35).

Even when we go forth at Christ's command, we need not expect to escape storms; for these disciples were going forth at Christ's command, yet they encountered the fiercest storm and were in great danger of being overwhelmed, so that they cried out in their distress for Christ's assistance.

Though Christ may delay His coming in our time of distress, it is only that our faith may be tried and strengthened, and that our prayers may be more intense, and that our desires for deliverance may be increased, so that when the deliverance does come we will appreciate it more fully.

Christ gave them a gentle rebuke, saying, "Where is your faith?" Why did you not shout victory in the very face of the storm, and say to the raging winds and rolling waves, "You can do no harm, for Christ, the mighty Savior is on board"?

It is much easier to trust when the sun is shining than when the storm is raging.

We never know how much real faith we have until it is put to the test in some fierce storm; and that is the reason why the Savior is on board.

If you are ever to be strong in the Lord and the power of His might, your strength will be born in some storm. SELECTED

With Christ in the vessel,
I smile at the storm.

Christ said, "Let us go to the other side"—not to the middle of the lake to be drowned. DAN CRAWFORD

June 4

The Lord caused the sea to go back ... all that night (Exod. 14:21).

In this verse there is a comforting message showing how God works in the dark. The real work of God for the children of Israel was not when they awakened and found that they could get over the Red Sea; but it was *"all that night."*

So there may be a great working in your life when it all seems dark and you cannot see or trace, but yet God is working. Just as truly did He work "all that night," as all the next day. The next day simply manifested what God had done during the night. Is there anyone reading these lines who may have gotten to a place where it seems dark? You believe to see, but you are not seeing. In your life-progress there is not constant victory; the daily, undisturbed communion is not there, and all seems dark.

"The Lord caused the sea to go back ... all that night." Do not forget that it was *"all that night."* God works all the night, until the light comes. You may not see it, but all that *"night"* in your life, as you believe God, He works. C. H. P.

> *"All that night" the Lord was working,*
> *Working in the tempest blast,*
> *Working with the swelling current,*
> *Flooding, flowing, free and fast.*
>
> *"All that night" God's children waited—*
> *Hearts, perhaps in agony—*
> *With the enemy behind them,*
> *And, in front, the cruel sea.*
>
> *"All that night" seemed blacker darkness*
> *Than they ever saw before,*
> *Though the light of God's own presence*
> *Near them was, and sheltered o'er.*
>
> *"All that night" that weary vigil*
> *Passed; the day at last did break,*
> *And they saw that God was working*
> *"All that night" a path to make.*
>
> *"All that night," O child of sorrow,*
> *Canst thou not thy heartbreak stay?*

Know thy God in darkest midnight
Works, as well as in the day.

L. S. P.

June 5

Make thy petition deep (Isa. 7:11, margin).

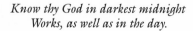

Make thy petition deep, O heart of mine,
Thy God can do much more
Than thou canst ask;
Launch out on the Divine,
Draw from His love-filled store.
Trust Him with everything;
Begin today,
And find the joy that comes
When Jesus has His way!

SELECTED

We must keep on *praying* and *waiting* upon the Lord, until the sound of a mighty rain is heard. There is no reason why we should not ask for large things; and without doubt we shall get large things if we ask in faith, and have the courage to wait with patient perseverance upon Him, meantime doing those things which lie within our power to do.

We cannot create the wind or set it in motion, but we can set our sails to catch it when it comes; we cannot make the electricity, but we can stretch the wire along upon which it is to run and do its work; we cannot, in a word, control the Spirit, but we can so place ourselves before the Lord, and so do the things He has bidden us do, that we will come under the influence and power of His mighty breath. SELECTED

"Cannot the same wonders be done now as of old? Where is the God of Elijah? He is *waiting* for Elijah to call on Him."

The greatest saints who ever lived, whether under the old or new dispensation, are on a level which is quite within our reach. The same forces of the spiritual world which were at their command, and the exertion of which made them such spiritual heroes, are open to us also. If we had the same faith, the same hope, the same love which they exhibited, we would achieve marvels as great as those which they achieved. A word of prayer in our mouths would be as potent to call down the gracious dews and melting fires of God's Spirit, as it was in Elijah's mouth to call down literal rain and fire, if we could only speak the word with that full assurance of faith wherewith he said it. DR. GOULBURN, DEAN OF NORWICH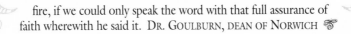

June 6

Watch unto prayer (1 Peter 4:7).

Go not, my friend, into the dangerous world without prayer. You kneel down at night to pray, drowsiness weighs down your eyelids; a hard day's work is a kind of excuse, and you shorten your prayer, and resign yourself softly to repose. The morning breaks; and it may be you rise late, and so your early devotions are not done, or are done with irregular haste.

No watching unto prayer! Wakefulness once more omitted; and now is that reparable? We solemnly believe not.

There has been that done which cannot be undone. You have given up your prayer, and you will suffer for it.

Temptation is before you, and you are not ready to meet it. There is a guilty feeling on the soul, and you linger at a distance from God. It is no marvel if that day in which you suffer drowsiness to interfere with prayer be a day in which you shrink from duty.

Moments of prayer intruded on by sloth cannot be made up. We may get experience, but we cannot get back the rich freshness and strength which were wrapped up in those moments. FREDERICK W. ROBERTSON

If Jesus, the strong Son of God, felt it necessary to rise before the breaking of the day to pour out His heart to God in prayer, how much more ought you to pray unto Him who is the Giver of every good and perfect gift, and who has promised all things necessary for our good.

What Jesus gathered into His life from His prayers we can never know; but this we do know, that the prayerless life is a powerless life. A prayerless life may be a noisy life, and fuss around a great deal; but such a life is far removed from Him who, by day and night, prayed to God. SELECTED

June 7

Where is God my maker, who giveth songs in the night? (Job 35:10).

Do you have sleepless nights, tossing on the hot pillow, and watching for the first glint of dawn? Ask the divine Spirit to enable you to fix your thoughts on God your Maker, and believe that He can fill those lonely, dreary hours with song.

Is yours the night of bereavement? Is it not often at such a time that God draws near, and assures the mourner that the Lord has need of the departed loved one, and called "the eager, earnest spirit to stand in the bright throng of the invisible, liberated, radiant, active, intent on some high mission"; and as the thought enters, is there not the beginning of a song?

Is yours the night of discouragement and fancied or actual failure? No one understands you, your friends reproach; but your Maker draws nigh, and gives you a song—a song of hope, the song which is harmonious with the strong, deep music of His providence. Be ready to sing the songs that your Maker gives. SELECTED

> *What then? Shall we sit idly down and say*
> *The night hath come; it is no longer day?*
> *Yet as the evening twilight fades away,*
> *The sky is filled with stars, invisible to day.*

The strength of the vessel can be demonstrated only by the hurricane, and the power of the gospel can be fully shown only when the Christian is subjected to some fiery trial. If God would make manifest the fact that "He giveth songs in the night," He must first make it night. WILLIAM TAYLOR

June 8

For every child of God overcomes the world: and the victorious principle which has overcome the world is our faith (1 John 5:4 WEYMOUTH).

At every turn in the road one can find something that will rob him of his victory and peace of mind, if he permits it. Satan is a long way from having retired from the business of deluding and ruining God's children if he can. At every milestone it is well to look carefully to the thermometer of one's experience, to see whether the temperature is well up.

Sometimes a person can, if he will, actually snatch victory from the very jaws of defeat, if he will resolutely put his faith up at just the right moment.

Faith can change any situation. No matter how dark it is, no matter what the trouble may be, a quick lifting of the heart to God in a moment of real, actual faith in Him, will alter the situation in a moment.

God is still on His throne, and He can turn defeat into victory in a second of time, if we really trust Him.

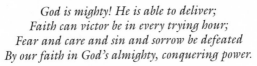

God is mighty! He is able to deliver;
Faith can victor be in every trying hour;
Fear and care and sin and sorrow be defeated
By our faith in God's almighty, conquering power.

Have faith in God, the sun will shine,
Though dark the clouds may be today;
His heart has planned your path and mine,
Have faith in God, have faith alway.

When one has faith, one does not retire; one stops the enemy where he finds him. MARSHAL FOCH

June 9

Feed on his faithfulness (Ps. 37:3 RV).

I once met a poor colored woman who earned a precarious living by hard daily labor, but who was a joyous triumphant Christian. "Ah, Nancy," said a gloomy Christian lady to her one day, "it is well enough to be happy now, but I should think the thoughts of your future would sober you.

"Only suppose, for instance, you should have a spell of sickness, and be unable to work; or suppose your present employers should move away, and no one else should give you anything to do; or suppose—"

"Stop!" cried Nancy. "I never supposes. De Lord is my Shepherd, and I knows I shall not want. And, Honey," she added, to her gloomy friend, "it's all dem *supposes* as is makin' you so mis'able. You'd better give dem all up, and just trust de Lord."

There is one text that will take all the "supposes" out of a believer's life if it be received and acted on in childlike faith; it is Hebrews 13:5–6: "Be content with such things as ye have: for *he* hath said, I will never leave thee, nor forsake thee. So that we may boldly say, The Lord is my helper, and I will not fear what man shall do unto me." H. W. S.

There's a stream of trouble across my path;
It is black and deep and wide.
Bitter the hour the future hath
When I cross its swelling tide.
But I smile and sing and say:
"I will hope and trust alway;
I'll bear the sorrow that comes tomorrow,
But I'll borrow none today."

Tomorrow's bridge is a dangerous thing;
I dare not cross it now.
I can see its timbers sway and swing,
And its arches reel and bow.
O heart, you must hope alway;
You must sing and trust and say:
"I'll bear the sorrow that comes tomorrow,
But I'll borrow none today."

The eagle that soars in the upper air does not worry itself as to how it is to cross rivers. SELECTED

June 10

And we know that all things work together for good to them that love God (Rom. 8:28).

How wide is this assertion of the apostle Paul! He does not say, "We know that *some* things," or *"most* things," or "*joyous* things," but "ALL things." From the minutest to the most momentous; from the humblest event in daily providence to the great crisis hours in grace.

And all things *"work"*—they *are* working; not all things *have* worked, or *shall* work; but it is a present operation.

At this very moment, when some voice may be saying, "Thy judgments are a great deep," the angels above, who are watching the development of the great plan, are with folded wings exclaiming, "The Lord is righteous in *all* his ways, and holy in *all* his works" (Ps. 145:17).

And then all things *"work together."* It is a beautiful blending. Many different colors, in themselves raw and unsightly, are required in order to weave the harmonious pattern.

Many separate tones and notes of music, even discords and dissonances, are required to make up the harmonious anthem.

Many separate wheels and joints are required to make the piece of machinery. Take a thread separately, or a note separately, or a wheel or a tooth of a wheel separately, and there may be neither use nor beauty discernible.

But *complete* the web, *combine* the notes, *put together* the separate parts of steel and iron, and you see how perfect and symmetrical is the result. Here is the lesson for faith: "What I do thou knowest not now, but thou shalt know hereafter." MACDUFF

In one thousand trials it is not five hundred of them that work for the believer's good, but nine hundred and ninety-nine of them, *and one beside.* GEORGE MUELLER

God meant it unto good (Gen. 50:20).

"God meant it unto good"—O blest assurance,
Falling like sunshine all across life's way,
Touching with Heaven's gold earth's darkest storm clouds,
Bringing fresh peace and comfort day by day.

'Twas not by chance the hands of faithless brethren
Sold Joseph captive to a foreign land;
Nor was it chance which, after years of suffering,
Brought him before the monarch's throne to stand.

One Eye all-seeing saw the need of thousands,
And planned to meet it through that one lone soul;
And through the weary days of prison bondage
Was working towards the great and glorious goal.

As yet the end was hidden from the captive,
The iron entered even to his soul;
His eye could scan the present path of sorrow,
Not yet his gaze might rest upon the whole.

Faith failed not through those long, dark days of waiting,
His trust in God was recompensed at last,
The moment came when God led forth his servant
To succour many, all his sufferings past.

"It was not you but God, that sent me hither,"
Witnessed triumphant faith in after days;
"God meant it unto good," no "second causes"
Mingled their discord with his song of praise.

"God means it unto good" for thee, beloved,
The God of Joseph is the same today;
His love permits afflictions strange and bitter,
His hand is guiding through the unknown way.

Thy Lord, who sees the end from the beginning,
Hath purposes for thee of love untold.
Then place thy hand in His and follow fearless,
Till thou the riches of His grace behold.

There, when thou standest in the Home of Glory,
And all life's path lies open to thy gaze,
Thine eyes shall SEE the hand which now thou trustest,
And magnify His love through endless days.

FREDA HANBURY ALLEN 🐝

June 11

The servant of the Lord must ... be gentle (2 Tim. 2:24).

⟨∽⟩

When God conquers us and takes all the flint out of our nature, and we get deep visions into the Spirit of Jesus, we then see as never before the great rarity of *gentleness of spirit* in this dark and unheavenly world.

The *graces* of the Spirit do not settle themselves down upon us by chance, and if we do not discern certain states of grace, and choose them, and in our thoughts nourish them, they never become fastened in our nature or behavior.

Every advance step in grace must be preceded by first apprehending it, and then a prayerful resolve to have it.

So few are willing to undergo the suffering out of which thorough gentleness comes. We must die before we are turned into gentleness, and crucifixion involves suffering; it is a real breaking and crushing of self, which wrings the heart and conquers the mind.

There is a good deal of mere mental and logical sanctification nowadays, which is only a religious fiction. It consists of mentally putting one's self on the altar, then mentally saying the altar sanctifies the gift, and then logically concluding therefore one is sanctified; and such a one goes forth with a gay, flippant, theological prattle about the deep things of God.

But the natural heartstrings have not been snapped, and the Adamic flint has not been ground to powder, and the bosom has not throbbed with the lonely, surging sighs of Gethsemane; and not having the real death marks of Calvary, there cannot be that soft, sweet, gentle, floating, victorious, overflowing, triumphant life that flows like a spring morning from an empty tomb. G. D. W. 🐝

And great grace was upon them all (Acts 4:33).

June 12

In everything ye are enriched by him (1 Cor. 1:5).

Have you ever seen men and women whom some disaster drove to a great act of prayer, and by and by the disaster was forgotten, but the sweetness of religion remained and warmed their souls?

So have I seen a storm in later spring; and all was black, save where the lightning tore the cloud with thundering rent.

The winds blew and the rains fell, as though heaven had opened its windows. What a devastation there was! Not a spider's web that was out of doors escaped the storm, which tore up even the strong-branched oak.

But ere long the lightning had gone by, the thunder was spent and silent, the rain was over, the western wind came up with its sweet breath, the clouds were chased away, and the retreating storm threw a scarf of rainbows over her fair shoulders and resplendent neck, and looked back and smiled, and so withdrew and passed out of sight.

But for weeks long the fields held up their hands full of ambrosial flowers, and all the summer through the grass was greener, the brooks were fuller, and the trees cast a more umbrageous shade, *because the storm passed by*—though all the rest of the earth had long ago forgotten the storm, its rainbows and its rain. THEODORE PARKER

> *God may not give us an easy journey to the promised land,*
> *but He will give us a safe one.* BONAR

It was a storm that occasioned the discovery of the gold mines of India. Hath not a storm driven some to the discovery of the richer mines of the love of God in Christ?

> *Is it raining, little flower?*
> *Be glad of rain;*
> *Too much sun would wither thee;*
> *'Twill shine again.*
> *The clouds are very black, 'tis true;*
> *But just behind them shines the blue.*
>
> *Art thou weary, tender heart?*
> *Be glad of pain:*
> *In sorrow sweetest virtues grow,*
> *As flowers in rain.*
> *God watches, and thou wilt have sun,*
> *When clouds their perfect work have done.*
>
> LUCY LARCOM

June 13

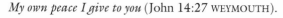

My own peace I give to you (John 14:27 WEYMOUTH).

Two painters each painted a picture to illustrate his conception of rest. The first chose for his scene a still, lone lake among the far-off mountains.

The second threw on his canvas a thundering waterfall, with a fragile birch tree bending over the foam; and at the fork of the branch, almost wet with the cataract's spray, sat a robin on its nest.

The first was only *stagnation;* the last was *rest.*

Christ's life outwardly was one of the most troubled lives that ever lived: tempest and tumult, tumult and tempest, the waves breaking over it all the time until the worn body was laid in the grave. But the inner life was a sea of glass. The great calm was always there.

At any moment you might have gone to Him and found rest. And even when the human bloodhounds were dogging Him in the streets of Jerusalem, He turned to His disciples and offered them, as a last legacy, "My peace."

Rest is not a hallowed feeling that comes over us in church; it is the repose of a heart set deep in God. DRUMMOND

> *My peace I give in times of deepest grief,*
> *Imparting calm and trust and My relief.*
>
> *My peace I give when prayer seems lost, unheard;*
> *Know that My promises are ever in My Word.*
>
> *My peace I give when thou art left alone—*
> *The nightingale at night has sweetest tone.*
>
> *My peace I give in time of utter loss,*
> *The way of glory leads right to the cross.*
>
> *My peace I give when enemies will blame,*
> *Thy fellowship is sweet through cruel shame.*
>
> *My peace I give in agony and sweat,*
> *For mine own brow with bloody drops was wet.*
>
> *My peace I give when nearest friend betrays—*
> *Peace that is merged in love, and for them prays.*
>
> *My peace I give when there's but death for thee—*
> *The gateway is the cross to get to Me.*

L. S. P.

June 14

I have prayed that your own faith may not fail (Luke 22:32).

Christian, take good care of thy faith, for recollect that *faith is the only means whereby thou canst obtain blessings.* Prayer cannot draw down answers from God's throne except it be the earnest prayer of the man who believes.

Faith is the telegraphic wire which links earth to heaven, on which God's messages of love fly so fast that before we call He answers, and while we are yet speaking He hears us. But if that telegraphic wire of faith be snapped, how can we obtain the promise?

Am I in trouble? I can obtain help for trouble by faith. Am I beaten about by the enemy? My soul on her dear Refuge leans by faith.

But take faith away, then in vain I call to God. There is no other road betwixt my soul and heaven. Blockade the road, and how can I communicate with the great King?

Faith links me with divinity. Faith clothes me with the power of Jehovah. Faith insures every attribute of God in my defense. It helps me to defy the hosts of hell. It makes me march triumphant over the necks of my enemies. But without faith how can I receive anything from the Lord?

Oh, then, Christian, watch well thy faith. "If thou canst believe, all things are possible to him that believeth." C. H. Spurgeon

We boast of being so practical a people that we want to have a surer thing than faith. But did not Paul say that the promise was by FAITH that it might be SURE? (Rom. 4:16). Dan Crawford

Faith honors God; God honors faith.

June 15

For God hath caused me to be fruitful in the land of my affliction (Gen. 41:52).

The summer showers are falling. The poet stands by the window watching them. They are beating and buffeting the earth with their fierce downpour. But the poet sees in his imaginings more than the showers which are falling before his eyes. He sees myriads of lovely flowers which shall be soon breaking forth from the watered earth, filling it with matchless beauty and fragrance. And so he sings:

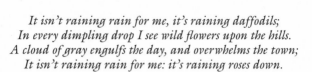

It isn't raining rain for me, it's raining daffodils;
In every dimpling drop I see wild flowers upon the hills.
A cloud of gray engulfs the day, and overwhelms the town;
It isn't raining rain for me: it's raining roses down.

Perchance some one of God's chastened children is even now saying, "O God, it is raining hard for me tonight.

"Testings are raining upon me which seem beyond my power to endure. Disappointments are raining fast, to the utter defeat of all my chosen plans. Bereavements are raining into my life which are making my shrinking heart quiver in its intensity of suffering. The rain of affliction is surely beating down upon my soul these days."

Withal, friend, you are mistaken. It isn't raining rain for you. *It's raining blessing.* For, if you will but believe your Father's Word, under that beating rain are springing up spiritual flowers of such fragrance and beauty as never before grew in that stormless, unchastened life of yours.

You indeed see the rain. But do you see also the flowers? You are pained by the testings. But God sees the sweet flower of faith which is upspringing in your life under those very trials.

You shrink from the suffering. But God sees the tender compassion for other sufferers which is finding birth in your soul.

Your heart winces under the sore bereavement. But God sees the deepening and enriching which that sorrow has brought to you.

It isn't raining afflictions for you. It is raining tenderness, love, compassion, patience, and a thousand other flowers and fruits of the blessed Spirit, which are bringing into your life such a spiritual enrichment as all the fullness of worldly prosperity and ease was never able to beget in your innermost soul. J. M. McC. 🖎

Songs Across the Storm

A harp stood in the moveless air,
Where showers of sunshine washed a thousand fragrant blooms;
A traveler bowed with loads of care
Essayed from morning till the dusk of evening glooms
To thrum sweet sounds from the songless strings;
The pilgrim strives in vain with each unanswering chord,
Until the tempest's thunder sings,
And, moving on the storm, the fingers of the Lord
A wondrous melody awakes;
And though the battling winds their soldier deeds perform,
Their trumpet-sound brave music makes
While God's assuring voice sings love across the storm.

June 16

My expectation is from him (Ps. 62:5).

Our too general neglect of looking for answers to what we ask, shows how little we are in earnest in our petitions. A husbandman is not content without the harvest; a marksman will observe whether the ball hits the target; a physician watches the effect of the medicine which he gives; and shall the Christian be careless about the effect of his labor?

Every prayer of the Christian, made in faith, according to the will of God, for which God has promised, offered up in the name of Jesus Christ, and under the influence of the Spirit, whether for temporal or for spiritual blessings, is, or will be fully answered.

God always answers the general design and intention of His people's prayers, in doing that which, all things considered, is most for His own glory and their spiritual and eternal welfare. As we never find that Jesus Christ rejected a single supplicant who came to Him for mercy, so we believe that no prayer made in His name will be in vain.

The answer to prayer may be approaching, though we discern not its coming. The seed that lies under ground in winter is taking root in order to see a spring and harvest, though it appears not above ground, but seems dead and lost. BICKERSTETH

Delayed answers to prayer are not only trials of faith, but they give us opportunities of honoring God by our steadfast confidence in Him under apparent repulses. C. H. SPURGEON

June 17

And there was a voice from the firmament that was over their heads, when they stood, and had let down their wings (Ezek. 1:25).

What is the letting down of the wings? People so often say, "How do you get the voice of the Lord?" Here is the secret. They heard the voice when they stood and let down their wings.

We have seen a bird with fluttering wings; though standing still, its wings are fluttering. But here we are told they heard the voice when they stood and had let down their wings.

Do we not sometimes kneel or sit before the Lord and yet feel conscious of a fluttering of our spirits? Not a real stillness in His presence.

A dear one told me several days ago of a certain thing she prayed about. "But," said she, "I did not wait until the answer came."

She did not get still enough to hear Him speak, but went away and followed her own thought in the matter. And the result proved disastrous and she had to retrace her steps.

Oh, how much energy is wasted! How much time is lost by not letting down the wings of our spirit and getting very quiet before Him! Oh, the calm, the rest, the peace which come as we wait in His presence until we hear from Him!

Then, ah then, we can go like lightning, and turn not as we go but go straight forward whithersoever the Spirit goes (See Ezek.1:14, 20).

Be still! Just now be still!
Something thy soul hath never heard,
Something unknown to any song of bird,
Something unknown to any wind, or wave, or star,
A message from the Fatherland afar,
That with sweet joy the homesick soul shall thrill,
Cometh to thee if thou canst be still.

Be still! Just now be still!
There comes a presence very mild and sweet;
White are the sandals of His noiseless feet.
It is the Comforter whom Jesus sent
To teach thee what the words He uttered meant.
The willing, waiting spirit, He doth fill.
If thou would'st hear His message,
Dear soul, be still!

June 18

Wherefore lift up the hands which hang down, and the feeble knees; and make straight paths for your feet, lest that which is lame be turned out of the way; but let it rather be healed (Heb. 12:12–13).

This is God's word of encouragement to us to lift up the hands of faith, and confirm the knees of prayer. Often our faith grows tired, languid, and relaxed, and our prayers lose their force and effectiveness.

The figure used here is a very striking one. The idea seems to be that we become discouraged and so timid that a little obstacle depresses and frightens us, and we are tempted to walk around it, and not face it: to take the easier way.

Perhaps it is some physical trouble that God is ready to heal, but the exertion is hard, or it is easier to secure some human help, or walk around in some other way.

There are many ways of walking around emergencies instead of going straight through them. How often we come up against something that appalls us, and we want to evade the issue with the excuse: "I am not quite ready for that now." Some sacrifice is to be made, some obedience demanded, some Jericho to be taken, some soul that we have not the courage to claim and carry through, some prayer that is hanging fire, or perhaps some physical trouble that is half-healed and we are walking around it.

God says, "Lift up the hands that hang down." March straight through the flood, and lo, the waters will divide, the Red Sea will open, the Jordan will part, and the Lord will lead you through to victory.

Don't let your feet "be turned out of the way," but let your body "be healed," your faith strengthened. Go right ahead and leave no Jericho behind you unconquered and no place where Satan can say that he was too much for you. This is a profitable lesson and an intensely practical one. How often have we been in that place. Perhaps you are there today. A. B. SIMPSON

Pay as little attention to discouragement as possible. Plough ahead as a steamer does, rough or smooth—rain or shine. To carry your cargo and make your port is the point. MALTBIE D. BABCOCK

June 19

Bread corn is bruised (Isa. 28:28).

Many of us cannot be used to become food for the world's hunger until we are broken in Christ's hands. "Bread corn is bruised." Christ's blessing ofttimes means sorrow, but even sorrow is not too great a price to pay for the privilege of touching other lives with benediction. The sweetest things in this world today have come to us through tears and pain. J. R. MILLER

187

God has made me bread for His elect, and if it be needful that the bread must be ground in the teeth of the lion to feed His children, blessed be the name of the Lord. IGNATIUS

"We must burn out before we can give out. We cease to bless when we cease to bleed."

"Poverty, hardship and misfortune have pressed many a life to moral heroism and spiritual greatness. Difficulty challenges energy and perseverance. It calls into activity the strongest qualities of the soul. It was the weights on father's old clock that kept it going. Many a headwind has been utilized to make port. God has appointed opposition as an incentive to faith and holy activity.

"The most illustrious characters of the Bible were bruised and threshed and ground into bread for the hungry. Abraham's diploma styles him as 'the father of the faithful.' That was because he stood at the head of his class in affliction and obedience.

"Jacob suffered severe threshings and grindings. Joseph was bruised and beaten and had to go through Potiphar's kitchen and Egypt's prison to get to his throne.

"David, hunted like a partridge on the mountain, bruised, weary and footsore, was ground into bread for a kingdom. Paul never could have been bread for Caesar's household if he had not endured the bruising, whippings and stonings. He was ground into fine flour for the royal family."

"Like combat, like victory. If for you He has appointed special trials, be assured that in His heart He has kept for you a special place. A soul sorely bruised is a soul elect."

June 20

Thine ears shall hear a word behind thee, saying, This is the way, walk ye in it, when ye turn to the right hand, and when ye turn to the left (Isa. 30:21).

When we are in doubt or difficulty, when many voices urge this course or the other, when prudence utters one advice and faith another, then let us be still, hushing each intruder, calming ourselves in the sacred hush of God's presence; let us study His Word in the attitude of devout attention; let us lift up our nature into the pure light of His face, eager only to know what God the Lord shall determine—and ere long a very distinct impression will be made, the unmistakable forthtelling of His secret counsel.

It is not wise in the earlier stages of Christian life to depend on this alone, but to wait for the corroboration of circumstances. But those who have had many dealings with God know well the value of secret fellowship with Him, to ascertain His will.

Are you in difficulty about your way? Go to God with your question; get direction from the light of His smile or the cloud of His refusal.

If you will only get alone, where the lights and shadows of earth cannot interfere, where human opinions fail to reach—and if you will dare to wait there silent and expectant, though all around you insist on immediate decision or action—the will of God will be made clear; and you will have a new conception of God, a deeper insight into His nature and heart of love, which shall be for yourself alone—a rapturous experience, to abide your precious perquisite forever, the rich guerdon of those long waiting hours. DAVID ॐ

> "STAND STILL," my soul, for so thy Lord commands:
> E'en when thy way seems blocked, leave it in His wise hands;
> His arm is mighty to divide the wave.
> "Stand still," my soul, "stand still" and thou shalt see
> How God can work the "impossible" for thee,
> For with a great deliverance He doth save.
>
> Be not impatient, but in stillness stand,
> Even when compassed 'round on every hand,
> In ways thy spirit does not comprehend.
> God cannot clear thy way till thou art still,
> That He may work in thee His blessed will,
> And all thy heart and will to Him do bend.
>
> "BE STILL," my soul, for just as thou art still,
> Can God reveal Himself to thee; until
> Through thee His love and light and life can freely flow;
> In stillness God can work through thee and reach
> The souls around thee. He then through thee can teach
> His lessons, and His power in weakness show.
>
> "BE STILL"—a deeper step in faith and rest.
> "Be still and know" thy Father knoweth best
> The way to lead His child to that fair land,
> A "summer" land, where quiet waters flow;
> Where longing souls are satisfied, and "know
> Their God," and praise for all that He has planned.
>   SELECTED ॐ

189

June 21

It was noised that he was in the house (Mark 2:1).

The polyps which construct the coral reefs, work away under water, never dreaming that they are building the foundation of a new island on which, by-and-by, plants and animals will live and children of God be born and fitted for eternal glory as joint-heirs of Christ.

If your place in God's ranks is a hidden and secluded one, beloved, do not murmur, do not complain, do not seek to get out of God's will, if He has placed you there; for without the polyps, the coral reefs would never be built, and God needs some who are willing to be spiritual polyps, and work away out of sight of men, but sustained by the Holy Ghost and in full view of heaven.

The day will come when Jesus will give the rewards, and He makes no mistakes, although some people may wonder how you came to merit such a reward, as they had never heard of you before. SELECTED

Just where you stand in the conflict,
There is your place.
Just where you think you are useless,
Hide not your face.
God placed you there for a purpose,
Whate'er it be;
Think He has chosen you for it;
Work loyally.
Gird on your armor! Be faithful
At toil or rest!
Whate'er it be, never doubting
God's way is best.
Out in the fight or on picket,
Stand firm and true;
This is the work which your Master
Gives you to do.

SELECTED

Safely we may leave the crowded meeting, the inspiring mountaintop, the helpful fellowship of "just men," and betake ourselves to our dim homely Emmaus, or to our dread public Colossae, or even to our far Macedonia in the mission field, quietly confident that just where He has placed us, in the usual round of life, He ordains that the borderland may be possessed, the victory won. NORTHCOTE DECK

June 22

Love covereth (Prov. 10:12).
Be eager in pursuit of this love (1 Cor. 13:7–13 WEYMOUTH).

Rehearse your troubles to God only. Not long ago I read in a paper a bit of personal experience from a precious child of God, and it made such an impression upon me that I record it here. She wrote:

"I found myself one midnight wholly sleepless as the surges of a cruel injustice swept over me, and the love which covers seemed to have crept out of my heart. Then I cried to God in an agony for the power to obey His injunction, 'Love covereth.'

"Immediately the Spirit began to work in me the power that brought about the forgetfulness.

"Mentally I dug a grave. Deliberately I threw up the earth until the excavation was deep.

"Sorrowfully I lowered into it the thing which wounded me. Quickly I shoveled in the clods.

"Over the mound I carefully laid the green sods. Then I covered it with white roses and forget-me-nots, and quickly walked away.

"Sweet sleep came. The wound which had been so nearly deadly was healed without a scar, and I know not today what caused my grief."

> There was a scar on yonder mountain-side,
> Gashed out where once the cruel storm had trod;
> A barren, desolate chasm, reaching wide
> Across the soft green sod.
>
> But years crept by beneath the purple pines,
> And veiled the scar with grass and moss once more,
> And left it fairer now with flowers and vines
> Than it had been before.
>
> There was a wound once in a gentle heart,
> Whence all life's sweetness seemed to ebb and die;
> And love's confiding changed to bitter smart,
> While slow, sad years went by.
>
> Yet as they passed, unseen an angel stole
> And laid a balm of healing on the pain,
> Till love grew purer in the heart made whole,
> And peace came back again.

June 23

When Peter was come down out of the ship, he walked on the water, to go to Jesus. But when he saw the wind boisterous, he was afraid; and beginning to sink, he cried, saying, Lord, save me (Matt. 14:29, 30).

Peter had a little faith in the midst of his doubts, says Bunyan; and so with crying and coming he was brought to Christ.

But here you see that sight was a hindrance; the waves were none of his business when once he had set out; all Peter had any concern with was the pathway of light that came gleaming across the darkness from where Christ stood. If it was tenfold Egypt beyond that, Peter had no call to look and see.

When the Lord shall call to you over the waters, "Come," step gladly forth. Look not for a moment away from Him.

Not by measuring the waves can you prevail; not by gauging the wind will you grow strong; to scan the danger may be to fall before it; to pause at the difficulties is to have them break above your head. Lift up your eyes unto the hills, and go forward—there is no other way.

> *Dost thou fear to launch away?*
> *Faith lets go to swim!*
> *Never will He let thee go;*
> *'Tis by trusting thou shalt know*
> *Fellowship with Him.*

June 24

Concerning the work of my hands command ye me (Isa. 45:11).

Our Lord spoke in this tone when He said, "Father, I will." Joshua used it when, in the supreme moment of triumph, he lifted up his spear toward the setting sun, and cried, "Sun, stand thou still!"

Elijah used it when he shut the heavens for three years and six months, and again opened them.

Luther used it when, kneeling by the dying Melanchthon, he forbade death to take his prey.

It is a marvelous relationship into which God bids us enter. We are familiar with words like those which follow in this paragraph: "I, even my hands, have stretched out the heavens, and all their host have I commanded." But that God should invite us to command Him, this is a change in relationship which is altogether startling!

What a difference there is between this attitude and the hesitating, halting, unbelieving prayers to which we are accustomed, and which by their perpetual repetition lose edge and point!

How often during His earthly life did Jesus put men into a position to command Him! When entering Jericho, He stood still, and said to the blind beggars:

"What will ye that I shall do unto you?" It was as though He said, "I am yours to command."

Can we ever forget how He yielded to the Syrophoenician woman the key to His resources and told her to help herself even as she would?

What mortal mind can realize the full significance of the position to which our God lovingly raises His little children? He seems to say, "All my resources are at your command." *"Whatsoever ye shall ask in my name, that will I do."* F. B. Meyer

> *Say to this mountain, "Go,*
> *Be cast into the sea";*
> *And doubt not in thine heart*
> *That it shall be to thee.*
> *It shall be done, doubt not His Word,*
> *Challenge thy mountain in the Lord!*
>
> *Claim thy redemption right,*
> *Purchased by precious blood;*
> *The Trinity unite*
> *To make it true and good.*
> *It shall be done, obey the Word,*
> *Challenge thy mountain in the Lord!*
>
> *Self, sickness, sorrow, sin,*
> *The Lord did meet that day*
> *On His beloved One,*
> *And thou art "loosed away."*
> *It has been done, rest on His Word,*
> *Challenge thy mountain in the Lord!*
>
> *Compass the frowning wall*
> *With silent prayer, then raise—*
> *Before its ramparts fall—*
> *The victor's shout of praise.*

It shall be done, faith rests assured,
Challenge thy mountain in the Lord!

The two-leaved gates of brass,
The bars of iron yield,
To let the faithful pass,
Conquerors in every field.
It shall be done, the foe ignored,
Challenge thy mountain in the Lord!

Take then the faith of God,
Free from the taint of doubt;
The miracle-working rod
That casts all reasoning out.
It shall be done, stand on the Word,
Challenge thy mountain in the Lord!

SELECTED

June 25

Speak unto the children of Israel, that they go forward (Exod. 14:15).

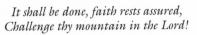

Imagine, O child of God, if you can, that triumphal march! The excited children restrained from ejaculations of wonder by the perpetual hush of their parents; the most uncontrollable excitement of the women as they found themselves suddenly saved from a fate worse than death; while the men followed or accompanied them ashamed or confounded that they had ever mistrusted God or murmured against Moses; and as you see those mighty walls of water piled by the outstretched hand of the Eternal, in response to the faith of a single man, learn what God will do for His own.

Dread not any result of implicit obedience to His command; fear not the angry waters which, in their proud insolence, forbid your progress. Above the voice of many waters, the mighty breakers of the sea, "the Lord sitteth King for ever."

A storm is only as the outskirts of His robe, the symptom of His advent, the environment of His presence.

Dare to trust Him; dare to follow Him! And discover that the very forces which barred your progress and threatened your life, at His bidding become the materials of which an avenue is made at liberty. F. B. MEYER

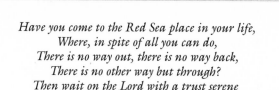

Have you come to the Red Sea place in your life,
Where, in spite of all you can do,
There is no way out, there is no way back,
There is no other way but through?
Then wait on the Lord with a trust serene
Till the night of your fear is gone;
He will send the wind, He will heap the floods,
When He says to your soul, "Go on."

And His hand will lead you through—clear through—
Ere the watery walls roll down,
No foe can reach you, no wave can touch,
No mightiest sea can drown;
The tossing billows may rear their crests,
Their foam at your feet may break,
But over their bed you shall walk dry shod
In the path that your Lord will make.

In the morning watch, 'neath the lifted cloud,
You shall see but the Lord alone,
When He leads you on from the place of the sea
To a land that you have not known;
And your fears shall pass as your foes have passed,
You shall be no more afraid;
You shall sing His praise in a better place,
A place that His hand has made.

ANNIE JOHNSON FLINT

June 26

For what if some did not believe? Shall their unbelief make the faith of God without effect? (Rom. 3:3).

I think that I can trace every scrap of sorrow in my life to simple unbelief. How could I be anything but quite happy if I believed always that all the past is forgiven, and all the present furnished with power, and all the future bright with hope because of the same abiding facts which do not change with my mood, do not stumble because I totter and stagger at the promise through unbelief, but stand firm and clear with their peaks of pearl cleaving the air of eternity, and the bases of their hills rooted unfathomable in the rock of God? Mont Blanc does not become a phantom or a mist because a climber grows dizzy on its side. JAMES SMETHAM 🐦

Is it any wonder that, when we stagger at any promise of God through unbelief, we do not receive it? Not that faith merits an answer, or in any way earns it, or works it out; but God has made *believing* a condition of receiving, and the Giver has a sovereign right to choose His own terms of gift. REV. SAMUEL HART 🐦

Unbelief says, "How can such and such things be?" It is full of "hows"; but faith has one great answer to the ten thousand "hows," and that answer is—GOD! C. H. M. 🐦

No praying man or woman accomplishes *so much* with *so little* expenditure of time as when he or she is praying.

If there should arise, it has been said—and the words are surely true to the thought of our Lord Jesus Christ in all His teaching on prayer—if there should arise ONE UTTERLY BELIEVING MAN, *the history of the world might be changed*.

Will YOU not be that one in the providence and guidance of God our Father? A. E. McADAM 🐦

Prayer without faith degenerates into objectless routine, or soulless hypocrisy. Prayer with faith brings omnipotence to back our petitions. Better not pray unless and until your whole being responds to the efficacy of your supplication. When the true prayer is breathed, earth and heaven, the past and the future, say Amen. And Christ prayed such prayers. P. C. M. 🐦

Nothing lies beyond the reach of prayer
except that which lies outside the will of God.

June 27

The Lord hath sent strength for thee (Ps. 68:28 PBV).

The Lord imparts unto us that primary strength of character which makes everything in life work with intensity and decision. We are "strengthened with might by his Spirit in the inner man." And the strength is continuous; reserves of power come to us which we cannot exhaust.

"As thy days, so shall thy strength be"—strength of will, strength of affection, strength of judgment, strength of ideals and achievement.

"The Lord is my strength" *to go on*. He gives us power to tread the dead level, to walk the long lane that seems never to have a turning, to go

through those long reaches of life which afford no pleasant surprise, and which depress the spirits in the sameness of a terrible drudgery.

"The Lord is my strength" *to go up*. He is to me the power by which
I can climb the Hill Difficulty and not be afraid.

"The Lord is my strength" *to go down*. It is when we leave the bracing heights, where the wind and the sun have been about us, and when
we begin to come down the hill into closer and more sultry spheres, that
the heart is apt to grow faint.

I heard a man say the other day concerning his growing physical frailty,
"It is the coming down that tires me!"

"The Lord is my strength" *to sit still*. And how difficult is the attainment! Do we not often say to one another, in seasons when we are compelled to be quiet, "If only I could do something!"

When the child is ill, and the mother stands by in comparative impotence, how severe is the test! But to do nothing, just to sit still and wait,
requires tremendous strength. "The Lord is my strength!" "Our sufficiency
is of God." FROM THE SILVER LINING

June 28

A door was opened in heaven (Rev. 4:1).

You must remember that John was in the Isle of Patmos, a lone, rocky,
inhospitable prison, for the Word of God and the testimony of Jesus. And
yet to him, under such circumstances, separated from all the loved ones of
Ephesus; debarred from the worship of church; condemned to the companionship of uncongenial fellow-captives, were vouchsafed these visions.
For him, also a door was opened.

We are reminded of Jacob, exiled from his father's house, who laid
himself down in a desert place to sleep, and in his dreams beheld a ladder
which united heaven with earth, and at the top stood God.

Not to these only, but to many more, doors have been opened into
heaven, when, so far as the world was concerned, it seemed as though their
circumstances were altogether unlikely for such revelations.

To prisoners and captives; to constant sufferers, bound by iron chains
of pain to sick couches; to lonely pilgrims and wanderers; to women
detained from the Lord's house by the demands of home, how often has
the door been opened to heaven.

But there are conditions. You must know what it is to be in the Spirit; you must be pure in heart and obedient in faith; you must be willing to count all things but loss for the excellency of the knowledge of Jesus Christ; then when God is all in all to us, when we live, move and have our being in His favor, to us also will the door be opened. FROM DAILY DEVOTIONAL COMMENTARY

God hath His mountains bleak and bare,
Where He doth bid us rest awhile;
Crags where we breathe a purer air,
Lone peaks that catch the day's first smile.

God hath His deserts broad and brown—
A solitude—a sea of sand,
Where He doth let heaven's curtain down,
Unknit by His Almighty hand.

June 29

There we saw the giants (Num. 13:33).

Yes, they saw the giants, but Caleb and Joshua saw God! Those who doubt say, *"We be not able to go up."* Those who believe say, *"Let us go up at once and possess it, for we are well able."*

Giants stand for great difficulties; and giants are stalking everywhere. They are in our families, in our churches, in our social life, in our own hearts; and we must overcome them or they will eat us up, as these men of old said of the giants of Canaan.

The men of faith said, "They are bread for us; we will eat them up." In other words, "We will be stronger by overcoming them than if there had been no giants to overcome."

Now the fact is, unless we have the overcoming faith we shall be eaten up, consumed by the giants in our path. Let us have the spirit of faith that these men of faith had, and see God, and He will take care of the difficulties. SELECTED

It is when we are in the way of *duty* that we find *giants*. It was when Israel was going *forward* that the giants appeared. When they turned back into the wilderness they found none.

There is a prevalent idea that the power of God in a human life should lift us above all trials and conflicts. The fact is, the power of God always

198

brings a conflict and a struggle. One would have thought that on his great missionary journey to Rome, Paul would have been carried by some mighty providence above the power of storms and tempests and enemies. But, on the contrary, it was one long, hard fight with persecuting Jews, with wild tempests, with venomous vipers and all the powers of earth and hell, and at last he was saved, as it seemed, by the narrowest margin, and had to swim ashore at Malta on a piece of wreckage and barely escape a watery grave.

Was that like a God of infinite power? Yes, just like Him. And so Paul tells us that when he took the Lord Jesus Christ as the life of his body, a severe conflict immediately came; indeed, a conflict that never ended, a pressure that was persistent, but out of which he always emerged victorious through the strength of Jesus Christ.

The language in which he describes this is most graphic. "We are troubled on every side, yet not distressed; perplexed, but not in despair; persecuted, but not forsaken; cast down, but not destroyed, always bearing about in the body the dying of the Lord Jesus, that the life also of Jesus might be manifested in our body."

What a ceaseless, strenuous struggle! It is impossible to express in English the forcible language of the original. There are five pictures in succession. In the first, the idea is crowding enemies pressing in from every side, and yet not crushing him because the police of heaven cleared the way just wide enough for him to get through. The literal translation would be, "We are crowded on every side, but not crushed."

The second picture is that of one whose way seems utterly closed and yet he has pressed through; there is light enough to show him the next step. The Revised Version translates it, "Perplexed but not unto despair." Rotherham still more literally renders it, "Without a way, but not without a by-way."

The third figure is that of an enemy in hot pursuit while the Divine Defender still stands by, and he is not left alone. Again we adopt the fine rendering of Rotherham, "Pursued but not abandoned."

The fourth figure is still more vivid and dramatic. The enemy has overtaken him, has struck him, has knocked him down. But it is not a fatal blow; he is able to rise again. It might be translated, "Overthrown but not overcome."

Once more the figure advances, and now it seems to be even death itself, "Always bearing about in the body the dying of the Lord Jesus." But he does not die, for "the life also of Jesus" now comes to his aid and he lives in the life of another until his life work is done.

The reason so many fail in this experience of divine healing is because they expect to have it all without a struggle, and when the conflict comes and the battle wages long, they become discouraged and surrender. God has nothing worth having that is easy. There are no cheap goods in the heavenly market. Our redemption cost all that God had to give, and everything worth having is expensive. Hard places are the very school of faith and character, and if we are to rise over mere human strength and prove the power of life divine in these mortal bodies, it must be through a process of conflict that may well be called the birth travail of a new life. It is the old figure of the bush that burned, but was not consumed, or of the vision in the house of the interpreter of the flame that would not expire, notwithstanding the fact that the demon ceaselessly poured water on it, because in the background stood an angel ever pouring oil and keeping the flame aglow.

No, dear suffering child of God, you cannot fail if only you dare to believe, to stand fast and refuse to be overcome. FROM A TRACT 🦥

June 30

There was silence, and I heard a still voice (Job 4:16, margin).

A score of years ago, a friend placed in my hand a book called *True Peace.* It was an old medieval message, and it had but one thought—that God was waiting in the depths of my being to talk to me if I would only get still enough to hear His voice.

I thought this would be a very easy matter, and so began to get still. But I had no sooner commenced than a perfect pandemonium of voices reached my ears, a thousand clamoring notes from without and within, until I could hear nothing but their noise and din.

Some were my own voices, my own questions, some my very prayers. Others were suggestions of the tempter and the voices from the world's turmoil.

In every direction I was pulled and pushed and greeted with noisy acclamations and unspeakable unrest. It seemed necessary for me to listen to some of them and to answer some of them; but God said, "Be still, and know that I am God." Then came the conflict of thoughts for tomorrow, and its duties and cares; but God said, "Be still."

And as I listened, and slowly learned to obey, and shut my ears to every sound, I found after a while that when the other voices ceased, or I ceased to hear them, there was a still small voice in the depths of my being that began to speak with an inexpressible tenderness, power and comfort.

As I listened, it became to me the voice of prayer, the voice of wisdom, the voice of duty, and I did not need to think so hard, or pray so hard, or trust so hard; but that "still small voice" of the Holy Spirit in my heart was God's prayer in my secret soul, was God's answer to all my questions, was God's life and strength for soul and body, and became the substance of all knowledge, and all prayer and all blessing: for it was the living GOD Himself as my life, my all.

It is thus that our spirit drinks in the life of our risen Lord, and we go forth to life's conflicts and duties like a flower that has drunk in, through the shades of night, the cool and crystal drops of dew. But as *dew never falls on a stormy night,* so the dews of His grace never come to the restless soul. A. B. SIMPSON

July 1

There shall be a performance (Luke 1:45).
My words shall be fulfilled in their season [their fixed appointed time] (Luke 1:20, Greek version).

There shall be a performance of those things
That loving heart hath waited long to see;
Those words shall be fulfilled to which she clings,
Because her God hath promised faithfully;
And, knowing Him, she ne'er can doubt His Word;
"He speaks and it is done." The mighty Lord!

There shall be a performance of those things,
O burdened heart, rest ever in His care;
In quietness beneath His shadowing wings
Await the answer to thy longing prayer.
When thou hast "cast thy care," the heart then sings,
There shall be a performance of those things.

There shall be a performance of those things,
O tired heart, believe and wait and pray;
At eventide the peaceful vesper rings,
Though cloud and rain and storm have filled the day.
Faith pierces through the mist of doubt that bars
The coming night sometimes, and finds the stars.

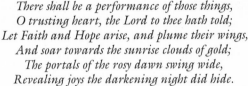

There shall be a performance of those things,
O trusting heart, the Lord to thee hath told;
Let Faith and Hope arise, and plume their wings,
And soar towards the sunrise clouds of gold;
The portals of the rosy dawn swing wide,
Revealing joys the darkening night did hide.

BESSIE PORTER

Matthew Henry says: "We must depend upon the performance of the promise, when all the ways leading up to it are shut up. 'For all the promises of God in him are yea [yes], and in him Amen [so be it], unto the glory of God by us'" (2 Cor. 1:20).

July 2

When thou goest, thy way shall be opened up before thee step by step (Prov. 4:12, free translation).

The Lord never builds a bridge of faith except under the feet of the faith-filled traveler. If He builds the bridge a rod ahead, it would not be a bridge of faith. That which is of sight is not of faith.

There is a self-opening gate which is sometimes used in country roads. It stands fast and firm across the road as a traveler approaches it. If he stops before he gets to it, it will not open. But if he will drive right at it, his wagon wheels press the springs below the roadway, and the gate swings back to let him through. He must push right on at the closed gate, or it will continue to be closed.

This illustrates the way to pass every barrier on the road of duty. Whether it is a river, a gate, or a mountain, all the child of Jesus has to do is to go for it. If it is a river, it will dry up when you are near enough to it, and are still pushing on. If it is a mountain, it will be lifted up and cast into a sea when you come squarely up without flinching, to where you thought it was.

Is there a great barrier across your path of duty just now? Just go for it, in the name of the Lord, and it won't be there. HENRY CLAY TRUMBULL

We sit and weep in vain. The voice of the Almighty said, "Up and onward forevermore." Let us move on and step out boldly, though it be into the night, and we can scarcely see the forest, or the alpine pass, which discloses but a few rods of its length from any single point of view. Press on! If necessary, we will find even the pillar of cloud and fire to mark our journey through the wilderness. There are guides and wayside inns along the road.

We will find food, clothes and friends at every stage of the journey, and as Rutherford so quaintly says: "However matters go, the worst will be a tired traveler and a joyful and sweet welcome home."

I'm going by the upper road, for that
still holds the sun,
I'm climbing through night's pastures where
the starry rivers run:
If you should think to seek me in my
old dark abode,
You'll find this writing on the door,
"He's on the Upper Road."

SELECTED

July 3

Doth the plowman plow all day to sow? (Isa. 28:24).

One day in early summer I walked past a beautiful meadow. The grass was as soft and thick and fine as an immense green Oriental rug. In one corner stood a fine old tree, a sanctuary for numberless wild birds; the crisp, sweet air was full of their happy songs. Two cows lay in the shade, the very picture of content.

Down by the roadside the saucy dandelion mingled his gold with the royal purple of the wild violet.

I leaned against the fence for a long time, feasting my hungry eyes, and thinking in my soul that God never made a fairer spot than my lovely meadow.

The next day I passed that way again, and lo! the hand of the despoiler had been there. A plowman and his great plow, now standing idle in the furrow, had in a day wrought a terrible havoc. Instead of the green grass there was turned up to view the ugly, bare, brown earth; instead of the singing birds there were only a few hens industriously scratching for worms. Gone were the dandelion and the pretty violet. I said in my grief, "How could anyone spoil a thing so fair?"

Then my eyes were opened by some unseen hand, and I saw a vision, a vision of a field of ripe corn ready for the harvest. I could see the giant, heavily laden stalks in the autumn sun; I could almost hear the music of the wind as it would sweep across the golden tassels. And before I was aware, the brown earth took on a splendor it had not had the day before.

Oh, that we might always catch the vision of an abundant harvest, when the great Master Plowman comes, as He often does, and furrows through our very souls, uprooting and turning under that which we thought most fair, and leaving for our tortured gaze only the bare and the unbeautiful. SELECTED 🖝

Why should I start at the plough of my Lord, that maketh the deep furrows on my soul? I know He is no idle husbandman, He purposeth a crop. SAMUEL RUTHERFORD 🖝

July 4

For the vision is yet for an appointed time ... though it tarry, wait for it; because it will surely come, it will not tarry (Hab. 2:3).

In the charming little booklet *Expectation Corner,* Adam Slowman was led into the Lord's treasure houses, and among many other wonders there revealed to him was the *"Delayed Blessing Office,"* where God kept certain things, prayed for, until the wise time came to send them.

It takes a long time for some pensioners to learn that *delays are not denials.* Ah, there are secrets of love and wisdom in the *"Delayed Blessings Department,"* which are little dreamt of! Men would pluck their mercies green when the Lord would have them ripe. *"Therefore will the Lord WAIT, that He may be gracious unto you"* (Isa. 30:18). He is watching in the hard places and will not allow one trial too many; He will let the dross be consumed, and then He will come gloriously to your help.

Do not grieve Him by doubting His love. Nay, lift up your head, and begin to praise Him *even now* for the deliverance which is on the way to you, and you will be abundantly rewarded for the delay which has tried your faith.

O Thou of little faith,
God hath not failed thee yet!
When all looks dark and gloomy,
Thou dost so soon forget—

Forget that He has led thee,
And gently cleared thy way;
On clouds has poured His sunshine,
And turned thy night to day.

And if He's helped thee hitherto,
He will not fail thee now;

How it must wound His loving heart
To see thy anxious brow!

Oh! doubt not any longer,
To Him commit thy way,
Whom in the past thou trusted,
And is "just the same today."

SELECTED

July 5

I will allure her, and bring her into the wilderness. . . . And I
will give her her vineyards from thence (Hos. 2:14–15).

A strange place to find vineyards—in the wilderness! And can it be that the riches which a soul needs can be obtained in the wilderness, which stands for a lonely place, out of which you can seldom find your way? It would seem so, and not only that, but the "Valley of Achor," which means bitterness, is called a door of hope. *And she shall sing there, as in the days of her youth!*

Yes, God knows our need of the wilderness experience. He knows where and how to bring out that which is enduring. The soul has been idolatrous, rebellious; has forgotten God, and with a perfect self-will has said, "I will follow after my lovers." But she did not overtake them. And, when she was hopeless and forsaken, God said, "I will allure her, and bring her into the wilderness, and speak comfortably unto her." What a loving God is ours! FROM CRUMBS

We never know where God hides His pools. We see a rock, and we cannot guess it is the home of the spring. We see a flinty place, and we cannot tell it is the hiding place of a fountain. God leads me into the hard places, and then I find I have gone into the dwelling place of eternal springs. SELECTED

July 6

Neither know we what to do; but our eyes are upon thee
(2 Chron. 20:12).

A life was lost in Israel because a pair of human hands were laid unbidden upon the ark of God. They were placed upon it with the best intent, to steady it when trembling and shaking as the oxen drew it along the rough way; but they touched God's work presumptuously, and they fell paralyzed and lifeless. *Much of the life of faith consists in letting things alone.*

If we wholly trust an interest to God, we must keep our hands off it; and He will guard it for us better than we can help Him. "Rest in the Lord, and wait patiently for him: fret not thyself because of him who prospereth in his way, because of the man who bringeth wicked devices to pass."

Things may seem to be going all wrong, but He knows as well as we; and He will arise in the right moment if we are really trusting Him so fully as to let Him work in His own way and time. There is nothing so masterly as inactivity in some things, and there is nothing so hurtful as restless working, for God has undertaken to work His sovereign will. A. B. SIMPSON

> *Being perplexed, I say,*
> *"Lord, make it right!*
> *Night is as day to Thee,*
> *Darkness as light.*
> *I am afraid to touch*
> *Things that involve so much;*
> *My trembling hand may shake,*
> *My skilless hand may break;*
> *Thine can make no mistake."*
>
> *Being in doubt I say,*
> *"Lord, make it plain;*
> *Which is the true, safe way?*
> *Which would be gain?*
> *I am not wise to know,*
> *Nor sure of foot to go;*
> *What is so clear to Thee,*
> *Lord, make it clear to me!"*

It is such a comfort to drop the tangles of life into God's hands and leave them there.

July 7

He hath ... made me a polished shaft (Isa. 49:2).

There is a very famous "Pebble Beach" at Pescadero, on the California coast. The lone line of white surf comes up with its everlasting roar, and rattles and thunders among the stones on the shore. They are caught in the arms of the pitiless waves, and tossed and rolled, and rubbed together, and ground against the sharp-grained cliffs. Day and night forever the ceaseless attrition goes on—never any rest. And the result?

Tourists from all the world flock thither to gather the round and beautiful stones. They are laid up in cabinets; they ornament the parlor mantels. But go yonder, around the point of the cliff that breaks off the face of the sea; and up in that quiet cove, sheltered from the storms, and lying ever in the sun, you shall find abundance of pebbles that have never been chosen by the traveler.

Why are these left all the years through unsought? For the simple reason that they have escaped all the turmoil and attrition of the waves, and the quiet and peace have left them as they found them, rough and angular and devoid of beauty. *Polish comes through trouble.*

Since God knows what niche we are to fill, let us trust Him to shape us to it. Since He knows what work we are to do, let us trust Him to drill us to the proper preparation.

> *O blows that smite! O hurts that pierce*
> *This shrinking heart of mine!*
> *What are ye but the Master's tools*
> *Forming a work Divine?*

Nearly all God's jewels are crystallized tears.

July 8

They shall mount up with wings as eagles (Isa. 40:31).

There is a fable about the way the birds got their wings at the beginning. They were first made without wings. Then God made the wings and put them down before the wingless birds and said to them, "Come, take up these burdens and bear them."

The birds had lovely plumage and sweet voices; they could sing, and their feathers gleamed in the sunshine, but they could not soar in the air. They hesitated at first when bidden to take up the burdens that lay at their feet, but soon they obeyed, and taking up the wings in their beaks, laid them on their shoulders to carry them.

For a little while the load seemed heavy and hard to bear, but presently, as they went on carrying the burdens, folding them over their hearts, the wings grew fast to their little bodies, and soon they discovered how to use them, and were lifted by them up into the air—*the weights became wings.*

It is a parable. We are the wingless birds, and our duties and tasks are the pinions God has made to lift us up and carry us heavenward. We look at our burdens and heavy loads, and shrink from them; but as we lift them and bind them about our hearts, they become wings, and on them we rise and soar toward God.

There is no burden which, if we lift it cheerfully and bear it with love in our hearts, will not become a blessing to us. God means our tasks to be our helpers; to refuse to bend our shoulders to receive a load, is to decline a new opportunity for growth. J. R. MILLER

Blessed is any weight, however overwhelming, which God has been so good as to fasten with His own hand upon our shoulders.

F. W. FABER

July 9

I have chosen thee in the furnace of affliction (Isa. 48:10).

Does not the Word come like a soft shower, assuaging the fury of the flame? Yes, is it not an asbestos armor, against which the heat has no power? Let the affliction come—God has *chosen* me. Poverty, thou mayest stride in at my door; but God is in the house already, and He has *chosen* me. Sickness, thou mayest intrude; but I have a balsam ready—God has *chosen* me. Whatever befall me in this vale of tears, I know that He has *chosen* me.

Fear not, Christian; Jesus is with thee. In all thy fiery trials, His presence is both thy comfort and safety. He will never leave one whom He has chosen for His own. "Fear not, for I am with thee," is His sure word of promise to His chosen ones in "the furnace of affliction." C. H. SPURGEON

> *Pain's furnace heat within me quivers,*
> *God's breath upon the flame doth blow;*
> *And all my heart in anguish shivers*
> *And trembles at the fiery glow;*
> *And yet I whisper, "As God will!"*
> *And in the hottest fire hold still.*

He comes and lays my heart, all heated,
On the hard anvil, minded so
Into His own fair shape to beat it
With His great hammer, blow on blow;
And yet I whisper, "As God will!"
And at His heaviest blows hold still.

He takes my softened heart and beats it;
The sparks fly off at every blow;
He turns it o'er and o'er and heats it,
And lets it cool, and makes it glow;
And yet I whisper, "As God will!"
And in His mighty hand hold still.

Why should I murmur? for the sorrow
Thus only longer-lived would be;
The end may come, and will tomorrow,
When God has done His work in me;
So I say trusting, "As God will!"
And, trusting to the end, hold still.

JULIUS STURM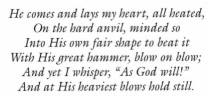

The burden of suffering seems a tombstone hung about our necks, while in reality it is only the weight which is necessary to keep down the diver while he is hunting for pearls. RICHTER

July 10

I called him, but he gave me no answer (Song of Sol. 5:6).

The Lord, when He hath given great faith, hath been known to try it by long delayings. He has suffered His servants' voices to echo in their ears as from a brazen sky. They have knocked at the golden gate, but it has remained unmovable, as though it were rusted upon its hinges. Like Jeremiah, they have cried, *"Thou hast covered thyself with a cloud, that our prayer should not pass through."* Thus have true saints continued long in patient waiting without reply, not because their prayers were not vehement, nor because they were unaccepted, but because it so pleased Him who is Sovereign, and who gives according to His own pleasure. If it pleases Him to bid our patience exercise itself, shall He not do as He will with His own!

No prayer is lost. Praying breath was never spent in vain. There is no such thing as prayer unanswered or unnoticed by God, and some things that we count refusals or denials are simply delays. H. BONAR

Christ sometimes delays His help that He may try our faith and quicken our prayers. The boat may be covered with the waves, and He sleeps on; but He will wake up before it sinks. He sleeps, but He never oversleeps; and there are no "too lates" with Him. ALEXANDER MACLAREN

Be still, sad soul! lift thou no passionate cry,
But spread the desert of thy being bare
To the full searching of the All-seeing eye;
Wait! and through dark misgiving, black despair,
God will come down in pity, and fill the dry
Dead place with light, and life, and vernal air.

J. C. SHAIRP

July 11

It came to pass after a while, that the brook dried up, because there had been no rain in the land (1 Kings 17:7).

Week after week, with unfaltering and steadfast spirit, Elijah watched the dwindling brook; often tempted to stagger through unbelief, but refusing to allow his circumstances to come between himself and God. Unbelief sees God through circumstances, as we sometimes see the sun shorn of his rays through smoky air; but faith puts God between itself and circumstances, and looks at them through Him. And so the dwindling brook became a silver thread; and the silver thread stood presently in pools at the foot of the largest boulders; and the pools shrank. The birds fled; the wild creatures of field and forest came no more to drink; the brook was dry. Only then to his patient and unwavering spirit, "the word of the Lord came saying, Arise, get thee to Zarephath."

Most of us would have gotten anxious and worn with planning long before that. We should have ceased our songs as soon as the streamlet caroled less musically over its rocky bed; and with harps swinging on the willows, we should have paced to and fro upon the withering grass, lost in pensive thought. And probably, long ere the brook was dry, we should have devised some plan, and asking God's blessing on it, would have started off elsewhere.

God often does extricate us, because His mercy endureth forever; but if we had only waited first to see the unfolding of His plans, we should never have found ourselves landed in such an inextricable labyrinth; and we should never have been compelled to retrace our steps with so many tears of shame. *Wait, patiently wait!* F. B. MEYER

July 12

He hath acquainted himself with my beaten path. When he hath searched me out, I shall come out shining (Job 23:10, free translation).

"Faith grows amid storms"—just four words, but oh, how full of import to the soul who has been in the storms!

Faith is that God-given faculty which, when exercised, brings the unseen into plain view, and by which the impossible things are made possible. It deals with supernaturals.

But it *"grows amid storms";* that is, where there are disturbances in the spiritual atmosphere. Storms are caused by the conflicts of elements; and the storms of the spiritual world are conflicts with hostile elements.

In such an atmosphere faith finds its most productive soil; in such an element it comes more quickly to full fruition.

The staunchest tree is not found in the shelter of the forest, but out in the open where the winds from every quarter beat upon it, and bend and twist it until it becomes a giant in stature—this is the tree which the mechanic wants his tools made of, and the wagon-maker seeks.

So in the spiritual world, when you see a giant, remember the road you must travel to come up to his side is not along the sunny lane where wildflowers ever bloom; but a steep, rocky, narrow pathway where the blasts of hell will almost blow you off your feet; where the sharp rocks cut the flesh, where the projecting thorns scratch the brow, and the venomous beasts hiss on every side.

It is a pathway of sorrow and joy, of suffering and healing balm, of tears and smiles, of trials and victories, of conflicts and triumphs, of hardships and perils and buffetings, of persecutions and misunderstandings, of troubles and distress; through all of which we are made more than conquerors through Him who loves us.

"Amid storms." Right in the midst where it is fiercest. You may shrink back from the ordeal of a fierce storm of trial … but go in! God is there to meet you in the center of all your trials, and to whisper His secrets which will make you come forth with a shining face and an indomitable faith that all the demons of hell shall never afterwards cause to waver. E. A. KILBOURNE

July 13

God ... calleth those things which be not as though they were (Rom. 4:17).

What does that mean? Why Abraham did this thing: he dared to believe God. It seemed an impossibility at his age that Abraham should become the father of a child; it looked incredible; and yet God called him a "father of many nations" before there was a sign of a child; and so Abraham called himself "father" because God called him so. That is faith; it is to believe and assert what God says. "Faith steps on seeming void, and finds the rock beneath."

Only say you have what God says you have, and He will make good to you all you believe. Only it must be real faith; all there is in you must go over in that act of faith to God. FROM CRUMBS

Be willing to live by believing and neither think nor desire to live in any other way. Be willing to see every outward light extinguished, to see the eclipse of every star in the blue heavens, leaving nothing but darkness and perils around, if God will only leave in thy soul the inner radiance, the pure bright lamp which faith has kindled. THOMAS C. UPHAM

The moment has come when you must get off the perch of distrust, out of the nest of seeming safety, and onto the wings of faith; just such a time as comes to the bird when it must begin to try the air. It may seem as though you must drop to the earth; so it may seem to the fledgling. It, too, may feel very like falling; but it does not fall—its pinions give it support, or, if they fail, the parent bird sweeps under and bears it upon its wings. Even so will God bear you. Only trust Him; "thou shalt be holden up." "Well, but," you say, "am I to cast myself upon nothing?" That is what the bird seems to have to do; but we know the *air is there*, and the air is not so unsubstantial as it seems. And *you* know the *promises of God are there*, and they are not unsubstantial at all. "But it seems an unlikely thing to come about that my poor weak soul should be girded with such strength." Has God said it shall? "That my tempted, yielding nature shall be victor in the strife." Has God said it shall? "That my timorous, trembling heart shall find peace?" Has God said it shall? For, if He has, you surely do not mean to give Him the lie! Hath He spoken, and shall He not do it? If you have gotten a word—"a sure word" of promise—take it implicitly, trust it absolutely. And this sure word you have; nay, you have more—you have Him who speaks the word confidently. "Yea, I say unto you," trust Him. J. B. FIGGIS, M.A.

July 14

Bind the sacrifice with cords, even unto the horns of the altar (Ps. 118:27).

Is not this altar inviting thee? Shall we not ask to be *bound* to it, that we may never be able to start back from our attitude of consecration? There are times when life is full of roseate light, and we choose the cross; at other times, when the sky is gray, we shrink from it. It is well to be *bound*.

Wilt Thou bind us, most blessed Spirit, and enamor us with the cross, and let us never leave it? Bind us with the scarlet cord of redemption, and the gold cord of love, and the silver cord of Advent-hope, so we will not go back from it, or wish for another lot than to be the humble partners with our Lord in His pain and sorrow!

The horns of the altar invite thee. Wilt thou come? Wilt thou dwell ever in a spirit of resigned humility, and give thyself wholly to the Lord? SELECTED

The story is told of a colored brother who, at a camp meeting, tried to give himself to God. Every night at the altar he consecrated himself; but every night before he left the meeting, the Devil would come to him and convince him that he did not *feel* any different and therefore he was not consecrated.

Again and again he was beaten back by the adversary. Finally, one evening he came to the meeting with an ax and a big stake. After consecrating himself, be drove the stake into the ground just where he had knelt. As he was leaving the building, the Devil came to him as usual and tried to make him believe that it was all a farce.

At once he went back to the stake and, pointing to it, said, "Look here, Mr. Devil, do you see that stake? Well, that's my witness that God has forever accepted me." Immediately the Devil left him, and he had no further doubts on the subject. FROM THE STILL SMALL VOICE

Beloved, if you are tempted to doubt the finality of your consecration, drive a stake down somewhere and let it be your witness before God and even the Devil that you have settled the question forever.

> *Are you groping for a blessing,*
> *Never getting there?*
> *Listen to a word in season,*
> *Get somewhere.*

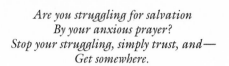

Are you struggling for salvation
By your anxious prayer?
Stop your struggling, simply trust, and—
Get somewhere.

Does the answer seem to linger
To your earnest prayer?
Turn your praying into praise, and—
Get somewhere.

You will never know His fulness
Till you boldly dare
To commit your all to Him, and—
Get somewhere.

Songs of the Spirit ☙

July 15

This is the victory that overcometh the world, even our faith
(1 John 5:4).

It is easy to love Him when the blue is in the sky,
When the summer winds are blowing, and we smell the roses nigh;
There is little effort needed to obey His precious will
When it leads through flower-decked valley, or over sun-kissed hill.

It is when the rain is falling, or the mist hangs in the air,
When the road is dark and rugged, and the wind no longer fair,
When the rosy dawn has settled in a shadowland of gray,
That we find it hard to trust Him, and are slower to obey.

It is easy to trust Him when the singing birds have come,
And their canticles are echoed in our heart and in our home;
But 'tis when we miss the music, and the days are dull and drear,
That we need a faith triumphant over every doubt and fear.

And our blessed Lord will give it; what we lack He will supply;
Let us ask in faith believing—on His promises rely;
He will ever be our Leader, whether smooth or rough the way,
And will prove Himself sufficient for the needs of every day.

To trust in spite of the look of being forsaken; to keep crying out into the vast, whence comes no returning voice, and where seems no hearing; to see the machinery of the world pauselessly grinding on as if self-moved, caring for no life, nor shifting a hairbreadth for all entreaty, and yet believe that God is awake and utterly loving; to desire nothing but what comes meant for us from His hand; to wait patiently, ready to die of hunger, fearing only lest faith should fail—such is the victory that overcometh the world, such is faith indeed. GEORGE MACDONALD ☙

July 16

Because thou hast done this thing, and hast not withheld thy son, thine only son. . . . I will multiply thy seed as the stars of the heaven; . . . because thou hast obeyed my voice (Gen. 22:16–18).

And from that day to this, men have been learning that when, at God's voice, they surrender up to Him the one thing above all else that was dearest to their very hearts, that same thing is returned to them by Him a thousand times over. Abraham gives up his one and only son, at God's call, and with this disappear all his hopes for the boy's life and manhood, and for a noble family bearing his name. But the boy is restored, the family becomes as the stars and sands in number, and out of it, in the fullness of time, appears Jesus Christ.

That is just the way God meets every real sacrifice of every child of His. We surrender all and accept poverty; and He sends wealth. We renounce a rich field of service; He sends us a richer one than we had dared to dream of. We give up all our cherished hopes, and die unto self; He sends us the life more abundant, and tingling joy. And the crown of it all is our Jesus Christ. For we can never know the fullness of the sacrifice. The earthly founder of the family of Christ must commence by losing himself and his only son, just as the heavenly Founder of that family did. We cannot be members of that family with the full privileges and joys of membership *upon any other basis.* C. G. TRUMBULL ☙

We sometimes seem to forget *that what God takes He takes in fire;* and that the only way to the resurrection life and the ascension mount is the way of the garden, the cross, and the grave.

Think not, O soul of man, that Abraham's was a unique and solitary experience. It is simply a specimen and pattern of God's dealings with all souls who are prepared to obey Him at whatever cost. After thou hast patiently endured, thou shalt receive the promise. The moment of supreme sacrifice shall be the moment of supreme and rapturous blessing. God's river, which is full of water, shall burst its banks, and pour upon thee a tide of wealth and grace. There is nothing, indeed, which God will not do for a man who dares to step out upon what seems to be the mist; though as he puts down his foot he finds a rock beneath him. F. B. MEYER

July 17

I will be still, and I will behold in my dwelling place (Isa. 18:4 RV).

Assyria was marching against Ethiopia, the people of which are described as tall and smooth. And as the armies advance, God makes no effort to arrest them; it seems as though they will be allowed to work their will. He is still watching them from His dwelling place, the sun still shines on them; but before the harvest, the whole of the proud army of Assyria is smitten as easily as when sprigs are cut off by the pruning hook of the husbandman.

Is not this a marvelous conception of God—being still and watching? His stillness is not acquiescence. His silence is not consent. He is only biding His time, and will arise, in the most opportune moment, and when the designs of the wicked seem on the point of success, to overwhelm them with disaster. As we look out on the evil of the world; as we think of the apparent success of wrongdoing; as we wince beneath the oppression of those that hate us, let us remember these marvelous words about God being still and beholding.

There is another side to this. Jesus beheld His disciples toiling at the oars through the stormy night; and watched though unseen, the successive steps of the anguish of Bethany, when Lazarus slowly passed through the stages of mortal sickness, until he succumbed and was borne to the rocky tomb. But He was only waiting the moment when He could interpose most effectually. Is He *still* to thee? He is not unobservant; He is beholding all things; He has His finger on thy pulse, keenly sensitive to all its fluctuations. He will come to save thee when the precise moment has arrived. FROM DAILY DEVOTIONAL COMMENTARY

Whatever His questions or His reticences, we may be absolutely sure of an unperplexed and undismayed Savior.

> *O troubled soul, beneath the rod,*
> *Thy Father speaks, be still, be still;*
> *Learn to be silent unto God,*
> *And let Him mould thee to His will.*

O praying soul, be still, be still,
He cannot break His plighted Word;
Sink down into His blessed will,
And wait in patience on the Lord.

O waiting soul, be still, be strong,
And though He tarry, trust and wait;
Doubt not, He will not wait too long,
Fear not, He will not come too late.

July 18

The eyes of the Lord run to and fro throughout the whole earth, to show himself strong in the behalf of them whose heart is perfect toward him (2 Chron. 16:9).

God is looking for a man or woman whose heart will be always set on Him, and who will trust Him for all He desires to do. God is eager to work more mightily now than He ever has through any soul. The clock of the centuries points to the eleventh hour.

"The world is waiting yet to see what God can do through a consecrated soul." Not the world alone, but God Himself is waiting for one who will be more fully devoted to Him than any who have ever lived; who will be willing to be nothing that Christ may be all; who will grasp God's own purposes; and taking His humility and His faith, His love and His power, will, without hindering, continue to let God do exploits. C. H. P.

There is no limit to what God can do with a man,
providing he will not touch the glory.

In an address given to ministers and workers after his ninetieth birthday, George Mueller spoke thus of himself: *"I was converted* in November, 1825, but I only came into *the full surrender of the heart* four years later, in July, 1829. The love of money was gone, the love of place was gone, the love of position was gone, the love of worldly pleasures and engagements was gone. God, God alone became my portion. I found my all in Him; I wanted nothing else. And by the grace of God this has remained, and has made me a happy man, an exceedingly happy man, and it led me to care only about the things of God. I ask affectionately, my beloved brethren, have you fully surrendered the heart to God, or is there this thing or that thing with which you are taken up irrespective of God? I read a little of the Scriptures before, but preferred other books; but since that time the revelation He has made of Himself has become unspeakably blessed to me, and I can say from my heart, God is an infinitely lovely Being. Oh, be not satisfied until in your own inmost soul you can say, God is an infinitely lovely Being!" SELECTED

I pray to God this day to make me an extraordinary Christian. WHITEFIELD

July 19

The cup which my Father hath given me, shall I not drink it? (John 18:11).

This was a greater thing to say and do than to calm the seas or raise the dead. Prophets and apostles could work wondrous miracles, but they could not always do and suffer the will of God. To do and suffer God's will is still the highest form of faith, the most sublime Christian achievement. To have the bright aspirations of a young life forever blasted; to bear a daily burden never congenial and to see no relief; to be pinched by poverty when you only desire a competency for the good and comfort of loved ones; to be fettered by some incurable physical disability; to be stripped bare of loved ones until you stand alone to meet the shocks of life—to be able to say in such a school of discipline, "The cup which my Father has given me, shall I not drink it?"—this is faith at its highest and spiritual success at the crowning point. Great faith is exhibited not so much in ability to do as to suffer. DR. CHARLES PARKHURST

To have a sympathizing God we must have a suffering Savior, and there is no true fellow-feeling with another save in the heart of him who has been afflicted like him.

We cannot do good to others save at a cost to ourselves, and our afflictions are the price we pay for our ability to sympathize. He who would be a helper, must first be a sufferer. He who would be a savior must somewhere and somehow have been upon a cross; and we cannot have the highest happiness of life in succoring others without tasting the cup which Jesus drank, and submitting to the baptism wherewith He was baptized.

The most comforting of David's psalms were pressed out by suffering; and if Paul had not had his thorn in the flesh we would have missed much of the tenderness which quivers in so many of his letters.

The present circumstance, which presses so hard against you (if surrendered to Christ), is the best-shaped tool in the Father's hand to chisel you for eternity. Trust Him, then. Do not push away the instrument lest you lose its work.

> *Strange and difficult indeed*
> *We may find it,*
> *But the blessing that we need*
> *Is behind it.*

The school of suffering graduates rare scholars.

July 20

Seeing then that we have a great high priest ... Jesus, the Son of God, let us hold fast our profession. Let us therefore come boldly unto the throne of grace, that we may obtain mercy, and find grace to help in time of need (Heb. 4:14, 16).

Our great Helper in prayer is the Lord Jesus Christ, our Advocate with the Father, our Great High Priest, whose chief ministry for us these centuries has been intercession and prayer. He it is who takes our imperfect petitions from our hands, cleanses them from their defects, corrects their faults, and then claims their answer from His Father on His own account and through His all-atoning merits and righteousness.

Brother, are you fainting in prayer? Look up. Your blessed Advocate has already claimed your answer, and you would grieve and disappoint Him if you were to give up the conflict in the very moment when victory is on its way to meet you. He has gone in for you into the inner chamber, and already holds up your name upon the palms of His hands; and the messenger, which is to bring you your blessing, is now on his way, and the Spirit is only waiting your trust to whisper in your heart the echo of the answer from the throne, *"It is done."* A. B. SIMPSON

The Spirit has much to do with acceptable prayer, and His work in prayer is too much neglected. He enlightens the mind to see its wants, softens the heart to feel them, quickens our desires after suitable supplies, gives clear views of God's power, wisdom, and grace to relieve us, and stirs up that confidence in His truth which excludes all wavering. Prayer is, therefore, a wonderful thing. In every acceptable prayer the whole Trinity is concerned. J. ANGELL JAMES

July 21

Let me prove, I pray thee, but this once with the fleece (Judg. 6:39).

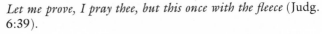

There are degrees to faith. At one stage of Christian experience we cannot believe unless we have some sign or some great manifestation of feeling. We feel our fleece, like Gideon, and if it is wet we are willing to trust God. This may be true faith, but it is imperfect. It always looks for feeling or some token beside the Word of God. It marks quite an advance in faith when we trust God without feelings. It is blessed to believe without having any emotion.

There is a third stage of faith which even transcends that of Gideon and his fleece. The first phase of faith believes when there are favorable emotions, the second believes when there is the absence of feeling, but this third form of faith believes God and His Word when circumstances, emotions, appearances, people, and human reason all urge to the contrary. Paul exercised this faith in Acts 27:20, 25, "And when neither sun nor stars in many days appeared, and no small tempest lay on us, all hope that we should be saved was then taken away." Notwithstanding all this Paul said, "Wherefore, sirs, be of good cheer; *for I believe God,* that it shall be even as it was told me."

May God give us faith to fully trust His Word though everything else witness the other way. C. H. P.

> *When is the time to trust?*
> *Is it when all is calm,*
> *When waves the victor's palm,*
> *And life is one glad psalm*
> *Of joy and praise?*
> *Nay! but the time to trust*
> *Is when the waves beat high,*
> *When storm clouds fill the sky,*
> *And prayer is one long cry,*
> *O help and save!*
>
> *When is the time to trust?*
> *Is it when friends are true?*
> *Is it when comforts woo,*
> *And in all we say and do*

We meet but praise?
Nay! but the time to trust
Is when we stand alone,
And summer birds have flown,
And every prop is gone,
All else but God.

What is the time to trust?
Is it some future day,
When you have tried your way,
And learned to trust and pray
By bitter woe?
Nay! but the time to trust
Is in this moment's need,
Poor, broken, bruised reed!
Poor, troubled soul, make speed
To trust thy God.

What is the time to trust?
Is it when hopes beat high,
When sunshine gilds the sky,
And joy and ecstasy
Fill all the heart?
Nay! but the time to trust
Is when our joy is fled,
When sorrow bows the head,
And all is cold and dead,
All else but God.

SELECTED

July 22

And therefore will the Lord wait, that he may be gracious unto you ... blessed are all they that wait for him (Isa. 30:18).

We must not only think of our waiting upon God, but also of what is more wonderful still, of God's waiting upon us. The vision of Him waiting on us will give new impulse and inspiration to our waiting upon Him. It will give us unspeakable confidence that our waiting cannot be in vain. Let us seek even now, at this moment, in the spirit of waiting on God, to find out something of what it means. He has inconceivably glorious purposes concerning every one of His children. And you ask, "How is it, if He waits to be gracious, that even after I come and wait upon Him, He does not give the help I seek, but waits on longer and longer?"

God is a wise husbandman, "who waiteth for the precious fruit of the earth, and hath long patience for it." He cannot gather the fruit till it is ripe. He knows when we are spiritually ready to receive the blessing to our profit and His glory. Waiting in the sunshine of His love is what will ripen the soul for His blessing. Waiting under the cloud of trial, that breaks in showers of blessings, is as needful. Be assured that if God waits longer than you could wish, it is only to make the blessing doubly precious. God waited four thousand years, till the fullness of time, ere He sent His Son. Our times are in His hands; He will avenge His elect speedily; He will make haste for our help, and not delay one hour too long. ANDREW MURRAY

July 23

Giving thanks always for all things unto God (Eph. 5:20).

No matter what the source of evil, if you are in God and surrounded by Him as by an atmosphere, all evil has to pass through Him before it comes to you. Therefore you can thank God for everything that comes, not for the sin of it, but for what God will bring out of it and through it. May God make our lives thanksgiving and perpetual praise, then He will make everything a blessing.

We once saw a man draw some black dots. We looked and could make nothing of them but an irregular assemblage of black dots. Then he drew a few lines, put in a few rests, then a clef at the beginning, and we saw these black dots were musical notes. On sounding them we were singing,

> *Praise God from whom all blessings flow,*
> *Praise Him all creatures here below.*

There are many black dots and black spots in our lives, and we cannot understand *why* they are there or *why* God permitted them to come. But if we let God come into our lives, and adjust the dots in the proper way, and draw the lines He wants, and separate this from that, and put in the rests at the proper places; out of the black dots and spots in our lives He will make a glorious harmony. Let us not hinder Him in this glorious work! C. H. P.

Would we know that the major chords were sweet,
If there were no minor key?
Would the painter's work be fair to our eyes,
Without shade on land or sea?

Would we know the meaning of happiness,
Would we feel that the day was bright,
If we'd never known what it was to grieve,
Nor gazed on the dark of night?

Many men owe the grandeur of their lives to their tremendous difficulties. C. H. SPURGEON

When the musician presses the black keys on the great organ, the music is as sweet as when he touches the white ones, but to get the capacity of the instrument he must touch them all. SELECTED

July 24

Then believed they his words; they sang his praise. They soon forgot his works; they waited not for his counsel; but lusted exceedingly in the wilderness, and tempted God in the desert. And he gave them their request; but sent leanness into their soul (Ps. 106:12–15).

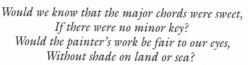

We read of Moses, that "he endured, as seeing him who is invisible." Exactly the opposite was true of the children of Israel in this record. They endured only when the circumstances were favorable; they were largely governed by the things that appealed to their senses, in place of resting in the invisible and eternal God.

In the present day there are those who live intermittent Christian lives because they have become occupied with the outward, and center in circumstances, in place of centering in God. God wants us more and more to see Him in everything, and to call nothing small if it bears us His message.

Here we read of the children of Israel, "*Then* they believed his words." They did not believe till *after* they saw—when they saw Him work, then they believed. They really doubted God when they came to the Red Sea; but when God opened the way and led them across and they *saw* Pharaoh and his host drowned—"then they believed."

They led an up-and-down life because of this kind of faith; it was a faith that depended upon circumstances. This is not the kind of faith God wants us to have.

The world says "seeing is believing," but God wants us to believe in order to see. The psalmist said, "I had fainted, unless I had *believed to see* the goodness of the Lord in the land of the living."

Do you believe God only when the circumstances are favorable, or do you believe no matter what the circumstances may be? C. H. P. 🐦

Faith is to believe what we do not see, and the reward of this faith is to see what we believe. SAINT AUGUSTINE 🐦

July 25

What I do thou knowest not now, but thou shalt know hereafter (John 13:7).

We have only a partial view here of God's dealings, His half-completed, half-developed plan: but all will stand out in fair and graceful proportions in the great finished temple of eternity! Go, in the reign of Israel's greatest king, to the heights of Lebanon. See that noble cedar, the pride of its compeers, an old wrestler with northern blasts! Summer loves to smile upon it, night spangles its feathery foliage with dewdrops, the birds nestle on its branches, the weary pilgrim or wandering shepherd reposes under its shadows from the midday heat or from the furious storm; but all at once it is marked out to fall. The aged denizen of the forest is doomed to succumb to the woodman's stroke!

As we see the ax making its first gash on its gnarled trunk, then the noble limbs stripped of their branches, and at last the "Tree of God," as was its distinctive epithet, coming with a crash to the ground, we exclaim against the wanton destruction, the demolition of this proud pillar in the temple of nature. We are tempted to cry with the prophet, as if inviting the sympathy of every lowlier stem—invoking inanimate things to resent the affront— *"Howl, fir tree; for the cedar has fallen!"*

But wait a little. Follow that gigantic trunk as the workmen of Hiram launch it down the mountainside; thence conveyed in rafts along the blue waters of the Mediterranean; and last of all, behold it set a glorious polished beam in the temple of God. As you see its destination, placed in the very Holy of Holies, in the diadem of the Great King—say, can you grudge that "the crown of Lebanon" was despoiled, in order that this jewel might have so noble a setting?

That cedar stood as a stately prop in nature's sanctuary, but "the glory of the latter house was greater than the glory of the former!"

How many of our souls are like these cedars of old! God's axes of trial have stripped and bared them. We see no reason for dealings so dark and mysterious, but He has a noble end and object in view; to set them as everlasting pillars and rafters in His heavenly Zion; to make them a "crown of glory in the hand of the Lord, and a royal diadem in the hand of our God." MACDUFF ☞

I do not ask my cross to understand,
My way to see—
Better in darkness just to feel Thy hand,
And follow Thee.

July 26

For we through the Spirit by faith wait for the hope of righteous-ness (Gal. 5:5 RV).

There are times when things look very dark to me—so dark that I have to wait even for hope. It is bad enough to wait *in* hope, to see no glimmer of a prospect and yet refuse to despair; to have nothing but night before the casement and yet to keep the casement open for possible stars; to have a vacant place in my heart and yet to allow that place to be filled by no inferior presence—that is the grandest patience in the universe. It is Job in the tempest; it is Abraham on the road to Moriah; it is Moses in the desert of Midian; it is the Son of Man in the Garden of Gethsemane.

There is no patience so hard as that which endures, "as seeing him who is invisible"; it is the waiting for hope.

Thou hast made waiting beautiful; Thou hast made patience divine. Thou hast taught us that the Father's will may be received just because it *is* His will. Thou hast revealed to us that a soul may see nothing but sorrow in the cup and yet may refuse to let it go, convinced that the eye of the Father sees further than its own.

Give me this divine power of Thine, the power of Gethsemane. Give me the power to wait for hope itself, to look out from the casement where there are no stars. Give me the power, when the very joy that was set before me is gone, to stand unconquered amid the night, and say, "To the eye of my Father it is perhaps shining still." I shall reach the climax of strength when I have learned to wait for hope. GEORGE MATHESON ☞

Strive to be one of those—so few—who walk the earth with ever-present consciousness—all mornings, middays, star-times—that the unknown which men call heaven is "close behind the visible scene of things."

July 27

Prove me now (Mal. 3:10).

What is God saying here but this: "My child, I still have windows in heaven. They are yet in service. The bolts slide as easily as of old. The hinges have not grown rusty. I would rather fling them open, and pour forth, than keep them shut, and hold back. I opened them for Moses, and the sea parted. I opened them for Joshua, and Jordan rolled back. I opened them for Gideon, and hosts fled. I will open them for you—*if you will only let Me*. On this side of the windows, heaven is the same rich storehouse as of old. The fountains and streams still overflow. The treasure rooms are still bursting with gifts. The lack is not on MY side. It is on yours. I am waiting. *Prove Me* now. Fulfill the conditions, on *your* part. Bring in the tithes. *Give Me a chance.* SELECTED

I can never forget my mother's very brief paraphrase of Malachi 3:10. The verse begins, "Bring ye the whole tithe in," and it ends up with "I will pour" the blessing *out* till you'll be embarrassed for space. Her paraphrase was this: "Give all He asks; take all He promises." S. D. GORDON

The ability of God is beyond our prayers, beyond our largest prayers! I have been thinking of some of the petitions that have entered into my supplication innumerable times. What have I asked for? I have asked for a cupful, and the ocean remains! I have asked for a sunbeam, and the sun abides! My best asking falls immeasurably short of my Father's giving: it is beyond what we can ask. J. H. JOWETT

All the rivers of Thy grace I claim,
Over every promise write my name. (Eph. 1:8–19)

July 28

The Lord hath his way in the whirlwind and in the storm (Nah. 1:3).

I recollect, when a lad, and while attending a classical institute in the vicinity of Mount Pleasant, sitting on an elevation of that mountain, and watching a storm as it came up the valley. The heavens were filled with blackness, and the earth was shaken by the voice of thunder. It seemed as

though that fair landscape was utterly changed, and its beauty gone, never to return.

But the storm swept on, and passed out of the valley; and if I had sat in the same place on the following day, and said, "Where is that terrible storm, with all its terrible blackness?" the grass would have said, "Part of it is in me," and the daisy would have said, "Part of it is in me," and the fruits and flowers and everything that grows out of the ground would have said, "Part of the storm is incandescent in me."

Have you asked to be made like your Lord? Have you longed for the fruit of the Spirit, and have you prayed for sweetness and gentleness and love? Then fear not the stormy tempest that is at this moment sweeping through your life. A blessing is in the storm, and there will be the rich fruitage in the "afterward." HENRY WARD BEECHER

> *The flowers live by the tears that fall*
> *From the sad face of the skies;*
> *And life would have no joys at all,*
> *Were there no watery eyes.*
> *Love thou thy sorrow: grief shall bring*
> *Its own excuse in after years;*
> *The rainbow!—see how fair a thing*
> *God hath built up from tears.*
>
> HENRY S. SUTTON

July 29

Hast thou seen the treasures of the hail, which I have reserved against the time of trouble? (Job 38:22–23).

Our trials are great opportunities. Too often we look on them as great obstacles. It would be a haven of rest and an inspiration of unspeakable power if each of us would henceforth recognize every difficult situation as one of God's chosen ways of proving to us His love and look around for the signals of His glorious manifestations; then, indeed, would every cloud become a rainbow, and every mountain a path of ascension and a scene of transfiguration.

If we will look back upon the past, many of us will find that the very time our heavenly Father has chosen to do the kindest things for us, and given us the richest blessings, has been the time we were strained and shut in on every side. God's jewels are often sent us in rough packages and by dark liveried servants, but within we find the very treasures of the King's palace and the Bridegroom's love. A. B. Simpson 🐦

Trust Him in the dark, honor Him with unwavering confidence even in the midst of mysterious dispensations, and the recompense of such faith will be like the molting of the eagle's plumes, which was said to give them a new lease of youth and strength. J. R. Macduff 🐦

If we could see beyond today
As God can see;
If all the clouds should roll away,
The shadows flee;
O'er present griefs we would not fret.
Each sorrow we would soon forget,
For many joys are waiting yet
For you and me.

If we could know beyond today
As God doth know,
Why dearest treasures pass away
And tears must flow;
And why the darkness leads to light,
Why dreary paths will soon grow bright;
Some day life's wrongs will be made right,
Faith tells us so.

"If we could see, if we could know,"
We often say,
But God in love a veil doth throw
Across our way;
We cannot see what lies before,
And so we cling to Him the more,
He leads us till this life is o'er
Trust and obey.

July 30

A cup of cold water only (Matt. 10:42).

⤫

What am I to do? I expect to pass through this world but once. Any good work, therefore, any kindness, or any service I can render to any soul of man or animal, let me do it now. Let me not neglect or defer it, for I shall not pass this way again. An Old Quaker saying 🐦

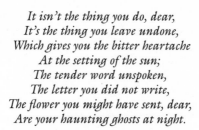

It isn't the thing you do, dear,
It's the thing you leave undone,
Which gives you the bitter heartache
At the setting of the sun;
The tender word unspoken,
The letter you did not write,
The flower you might have sent, dear,
Are your haunting ghosts at night.

The stone you might have lifted
Out of your brother's way,
The bit of heartsome counsel
You were hurried too much to say;
The loving touch of the hand, dear,
The gentle and winsome tone,
That you had no time or thought for,
With troubles enough of your own.

These little acts of kindness,
So easily out of mind,
These chances to be angels,
Which even mortals find—
They come in night and silence,
Each chill reproachful wraith,
When hope is faint and flagging,
And a blight has dropped on faith.

For life is all too short, dear.
And sorrow is all too great,
To suffer our slow compassion
That tarries until too late.
And it's not the thing you do, dear,
It's the thing you leave undone,
Which gives you the bitter heartache,
At the setting of the sun.

ADELAIDE PROCTOR

Give what you have; to someone it may be better than you dare to
think. LONGFELLOW

July 31

He . . . guided them by the skillfulness of his hands (Ps. 78:72).

When you are doubtful as to your course, submit your judgment absolutely to the Spirit of God, and ask Him to shut against you every door but the right one.... Meanwhile keep on as you are, and consider the absence of indication to be the indication of God's will that you are on His track.... As you go down the long corridor, you will find that He has preceded you, and locked many doors which you would fain have entered; but be sure that beyond these there is one which He has left unlocked. Open it and enter, and you will find yourself face-to-face with a bend of the river of opportunity, broader and deeper than anything you had dared to imagine in your sunniest dreams. Launch forth upon it; it conducts to the open sea.

God guides us, often by circumstances. At one moment the way may seem utterly blocked; and then shortly afterward some trivial incident occurs, which might not seem much to others, but which to the keen eye of faith speaks volumes. Sometimes these things are repeated in various ways, in answer to prayer. They are not haphazard results of chance, but the opening up of circumstances in the direction in which we would walk. *And they begin to multiply as we advance toward our goal,* just as the lights do as we near a populous town, when darting through the land by night express. F. B. MEYER

If you go to Him to be guided, He will guide you; but He will not comfort your distrust or half-trust of Him by showing you the chart of all His purposes concerning you. He will show you only into a way where, if you go cheerfully and trustfully forward, He will show you on still farther. HORACE BUSHNELL

As moves my fragile bark across the storm-swept sea,
Great waves beat o'er her side, as north wind blows;
Deep in the darkness hid lie threat'ning rocks and shoals;
But all of these, and more, my Pilot knows.

Sometimes when dark the night, and every light gone out,
I wonder to what port my frail ship goes;
Still though the night be long, and restless all my hours,
My distant goal, I'm sure, my Pilot knows.

THOMAS CURTIS CLARK

August 1

Surrender your very selves to God as living men who have risen from the dead (Rom. 6:13 WEYMOUTH).

I went one night to hear an address on consecration. No special message came to me from it, but as the speaker kneeled to pray, he dropped this sentence: "O Lord, Thou knowest we can trust the Man that died for us." And that was my message. I rose and walked down the street to the train; and as I walked, I pondered deeply all that consecration might mean to my life and—I was afraid. And then, above the noise and clatter of the street traffic came to me the message: "You can trust the Man that died for you."

I got into the train to ride homeward; and as I rode, I thought of the changes, the sacrifices, the disappointments which consecration might mean to me and—I was afraid.

I reached home and sought my room, and there upon my knees I saw my past life. I had been a Christian, an officer in the church, a Sunday school superintendent, but had never definitely yielded my life to God.

Yet as I thought of the darling plans which might be baffled, of the cherished hopes to be surrendered, and the chosen profession which I might have to abandon—*I was afraid.*

I did not see the better things God had for me, so my soul was shrinking back; and then for the last time, with a swift rush of convicting power, came to my innermost heart that searching message:

"My child, you can trust the Man that died for you. If you cannot trust Him, whom can you trust?"

That settled it for me, for in a flash I saw the Man who so loved me as to die for me could be absolutely trusted with all the concerns of the life He had saved.

Friend, you can trust the Man that died for you. You can trust Him to baffle no plan which is not best to be foiled, and to carry out every one which is for God's glory and your highest good. You can trust Him to lead you in the path which is the very best in this world for you. J. H. McC. ☞

> *Just as I am, thy love unknown,*
> *Has broken every barrier down,*
> *Now to be Thine, yea, Thine ALONE,*
> *O Lamb of God, I come!*

> *Life is not salvage to be saved out of the world,*
> *but an investment to be used in the world.*

August 2

I will make all my mountains a way (Isa. 49:11).

God will make obstacles serve His purpose. We all have mountains in our lives. There are people and things that threaten to bar our progress in the divine life. Those heavy claims, that uncongenial occupation, that thorn in the flesh, that daily cross—we think that if only these were removed we might live purer, tenderer, holier lives; and often we pray for their removal.

"Oh, fools, and slow of heart!" These are the very conditions of achievement; they have been put into our lives as the means to the very graces and virtues for which we have been praying so long. Thou hast prayed for patience through long years, but there is something that tries thee beyond endurance; thou hast fled from it, evaded it, accounted it an unsurmountable obstacle to the desired attainment, and supposed that its removal would secure thy immediate deliverance and victory.

Not so! Thou wouldest gain only the cessation of temptations to impatience. But this would not be patience. Patience can be acquired only through just such trials as now seem unbearable.

Go back; submit thyself. Claim to be a partaker in the patience of Jesus. Meet thy trials in Him. There is nothing in life which harasses and annoys that may not become subservient to the highest ends. They are *His* mountains. He puts them there. We know that God will not fail to keep His promise. "God understandeth the way thereof and knoweth the place thereof. For he looketh to the ends of the earth, and seeth under the whole heaven"; and when we come to the foot of the mountains, we shall find the way. From *Christ in Isaiah*, by Meyer

The meaning of trial is not only to test worthiness, but to increase it; as the oak is not only tested by the storms, but toughened by them.

August 3

Quit you like men, be strong (1 Cor. 16:13).

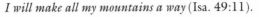

Do not pray for easy lives! Pray to be stronger men. Do not pray for tasks equal to your powers. Pray for powers equal to your tasks. Then the doing of your work shall be no miracle, but you shall be a miracle. Phillips Brooks

We must remember that it is not in any easy or self-indulgent life that Christ will lead us to greatness. The easy life leads not upward, but downward. Heaven always is above us, and we must ever be looking up toward it. There are some people who always avoid things that are costly, that require self-denial, or self-restraint and sacrifice, but toil and hardship show us the only way to nobleness. Greatness comes not by having a mossy path made for you through the meadow, but by being sent to hew out a roadway by your own hands. Are you going to reach the mountain splendors? SELECTED 🦜

Be strong!
We are not here to play, to dream, to drift;
We have hard work to do, and loads to lift.
Shun not the struggle; face it.
'Tis God's gift.

Be strong!
Say not the days are evil—Who's to blame?
And fold the hands and acquiesce—O shame!
Stand up, speak out, and bravely,
In God's name.

Be strong!
It matters not how deep entrenched the wrong,
How hard the battle goes, the day how long,
Faint not, fight on!
Tomorrow comes the song.

MALTBIE D. BABCOCK 🦜

August 4

And Jesus lifted up his eyes, and said, Father, I thank thee that thou hast heard me (John 11:41).

⟿

This is a very strange and unusual order. Lazarus is still in the grave, and the thanksgiving *precedes* the miracle of resurrection. I thought that the thanksgiving would have risen when the great deed had been wrought, and Lazarus was restored to life again. But Jesus gives thanks for what He is about to receive. The gratitude breaks forth *before* the bounty has arrived, in the assurance that it is certainly on the way. The song of victory is sung *before* the battle has been fought. It is the sower who is singing the song of the harvest home. It is thanksgiving before the miracle!

Who thinks of announcing a victory-psalm when the crusaders are just starting out for the field? Where can we hear the grateful song for the answer which has not yet been received? And after all, there is nothing strange or forced, or unreasonable to the Master's order. *Praise* is really the most vital preparatory ministry to the working of the miracles. Miracles are wrought by spiritual power. Spiritual power is always proportioned to our *faith*. Dr. Jowett

Praise Changes Things

Nothing so pleases God in connection with our prayer and our praise, and nothing so blesses the man who prays as the praise which he offers. I got a great blessing once in China in this connection. I had received bad and sad news from home, and deep shadows had covered my soul. I prayed, but the darkness did not vanish. I summoned myself to endure, but the darkness only deepened. Just then I went to an inland station and saw on the wall of the mission home these words: "Try Thanksgiving." I did, and in a moment every shadow was gone, not to return. Yes, the psalmist was right, "It is a good thing to give thanks unto the Lord." Rev. Henry W. Frost

August 5

Is (2 Cor. 12:9).

It had pleased God to remove my youngest child under circumstances of peculiar trial and pain; and as I had just laid my little one's body in the churchyard, on return home, I felt it my duty to preach to my people on the meaning of trial.

Finding that this text was in the lesson for the following Sabbath, I chose it as my Master's message to them and myself; but on trying to prepare the notes, I found that in honesty I could not say that the words were true; and therefore I knelt down and asked God to let His grace be sufficient for me. While I was thus pleading, I opened my eyes and saw a framed illuminated text, which my mother had given me only a few days before, and which I had told my servant to place upon the wall during my absence at the holiday resort where my little one was taken away from us.

I did not notice the words on returning to my house; but as I looked up and wiped my eyes, the words met my gaze, "My grace *is* sufficient for thee."

The "is" was picked out in bright green while the "My" and the "thee" were painted in another color.

In one moment the message came straight to my soul as a rebuke for offering such a prayer as, "Lord, let Thy grace be sufficient for me"; for the answer was almost as an audible voice, "How dare you ask that which is?" God cannot make it any more sufficient than He has made it; get up and believe it, and you will find it true, because the Lord says it in the simplest way: "My grace *is* (not shall be or may be) sufficient for thee."

"My," "is," and "thee" were from that moment, I hope, indelibly fixed upon my heart; and I (thank God) have been trying to live in the reality of the message from that day forward to the present time.

The lesson that came to me, and which I seek to convey to others, is, *Never turn God's facts into hopes, or prayers, but simply use them as realities, and you will find them powerful as you believe them.* PREBENDARY H. W. WEBB PEPLOE

> *He giveth more grace when the burdens grow greater,*
> *He sendeth more strength when the labors increase;*
> *To added affliction He addeth His mercies,*
> *To multiplied trials His multiplied peace.*
>
> *When we have exhausted our store of endurance,*
> *When our strength has failed ere the day is half done,*
> *When we reach the end of our hoarded resources*
> *Our Father's full giving is only begun.*
>
> *His love has no limit, His grace has no measure,*
> *His power no boundary known unto men;*
> *For out of His infinite riches in Jesus*
> *He giveth and giveth and giveth again.*
>   ANNIE JOHNSON FLINT

August 6

Awake, O north wind; and come, thou south, blow upon my garden, that the spices thereof may flow out! (Song of Sol. 4:16).

Look at the meaning of this prayer a moment. Its root is found in the fact that, as delicious odors may lie *latent* in a spice tree, so *graces* may lie unexercised and undeveloped in a Christian's heart. There is many a plant of profession; but from the ground there breathes forth no fragrance of holy affections or of godly deeds. The same winds blow on the thistle bush and on the spice tree, but it is only *one* of them which gives out rich odors.

Sometimes God sends severe blasts of trial upon His children to develop their graces. Just as torches burn most brightly when swung to and fro; just as the juniper plant smells sweetest when flung into the flames; so the richest qualities of a Christian often come out under the north wind of suffering and adversity. Bruised hearts often emit the fragrance that God loveth to smell.

> *I had a tiny box, a precious box*
> *Of human love—my spikenard of great price;*
> *I kept it close within my heart of hearts*
> *And scarce would lift the lid lest it should waste*
> *Its perfume on the air. One day a strange*
> *Deep sorrow came with crushing weight, and fell*
> *Upon my costly treasure, sweet and rare*
> *And broke the box to atoms. All my heart*
> *Rose in dismay and sorrow at this waste,*
> *But as I mourned, behold a miracle*
> *Of grace Divine. My human love was changed*
> *To Heaven's own, and poured in healing streams*
> *On other broken hearts, while soft and clear*
> *A voice above me whispered, "Child of Mine,*
> *With comfort wherewith thou art comforted,*
> *From this time forth, go comfort others,*
> *And thou shalt know blest fellowship with Me,*
> *Whose broken heart of love hath healed the world."*

August 7

And when they had prayed, the place was shaken where they were assembled together, and they were all filled with the Holy Ghost and they spake the word of God with boldness. And with great power gave the apostles witness of the resurrection (Acts 4:31, 33).

Christmas Evans tells us in his diary that one Sunday afternoon he was traveling a very lonely road to attend an appointment, and he was convicted of a cold heart. He says, "I tethered my horse and went to a sequestered spot, where I walked to and fro in an agony as I reviewed my life. I waited three hours before God, broken with sorrow, until there broke over me a sweet sense of His forgiving love. I received from God a new baptism of the Holy Ghost. As the sun was westering, I went back to the road, found my horse, mounted it and went to my appointment. On the following day I preached with such new power to a vast concourse of people gathered on the hillside, that a revival broke out that day and spread through all Wales."

The greatest question that can be asked of the "twice born" ones is, *"Have ye received the Holy Ghost since ye believed?"*

This was the password into the early church.

O the Spirit filled life; is it thine, is it thine?
Is thy soul wholly filled with the Spirit Divine?
O thou child of the King, has He fallen on thee?
Does He reign in thy soul, so that all men may see
The dear Savior's blest image reflected in thee?

Has He swept through thy soul like the waves of the sea?
Does the Spirit of God daily rest upon thee?
Does He sweeten thy life, does He keep thee from care?
Does He guide thee and bless thee in answer to prayer?
Is it joy to be led of the Lord anywhere?

Is He near thee each hour, does He stand at thy side?
Does He gird thee with strength, has He come to abide?
Does He give thee to know that all things may be done
Through the grace and the power of the Crucified One?
Does He witness to thee of the glorified Son?

Has He purged thee of dross with the fire from above?
Is He first in thy thoughts, has He all of thy love?
Is His service thy choice, and is sacrifice sweet?
Is the doing His will both thy drink and thy meat?
Dost thou run at His bidding with glad eager feet?

Has He freed thee from self and from all of thy greed?
Dost thou hasten to succor thy brother in need?
As a soldier of Christ dost thou hardness endure?
Is thy hope in the Lord everlasting and sure?
Hast thou patience and meekness, art tender and pure?

O the Spirit-filled life may be thine, may be thine,
In thy soul evermore the Shekinah may shine;
It is thine to live with the tempests all stilled,
It is thine with the blessed Holy Ghost to be filled;
It is thine, even thine, for thy Lord has so willed.

August 8

Thou art my king, O God: Command deliverance [victories, in margin] for Jacob (Ps. 44:4 RV).

There is no foe to your growth in grace, no enemy in your Christian work, which was not included in your Savior's conquests.

You need not be afraid of them. When you touch them, they will flee before you. God has promised to deliver them up before you. Only be strong and very courageous! Fear not, nor be dismayed! The Lord is with you, O mighty men of valor—mighty because you are one with the Mightiest. Claim victory!

Whenever your enemies close in upon you, *claim victory!* Whenever heart and flesh fail, look up and claim VICTORY!

Be sure that you have a share in that triumph which Jesus won, not for Himself alone, but for us all; remember that you were in Him when He won it, and *claim victory!*

Reckon that it is yours, and gather spoil. Neither the Anakim nor fenced cities need daunt or abash you. You are one of the conquering legion. *Claim your share in the Savior's victory.* FROM JOSHUA, BY MEYER

We are children of the King. In which way do we most honor our divine Sovereign, by failing to claim our rights and even doubting whether they belong to us, or by asserting our privilege as children of the Royal Family and demanding the rights which belong to our heirship?

August 9

Blessed is the man whose strength is in thee ... who passing through the valley of Baca, make it a well (Ps. 84:5–6).

Comfort does not come to the lighthearted and merry. We must go down into "depths" if we would experience this most precious of God's gifts—comfort, and thus be prepared to be co-workers together with Him.

When night—needful night—gathers over the garden of our souls, when the leaves close up, and the flowers no longer hold any sunlight within their folded petals, there shall never be wanting, even in the thickest darkness, drops of heavenly dew—dew which falls only when the sun has gone.

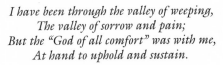

I have been through the valley of weeping,
The valley of sorrow and pain;
But the "God of all comfort" was with me,
At hand to uphold and sustain.

As the earth needs the clouds and sunshine,
Our souls need both sorrow and joy;
So He places us oft in the furnace,
The dross from the gold to destroy.

When he leads thro' some valley of trouble,
His omnipotent hand we trace;
For the trials and sorrows He sends us,
Are part of His lessons in grace.

Oft we shrink from the purging and pruning,
Forgetting the Husbandman knows
That the deeper the cutting and paring,
The richer the cluster that grows.

Well He knows that affliction is needed;
He has a wise purpose in view,
And in the dark valley He whispers,
"Hereafter Thou'lt know what I do."

As we travel thro' life's shadow'd valley,
Fresh springs of His love ever rise;
And we learn that our sorrows and losses,
Are blessings just sent in disguise.

So we'll follow wherever He leadeth,
Let the path be dreary or bright;
For we've proved that our God can give comfort;
Our God can give songs in the night.

August 10

When he had heard therefore that he was sick, he abode two days
still in the same place where he was (John 11:6).

In the forefront of this marvelous chapter stands the affirmation, "Jesus loved Martha, and her sister, and Lazarus," as if to teach us that at the very heart and foundation of all God's dealings with us, however dark and mysterious they may be, we must dare to believe in and assert the infinite, unmerited, and unchanging love of God. Love permits pain. The sisters never doubted that He would speed at all hazards and stay their brother from death, but, "When he had heard *therefore* that he was sick, he abode two days still in the same place where he was."

What a startling *"therefore"*! He abstained from going, not because He did not love them, but because He did love them. His love alone kept Him back from hasting at once to the dear and stricken home. Anything less than infinite love must have rushed instantly to the relief of those loved and troubled hearts, to stay their grief and to have the luxury of wiping and stanching their tears and causing sorrow and sighing to flee away. Divine love could alone hold back the impetuosity of the Savior's tender-heartedness until the angel of pain had done her work.

Who can estimate how much we owe to suffering and pain? But for them we should have little scope for many of the chief virtues of the Christian life. Where was faith, without trial to test it; or patience, with nothing to bear; or experience, without tribulation to develop it? SELECTED

Loved! then the way will not be drear;
For One we know is ever near,
Proving it to our hearts so clear
That we are loved.

Loved when our sky is clouded o'er,
And days of sorrow press us sore;
Still we will trust Him evermore,
For we are loved.

Time, that affects all things below,
Can never change the love He'll show;
The heart of Christ with love will flow,
And we are loved.

August 11

Although the fig tree shall not blossom, neither shall fruit be in the vines; the labor of the olive shall fail, and the fields shall yield no meat; the flock shall be cut off from the fold, and there shall be no herd in the stalls: yet I will rejoice in the Lord, I will joy in the God of my salvation (Hab. 3:17–18).

Observe, I entreat you, how calamitous a circumstance is here supposed, and how heroic a faith is expressed. It is really as if he said, "Though I should be reduced to so great extremity as not to know where to find my necessary food, though I should look around about me on an empty house and a desolate field, and see the marks of the divine scourge where I had once seen the fruits of God's bounty, *yet I will rejoice in the Lord.*"

Methinks these words are worthy of being *written as with a diamond on a rock* forever. Oh, that by divine grace they might be deeply engraven on each of our hearts! Concise as the form of speaking in the text is, it evidently implies or expresses the following particulars: That in the day of his distress he would fly to God; that he would maintain a holy composure of spirit under this dark dispensation, nay, that in the midst of all he would indulge in a sacred joy in God, and a cheerful expectation from Him. Heroic confidence! Illustrious faith! Unconquerable love! DODDRIDGE 🖎

> *Last night I heard a robin singing in the rain,*
> *And the raindrops' patter made a sweet refrain,*
> *Making all the sweeter the music of the strain.*
>
> *So, I thought, when trouble comes, as trouble will,*
> *Why should I stop singing? Just beyond the hill*
> *It may be that sunshine floods the green world still.*
>
> *He who faces the trouble with a heart of cheer*
> *Makes the burden lighter. If there falls a tear,*
> *Sweeter is the cadence in the song we hear.*
>
> *I have learned your lesson, bird with dappled wing,*
> *Listening to your music with its lilt of spring—*
> *When the storm-cloud darkens, then's the TIME to sing.*
>
> EBEN E. REXFORD 🖎

August 12

Whereby are given unto us exceeding great and precious promises (2 Peter 1:4).

When a shipwright builds a vessel, does he build it to keep it upon the stocks? Nay, he builds it for the sea and the storm. When he was making it, he thought of tempests and hurricanes; if he did not, he was a poor shipbuilder. When God made thee a believer, He meant to try thee; and when He gave thee promises, and bade thee trust them, He gave such promises as are suitable for times of tempest and tossing. Dost thou think that God makes shams like some that have made belts for swimming, which were good to exhibit in a shop, but of no use in the sea?

We have all heard of swords which were useless in war; and even of shoes which were made to sell, but were never meant to walk in. God's shoes are of iron and brass, and you can walk to heaven in them without their ever wearing out; and His lifebelts, you may swim a thousand Atlantics upon them, and there will be no fear of your sinking. His Word of promise is meant to be tried and proved.

There is nothing Christ dislikes more than for His people to make a show-thing of Him, and not to use Him. He loves to be employed by us. Covenant blessings are not meant to be looked at only, but to be appropriated. Even our Lord Jesus is given to us for our present use. Thou dost not make use of Christ as thou oughtest to do.

O man, I beseech you do not treat God's promises as if they were curiosities for a museum; but use them as everyday sources of comfort. Trust the Lord whenever your time of need comes on. C. H. SPURGEON

Go to the deeps of God's promise,
And claim whatsoever ye will;
The blessing of God will not fail thee,
His Word He will surely fulfill.

How can God say no to something He has promised?

August 13

If the clouds be full of rain, they empty themselves upon the earth
(Eccles. 11:3).

Why, then, do we dread the clouds which now darken our sky? True, for a while they hide the sun, but the sun is not quenched; he will be out again before long. Meanwhile those black clouds are filled with rain; and the blacker they are, the more likely they will yield plentiful showers.

How can we have rain without clouds? Our troubles have always brought us blessings, and they always will. They are the dark chariots of bright grace. These clouds will empty themselves before long, and every tender herb will be gladder for the shower. Our God may drench us with grief, but He will refresh us with mercy. Our Lord's love letters often come to us in black-edged envelopes. His wagons rumble, but they are loaded with benefits. His rod blossoms with sweet flowers and nourishing fruits. Let us not worry about the clouds, but sing because May flowers are brought to us through the April clouds and showers.

O Lord, the clouds are the dust of Thy feet! How near Thou art in the cloudy and dark day! Love beholds Thee, and is glad. Faith sees the clouds emptying themselves and making the little hills rejoice on every side. C. H. SPURGEON

> *What seems so dark to thy dim sight*
> *May be a shadow, seen aright*
> *Making some brightness doubly bright.*
>
> *The flash that struck thy tree—no more*
> *To shelter thee—lets heaven's blue floor*
> *Shine where it never shone before.*
>
> *The cry wrung from thy spirit's pain*
> *May echo on some far-off plain,*
> *And guide a wanderer home again.*
>
> *The blue of heaven is larger than the clouds.*

August 14

Thou couldst have no power at all against me, except it were given thee from above (John 19:11).

Nothing that is not God's will can come into the life of one who trusts and obeys God. This fact is enough to make our life one of ceaseless thanksgiving and joy. For "God's will is the one hopeful, glad, and glorious thing in the world"; and it is working in the omnipotence for us all the time, with nothing to prevent it *if we* are surrendered and believing.

One who was passing through deep waters of affliction wrote to a friend: "Is it not a glorious thing to know that, no difference how unjust a thing may be, or how absolutely it may seem to be from Satan, *by the time it reaches us it is God's will for us,* and will work for good to us? For *all things* work together for good to us who love God. And even of the betrayal, Christ said, *"The cup which my Father gave me, shall I not drink it?"* We live charmed lives if we are living in the center of God's will. All the attacks that Satan, through others' sin, can hurl against us are not only powerless to harm us, but are turned into blessings on the way. H. W. S.

In the center of the circle
Of the Will of God I stand:
There can come no second causes,
All must come from His dear hand.
All is well! for 'tis my Father
Who my life hath planned.

Shall I pass through waves of sorrow?
Then I know it will be best;
Though I cannot tell the reason,
I can trust, and so am blest.
God is Love, and God is faithful.
So in perfect Peace I rest.

With the shade and with the sunshine,
With the joy and with the pain,
Lord, I trust Thee! both are needed,
Each Thy wayward child to train,
Earthly loss, did we but know it,
Often means our heavenly gain.

I. G. W.

August 15

We must through much tribulation enter into the kingdom of God (Acts 14:22).

The best things of life come out of wounding. Wheat is crushed before it becomes bread. Incense must be cast upon the fire before its odors are set free. The ground must be broken with the sharp plough before it is ready to receive the seed. It is the broken heart that pleases God. The sweetest joys in life are the fruits of sorrow. Human nature seems to need suffering to fit it for being a blessing to the world.

Beside my cottage door it grows,
The loveliest, daintiest flower that blows,
A sweetbriar rose.

At dewy morn or twilight's close,
The rarest perfume from it flows,
This strange wild rose.

But when the rain-drops on it beat,
Ah, then, its odors grow more sweet,
About my feet.

Ofttimes with loving tenderness,
Its soft green leaves I gently press,
In sweet caress.

A still more wondrous fragrance flows
The more my fingers close
And crush the rose.

Dear Lord, oh, let my life be so
Its perfume when tempests blow,
The sweeter flow.

And should it be Thy blessed will,
With crushing grief my soul to fill,
Press harder still.

And while its dying fragrance flows
I'll whisper low, "He loves and knows
His crushed briar rose."

If you aspire to be a son of consolation; if you would partake of the priestly gift of sympathy; if you would pour something beyond commonplace consolation into a tempted heart; if you would pass through the intercourse of daily life with the delicate tact that never inflicts pain; you must be content to pay the price of a costly education—like Him, you must suffer. F. W. ROBERTSON

August 16

In waiting, I waited, for the Lord (Ps. 40:1, margin).

Waiting is much more difficult than walking. Waiting requires patience, and patience is a rare virtue. It is fine to know that God builds hedges around His people—when the hedge is looked at from the viewpoint of protection. But when the hedge is kept around one until it grows so high that he cannot see over the top, and wonders whether he is ever to get out of the little sphere of influence and service in which he is pent up, it is hard for him sometimes to understand why he may not have a larger environment—hard for him to "brighten the corner" where he is.

But God has a purpose in all HIS holdups. "The steps of a good man are ordered by the Lord," reads Psalm 37:23.

On the margin of his Bible at this verse George Mueller had a notation, "And the *stops* also." It is a sad mistake for men to break through God's hedges. It is a vital principle of guidance for a Christian never to move out of the place in which he is sure God has placed him, until the Pillar of Cloud moves. From Sunday School Times

When we learn to wait for our Lord's lead in everything, we shall know the strength that finds *its climax in an even, steady walk.* Many of us are lacking in the strength we so covet. But God gives full power for every task He appoints. Waiting, holding oneself true to His lead—this is the secret of strength. And anything that falls out of the line of obedience is a waste of time and strength. Watch for His leading. S. D. Gordon

Must life be a failure for one compelled to stand still in enforced inaction and see the great throbbing tides of life go by? No; victory is then to be gotten by standing still, by quiet waiting. It is a thousand times harder to do this than it was in the active days to rush on in the columns of stirring life. It requires a grander heroism to stand and wait and not lose heart and not lose hope, to submit to the will of God, to give up work and honors to others, to be quiet, confident and rejoicing, while the happy, busy multitude go on and away. It is the grandest life "having done all, to stand." J. R. Miller

August 17

I believe God, that it shall be even as it was told me (Acts 27:25).

I went to America some years ago with the captain of a steamer, who was a very devoted Christian. When off the coast of Newfoundland he said to me, "The last time I crossed here, five weeks ago, something happened which revolutionized the whole of my Christian life. We had George Mueller of Bristol on board. I had been on the bridge twenty-four hours and never left it. George Mueller came to me, and said, "Captain, I have come to tell you that I must be in Quebec Saturday afternoon." "It is impossible," I said. "Very well, if your ship cannot take me, God will find some other way. I have never broken an engagement for fifty-seven years. Let us go down into the chartroom and pray."

I looked at that man of God, and thought to myself, what lunatic asylum can that man have come from? I never heard of such a thing as this. "Mr. Mueller," I said, "do you know how dense this fog is?" "No," he replied, *"my eye is not on the density of the fog, but on the living God, who controls every circumstance of my life."*

He knelt down and prayed one of the most simple prayers, and when he had finished I was going to pray: but he put his hand on my shoulder, and told me *not* to pray. "First, you do not believe He will answer; and second I BELIEVE HE HAS, and there is no need whatever for you to pray about it."

I looked at him, and he said, "Captain, I have known my Lord for fifty-seven years, and there has never been a single day that I have failed to get audience with the King. Get up, Captain and open the door, and you will find the fog gone." I got up, and the fog was indeed gone. On Saturday afternoon George Mueller was in Quebec for his engagement. SELECTED

If our love were but more simple,
We should take Him at His word;
And our lives would be all sunshine,
In the sweetness of our Lord.

August 18

Alone (Deut. 32:12).

The hill was steep, but cheered along the way
By converse sweet, I mounted on the thought
That so it might be till the height was reached;
But suddenly a narrow winding path
Appeared, and then the Master said, "My child,
Here thou wilt safest walk with Me alone."

I trembled, yet my heart's deep trust replied,
"So be it, Lord." He took my feeble hand
In His, accepting thus my will to yield Him
All, and to find all in Him.
One long, dark moment,
And no friend I saw, save Jesus only.

But oh! so tenderly He led me on
And up, and spoke to me such words of cheer,
Such secret whisperings of His wondrous love,
That soon I told Him all my grief and fear,
And leaned on His strong arm confidingly.

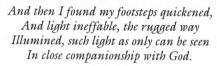

And then I found my footsteps quickened,
And light ineffable, the rugged way
Illumined, such light as only can be seen
In close companionship with God.

A little while, and we shall meet again
The loved and lost; but in the rapturous joy
Of greetings, such as here we cannot know,
And happy song, and heavenly embraces,
And tender recollections rushing back
Of pilgrim life, methinks one memory
More dear and sacred than the rest, shall rise
And we who gather in the golden streets,
Shall oft be stirred to speak with grateful love
Of that dark day when Jesus bade us climb
Some narrow steep, leaning on Him alone.

"There is no high hill but beside some deep valley. There is no birth without a pang." DAN CRAWFORD 🦋

August 19

As sorrowful, yet always rejoicing (2 Cor. 6:10).

Sorrow was beautiful, but her beauty was the beauty of the moonlight shining through the leafy branches of the trees in the wood, and making little pools of silver here and there on the soft green moss below.

When Sorrow sang, her notes were like the low sweet call of the nightingale, and in her eyes was the unexpectant gaze of one who has ceased to look for coming gladness. She could weep in tender sympathy with those who weep, but to rejoice with those who rejoice was unknown to her.

Joy was beautiful, too, but his was the radiant beauty of the summer morning. His eyes still held the glad laughter of childhood, and his hair had the glint of the sunshine's kiss. When Joy sang his voice soared upward as the lark's, and his step was the step of a conqueror who has never known defeat. He could rejoice with all who rejoice, but to weep with those who weep was unknown to him.

"But we can never be united," said Sorrow wistfully.

"No, never." And Joy's eyes shadowed as he spoke. "*My* path lies through the sunlit meadows, the sweetest roses bloom for my gathering, and the blackbirds and thrushes await my coming to pour forth their most joyous lays."

"*My* path," said Sorrow, turning slowly away, "leads through the darkening woods; with moonflowers only shall my hands be filled. Yet the sweetest of all earth songs—the love song of the night—shall be mine; farewell, Joy, farewell."

Even as she spoke they became conscious of a form standing beside them; dimly seen, but of a kingly Presence, and a great and holy awe stole over them as they sank on their knees before Him.

"I see Him as the King of Joy," whispered Sorrow, "for on His head are many crowns, and the nailprints in His hands and feet are the scars of a great victory. Before Him all my sorrow is melting away into deathless love and gladness, and I give myself to Him forever."

"Nay, Sorrow," said Joy softly, "but I see Him as the King of Sorrow, and the crown on His head is a crown of thorns, and the nailprints in His hands and feet are the scars of a great agony. I, too, give myself to Him forever, for sorrow with Him must be sweeter than any joy that I have known."

"Then we are *one* in Him," they cried in gladness, "for none but He could unite Joy and Sorrow."

Hand in hand they passed out into the world to follow Him through storm and sunshine, in the bleakness of winter cold and the warmth of summer gladness, "as sorrowful yet always rejoicing."

> *Should Sorrow lay her hand upon thy shoulder,*
> *And walk with thee in silence on life's way,*
> *While Joy, thy bright companion once, grown colder,*
> *Becomes to thee more distant day by day?*
> *Shrink not from the companionship of Sorrow,*
> *She is the messenger of God to thee;*
> *And thou wilt thank Him in His great tomorrow—*
> *For what thou knowest not now, thou then shalt see;*
> *She is God's angel, clad in weeds of night,*
> *With "whom we walk by faith and not by sight."*

August 20

And Jacob was left alone; and there wrestled a man with him until the breaking of the day (Gen. 32:24).

God is wrestling with Jacob more than Jacob is wrestling with God. It was the Son of Man, the Angel of the Covenant. It was God in human form pressing down and pressing out the old Jacob life; and ere the morning broke, God had prevailed and Jacob fell with his thigh dislocated. But as he fell, he fell into the arms of God, and there he clung and wrestled, too, until the blessing came; and the new life was born and he arose from the earthly to the heavenly, the human to the divine, the natural to the supernatural. And as he went forth that morning he was a weak and broken man, but God was there instead; and the heavenly voice proclaimed, *"Thy name shall be called no more Jacob, but Israel; for as a prince hast thou power with God and with men, and hast prevailed."*

Beloved, this must ever be a typical scene in every transformed life. There comes a crisis hour to each of us, if God has called us to the highest and best, when all resources fail; when we face either ruin or something higher than we ever dreamed; when we must have infinite help from God and yet, ere we can have it, we must let something go; we must surrender completely; we must cease from our own wisdom, strength, and righteousness, and become crucified with Christ and alive in Him. God knows how to lead us up to this crisis, and He knows how to lead us through.

Is He leading you thus? Is this the meaning of your deep trial, or your difficult surroundings, or that impossible situation, or that trying place through which you cannot go without Him, and yet you have not enough of Him to give you the victory?

Oh, turn to Jacob's God! Cast yourself helplessly at His feet. Die to your strength and wisdom in His loving arms and rise, like Jacob, into His strength and all-sufficiency. There is no way out of your hard and narrow place but at the top. You must get deliverance by rising higher and coming into a new experience with God. Oh, may it bring you into all that is meant by the revelation of the Mighty One of Jacob!—*But God.*

> *At Thy feet I fall,*
> *Yield Thee up my ALL,*
> *To SUFFER, LIVE, OR DIE*
> *For my Lord crucified.*

August 21

He brought me forth also into a large place; he delivered me, because he delighted in me (Ps. 18:19).

And what is this "large place"? What can it be but God Himself, that infinite Being in whom all other beings and all other streams of life terminate? God is a large place indeed. And it was through humiliation, through abasement, through nothingness that David was brought into it. MADAME GUYON

I bare you on eagles' wings, and brought you unto myself (Exod. 19:4).

Fearing to launch on "full surrender's" tide,
I asked the Lord where would its waters glide
My little bark, "To troubled seas I dread?"
"Unto Myself," He said.

Weeping beside an open grave I stood,
In bitterness of soul I cried to God:
"Where leads this path of sorrow that I tread?"
"Unto Myself," He said.

Striving for souls, I loved the work too well;
Then disappointments came; I could not tell
The reason, till He said, "I am thine all;
Unto Myself I call."

Watching my heroes—those I love the best—
I saw them fail; they could not stand the test,
Even by this the Lord, through tears not few,
Unto Himself me drew.

Unto Himself! Nor earthly tongue can tell
The bliss I find, since in His heart I dwell;
The things that charmed me once seem all as naught;
Unto Himself I'm brought.

SELECTED

August 22

And the rest, some on boards, some on broken pieces of the ship. And so it came to pass that they escaped all safe to land (Acts 27:44).

The marvelous story of Paul's voyage to Rome, with its trials and triumphs, is a fine pattern of the lights and shades of the way of faith all through the story of human life. The remarkable feature of it is the hard

and narrow places which we find intermingled with God's most extraordinary interpositions and providences.

It is the common idea that the pathway of faith is strewn with flowers, and that when God interposes in the life of His people, He does it on a scale so grand that He lifts us quite out of the plane of difficulties. The actual fact, however, is that the real experience is quite contrary. The story of the Bible is one of alternate trial and triumph in the case of everyone of the cloud of witnesses from Abel down to the latest martyr.

Paul, more than anyone else, was an example of how much a child of God can suffer without being crushed or broken in spirit. On account of his testifying in Damascus, he was hunted down by persecutors and obliged to flee for his life, but we behold no heavenly chariot transporting the holy apostle amid thunderbolts of flame from the reach of his foes, but "through a window in a basket," was he let down over the walls of Damascus and so escaped their hands. In an old clothes basket, like a bundle of laundry, or groceries, the servant of Jesus Christ was dropped from the window and ignominiously fled from the hate of his foes.

Again we find him left for months in the lonely dungeons; we find him telling of his watchings, his fastings, and his desertion by friends, of his brutal and shameful beatings, and here even after God has promised to deliver him, we see him for days left to toss upon a stormy sea, obliged to stand guard over the treacherous seamen, and at last when the deliverance comes, there is no heavenly galley sailing from the skies to take off the noble prisoner; there is no angel form walking along the waters and stilling the raging breakers; there is no supernatural sign of the transcendent miracle that is being wrought; but one is compelled to seize a spar, another a floating plank, another to climb on a fragment of the wreck, another to strike out and swim for his life.

Here is God's pattern for our own lives. Here is a gospel of help for people that have to live in this everyday world with real and ordinary surroundings, and a thousand practical conditions which have to be met in a thoroughly practical way.

God's promises and God's providences do not lift us out of the plane of common sense and commonplace trial, but it is through these very things that faith is perfected, and that God loves to interweave the golden threads of His love along the warp and woof of our everyday experience.
FROM HARD PLACES IN THE WAY OF FAITH

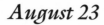

August 23

He went out, not knowing whither he went (Heb. 11:8).

It is faith without sight. When we can *see,* it is not faith, but reasoning. In crossing the Atlantic we observed this very principle of faith. We *saw* no path upon the sea, nor sign of the shore. And yet day by day we were marking our path upon the chart as exactly as if there had followed us a great chalk line upon the sea. And when we came within twenty miles of land, we knew where we were as exactly as if we had seen it all three thousand miles ahead.

How had we measured and marked our course? Day by day our captain had taken his instruments and, looking up to the sky, had fixed his course by the sun. He was sailing by the heavenly, not the earthly lights.

So faith looks up and sails on, by God's great Sun, not *seeing* one shoreline or earthly lighthouse or path upon the way. Often its steps seem to lead into utter uncertainty, and even darkness and disaster; but He opens the way, and often makes such midnight hours the very gates of day. Let us go forth this day, not knowing, but trusting. FROM DAYS OF HEAVEN UPON EARTH

"Too many of us want to see our way through before starting new enterprises. If we could and did, from whence would come the development of our Christian graces? Faith, hope and love cannot be plucked from trees like ripe apples. After the words 'In the beginning' comes the word 'God.' The first step turns the key into God's powerhouse, and it is not only true that God helps those who help themselves, but He also helps those who cannot help themselves. You can depend upon Him every time."

"*Waiting* on God brings us to our journey's end quicker than our feet."

The opportunity is often lost by deliberation.

August 24

I have all, and abound (Phil. 4:18).

In one of my garden books there is a chapter with a very interesting heading, *"Flowers that Grow in the Gloom."* It deals with those patches in a garden which never catch the sunlight. And my guide tells me the sort of flowers which are not afraid of these dingy corners—may rather like them and flourish in them.

And there are similar things in the world of the spirit. They come out when material circumstances become stern and severe. They grow in the gloom. How can we otherwise explain some of the experiences of the Apostle Paul?

Here he is in captivity at Rome. The supreme mission of his life appears to be broken. But it is just in this besetting dinginess that flowers begin to show their faces in bright and fascinating glory. He may have seen them before, growing in the open road, but never as they now appeared in incomparable strength and beauty. Words of promise opened out their treasures as he had never seen them before.

Among those treasures were such wonderful things as the grace of Christ, the love of Christ, the joy and peace of Christ; and it seemed as though they needed an "encircling gloom" to draw out their secret and their inner glory. At any rate the realm of gloom became the home of revelation, and Paul began to realize as never before the range and wealth of his spiritual inheritance.

Who has not known men and women who, when they arrive at seasons of gloom and solitude, put on strength and hopefulness like a robe? You may imprison such folk where you please; but you shut up their treasure with them. You cannot shut it out. You may make their material lot a desert, but "the wilderness and the solitary place shall be glad, and the desert shall rejoice and blossom as the rose." Dr. Jowett

"Every flower, even the fairest, has its shadow beneath it as it swings in the sunlight."

Where there is much light there is much shade.

August 25

Shut up unto the faith (Gal. 3:23).

God, in olden time suffered man to be kept in ward by the law that he might learn the more excellent way of faith. For by the law he would see God's holy standard and by the law he would see his own utter helplessness; then he would be glad to learn God's way of faith.

God still shuts us up to faith. Our natures, our circumstances, trials, disappointments, all serve to shut us up and keep us in ward till we see that the only way out is God's way of faith. Moses tried by self-effort, by personal influence, even by violence, to bring about the deliverance of his people. God had to shut him up forty years in the wilderness before he was prepared for God's work.

Paul and Silas were bidden of God to preach the gospel in Europe. They landed and proceeded to Philippi. They were flogged, they were shut up in prison, their feet were put fast in the stocks. They were shut up to faith. They trusted God. They sang praises to Him in the darkest hour, and God wrought deliverance and salvation.

John was banished to the Isle of Patmos. He was shut up to faith. Had he not been so shut up, he would never have seen such glorious visions of God.

Dear reader, are you in some great trouble? Have you had some great disappointment, have you met some sorrow, some unspeakable loss? Are you in a hard place? Cheer up! You are shut up to faith. Take your trouble the right way. Commit it to God. Praise Him that He maketh "all things work together for good," and that "God worketh for him that waiteth for him." There will be blessings, help, and revelations of God that will come to you that never could otherwise have come; and many besides yourself will receive great light and blessing because you were shut up to faith. C. H. P.

Great things are done when men and mountains meet,
These are not done by jostling in the street.

August 26

It is not in me (Job 28:14).

I remember a summer in which I said, "It is the ocean I need," and I went to the ocean; but it seemed to say, *"It is not in me!"* The ocean did not do for me what I thought it would. Then I said, "The mountains will rest me," and I went to the mountains, and when I awoke in the morning there stood the grand mountain that I had wanted so much to see; but it said, *"It is not in me!"* It did not satisfy. Ah! I needed the ocean of His love, and the high mountains of His truth within. It was *wisdom* that the "depths" said they did not contain, and that could not be compared with jewels or gold or precious stones. *Christ is wisdom and our deepest need.* Our restlessness within can only be met by the revelation of His eternal friendship and love for us. MARGARET BOTTOME

My heart is there!
Where, on eternal hills, my loved one dwells
Among the lilies and asphodels;
Clad in the brightness of the Great White Throne,
Glad in the smile of Him who sits thereon,
The glory gilding all His wealth of hair
And making His immortal face more fair—
THERE IS MY TREASURE and my heart is there.

My heart is there!
With Him who made all earthly life so sweet,
So fit to live, and yet to die so meet;
So mild, so grand, so gentle and so brave,
So ready to forgive, so strong to save.
His fair, pure Spirit makes the Heavens more fair,
And thither rises all my longing prayer—
THERE IS MY TREASURE and my heart is there.

FAVORITE POEM OF THE LATE CHAS. E. COWMAN

You cannot detain the eagle in the forest. You may gather around him a chorus of the choicest birds; you may give him a perch on the goodliest pine; you may charge winged messengers to bring him choicest dainties; but he will spurn them all. Spreading his lofty wings, and with his eye on the alpine cliff, he will soar away to his own ancestral halls amid the munition of rocks and the wild music of tempest and waterfall.

The soul of man, in its eagle soarings, will rest with nothing short of the Rock of Ages. Its ancestral halls are the halls of heaven. Its munitions of rocks are the attributes of God. The sweep of its majestic flight is eternity! "Lord, THOU hast been our dwelling place in all generations." MACDUFF

"My Home is God Himself"; Christ brought me there.
I laid me down within His mighty arms;
He took me up, and safe from all alarms
He bore me "where no foot but His hath trod,"
Within the holiest at Home with God,
And bade me dwell in Him, rejoicing there.
O Holy Place! O Home divinely fair!
And we, God's little ones, abiding there.

"My Home is God Himself"; it was not so!
A long, long road I traveled night and day,
And sought to find within myself some way,
Aught I could do, or feel to bring me near;

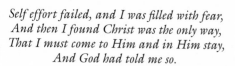

Self effort failed, and I was filled with fear,
And then I found Christ was the only way,
That I must come to Him and in Him stay,
And God had told me so.

And now "my Home is God," and sheltered there,
God meets the trials of my earthly life,
God compasses me round from storm and strife,
God takes the burden of my daily care.
O Wondrous Place! O Home divinely fair!
And I, God's little one, safe hidden there.
Lord, as I dwell in Thee and Thou in me,
So make me dead to everything but Thee;
That as I rest within my Home most fair,
My soul may evermore and only see
My God in everything and everywhere;
My Home is God.

UNKNOWN 🖎

August 27

And he took him aside from the multitude (Mark 7:33).

Paul not only stood the tests in Christian activity, but in the solitude of captivity. You may stand the strain of the most intense labor, coupled with severe suffering, and yet break down utterly when laid aside from all religious activities; when forced into close confinement in some prison house.

That noble bird, soaring the highest above the clouds and enduring the longest flights, sinks into despair when in a cage where it is forced to beat its helpless wings against its prison bars. You have seen the great eagle languish in its narrow cell with bowed head and drooping wings. What a picture of the sorrow in inactivity.

Paul in prison. That was another side of life. Do you want to see how he takes it? I see him looking out over the top of his prison wall and over the heads of his enemies. I see him write a document and sign his name— not the prisoner of Festus, nor of Caesar; not the victim of the Sanhedrin; but the—"prisoner of the Lord." He saw only the hand of God in it all. To him the prison becomes a palace. Its corridors ring with shouts of triumphant praise and joy.

Restrained from the missionary work he loved so well, he now built a new pulpit—a new witness stand—and from that place of bondage come some of the sweetest and most helpful ministries of Christian liberty. What precious messages of light come from those dark shadows of captivity.

Think of the long train of imprisoned saints who have followed in Paul's wake. For twelve long years Bunyan's lips were silenced in Bedford jail. It was there that he did the greatest and best work of his life. There he wrote the book that has been read next to the Bible. He says, "I was at home in prison and I sat me down and wrote, and wrote, for joy did make me write."

The wonderful dream of that long night has lighted the pathway of millions of weary pilgrims. That sweet-spirited French lady, Madam Guyon, lay long between prison walls. Like some caged birds that sing the sweeter for their confinement, the music of her soul has gone out far beyond the dungeon walls and scattered the desolation of many drooping hearts.

Oh, the heavenly consolation that has poured forth from places of solitude! S. C. REES

Taken aside by Jesus,
To feel the touch of His hand;
To rest for a while in the shadow
Of the Rock in a weary land.

Taken aside by Jesus,
In the loneliness dark and drear,
Where no other comfort may reach me,
Than His voice to my heart so dear.

Taken aside by Jesus,
To be quite alone with Him,
To hear His wonderful tones of love
'Mid the silence and shadows dim.

Taken aside by Jesus,
Shall I shrink from the desert place;
When I hear as I never heard before,
And see Him "face to face"?

August 28

There he proved them (Exod. 15:25).

I stood once in the test room of a great steel mill. All around me were little partitions and compartments. Steel had been tested to the limit and marked with figures that showed its breaking point. Some pieces had been twisted until they broke, and the strength of torsion was marked on them. Some had been stretched to the breaking point and their tensile strength indicated. Some had been compressed to the crushing point and also marked. The master of the steel mill knew just what these pieces of steel would stand under strain. He knew just what they would bear if placed in the great ship, building, or bridge. He knew this because his testing room revealed it.

It is often so with God's children. God does not want us to be like vases of glass or porcelain. He would have us like these toughened pieces of steel, able to bear twisting and crushing to the uttermost without collapse.

He wants us to be, not hothouse plants, but storm-beaten oaks; not sand dunes driven with every gust of wind, but granite rocks withstanding the fiercest storms. To make us such He must needs bring us into His testing room of suffering. Many of us need no other argument than our own experiences to prove that suffering is indeed God's testing room of faith. J. H. McC. ✺

It is very easy for us to speak and theorize about faith, but God often casts us into crucibles to try our gold, and to separate it from the dross and alloy. Oh, happy are we if the hurricanes that ripple life's unquiet sea have the effect of making Jesus more precious. Better the storm with Christ than smooth waters without Him. MACDUFF ✺

What if God could not manage to ripen your life without suffering?

August 29

And he went out carrying his own cross (John 19:17).

There is a poem called "The Changed Cross." It represents a weary one who thought that her cross was surely heavier than those of others whom she saw about her, and she wished that she might choose another instead of her own. She slept, and in her dream she was led to a place where many crosses lay, crosses of different shapes and sizes. There was a little one most beauteous to behold, set in jewels and gold. "Ah, this I can wear with comfort," she said. So she took it up, but her weak form shook beneath it. The jewels and the gold were beautiful, but they were far too heavy for her.

Next she saw a lovely cross with fair flowers entwined around its sculptured form. Surely that was the one for her. She lifted it, but beneath the flowers were piercing thorns which tore her flesh.

At last, as she went on, she came to a plain cross, without jewels, without carvings, with only a few words of love inscribed upon it. This she took up and it proved the best of all, the easiest to be borne. And as she looked upon it, bathed in the radiance that fell from heaven, she recognized her own old cross. She had found it again, and it was the best of all and lightest for her.

God knows best what cross we need to bear. We do not know how heavy other people's crosses are. We envy someone who is rich; his is a golden cross set with jewels, but we do not know how heavy it is. Here is another whose life seems very lovely. She bears a cross twined with flowers. If we could try all the other crosses that we think lighter than our own, we would at last find that not one of them suited us so well as our own.
FROM GLIMPSES THROUGH LIFE'S WINDOWS 🥢

> *If thou, impatient, dost let slip thy cross,*
> *Thou wilt not find it in this world again;*
> *Nor in another: here and here alone*
> *Is given thee to suffer for God's sake.*
> *In other worlds we may more perfectly*
> *Love Him and serve Him, praise Him,*
> *Grow nearer and nearer to Him with delight.*
> *But then we shall not any more*
> *Be called to suffer, which is our appointment here.*
> *Canst thou not suffer, then, one hour or two?*
> *If He should call thee from thy cross today,*
> *Saying: "It is finished—that hard cross of thine*
> *From which thou prayest for deliverance,"*
> *Thinkest thou not some passion of regret*
> *Would overcome thee? Thou would'st say,*
> *"So soon? Let me go back and suffer yet awhile*
> *More patiently. I have not yet praised God."*
> *Whensoe'er it comes, that summons that we look for,*
> *It will seem soon, too soon. Let us take heed in time*
> *That God may now be glorified in us.*
> UGO BASSI'S SERMON IN A HOSPITAL 🥢

August 30

They that go down to the sea in ships, that do business in great waters; these see the works of the Lord, and his wonders in the deep (Ps. 107:23–24).

He is but an apprentice and no master in the art, who has not learned that every wind that blows is fair for heaven. The only thing that helps nobody, is a dead calm. North or south, east or west, it matters not, every wind may help toward that blessed port. Seek one thing only: *keep well out to sea*, and then have no fear of stormy winds. Let our prayer be that of an old Cornishman: "O Lord, send us out to sea—out in the deep water. Here we are so close to the rocks that the first bit of breeze with the Devil, we are all knocked to pieces. Lord, send us out to sea—out in the deep water, where we shall have room enough to get a glorious victory." MARK GUY PEARSE

Remember that we have no more faith at any time than we have in the hour of trial. All that will not bear to be tested is mere carnal confidence. Fair-weather faith is no faith. C. H. SPURGEON

August 31

Blessed are they that have not seen, and yet have believed (John 20:29).

How strong is the snare of the things that are seen, and how necessary for God to keep us in the things that are unseen! If Peter is to walk on the water, he must walk; if he is going to swim, he must swim, but he cannot do both. If the bird is going to fly, it must keep away from fences and the trees, and trust to its buoyant wings. But if it tries to keep within easy reach of the ground, it will make poor work of flying.

God had to bring Abraham to the end of his own strength, and to let him see that in his own body he could do nothing. He had to consider his own body as good as dead and then take God for the whole work; and when he looked away from himself, and trusted God alone, then he became fully persuaded that what He had promised, He was able to perform. That is what God is teaching us, and He has to keep away encouraging results until we learn to trust without them, and then He loves to make His Word real in fact as well as faith. A. B. SIMPSON

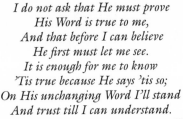

I do not ask that He must prove
His Word is true to me,
And that before I can believe
He first must let me see.
It is enough for me to know
'Tis true because He says 'tis so;
On His unchanging Word I'll stand
And trust till I can understand.

E. M. WINTER

September 1

I will lay thy stones with fair colors (Isa. 54:11).

The stones from the wall said, "We come from the mountains far away, from the sides of the craggy hills. Fire and water have worked on us for ages but made us only crags. Human hands have made us into a dwelling where the children of your immortal race are born, and suffer, and rejoice, and find rest and shelter, and learn the lessons set them by our Maker and yours. But we have passed through much to fit us for this. Gunpowder has rent our very heart; pickaxes have cleaved and broken us, it seemed to us often without design or meaning, as we lay misshapen stones in the quarry; but gradually we were cut into blocks, and some of us were chiseled with finer instruments to a sharper edge. But we are complete now, and are in our places, and are of service."

You are in the quarry still, and not complete, and therefore to you, as once to us, much is inexplicable. But you are destined for a higher building, and one day you will be placed in it by hands not human, a living stone in a heavenly temple.

In the still air the music lies unheard;
In the rough marble beauty hides unseen;
To make the music and the beauty needs
The master's touch, the sculptor's chisel keen.

Great Master, touch us with Thy skillful hands;
Let not the music that is in us die!
Great Sculptor, hew and polish us; nor let,
Hidden and lost, thy form within us lie!

September 2

Unto you it is given ... to suffer (Phil. 1:29).

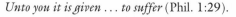

God keeps a costly school. Many of its lessons are spelled out through tears. Richard Baxter said, "O God, I thank Thee for a bodily discipline of eight and fifty years"; and he is not the only man who has turned a trouble into triumph.

This school of our heavenly Father will soon close for us; the term time is shortening every day. Let us not shrink from a hard lesson or wince under any rod of chastisement. The richer will be the crown, and the sweeter will be heaven, if we endure cheerfully to the end and graduate in glory. THEODORE L. CUYLER

The finest china in the world is burned at least three times, some of it more than three times. Dresden china is always burned three times. *Why* does it go through that intense fire? Once ought to be enough; twice ought to be enough. No, three times are necessary to burn that china so that the gold and the crimson are brought out more beautifully and then fastened there to stay.

We are fashioned after the same principle in human life. Our trials are burned into us once, twice, thrice; and by God's grace these beautiful colors are there and they are there to stay forever. CORTLAND MYERS

> *Earth's fairest flowers grow not on sunny plain,*
> *But where some vast upheaval rent in twain*
> *The smiling land....*
> *After the whirlwind's devastating blast,*
> *After the molten fire and ashen pall,*
> *God's still small voice breathes healing over all.*
> *From riven rocks and fern-clad chasms deep,*
> *Flow living waters as from hearts that weep,*
> *There in the afterglow soft dews distill*
> *And angels tend God's plants when night falls still,*
> *And the Beloved passing by the way*
> *Will gather lilies at the break of day.*
>
> J. H. D.

September 3

And he saw them toiling in rowing (Mark 6:48).

Straining, driving effort does not accomplish the work God gives man to do. Only God Himself, who always works without strain, and who never overworks, can do the work that He assigns to His children. When they restfully trust Him to do it, it will be well done and completely done. The way to let Him do His work through us is to partake of Christ so fully, by faith, that He more than fills our life.

A man who had learned this secret once said: "I came to Jesus and I drank, and I do not think that I shall ever be thirsty again. I have taken for my motto, *'Not overwork, but overflow';* and already it has made all the difference in my life."

There is no effort in overflow. It is quietly irresistible. It is the normal life of omnipotent and ceaseless accomplishment into which Christ invites us today and always. FROM SUNDAY SCHOOL TIMES

> *Be all at rest, my soul, O blessed secret,*
> *Of the true life that glorifies the Lord:*
> *Not always doth the busiest soul best serve Him,*
> *But he that resteth on His faithful Word.*
>
> *Be all at rest, let not your heart be rippled,*
> *For tiny wavelets mar the image fair,*
> *Which the still pool reflects of heaven's glory—*
> *And thus the image He would have thee bear.*
>
> *Be all at rest, my soul, for rest is service,*
> *To the still heart God doth His secrets tell;*
> *Thus shalt thou learn to wait, and watch, and labor,*
> *Strengthened to bear, since Christ in thee doth dwell.*
>
> *For what is service but the life of Jesus,*
> *Lived through a vessel of earth's fragile clay,*
> *Loving and giving and poured forth for others,*
> *A living sacrifice from day to day.*
>
> *Be all at rest, so shalt thou be an answer*
> *To those who question, "Who is God and where?"*
> *For God is rest, and where He dwells is stillness,*
> *And they who dwell in Him, His rest shall share.*

And what shall meet the deep unrest around thee,
But the calm peace of God that filled His breast?
For still a living Voice calls to the weary,
From Him who said, "Come unto Me and rest."

FREDA HANBURY ALLEN

"In resurrection stillness there is resurrection power."

September 4

And when you hear the sound of the trumpet, all the people shall shout with a great shout; and the wall of the city shall fall down flat, and the people shall ascend up every man straight before him (Josh. 6:5).

The shout of steadfast faith is in direct contrast to the moans of wavering faith, and to the wails of discouraged hearts. Among the many "secrets of the Lord," I do not know of any that are more valuable than the secret of this *shout of faith*. The Lord said to Joshua, "See, I have given into thine hand Jericho, and the king thereof, and the mighty men of valour." He had not said, "I *will* give," but "I *have* given." It belonged to them already; and now they were called to take possession of it. But the great question was, How? It looked impossible, but the Lord declared His plan.

Now, no one can suppose for a moment that this shout caused the walls to fall. And yet the *secret* of their victory lay in just this shout, for it was the shout of a faith which dared, on the authority of God's Word alone, to claim a promised victory, while as yet there were no signs of this victory being accomplished. And according to their faith God did unto them; so that, when they shouted, He made the walls to fall.

God had declared that He *had given* them the city, and faith reckoned this to be true. And long centuries afterward the Holy Ghost recorded this triumph of faith in Hebrews: "By faith the walls of Jericho fell down, after they were compassed about seven days." HANNAH WHITALL SMITH

Faith can never reach its consummation,
Till the victor's thankful song we raise:
In the glorious city of salvation,
God has told us all the gates are praise.

September 5

Blessed are all they that wait for him (Isa. 30:18).

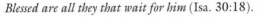

We hear a great deal about waiting on God. There is, however, another side. When we wait *on* God, He is waiting till we are ready; when we wait *for* God, we are waiting till He is ready.

There are some people who say, and many more who believe, that as soon as we meet all the conditions, God will answer our prayers. They say that God lives in an eternal *now;* with Him there is no past nor future; and that if we could fulfill all that He requires in the way of obedience to His will, *immediately* our needs would be supplied, our desires fulfilled, our prayers answered.

There is much truth in this belief, and yet it expresses only one side of the truth. While God *lives* in an eternal *now,* yet He *works* out His purposes in *time.* A petition presented before God is like a seed dropped in the ground. Forces above and beyond our control must work upon it, till the true fruition of the answer is given. FROM THE STILL SMALL VOICE

> *I longed to walk along an easy road,*
> *And leave behind the dull routine of home,*
> *Thinking in other fields to serve my God;*
> *But Jesus said, "My time has not yet come."*
>
> *I longed to sow the seed in other soil,*
> *To be unfettered in the work, and free,*
> *To join with other laborers in their toil;*
> *But Jesus said, "'Tis not My choice for thee."*
>
> *I longed to leave the desert, and be led*
> *To work where souls were sunk in sin and shame,*
> *That I might win them; but the Master said,*
> *"I have not called thee, publish here My name."*
>
> *I longed to fight the battles of my King,*
> *Lift high His standards in the thickest strife;*
> *But my great Captain bade me wait and sing*
> *Songs of His conquests in my quiet life.*
>
> *I longed to leave the uncongenial sphere,*
> *Where all alone I seemed to stand and wait,*
> *To feel I had some human helper near,*
> *But Jesus bade me guard one lonely gate.*

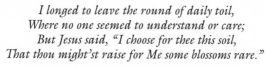

I longed to leave the round of daily toil,
Where no one seemed to understand or care;
But Jesus said, "I choose for thee this soil,
That thou might'st raise for Me some blossoms rare."

And now I have no longing but to do
At home, or else afar, His blessed will,
To work amid the many or the few;
Thus, "choosing not to choose," my heart is still.
SELECTED ☞

And Patience was willing to wait.
FROM PILGRIM'S PROGRESS ☞

September 6

Thou remainest (Heb. 1:11).

There are always lone hearth fires; so many! And those who sit beside them, with the empty chair, cannot restrain the tears that *will* come. One sits *alone* so much. There *is* some One unseen, just here within reach. But somehow we don't *realize* His presence. Realizing is blessed, but—*rare*. It belongs to the mood, to the feelings. It is dependent on weather conditions and bodily conditions. The rain, the heavy fog outside, the poor sleep, the twinging pain, these make one's mood so much, they seem to blur out the realizing. But there is something a little higher up than realizing. It is yet more blessed. It is independent of these outer conditions, it is something that abides. It is this: *recognizing* that Presence unseen, so wondrous and quieting, so soothing and calming and warming. *Recognize His* presence—the Master's own. He is here, close by; His presence is real. Recognizing will help realizing, too, but it never depends on it. Aye, more, immensely more, the truth is presence, not a thing, a fact, a statement. Some *One* is present, a warm-hearted Friend, an all-powerful Lord. And this is the joyful truth for weeping hearts everywhere, whatever be the hand that has drawn the tears; by whatever stream it be that your weeping willow is planted. S. D. GORDON ☞

When from my life the old-time joys have vanished,
Treasures once mine, I may no longer claim,
This truth may feed my hungry heart, and famished:
Lord, THOU REMAINEST! THOU art still the same!

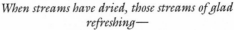

*When streams have dried, those streams of glad
refreshing—*
Friendships so blest, so rich, so free;
When sun-kissed skies give place to clouds depressing,
Lord, THOU REMAINEST! Still my heart hath THEE.

When strength hath failed, and feet, now worn and weary,
On gladsome errands may no longer go,
Why should I sigh, or let the days be dreary?
Lord, THOU REMAINEST! Could'st THOU more bestow?

Thus through life's days—whoe'er or what may fail me,
Friends, friendships, joys, in small or great degree,
Songs may be mine, no sadness need assail me,
Lord, THOU REMAINEST! Still my heart hath THEE.
                                       J. DANSON SMITH

September 7

God is our refuge and strength, a very present help in trouble
(Ps. 46:1).

The question often comes, "Why didn't He help me sooner?" It is not
His order. He must first adjust you to the trouble and cause you to learn
your lesson from it. His promise is, "I will be with him *in* trouble; I will
deliver him and honor him." He must be with you *in* the trouble first all
day and all night. Then He will take you out of it. This will not come till
you have stopped being restless and fretful about it and become calm and
quiet. Then He will say, "It is enough."

God uses trouble to teach His children precious lessons. They are
intended to educate us. When their good work is done, a glorious recompense
will come to us through them. There is a sweet joy and a real value in them.
He does not regard them as difficulties but as opportunities. SELECTED

> *Not always OUT of our troublous times,*
> *And the struggles fierce and grim,*
> *But IN—deeper IN—to our sure rest,*
> *The place of our peace, in Him.*
>   ANNIE JOHNSON FLINT

We once heard a simple old colored man say something that we have
never forgotten: "When God tests you, it is a good time for you to test Him

by putting His promises to the proof, and claiming from Him just as much as your trials have rendered necessary."

There are two ways of getting out of a trial. One is to simply try to get rid of the trial, and be thankful when it is over. The other is to recognize the trial as a challenge from God to claim a larger blessing than we have ever had, and to hail it with delight as an opportunity of obtaining a larger measure of divine grace. Thus even the adversary becomes an auxiliary, and the things that seem to be against us turn out to be for the furtherance of our way. Surely, this is to be more than conquerors through Him who loved us. A. B. SIMPSON

September 8

Thou hast enlarged me when I was in distress (Ps. 4:1).

This is one of the grandest testimonies ever given by man to the moral government of God. It is not a man's thanksgiving that he has been set free from suffering. It is a thanksgiving that he has been set free through suffering: "Thou hast enlarged me when I was in distress." He declares the sorrows of life to have been themselves the source of life's enlargement.

And have not you and I a thousand times felt this to be true? It is written of Joseph in the dungeon that "the iron entered into his soul." We all feel that what Joseph needed for his soul was just the iron. He had seen only the glitter of the gold. He had been rejoicing in youthful dreams; and dreaming hardens the heart. He who sheds tears over a romance will not be most apt to help reality; real sorrow will be too unpoetic for him. We need the iron to enlarge our nature. The gold is but a vision; the iron is an experience. The chain which unites me to humanity must be an iron chain. That touch of nature which makes the world akin is not joy, but sorrow; gold is partial, but iron is universal.

My soul, if thou wouldst be enlarged into human sympathy, thou must be narrowed into limits of human suffering. Joseph's dungeon is the road to Joseph's throne. Thou canst not lift the iron load of thy brother if the iron hath not entered into thee. It is thy limit that is thine enlargement. It is the shadows of thy life that are the real fulfillment of thy dreams of glory. Murmur not at the shadows; they are better revelations than thy dreams. Say not that the shades of the prison-house have fettered thee; thy fetters are wings—wings of flight into the bosom of humanity. The door of thy prison-house is a door into the heart of the universe. God has enlarged thee by the binding of sorrow's chain. GEORGE MATHESON

If Joseph had not been Egypt's prisoner, he never would have been Egypt's governor. The iron chain about his feet ushered in the golden chain about his neck. SELECTED

September 9

Not much earth (Matt. 13:5).

Shallow! It would seem from the teaching of this parable that we have something to do with the soil. The fruitful seed fell into "good and honest hearts." I suppose the shallow people are the *soil without much earth*—those who have no real purpose, are moved by a tender appeal, a good sermon, a pathetic melody, and at first it looks as if they would amount to something; but *not much earth*—no depth, no deep, honest purpose, no earnest desire to know duty in order to do it. Let us look after the soil of our hearts.

When a Roman soldier was told by his guide that if he insisted on taking a certain journey it would probably be fatal, he answered, "It is necessary for me to go; it is not necessary for me to live."

This was depth. When we are convicted something like that we shall come to something. The shallow nature lives in its impulses, its impressions, its intuitions, its instincts, and very largely its surroundings. The profound character looks beyond all these and moves steadily on, sailing past all storms and clouds into the clear sunshine which is always on the other side, and waiting for the afterwards which always brings the reversion of sorrow, seeming defeat and failure.

When God has deepened us, then He can give us His deeper truths, His profoundest secrets, and His mightier trusts. Lord, lead me into the depths of Thy life and save me from a shallow experience!

> *On to broader fields of holy vision;*
> *On to loftier heights of faith and love;*
> *Onward, upward, apprehending wholly,*
> *All for which He calls thee from above.*
>
> A. B. SIMPSON

September 10

The Lord will perfect that which concerneth me (Ps. 138:8).

There is a divine mystery in suffering, a strange and supernatural power in it, which has never been fathomed by the human
reason. There never has been known great saintliness of soul which did
not pass through great suffering. When the suffering soul reaches a calm
sweet carelessness, when it can inwardly smile at its own suffering, and does
not even ask God to deliver it from suffering, then it has wrought its blessed
ministry; then patience has its perfect work; then the crucifixion begins to
weave itself into a crown.

It is in this state of the perfection of suffering that the Holy Spirit works
many marvelous things in our souls. In such a condition, our whole being
lies perfectly still under the hand of God; every faculty of the mind and will
and heart are at last subdued; a quietness of eternity settles down into the
whole being; the tongue grows still and has but few words to say; it stops
asking God questions; it stops crying, "Why hast thou forsaken me?"

The imagination stops building air castles, or running off on foolish
lines; the reason is tame and gentle; the choices are annihilated; it has no
choice in anything but the purpose of God. The affections are weaned from
all creatures and all things; it is so dead that nothing can hurt it, nothing
can offend it, nothing can hinder it, nothing can get in its way; for let the
circumstances be what they may, it seeks only for God and His will, and it
feels assured that God is making everything in the universe, good or bad,
past or present, work together for its good.

Oh, the blessedness of being absolutely conquered! of losing our own
strength, and wisdom, and plans, and desires, and being where every atom
of our nature is like placid Galilee under the omnipotent feet of our Jesus.
FROM SOUL FOOD 🍃

The great thing is to suffer without being discouraged. FENELON 🍃

The heart that serves, and loves, and clings,
Hears everywhere the rush of angel wings.

September 11

And so, after he had patiently endured, he obtained the promise
(Heb. 6:15).

Abraham was long tried, but he was richly rewarded. The Lord tried
him by delaying to fulfill His promise. Satan tried him by temptation; men
tried him by jealousy, distrust, and opposition; Sarah tried him by her peev-
ishness. But he patiently endured. He did not question God's veracity, nor

limit His power, nor doubt His faithfulness, nor grieve His love; but he bowed to divine sovereignty, submitted to infinite wisdom, and was silent under delays, waiting the Lord's time. And so, having patiently endured, he obtained the promise.

God's promises cannot fail of their accomplishment. Patient waiters cannot be disappointed. Believing expectation shall be realized.

Beloved, Abraham's conduct condemns a hasty spirit, reproves a murmuring one, commends a patient one, and encourages quiet submission to God's will and way. Remember, Abraham was tried; he patiently waited; he received the promise and was satisfied. Imitate his example, and you will share the same blessing. SELECTED

September 12

Who is this that cometh up from the wilderness, leaning upon her beloved? (Song of Sol. 8:5).

Someone gained a good lesson from a southern prayer meeting. A colored brother asked the Lord for various blessings—as you and I do, and thanked the Lord for many already received—as you and I do; but he closed with this unusual petition: "And, O Lord, support us! Yes, support us Lord on every leanin' side!" Have you any leaning sides? This humble man's prayer pictures them in a new way and shows the Great Supporter in a new light also. He is always walking by the Christian, ready to extend His mighty arm and steady the weak one on "every *leanin'* side."

> *Child of My love, lean hard*
> *And let Me feel the pressure of thy care;*
> *I know thy burden, child. I shaped it;*
> *Poised it in Mine Own hand; made no proportion*
> *In its weight to thine unaided strength,*
> *For even as I laid it on, I said,*
> *"I shall be near, and while she leans on Me,*
> *This burden shall be Mine, not hers;*
> *So shall I keep My child within the circling arms*
> *Of My Own love." Here lay it down, nor fear*
> *To impose it on a shoulder which upholds*
> *The government of worlds. Yet closer come:*
> *Thou art not near enough. I would embrace thy care;*
> *So I might feel My child reposing on My breast.*

Thou lovest Me? I knew it. Doubt not then;
But loving Me, lean hard.

September 13

Come up in the morning ... and present thyself there to me in
the top of the mount (Exod. 34:2).

The *morning* is the time fixed for my meeting the Lord. The very word *morning* is as a cluster of rich grapes. Let us crush them, and drink the sacred wine. In the morning! Then God means me to be at my best in strength and hope. I have not to climb in my weakness. In the night I have buried yesterday's fatigue, and in the morning take a new lease of energy. Blessed is the day whose morning is sanctified! Successful is the day whose first victory was won in prayer! Holy is the day whose dawn finds thee on the top of the mount!

My Father, I am coming. Nothing on the mean plain shall keep me away from the holy heights. At Thy bidding I come, so Thou wilt meet me. Morning on the mount! It will make me strong and glad all the rest of the day so well begun. JOSEPH PARKER

Still, still with Thee, when purple morning breaketh,
When the bird waketh, and the shadows flee;
Fairer than morning, lovelier than daylight,
Dawns the sweet consciousness, I am with Thee.

Alone with Thee, amid the mystic shadows,
The solemn hush of nature newly born;
Alone with Thee in breathless adoration,
In the calm dew and freshness of the morn.

As in the dawning o'er the waveless ocean,
The image of the morning-star doth rest,
So in this stillness, Thou beholdest only
Thine image in the waters of my breast.

When sinks the soul, subdued by toil, to slumber,
Its closing eyes look up to Thee in prayer;
Sweet the repose, beneath Thy wings o'er shadowing,
But sweeter still to wake and find Thee there.
HARRIET BEECHER STOWE

My mother's habit was every day, immediately after breakfast, to withdraw for an hour to her own room, and to spend that hour in reading the Bible, in meditation and prayer. From that hour, as from a pure fountain, she drew the strength and sweetness which enabled her to fulfill all her duties and to remain unruffled by the worries and pettinesses which are so often the trial of narrow neighborhoods. As I think of her life and all it had to bear, I see the absolute triumph of Christian grace in the lovely ideal of a Christian lady. I never saw her temper disturbed; I never heard her speak one word of anger, of calumny, or of idle gossip; I never observed in her any sign of a single sentiment unbecoming to a soul which had drunk of the river of the water of life and which had fed upon manna in the barren wilderness. FARRAR

Give God the blossom of the day. Do not put Him off with faded leaves.

September 14

Whosoever will come after me, let him deny himself, and take up his cross, and follow me (Mark 8:34).

The cross which my Lord bids me take up and carry may assume different shapes. I may have to content myself with a lowly and narrow sphere, when I feel that I have capacities for much higher work. I may have to go on cultivating year after year, a field which seems to yield me no harvests whatsoever. I may be bidden to cherish kind and loving thoughts about someone who has wronged me—be bidden speak to him tenderly, and take his part against all who oppose him, and crown him with sympathy and succor. I may have to confess my Master amongst those who do not wish to be reminded of Him and His claims. I may be called to "move among my race, and show a glorious morning face," when my heart is breaking.

There are many crosses, and every one of them is sore and heavy. None of them is likely to be sought out by me of my own accord. But never is Jesus so near me as when I lift my cross, and lay it submissively on my shoulder, and give it the welcome of a patient and unmurmuring spirit.

He draws close, to ripen my wisdom, to deepen my peace, to increase my courage, to augment my power to be of use to others, through the very experience which is so grievous and distressing, and then—as I read on the seal of one of those Scottish Covenanters whom Claverhouse imprisoned on the lonely Bass, with the sea surging and sobbing round—*I grow under the load*. ALEXANDER SMELLIE

*"Use your cross as a crutch to help you on, and not as a
stumbling block to cast you down."*

*You may others from sadness to gladness beguile,
If you carry your cross with a smile.*

September 15

Blow upon my garden that the spices may thereof flow out (Song
of Sol. 4:16).

Some of the spices mentioned in this chapter are quite suggestive. The
aloe was a bitter spice, and it tells of the sweetness of bitter things, the bit-
ter-sweet, which has its own fine application that only those can understand
who have felt it. The myrrh was used to embalm the dead, and it tells of
death to something. It is the sweetness which comes to the heart after it
has died to its self-will and pride and sin.

Oh, the inexpressible charm that hovers about some Christians simply
because they bear upon the chastened countenance and mellow spirit the
impress of the cross, the holy evidence of having died to something that
was once proud and strong, but is now forever at the feet of Jesus. It is the
heavenly charm of a broken spirit and a contrite heart, the music that
springs from the minor key, the sweetness that comes from the touch of the
frost upon the ripened fruit.

And then the frankincense was a fragrance that came from the touch
of the fire. It was the burning powder that rose in clouds of sweetness from
the bosom of the flames. It tells of the heart whose sweetness has been
called forth, perhaps by the flames of affliction, until the holy place of the
soul is filled with clouds of praise and prayer. Beloved, are we giving out
the spices, the perfumes, the sweet odors of the heart? FROM THE LOVE-
LIFE OF OUR LORD

*A Persian fable says: One day
A wanderer found a lump of clay
So redolent of sweet perfume
Its odors scented all the room.
"What are thou?" was his quick demand,
"Art thou some gem from Samarcand,
Or spikenard in this rude disguise,
Or other costly merchandise?"
"Nay: I am but a lump of clay."*

"Then whence this wondrous perfume—say!"
"Friend, if the secret I disclose,
I have been dwelling with the rose."
Sweet parable! and will not those
Who love to dwell with Sharon's rose,
Distill sweet odors all around,
Though low and mean themselves are found?
Dear Lord, abide with us that we
May draw our perfume fresh from Thee.

September 16

Hide thyself by the brook Cherith (1 Kings 17:3).

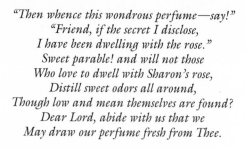

God's servants must be taught the value of the hidden life. The man who is to take a high place before his fellows must take a low place before his God. We must not be surprised if sometimes our Father says: "There, child, thou hast had enough of this hurry, and publicity, and excitement; get thee hence, and hide thyself by the brook—hide thyself in the Cherith of the sick chamber, or in the Cherith of bereavement, or in some solitude from which the crowds have ebbed away."

Happy is he who can reply, "This Thy will is also mine; I flee unto Thee to hide me. Hide me in the secret of Thy tabernacle, and beneath the cover of Thy wings!"

Every saintly soul that would wield great power with men must win it in some hidden Cherith. The acquisition of spiritual power is impossible, unless we can hide ourselves from men and from ourselves in some deep gorge where we may absorb the power of the eternal God; as vegetation through long ages absorbed these qualities of sunshine, which it now gives back through burning coal.

Bishop Andrews had his Cherith, in which he spent five hours every day in prayer and devotion. John Welsh had it—who thought the day ill spent which did not witness eight or ten hours of closet communion. David Brainerd had it in the woods of North America. Christmas Evans had it in his long and lonely journeys amid the hills of Wales.

Or, passing back to the blessed age from which we date the centuries: Patmos, the seclusion of the Roman prisons, the Arabian desert, the hills and vales of Palestine, are forever memorable as the Cheriths of those who have made our modern world.

Our Lord found His Cherith at Nazareth, and in the wilderness of Judea; amid the olives of Bethany, and the solitude of Gadara. None of us, therefore, can dispense with some Cherith where the sounds of human voices are exchanged for the waters of quietness which are fed from the throne; and where we may taste the sweets and imbibe the power of a life hidden with Christ. FROM ELIJAH, BY MEYER ❧

September 17

It is the Lord: let him do what seemeth him good (1 Sam. 3:18).

See God in everything, and God will calm and color all that thou dost see!" It may be that the circumstances of our sorrows will not be removed, their condition will remain unchanged; but if Christ, as Lord and Master of our life, is brought into our grief and gloom, "HE will compass us about with songs of deliverance." To see HIM, and to be sure that His wisdom cannot err, His power cannot fail, His love can never change; to know that even His direst dealings with us are for our deepest spiritual gain, is to be able to say, in the midst of bereavement, sorrow, pain, and loss, "The Lord gave, and the Lord hath taken away; blessed be the name of the Lord."

Nothing else but *seeing God in everything* will make us loving and patient with those who annoy and trouble us. They will be to us then only instruments for accomplishing His tender and wise purposes toward us, and we shall even find ourselves at last inwardly thanking them for the blessing they bring us. Nothing else will completely put an end to all murmuring or rebelling thoughts. H. W. SMITH ❧

"Give me a new idea," I said,
While musing on a sleepless bed;
"A new idea that'll bring to earth
A balm for souls of priceless worth;
That'll give men thoughts of things above,
And teach them how to serve and love,
That'll banish every selfish thought,
And rid men of the sins they've fought."

The new thought came, just how, I'll tell:
'Twas when on bended knee I fell,
And sought from HIM who knows full well
The way our sorrow to expel.

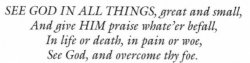

SEE GOD IN ALL THINGS, great and small,
And give HIM praise whate'er befall,
In life or death, in pain or woe,
See God, and overcome thy foe.

I saw HIM in the morning light,
HE made the day shine clear and bright;
I saw HIM in the noontide hour,
And gained from HIM refreshing shower.
At eventide, when worn and sad,
HE gave me help, and made me glad.
At midnight, when on tossing bed
My weary soul to sleep HE led.

I saw HIM when great losses came,
And found HE loved me just the same.
When heavy loads I had to bear,
I found HE lightened every care.
By sickness, sorrow, sore distress,
HE calmed my mind and gave me rest.
HE's filled my heart with gladsome praise
Since I gave HIM the upward gaze.

'Twas new to me, yet old to some,
This thought that to me has become
A revelation of the way
We all should live throughout the day;
For as each day unfolds its light,
We'll walk by faith and not by sight.
Life will, indeed, a blessing bring,
If we SEE GOD IN EVERYTHING.

A. E. FINN

September 18

Where there is no vision, the people perish (Prov. 29:18).

Waiting upon God is necessary in order to see Him to have a vision of Him. The *time element* in vision is essential. Our hearts are like a sensitive photographer's plate; and in order to have God revealed there, we must sit at His feet a long time. The troubled surface of a lake will not reflect an object.

Our lives must be quiet and restful if we would see God.

There is power in the sight of some things to affect one's life. A quiet sunset will bring peace to a troubled heart. Thus the vision of God always transforms human life.

Jacob saw God at Jabbok's ford, and became Israel. The vision of God transformed Gideon from a coward into a valiant soldier. The vision of Christ changed Thomas from a doubting follower into a loyal, devout disciple.

But men have had visions of God since Bible times. William Carey saw God, and left his shoemaker's bench and went to India. David Livingstone saw God, and left all to follow Him through the jungles of dark Africa. Scores and hundreds have had visions of God, and are today in the uttermost parts of the earth working for the speedy evangelization of the heathen. DR. PARDINGTON 🦚

There is hardly ever a complete silence in the soul. God is whispering to us well-nigh incessantly. Whenever the sounds of the world die out in the soul, or sink low, then we hear the whisperings of God. He is always whispering to us, only we do not hear, because of the noise, hurry, and distraction which life causes as it rushes on. F. W. FABER 🦚

Speak, Lord, in the stillness,
While I wait on Thee;
Hushed my heart to listen
In expectancy.

Speak, O blessed Master,
In this quiet hour;
Let me see Thy face, Lord,
Feel Thy touch of power.

For the words Thou speakest,
"They are life," indeed;
Living bread from Heaven
Now my spirit feed!

Speak, Thy servant heareth!
Be not silent, Lord;
Waits my soul upon Thee
For the quickening word!

September 19

My Father is the husbandman (John 15:1).

It is comforting to think of trouble, in whatever form it may come to us, as a heavenly messenger, bringing us something from God. In its earthly aspect it may seem hurtful, even destructive; but in its spiritual out-working it yields blessing. Many of the richest blessings which have come down to us from the past are the fruit of sorrow or pain. We should never forget that redemption, the world's greatest blessing, is the fruit of the world's greatest sorrow. In every time of sharp pruning, when the knife is deep and the pain is sore, it is an unspeakable comfort to read, "My Father is the husbandman."

Doctor Vincent tells of being in a great hothouse where luscious clusters of grapes were hanging on every side. The owner said, "When my new gardener came, he said he would have nothing to do with these vines unless he could cut them clean down to the stalk; and he did, and we had no grapes for two years, but this is the result."

There is rich suggestiveness in this interpretation of the pruning process, as we apply it to the Christian life. Pruning *seems* to be destroying the vine, the gardener *appears* to be cutting it all away; but he looks on into the future and knows that the final outcome will be the enrichment of its life and greater abundance of fruit.

There are blessings we can never have unless we are ready to pay the price of pain. There is no way to reach them save through suffering. DR. MILLER

> *I walked a mile with Pleasure,*
> *She chattered all the way;*
> *But left me none the wiser*
> *For all she had to say.*
>
> *I walked a mile with Sorrow,*
> *And ne'er a word said she;*
> *But, oh, the things I learned from her*
> *When sorrow walked with me.*

September 20

Said I not unto thee, that, if thou wouldest believe, thou shouldest see the glory of God? (John 11:40).

Mary and Martha could not understand what their Lord was doing. Both of them said to Him, *"Lord, if thou hadst been here, my brother had not died."* Back of it all we seem to read their thought: "Lord, we do not understand *why* you have stayed away so long. We do not understand *how* you could let death come to the man whom you loved. We do not understand how you could let sorrow and suffering ravage our lives when your presence might have stayed it all. *Why* did you not come? It is too late now, for already he has been dead four days!"

And to it all Jesus had but one great truth: "You may not understand; but I tell you if you *believe*, you will *see.*"

Abraham could not understand *why* God should ask the sacrifice of the boy; but he trusted. And he *saw* the glory of God in his restoration to his love. Moses could not understand *why* God should keep him forty years in the wilderness, but he trusted; and he *saw* when God called him to lead forth Israel from bondage.

Joseph could not understand the cruelty of his brethren, the false witness of a perfidious woman, and the long years of an unjust imprisonment; but he trusted, and he *saw* at last the glory of God in it all.

Jacob could not understand the strange providence which permitted the same Joseph to be torn from his father's love, but he *saw* the glory of God when he looked into the face of that same Joseph as the viceroy of a great king, and the preserver of his own life and the lives of a great nation.

And so, perhaps in your life. You say, "I do not understand why God let my dear one be taken. I do not understand why affliction has been permitted to smite me. I do not understand the devious paths by which the Lord is leading me. I do not understand why plans and purposes that seemed good to my eyes should be baffled. I do not understand why blessings I so much need are so long delayed."

Friend, you do not *have* to understand all God's ways with you. God does not expect you to understand them. You do not expect *your* child to understand, only believe. Some day you will *see* the glory of God in the things which you do not understand. J. H. McC. 🐚

> *If we could push ajar the gates of life,*
> *And stand within, and all God's working see,*
> *We might interpret all this doubt and strife,*
> *And for each mystery could find a key.*
>
> *But not today. Then be content, poor heart;*
> *God's plans, like lilies pure and white, unfold,*
> *We must not tear the close-shut leaves apart—*
> *Time will reveal the calyxes of gold.*

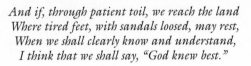

And if, through patient toil, we reach the land
Where tired feet, with sandals loosed, may rest,
When we shall clearly know and understand,
I think that we shall say, "God knew best."

September 21

I count all things but loss for the excellency of the knowledge of
Christ Jesus, my Lord (Phil. 3:8).

This is the happy season of ripening cornfields, of the merry song of the reapers, of the secured and garnered grain. But let me hearken to the sermon of the field. This is its solemn word to me. You must die in order to live. You must refuse to consult your own ease and well-being. You must be crucified, not only in desires and habits which are sinful, but in many more which appear innocent and right.

If you would save others, you cannot save yourself. If you would bear much fruit, you must be buried in darkness and solitude.

My heart fails me as I listen. But, when Jesus asks it, let me tell myself that it is my high dignity to enter into the fellowship of His sufferings; and thus I am in the best of company. And let me tell myself again that it is all meant to make me a vessel meet for His use. His own Calvary has blossomed into fertility; and so shall mine. Plenty out of pain, life out of death: is it not the law of the kingdom? FROM IN THE HOUR OF SILENCE

Do we call it dying when the bud bursts into flower? SELECTED

Finding, following, keeping, struggling,
Is He sure to bless?
Saints, apostles, prophets, martyrs,
Answer, "Yes."

September 22

And the Lord said . . . Satan hath desired to have you, that he
may sift you as wheat; but I have prayed for thee, that thy faith
fail not (Luke 22:31–32).

Our faith is the center of the target at which God doth shoot when He tries us; and if any other grace shall escape untried, certainly faith shall not.

There is no way of piercing faith to its very marrow like the sticking of the arrow of desertion into it; this finds it out whether it be of immortals or no. Strip it of its armor of conscious enjoyment, and suffer the terrors of the Lord to set themselves in array against it; and that is faith indeed which can escape unhurt from the midst of the attack. Faith must be tried, and seeming desertion is the furnace, heated seven times, into which it might be thrust. Blest is the man who can endure the ordeal! C. H. SPURGEON 🦅

Paul said, "I have kept the faith," but he lost his head! They cut that off, but it didn't touch his faith. He rejoiced in three things—this great apostle to the Gentiles; he had "fought a good fight," he had "finished his course," he had "kept the faith." What did all the rest amount to? Saint Paul won the race; he gained the prize, and he has not only the admiration of earth today, but the admiration of heaven. Why do we not act as if it paid to lose all to win Christ? Why are we not loyal to truth as he was? Ah, we haven't his arithmetic. He counted differently from us; we count the things *gain* that he counted *loss*. We must have his faith, and keep it if we would wear the same crown.

September 23

He that believeth on me, as the scripture hath said, out of his belly shall flow rivers of living water (John 7:38).

Some of us are shivering and wondering why the Holy Spirit does not fill us. We have plenty coming in, but we do not give it out. Give out the blessing that you have, start larger plans for service and blessing, and you will soon find that the Holy Ghost is before you, and He will present you with blessings for service, and give you all that He can trust you to give away to others.

There is a beautiful fact in nature which has its spiritual parallels. There is no music so heavenly as an aeolian harp, and the aeolian harp is nothing but a set of musical chords arranged in harmony and then left to be touched by the unseen fingers of the wandering winds. And as the breath of heaven floats over the chords, it is said that notes almost divine float out upon the air, as if a choir of angels were wandering around and touching the strings.

And so it is possible to keep our hearts so open to the touch of the Holy Spirit that He can play upon them at will, as we quietly wait in the pathway of His service. FROM DAYS OF HEAVEN UPON EARTH 🦅

When the apostles received the baptism with the Holy Ghost
they did not rent the upper room and stay there to hold holiness
meetings, but went everywhere preaching the gospel. WILL HUFF

> *"If I have eaten my morsel alone,"*
> *The patriarch spoke with scorn;*
> *What would he think of the Church were he shown*
> *Heathendom—huge, forlorn,*
> *Godless, Christless, with soul unfed,*
> *While the Church's ailment is fullness of bread,*
> *Eating her morsel alone?*

> *"Freely ye have received, so give,"*
> *He bade, who hath given us all.*
> *How shall the soul in us longer live*
> *Deaf to their starving call,*
> *For whom the blood of the Lord was shed,*
> *And His body broken to give them bread,*
> *If we eat our morsel alone!*
>
> ARCHBISHOP ALEXANDER

Where is Abel thy brother? (Gen. 4:9).

September 24

After they were come to Mysia, they assayed to go into Bithynia:
but the Spirit suffered them not (Acts 16:7).

What a strange prohibition! These men were going into Bithynia just
to do Christ's work, and the door is shut against them by Christ's own
Spirit. I, too, have experienced this in certain moments. I have sometimes
found myself interrupted in what seemed to me a career of usefulness.
Opposition came and forced me to go back, or sickness came and compelled me to retire into a desert apart.

It was hard at such times to leave my work undone when I believed
that work to be the service of the Spirit. But I came to remember that the
Spirit has not only a service of work, but a service of waiting. I came to see
that in the kingdom of Christ there are not only times for action, but times
in which to forbear acting. I came to learn that the desert place apart is
often the most useful spot in the varied life of man—more rich in harvest
than the seasons in which the corn and wine abounded. I have been taught

to thank the blessed Spirit that many a darling Bithynia had to be left unvisited by me.

And so, Thou divine Spirit, would I still be led by Thee. Still there come to me disappointed prospects of usefulness. Today the door seems to open into life and work for Thee; tomorrow it closes before me just as I am about to enter.

Teach me to see another door in the very inaction of the hour. Help me to find in the very prohibition thus to serve Thee, a new opening into Thy service. Inspire me with the knowledge that a man may at times be called to do his duty by doing nothing, to work by keeping still, to serve by waiting. When I remember the power of the "still small voice," I shall not murmur that sometimes the Spirit suffers me *not* to go. GEORGE MATHESON

When I cannot understand my Father's leading.
And it seems to be but hard and cruel fate,
Still I hear that gentle whisper ever pleading,
God is working, God is faithful, ONLY WAIT.

September 25

Why go I mourning? (Ps. 42:9).

Canst thou answer this, believer? Canst thou find any reason why thou art so often mourning instead of rejoicing? Why yield to gloomy anticipations? Who told thee that the night would never end in day? Who told thee that the winter of thy discontent would proceed from frost to frost, from snow and ice, and hail, to deeper snow, and yet more heavy tempest of despair? Knowest thou not that day follows night, that flood comes after ebb, that spring and summer succeed winter? Hope thou then! Hope thou ever! for God fails thee not. C. H. SPURGEON

He was better to me than all my hopes;
He was better than all my fears;
He made a bridge of my broken works,
And a rainbow of my tears.
The billows that guarded my sea-girt path,
But carried my Lord on their crest;
When I dwell on the days of my wilderness march
I can lean on His love for the rest.

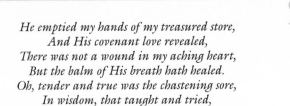

He emptied my hands of my treasured store,
And His covenant love revealed,
There was not a wound in my aching heart,
But the balm of His breath hath healed.
Oh, tender and true was the chastening sore,
In wisdom, that taught and tried,
Till the soul that He sought was trusting in Him,
And nothing on earth beside.

He guided my paths that I could not see,
By ways that I have not known;
The crooked was straight, and the rough was plain
As I followed the Lord alone.
I praise Him still for the pleasant palms,
And the water-springs by the way,
For the glowing pillar of flame by night,
And the sheltering cloud by day.

Never a watch on the dreariest halt,
But some promise of love endears;
I read from the past, that my future shall be
Far better than all my fears.
Like the golden pot, of the wilderness bread,
Laid up with the blossoming rod,
All safe in the ark, with the law of the Lord,
Is the covenant care of my God.

September 26

We walk by faith, not by appearance (2 Cor. 5:7 RV).

By faith, not appearance; God never wants us to look at our feelings. Self may want us to; and Satan may want us to. But God wants us to face facts, not feelings; the facts of Christ and of His finished and perfect work for us.

When we face these precious facts and believe them because God says they are facts, God will take care of our feelings.

God never gives feeling to enable us to trust Him; God never gives feeling to encourage us to trust Him; God never gives feeling to show that we have already and utterly trusted Him.

God gives feeling only when He sees that we trust Him apart from all feeling, resting on His own Word and on His own faithfulness to His promise.

Never until then can the feeling (which is from God) possibly come; and God will give the feeling in such a measure and at such a time as His love sees best for the individual case.

We must choose between facing toward our feelings and facing toward God's facts. Our feelings may be as uncertain as the sea or the shifting sands. God's facts are as certain as the Rock of Ages, even Christ Himself, who is the same yesterday, today, and forever.

> *When darkness veils His lovely face*
> *I rest on His unchanging grace;*
> *In every high and stormy gale,*
> *My anchor holds within the veil.*

September 27

I have found an atonement (Job 33:24, margin).

Divine healing is just divine life. It is the headship of Christ over the body. It is the life of Christ in the frame. It is the union of our members with the very body of Christ and the inflowing life of Christ in our living members. It is as real as His risen and glorified body. It is as reasonable as the fact that He was raised from the dead and is a living Man with a true body and a rational soul today at God's right hand.

That living Christ belongs to us in all His attributes and powers. We are members of His body, His flesh, and His bones, and if we can only believe and receive it, we may live upon the very life of the Son of God. Lord, help me to know "the Lord for the body and the body for the Lord." A. B. SIMPSON

"The Lord thy God in the midst of thee is mighty" (Zeph. 3:17). This was the text that first flashed the truth of divine healing into my mind and worn-out body nearly a quarter century ago. It is still the door, wide open more than ever, through which the living Christ passes moment by moment into my redeemed body, filling, energizing, vitalizing it with the presence and power of His own personality, turning my whole being into a "new heaven and new earth." *"The Lord, thy God."* Thy God, my God. Then all that is in God Almighty is mine and in me just as far as I am able and willing to appropriate Him and all that belongs to Him. This God, "Mighty," ALL Mighty God, is our INSIDE God. He is, as Father, Son, and Holy Spirit, in the midst of me, just as really as the sun is in the center of the heavens, or like the great dynamo in the center of the powerhouse of my threefold being.

He is in the midst, at the center of my physical being. He is in the midst of my brain. He is in the midst of my nerve centers.

For twenty-one years it has been not only a living reality to me, but a reality growing deeper and richer, until now at the age of seventy years, I am in every sense a younger, fresher man than I was at thirty. At this present time I am in the strength of God, doing full twice as much work, mental and physical, as I have ever done in the best days of the past, and this observe, with less than half the effort then necessary. My life, physical, mental, and spiritual, is like an artesian well—always full, overflowing. To speak, teach, travel by night and day in all weather and through all the sudden and violent changes of our variable climate, is no more effort to me than it is for the mill-wheel to turn when the stream is full or for the pipe to let the water run through.

My body, soul and spirit thus redeemed,
Sanctified and healed I give, O Lord, to Thee,
A consecrated offering Thine ever more to be.
That all my powers with all their might
In Thy sole glory may unite—Hallelujah!

DR. HENRY WILSON

September 28

In me . . . peace (John 16:33).

There is a vast difference between happiness and blessedness. Paul had imprisonments and pains, sacrifice and suffering up to the very limit; but in the midst of it all, he was blessed. All the beatitudes came into his heart and life *in the midst* of those very conditions.

Paganini, the great violinist, came out before his audience one day and made the discovery just as they ended their applause that there was something wrong with his violin. He looked at it a second and then saw that it was not his famous and valuable one.

He felt paralyzed for a moment, then turned to his audience and told them there had been some mistake and he did not have his own violin. He stepped back behind the curtain thinking that it was still where he had left it, but discovered that someone had stolen his and left that old secondhand one in its place. He remained back of the curtain a moment, then came out before his audience and said: "Ladies and Gentlemen: I will show you that the music is not in the instrument, but in the soul." And he played as he had never played before; and out of that secondhand instrument, the music poured forth until the audience was enraptured with enthusiasm and the applause almost lifted the ceiling of the building, because the man had revealed to them that music was not in the machine but in his own soul.

It is your mission, tested and tried one, to walk out on the stage of this world and reveal to all earth and heaven that the music is not in conditions, not in the things, not in externals, but the music of life is in your own soul.

> *If peace be in the heart,*
> *The wildest winter storm is full of solemn beauty,*
> *The midnight flash but shows the path of duty,*
> *Each living creature tells some new and joyous story,*
> *The very trees and stones all catch a ray of glory,*
> *If peace be in the heart.*
>
> CHARLES FRANCIS RICHARDSON

September 29

I will give myself unto prayer (Ps. 109:4).

We are often in a *religious hurry* in our devotions. How much *time* do we spend in them daily? Can it not be easily reckoned in minutes? Who ever knew an eminently holy man who did *not* spend much of his time in prayer? Did ever a man exhibit *much* of the *spirit* of prayer, who did not devote much time in his closet?

Whitefield says, "Whole days and weeks have I spent prostrate on the ground, in silent or vocal prayer." "Fall upon your knees and *grow* there," is the language of another, who knew whereof he affirmed.

It has been said that no great work in literature or science was ever wrought by a man who did not love solitude. We may lay it down as an elemental principle of religion, that no large growth in holiness was ever gained by one who did not *take* time to be often, and long, *alone with God.*
FROM THE STILL HOUR

> *"Come, come," He saith, "O soul oppressed and weary,*
> *Come to the shadows of my desert rest;*
> *Come walk with Me far from life's babbling discords,*
> *And peace shall breathe like music in thy breast."*

September 30

As an eagle stirreth up her nest, fluttereth over her young, spreadeth abroad her wings, taketh them, beareth them on her wings: so the Lord alone did lead him, and there was no strange god with him (Deut. 32:11, 12).

Our Almighty Parent delights to conduct the tender nestlings of His care to the very edge of the precipice, and even to thrust them off into the steeps of air, that they may learn their possession of unrealized power of flight, to be forever a luxury; and if, in the attempt, they be exposed to unwonted peril, He is prepared to swoop beneath them, and to bear them upward on His mighty pinions. When God brings any of His children into a position of unparalleled difficulty, they may always count upon Him to deliver them. From The Song of Victory 🐝

"When God puts a burden upon you He puts His own arm underneath."

There is a little plant, small and stunted, growing under the shade of a broad-spreading oak; and this little plant values the shade which covers it, and greatly does it esteem the quiet rest which its noble friend affords. But a blessing is designed for this little plant.

Once upon a time there comes along the woodman, and with his sharp ax he fells the oak. The plant weeps and cries, "My shelter is departed; every rough wind will blow upon me, and every storm will seek to uproot me!"

"No, no," saith the angel of that flower, "now will the sun get at thee; now will the shower fall on thee in more copious abundance than before; now thy stunted form shall spring up into loveliness, and thy flower, which could never have expanded itself to perfection shall now laugh in the sunshine, and men shall say, "How greatly hath that plant increased! How glorious hath become its beauty, through the removal of that which was its shade and its delight!"

See you not, then, that God may take away your comforts and your privileges, to make you the better Christians? Why the Lord always trains His soldiers, not by letting them lie on feather beds, but by turning them out, and using them to forced marches and hard service. He makes them ford through streams, and swim through rivers, and climb mountains, and walk many a long march with heavy knapsacks of sorrow on their backs. This is the way in which He makes them soldiers—not by dressing them up in fine uniforms, to swagger at the barrack gates, and to be fine gentlemen in the eyes of the loungers in the park. God knows that soldiers are only to be made in battle; they are not to be grown in peaceful times. We may grow the stuff of which soldiers are made; but warriors are really educated by the smell of powder, in the midst of whizzing bullets and roaring cannonades, not in soft and peaceful times. Well, Christian, may not this account for it all? Is not thy Lord bringing out thy graces and making them grow? Is He not developing in you the qualities of the soldier by throwing you into the heat of battle, and should you not use every appliance to come off conqueror? SPURGEON

October 1

It is good for me that I have been afflicted (Ps. 119:71).

It is a remarkable circumstance that the most brilliant colors of plants are to be seen on the highest mountains, in spots that are most exposed to the wildest weather. The brightest lichens and mosses, the loveliest gems of wildflowers, abound far up on the bleak, storm-scalped peak.

One of the richest displays of organic coloring I ever beheld was near the summit of Mount Chenebettaz, a hill about 10,000 feet high, immediately above the great Saint Bernard Hospice. The whole face of an extensive rock was covered with a most vivid yellow lichen which shone in the sunshine like the golden battlement of an enchanted castle.

There, in that lofty region, amid the most frowning desolation, exposed to the fiercest tempest of the sky, this lichen exhibited a glory of color such as it never showed in the sheltered valley. I have two specimens of the same lichen before me while I write these lines, one from the great Saint Bernard, and the other from the wall of a Scottish castle, deeply embossed among sycamore trees; and the difference in point of form and coloring between them is most striking.

The specimen nurtured amid the wild storms of the mountain peak is of a lovely primrose hue, and is smooth in texture and complete in outline, while the specimen nurtured amid the soft airs and the delicate showers of the lowland valley is of a dim rusty hue, and is scurfy in texture, and broken in outline.

And is it not so with the Christian who is afflicted, tempest-tossed, and not comforted? Till the storms and vicissitudes of God's providence beat upon him again and again, his character appears marred and clouded; but trials clear away the obscurity, perfect the outlines of his disposition, and give brightness and blessing to his life.

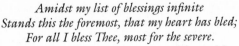

Amidst my list of blessings infinite
Stands this the foremost, that my heart has bled;
For all I bless Thee, most for the severe.

HUGH MACMILLAN

October 2

And he took them, and went aside privately into a desert place
(Luke 9:10).

In order to grow in grace, we must be much alone. It is not in society
that the soul grows most vigorously. In one single quiet hour of prayer it will
often make more progress than in days of company with others. It is in the
desert that the dew falls freshest and the air is purest. ANDREW BONAR

> *Come ye yourselves apart and rest awhile,*
> *Weary, I know it, of the press and throng,*
> *Wipe from your brow the sweat and dust of toil,*
> *And in My quiet strength again be strong.*
>
> *Come ye aside from all the world holds dear,*
> *For converse which the world has never known,*
> *Alone with Me, and with My Father here,*
> *With Me and with My Father not alone.*
>
> *Come, tell Me all that ye have said and done,*
> *Your victories and failures, hopes and fears.*
> *I know how hearty souls are wooed and won;*
> *My choicest wreaths are always wet with tears.*
>
> *Come ye and rest; the journey is too great,*
> *And ye will faint beside the way and sink;*
> *The bread of life is here for you to eat,*
> *And here for you the wine of love to drink.*
>
> *Then fresh from converse with your Lord return,*
> *And work till daylight softens into even:*
> *The brief hours are not lost in which ye learn*
> *More of your Master and His rest in Heaven.*

October 3

And after the earthquake a fire; and after the fire a sound of gentle stillness (1 Kings 19:12, margin RV).

A soul, who made rapid progress in her understanding of the Lord, was once asked the secret of her easy advancement. She replied tersely, *"Mind the checks."* And the reason that many of us do not know and better understand Him is, we do not give heed to His gentle checks, His delicate restraints and constraints. His is a still, small voice. A still voice can hardly be heard. It must be felt: a steady, gentle pressure upon the heart and mind like the touch of a morning zephyr in one's heart, but if heeded growing noiselessly clearer to your inner ear. His voice is for the ear of love, and love is intent upon hearing even faintest whispers. There comes a time also when love ceases to speak if not responded to, or believed in. He is love, and if you would know Him and His voice, give constant ear to His gentle touches. In conversation, when about to utter some word, give heed to that gentle voice, mind the check and refrain from speech. When about to pursue some course that seems all clear and right and there comes quietly to your spirit a suggestion that has in it the force almost of a conviction, give heed, even if changed plans seem highest folly from the standpoint of human wisdom. Learn also to wait on God for the unfolding of His will. Let God form your plans about everything in your mind and heart and then let Him execute them. Do not possess any wisdom of your own. For many times His execution will seem so contradictory to the plan He gave. He will seem to work against Himself. Simply listen, obey, and trust God even when it seems highest folly so to do. He will in the end make "all things work together," but so many times in the first appearance of the outworking of His plans,

> *In His own world He is content*
> *To play a losing game.*

So if you would know His voice, never consider results or possible effects. Obey even when He asks you to move in the dark. He Himself will be gloriously light in you. And there will spring up rapidly in your heart an acquaintanceship and a fellowship with God which will be overpowering in itself to hold you and Him together, even in severest testings and under most terrible pressures. FROM WAY OF FAITH

October 4

So the Lord blessed the latter end of Job more than his beginning
(Job 42:12).

Through his griefs Job came to his heritage. He was tried that his godliness might be confirmed. Are not my troubles intended to deepen my character and to robe me in graces I had little of before? I come to my glory through eclipses, tears, death. My ripest fruit grows against the roughest wall. Job's afflictions left him with higher conceptions of God and lowlier thoughts of himself. *"Now,"* he cried, *"mine eye seeth thee."*

And if, through pain and loss, I feel God so near in His majesty that I bend low before Him and pray, *"Thy will be done,"* I gain very much. God gave Job glimpses of the future glory. In those wearisome days and nights, he penetrated within the veil, and could say, *"I know that my Redeemer liveth."* Surely the latter end of Job was more blessed than the beginning. FROM IN THE HOUR OF SILENCE 🖋

"Trouble never comes to a man unless she brings a nugget of gold in her hand."

Apparent adversity will finally turn out to be the advantage of the right if we are only willing to keep on working and to wait patiently. How steadfastly the great victor souls have kept at their work, dauntless and unafraid! There are blessings which we cannot obtain if we cannot accept and endure suffering. There are joys that can come to us only through sorrow. There are revelings of divine truth which we can get only when earth's lights have gone out. There are harvests which can grow only after the plowshare has done its work. SELECTED 🖋

Out of suffering have emerged the strongest souls; the most massive characters are seamed with scars; martyrs have put on their coronation robes glittering with fire, and through their tears have the sorrowful first seen the gates of heaven. CHAPIN 🖋

I shall know by the gleam and glitter
Of the golden chain you wear,
By your heart's calm strength in loving,
Of the fire you have had to bear.
Beat on, true heart, forever;
Shine bright, strong golden chain;
And bless the cleansing fire
And the furnace of living pain!

ADELAIDE PROCTOR 🖋

October 5

It came to pass ... that the brook dried up (1 Kings 17:7).

The education of our faith is incomplete if we have not learned that there is a providence of loss, a ministry of failing and of fading things, a gift of emptiness. The material insecurities of life make for its spiritual establishment. The dwindling stream by which Elijah sat and mused is a true picture of the life of each of us. *"It came to pass ... that the brook dried up"*—that is the history of our yesterday, and a prophecy of our morrows.

In some way or other we will have to learn the difference between trusting in the gift and trusting in the Giver. The gift may be good for a while, but the Giver is the eternal love.

Cherith was a difficult problem to Elijah until he got to Zarephath, and then it was all as clear as daylight. God's hard words are never His last words. The woe and the waste and the tears of life belong to the interlude and not to the finale.

Had Elijah been led straight to Zarephath he would have missed something that helped to make him a wiser prophet and a better man. He lived by faith at Cherith. And whensoever in your life and mine some spring of earthly and outward resource has dried up, it has been that we might learn that our hope and help are in God who made heaven and earth. F. B. MEYER

Perchance thou, too, hast camped by such sweet waters,
And quenched with joy thy weary, parched soul's thirst;
To find, as time goes on, thy streamlet alters
From what it was at first.

Hearts that have cheered, or soothed, or blest, or stengthened;
Loves that have lavished so unstintedly;
Joys, treasured joys—have passed, as time hath lengthened,
Into obscurity.

If thus, ah soul, the brook thy heart hath cherished
Doth fail thee now—no more thy thirst assuage—
If its once glad refreshing streams have perished,
Let HIM thy heart engage.

He will not fail, nor mock, nor disappoint thee;
His consolations change not with the years;
With oil of joy He surely will anoint thee,
And wipe away thy tears.

J. DANSON SMITH

October 6

He opened not his mouth (Isa. 53:7).

How much grace it requires to bear a misunderstanding rightly, and to receive an unkind judgment in holy sweetness! Nothing tests the Christian character more than to have some evil thing said about him. This is the file that soon proves whether we are electroplate or solid gold. If we could only know the blessings that lie hidden in our trials we would say like David, when Shimei cursed him, "Let him curse; . . . it may be . . . that the Lord will requite me good for his cursing this day."

Some people get easily turned aside from the grandeur of their lifework by pursuing their own grievances and enemies, until their life gets turned into one little petty whirl of warfare. It is like a nest of hornets. You may disperse the hornets, but you will probably get terribly stung, and get nothing for your pains, for even their honey is not worth a search.

God give us more of His Spirit, "who, when he was reviled, reviled not again"; but "committed himself to him that judgeth righteously." "Consider him that endureth such contradiction of sinners against himself." A. B. SIMPSON

> *"Before you" He trod all the path of woe,*
> *He took the sharp thrusts with His head bent low.*
> *He knew deepest sorrow and pain and grief,*
> *He knew long endurance without relief,*
> *He took all the bitter from death's deep cup,*
> *He kept not a blood-drop but gave all up.*
> *"Before you" and for you, He won the fight*
> *To bring you to glory and realms of light.*

L. S. P.

October 7

Who is among you that feareth Jehovah, that obeyeth the voice of his servant? He that walketh in darkness and hath no light, let him trust in the name of Jehovah and rely upon his God (Isa. 50:10 RV).

What shall the believer do in times of darkness—the darkness of perplexity and confusion, not of heart but of mind? Times of darkness come

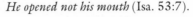

296

to the faithful and believing disciple who is walking obediently in the will of God; seasons when he does not know what to do, nor which way to turn. The sky is overcast with clouds. The clear light of heaven does not shine upon his pathway. One feels as if he were groping his way in darkness.

Beloved, is this you? What shall the believer do in times of darkness? Listen! "Let him trust in the name of the Lord, and rely upon his God."

The first thing to do is do nothing. This is hard for poor human nature to do. In the West there is a saying that runs thus, "When you're rattled, don't rush"; in other words, "When you don't know what to do, don't do it."

When you run into a spiritual fog bank, don't tear ahead; slow down the machinery of your life. If necessary, anchor your bark or let it swing at its moorings. We are to simply trust God. While we trust, God can work. Worry prevents Him from doing anything for us. If the darkness that overshadows us strikes terror to us; if we run hither and yon in a vain effort to find some way of escape out of a dark place of trial, where divine providence has put us, the Lord can do nothing for us.

The peace of God must quiet our minds and rest our hearts. We must put our hand in the hand of God like a little child, and let Him lead us out into the bright sunshine of His love.

He knows the way out of the woods. Let us climb up into His arms and trust Him to take us out by the shortest and surest road.
DR. PARDINGTON ❧

Remember we are never without a pilot when we know not how to steer.

> *Hold on, my heart, in thy believing—*
> *The steadfast only wins the crown;*
> *He who, when stormy winds are heaving,*
> *Parts with its anchor, shall go down;*
> *But he who Jesus holds through all,*
> *Shall stand, though Heaven and earth should fall.*
>
> *Hold out! There comes an end to sorrow;*
> *Hope from the dust shall conquering rise;*
> *The storm foretells a summer's morrow;*
> *The Cross points on to Paradise;*
> *The Father reigneth! cease all doubt;*
> *Hold on, my heart, hold on, hold on.*

October 8

Do not begin to be anxious (Phil. 4:6 PBV).

Not a few Christians live in a state of unbroken anxiety, and others fret and fume terribly. To be perfectly at peace amid the hurly-burly of daily life is a secret worth knowing. What is the use of worrying? It never made anybody strong; never helped anybody to do God's will; never made a way of escape for anyone out of perplexity. Worry spoils lives which would otherwise be useful and beautiful. Restlessness, anxiety, and care are absolutely forbidden by our Lord, who said: "Take no thought," that is, no anxious thought, "saying what shall we eat, or what shall we drink, or wherewithal shall we be clothed?" He does not mean that we are not to take forethought and that our life is to be without plan or method; but that we are not to worry about these things. People know you live in the realm of anxious care by the lines on your face, the tones of your voice, the minor key in your life, and the lack of joy in your spirit. Scale the heights of a life abandoned to God, then you will look down on the clouds beneath your feet. REV. DARLOW SARGEANT

It is always weakness to be fretting and worrying, questioning and mistrusting. Can we gain anything by it? Do we not unfit ourselves for action, and unhinge our minds for wise decision? We are sinking by our struggles when we might float by faith.

Oh, for grace to be quiet! Oh, to be still and know that Jehovah is God! The Holy One of Israel must defend and deliver His own. We may be sure that every word of His will stand, though the mountains should depart. He deserves to be confided in. Come, my soul, return unto thy rest, and lean thy head upon the bosom of the Lord Jesus. SELECTED

> *Peace thy inmost soul shall fill*
> *Lying still!*

October 9

Therefore will the Lord wait, that he may be gracious unto you (Isa. 30:18).

Where showers fall most, there the grass is greenest. I suppose the fogs and mists of Ireland make it "the Emerald Isle"; and whenever you find great fogs of trouble, and mists of sorrow, you always find emerald green hearts; full of the beautiful verdure of the comfort and love of God. O Christian, do not thou be saying, "Where are the swallows gone? They are gone; they are dead." They are not dead; they have skimmed the purple sea, and gone to a far-off land; but they will be back again by and by. Child of God, say not the flowers are dead; say not the winter has killed them, and they are gone. Ah, no! though winter hath coated them with the ermine of its snow; they will put up their heads again, and will be alive very soon. Say not, child of God, that the sun is quenched, because the cloud hath hidden it. Ah, no; he is behind there, brewing summer for thee; for when he cometh out again, he will have made the clouds fit to drop in April showers, all of them mothers of the sweet May flowers. And oh! above all, when thy God hides His face, say not that He hath forgotten thee. He is but tarrying a little while to make thee love Him better; and when He cometh, thou shalt have joy in the Lord, and shalt rejoice with joy unspeakable. Waiting exercises our grace; waiting tries our faith; therefore, wait on in hope; for though the promise tarry, it can never come too late. C. H. SPURGEON

Oh, every year hath its winter,
And every year hath its rain—
But a day is always coming
When the birds go north again.

When new leaves swell in the forest,
And grass springs green on the plain,
And alders' veins turn crimson—
And the birds go north again.

Oh, every heart hath its sorrow,
And every heart hath its pain—
But a day is always coming
When the birds go north again.

'Tis the sweetest thing to remember,
If courage be on the wane,
When the cold, dark days are over—
Why, the birds go north again.

October 10

Fret not (Ps. 37:1).

This to me is a divine command; the same as *"Thou shalt not steal."* Now let us get to the definition of fretting. One good definition is, "Made rough on the surface." "Rubbed, or worn away"; and a peevish, irrational, fault-finding person not only wears himself out, but is very wearing to others. To fret is to be in a state of vexation, and in this psalm we are not only told not to fret because of evildoers, but to fret not "in anywise." It is injurious, and God does not want us to hurt ourselves.

A physician will tell you that a fit of anger is more injurious to the system than a fever, and a fretful disposition is not conducive to a healthy body; and you know rules are apt to work both ways, and the next step down from fretting is crossness, and that amounts to anger. Let us settle this matter, and be obedient to the command, *"Fret not."* MARGARET BOTTOME

Overheard in an Orchard

Said the Robin to the Sparrow:
"I should really like to know
Why these anxious human beings
Rush about and worry so."

Said the Sparrow to the Robin:
"Friend, I think that it must be
That they have no Heavenly Father
Such as cares for you and me."

ELIZABETH CHENEY

October 11

As dying and behold we live (2 Cor. 6:9).

I had a bed of asters last summer that reached clear across my garden in the country. Oh, how gaily they bloomed. They were planted late. On the sides were yet fresh blossoming flowers, while the tops had gone to seed. Early frosts came, and I found one day that that long line of radiant beauty was seared, and I said, "Ah! the season is too much for them; they have perished"; and I bade them farewell.

I disliked to go and look at the bed, it looked so like a grave-yard of flowers. But, four or five weeks ago one of my men called my attention to the fact that along the whole line of that bed there were asters coming up in the greatest abundance; and I looked, and behold, for every plant that I thought the winter had destroyed there were fifty plants that it had planted. What did those frosts and surly winds do?

They caught my flowers, they slew them, they cast them to the ground, they trod with snowy feet upon them, and they said, leaving their work, *"This is the end of you."* And the next spring there were for every root, fifty witnesses to rise up and say, *"By death we live."*

And as it is in the floral tribe, so it is in God's kingdom. By death came everlasting life. By crucifixion and the sepulchre came the throne and the palace of the eternal God. By overthrow came victory.

Do not be afraid to suffer. Do not be afraid to be overthrown.

It is by being cast down and not destroyed; it is by being shaken to pieces, and the pieces torn to shreds, that men become men of might, and that one a host; whereas men that yield to the appearance of things, and go with the world, have their quick blossoming, their momentary prosperity and then their end, which is an end forever. BEECHER

Measure thy life by loss and not by gain,
Not by the wine drunk, but by the wine poured forth.
For love's strength standeth in love's sacrifice,
And he who suffers most has most to give.

October 12

And Joseph's master took him, and put him into the prison. . . .
But the Lord was with Joseph . . . and that which he did, the Lord
made it to prosper (Gen. 39:20, 21, 23).

When God lets us go to prison because we have been serving Him, and goes there with us, prison is about the most blessed place in the world that we could be in. Joseph seems to have known that. He did not sulk and grow discouraged and rebellious because "everything was against him." If he had, the prison-keeper would never have trusted him so. Joseph does not even seem to have pitied himself.

Let us remember that if *self-pity* is allowed to set in, that is the end of us—until it is cast utterly from us. Joseph just turned over everything in joyous trust to God, and so the keeper of the prison turned over everything to

Joseph. Lord Jesus, when the prison doors close in on me, keep me trusting, and keep my joy full and abounding. Prosper Thy work through me in prison: even there, make me free indeed. SELECTED

A little bird I am,
Shut from the fields of air,
And in my cage I sit and sing
To Him who placed me there;
Well pleased a prisoner to be,
Because, My God, it pleaseth Thee.

My cage confines me round,
Abroad I cannot fly,
But though my wing is closely bound,
My soul is at liberty;
For prison walls cannot control
The flight, the freedom of the soul.

I have learnt to love the darkness of sorrow; there you see the brightness of His face. MADAME GUYON

October 13

In nothing be anxious (Phil. 4:6).

No anxiety ought to be found in a believer. Great, many, and varied may be our trials, our afflictions, our difficulties, and yet there should be no anxiety under any circumstances, because we have a Father in heaven who is almighty, who loves His children as He loves His only-begotten Son, and whose very joy and delight it is to succor and help them at all times and under all circumstances. We should attend to the Word, "In nothing be anxious, but in everything by prayer and supplication with thanksgiving let your requests be made known unto God."

"In everything," that is not merely when the house is on fire, not merely when the beloved wife and children are on the brink of the grave, but in the smallest matters of life, bring everything before God, the little things, the very little things, what the world calls trifling things—*everything*—living in holy communion with our heavenly Father and with our precious Lord Jesus all day long. And when we awake at night, by a kind of spiritual instinct again turning to Him, and speaking to Him, bringing our various little matters before Him in the sleepless night, the difficulties

in connection with the family, our trade, our profession. Whatever tries us in any way, speak to the Lord about it.

"By prayer and supplication," taking the place of beggars, with earnestness, with perseverance, going on and waiting, waiting, waiting on God.

"With thanksgiving." We should at all times lay a good foundation with thanksgiving. If everything else were wanting, this is always present, that He has saved us from hell. Then, that He has given us His Holy Word—His Son, His choicest gift—and the Holy Spirit. Therefore we have abundant reason for thanksgiving. O let us aim at this!

"And the peace of God which passeth all understanding, shall keep your hearts and minds in Christ Jesus." And this is so great a blessing, so real a blessing, so precious a blessing, that it must be known *experimentally* to be entered into, for it passeth understanding. O, let us lay these things to heart, and the result will be, if we habitually walk in this spirit, we shall far more abundantly glorify God, than as yet we have done. FROM GEORGE MUELLER, IN LIFE OF TRUST ☞

Twice or thrice a day, look to see if your heart is not disquieted about something; and if you find that it is, take care forthwith to restore it to calm. FRANCIS DE SALES ☞

October 14

The angel of the Lord came upon him [Peter] and a light shined in the prison; and he smote Peter on the side, and raised him up, saying, Arise up quickly. And his chains fell off (Acts 12:7). *And at midnight Paul and Silas prayed and sang praises unto God.... And suddenly there was a great earthquake, so that the foundations of the prison were shaken; and immediately all the doors were opened and every one's bands were loosed* (Acts 16:25, 26).

This is God's way. In the darkest hours of the night, His tread draws near across the billows. As the day of execution is breaking, the angel comes to Peter's cell. When the scaffold for Mordecai is complete, the royal sleeplessness leads to a reaction in favor of the favored race.

Ah, soul, it may have to come to the worst with thee ere thou art delivered; but thou wilt be delivered! God may keep thee waiting, but He will ever be mindful of His covenant, and will appear to fulfill His inviolable Word. F. B. MEYER ☞

There's a simplicity about God in working out His plans, yet a resourcefulness equal to any difficulty, and an unswerving faithfulness to His trusting child, and an unforgetting steadiness in holding to His purpose. Through a fellow-prisoner, then a dream, He lifts Joseph from a prison to a premiership. And the length of stay in the prison prevents dizziness in the premier. It's safe to trust God's methods and to go by His clock. S. D. GORDON

Providence hath a thousand keys to open a thousand sundry doors for the deliverance of His own, when it is even come to a desperate case. Let us be faithful; and care for our own part which is to suffer for Him, and lay Christ's part on Himself, and leave it there. GEORGE MACDONALD

Difficulty is the very atmosphere of miracle—it is a miracle in its first stage. If it is to be a great miracle, the condition is not difficulty but impossibility.

The clinging hand of His child makes a desperate situation a delight to Him.

October 15

By reason of breakings they purify themselves (Job 41:25).

God uses most for His glory those people and things which are most perfectly broken. The sacrifices He accepts are broken and contrite hearts. It was the breaking down of Jacob's natural strength at Peniel that got him where God could clothe him with spiritual power. It was breaking the surface of the rock at Horeb, by the stroke of Moses' rod, that let out the cool waters to thirsty people.

It was when the three hundred elect soldiers under Gideon broke their pitchers, a type of breaking themselves, that the hidden lights shone forth to the consternation of their adversaries. It was when the poor widow broke the seal of the little pot of oil, and poured it forth, that God multiplied it to pay her debts and supply means of support.

It was when Esther risked her life and broke through the rigid etiquette of a heathen court, that she obtained favor to rescue her people from death. It was when Jesus took the five loaves and broke them, that the bread was multiplied in the very act of breaking, sufficient to feed five thousand. It was when Mary broke her beautiful alabaster box, rendering it henceforth useless, that the pent-up perfume filled the house. It was when Jesus allowed His precious body to be broken to pieces by thorns and nails and spear, that His inner life was poured out, like a crystal ocean, for thirsty sinners to drink and live.

It is when a beautiful grain of corn is broken up in the earth by DEATH, that its inner heart sprouts forth and bears hundreds of other grains. And thus, on and on, through history, and all biography, and all vegetation, and all spiritual life, God must have BROKEN THINGS.

Those who are broken in wealth, and broken in self-will, and broken in their ambitions, and broken in their beautiful ideals, and broken in worldly reputation, and broken in their affections, and broken ofttimes in health; those who are despised and seem utterly forlorn and helpless, the Holy Ghost is seizing upon, and using for God's glory. "The lame take the prey," Isaiah tells us.

O break my heart; but break it as a field
Is by the plough up-broken for the corn;
O break it as the buds, by green leaf sealed,
Are, to unloose the golden blossom, torn;
Love would I offer unto Love's great Master,
Set free the odor, break the alabaster.

O break my heart; break it victorious God,
That life's eternal well may flash abroad;
O let it break as when the captive trees,
Breaking cold bonds, regain their liberties;
And as thought's sacred grove to life is springing,
Be joys, like birds, their hope, Thy victory singing.

THOMAS TOKE BUNCH

October 16

Let us lay aside every weight, and the sin which doth so easily beset us, and let us run with patience the race that is set before us (Heb. 12:1).

There are weights which are not sins themselves, but which become distractions and stumbling blocks in our Christian progress. One of the worst of these is despondency. The heavy heart is indeed a weight that will surely drag us down in our holiness and usefulness.

The failure of Israel to enter the land of promise began in murmuring, or, as the text in Numbers literally puts it, *"as it were murmured."* Just a faint desire to complain and be discontented. This led on until it blossomed and ripened into rebellion and ruin. Let us give ourselves no liberty ever to doubt God or His love and faithfulness to us in everything and forever.

We can set our will against doubt just as we do against any other sin; and as we stand firm and refuse to doubt, the Holy Spirit will come to our aid and give us the faith of God and crown us with victory.

It is very easy to fall into the habit of doubting, fretting, and wondering if God has forsaken us and if, after all, our hopes are to end in failure. Let us refuse to be discouraged. Let us refuse to be unhappy. Let us "count it all joy" when we cannot feel one emotion of happiness. Let us rejoice by faith, by resolution, by reckoning, and we shall surely find that God will make the reckoning real. SELECTED

The Devil has two master tricks. One is *to get us discouraged;* then for a time at least we can be of no service to others, and so are defeated. The other is to *make us doubt,* thus breaking the faith link by which we are bound to our Father. Look out! Do not be tricked either way. G. E. M.

Gladness! I like to cultivate the spirit of gladness! It puts the soul so in tune again, and keeps it in tune, so that Satan is shy of touching it—the chords of the soul become too warm, or too full of heavenly electricity, for his infernal fingers, and he goes off somewhere else! Satan is always very shy of meddling with me when my heart is full of gladness and joy in the Holy Ghost.

My plan is to shun the spirit of *sadness* as I would Satan; but, alas! I am not always successful. Like the Devil himself it meets me on the highway of *usefulness,* looks me so fully in my face, till my poor soul changes color!

Sadness discolors everything; it leaves all objects *charmless;* it involves future prospects in darkness; it deprives the soul of all its aspirations, enchains all its powers, and produces a mental paralysis!

An *old believer* remarked, that *cheerfulness* in religion makes all its services come off with delight; and that we are never carried forward so swiftly in the ways of duty as when borne on the wings of *delight;* adding, that *melancholy* clips such wings; or, to alter the figure, takes off our chariot wheels in duty, and makes them, like those of the Egyptians, drag heavily.

October 17

God forbid that I should glory, save in the cross of our Lord Jesus Christ, by whom the world is crucified unto me, and I unto the world (Gal. 6:14).

They were living to themselves; self with its hopes, and promises and dreams, still had hold of them; but the Lord began to fulfill their prayers. They had asked for contrition and had surrendered for it to be given them at any cost, and He sent them sorrow; they had asked for purity, and He sent them thrilling anguish; they had asked to be meek, and He had broken their hearts; they had asked to be dead to the world, and He slew all their living hopes; they had asked to be made like unto Him, and He placed them in the furnace, sitting by "as a refiner and purifier of silver," until they should reflect His image; they had asked to lay hold of His cross, and when He had reached it to them it lacerated their hands.

They had asked they knew not what, nor how, but He had taken them at their word and granted them all their petitions. They were hardly willing to follow Him so far or to draw so nigh to Him. They had upon them an awe and fear, as Jacob at Bethel, or Eliphaz in the night visions, or as the apostles when they thought that they had seen a spirit and knew not that it was Jesus. They could almost pray Him to depart from them, or to hide His awfulness. They found it easier to obey than to suffer, to do than to give up, to bear the cross than to hang upon it. But they cannot go back, for they have come too near the unseen cross, and its virtues have pierced too deeply within them. He is fulfilling to them His promise, "And I, if I be lifted up from the earth, will draw all men unto me" (John 12:32).

But now at last their turn has come. Before, they had only heard of the mystery, but now they feel it. He has fastened on them His look of love, as He did on Mary and Peter, and they can but choose to follow.

Little by little, from time to time, by flitting gleams, the mystery of His cross shines out upon them. They behold Him lifted up, they gaze on the glory which rays from the wounds of His holy passion; and as they gaze they advance and are changed into His likeness, and His name shines out through them, for He dwells in them. They live alone with Him above, in unspeakable fellowship; willing to lack what others own (and what they might have had), and to be unlike all, so that they are only like Him.

Such are they in all ages "who follow the Lamb whithersoever he goeth."

Had they chosen for themselves, or their friends chosen for them, they would have chosen otherwise. They would have been brighter here but less glorious in His kingdom. They would have had Lot's portion, not Abraham's. If they had halted anywhere—if God had taken off His hand and let them stray back—what would they not have lost? What forfeits in the resurrection?

But He stayed them up, even against themselves. Many a time their foot had well nigh slipped; but He in mercy held them up. Now, even in this life, they know that all He did was done well. It was good to suffer here, that they might reign hereafter; to bear the cross below, for they shall wear the crown above; and that not their will but His was done on them and in them. ANONYMOUS ❧

October 18

Know of a surety that thy seed shall be a stranger in a land that is not theirs; ... they shall afflict them four hundred years; ... and afterward shall they come out with great substance (Gen. 15:13–14).

An assured part of God's pledged blessing to us is delay and suffering. A delay in Abram's own lifetime that seemed to put God's pledge beyond fulfillment was followed by seemingly unendurable delay of Abram's descendants. But it was only a delay: they *"came out with great substance."* The pledge was redeemed.

God is going to test me with delays; and with the delays will come suffering, but through it all stands God's pledge: His new covenant with me in Christ, and His inviolable promise of every lesser blessing that I need. The delay and the suffering are part of the promised blessing; let me praise Him for them today; and let me wait on the Lord and be of good courage, and He will strengthen my heart. C. G. TRUMBULL

> *Unanswered yet the prayer your lips have pleaded*
> *In agony of heart these many years?*
> *Does faith begin to fail? Is hope departing?*
> *And think you all in vain those falling tears?*
> *Say not the Father hath not heard your prayer;*
> *You shall have your desire sometime, somewhere.*
>
> *Unanswered yet? Nay do not say ungranted;*
> *Perhaps your work is not yet wholly done.*
> *The work began when first your prayer was uttered,*
> *And God will finish what He has begun.*
> *If you will keep the incense burning there,*
> *His glory you shall see sometime, somewhere.*
>
> *Unanswered yet? Faith cannot be unanswered,*
> *Her feet are firmly planted on the Rock;*
> *Amid the wildest storms she stands undaunted,*
> *Nor quails before the loudest thunder shock.*
> *She knows Omnipotence has heard her prayer,*
> *And cries, "It shall be done"—sometime, somewhere.*
>
> MISS OPHELIA G. BROWNING

October 19

The ark of the covenant of the Lord went before them (Num. 10:33).

God does give us impressions, but not that we should act on them as impressions. If the impression be from God, He will Himself give sufficient evidence to establish it beyond the possibility of a doubt.

How beautiful is the story of Jeremiah, of the impression that came to him respecting the purchase of the field of Anathoth. But Jeremiah did not act upon this impression until after the following day, when his uncle's son came to him and brought him external evidence by making a proposal for the purchase. Then Jeremiah said: *"I knew this was the word of the Lord."*

He waited until God seconded the impression by a providence, and then he acted in full view of the open facts, which could bring conviction unto others as well as to himself. God wants us to act according to His mind. We are not to ignore the Shepherd's personal voice but, like Paul and his companions at Troas, we are to listen to all the voices that speak and "gather" from all the circumstances, as they did, the full mind of the Lord. Dr. Simpson

Where God's finger points, there God's hand will make the way.

Do not say in thine heart what thou wilt or wilt not do, but wait upon God until He makes known His way. So long as that way is hidden it is clear that there is no need of action, and that *He accounts Himself responsible for all the results of keeping thee where thou art.* Selected

For God through ways we have not known,
Will lead His own.

October 20

And the peace of God, which transcends all our powers of thought, will be a garrison to guard your hearts and minds in Christ Jesus (Phil. 4:7 weymouth).

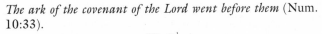

There is what is called the "cushion of the sea." Down beneath the surface that is agitated by storms, and driven about with winds, there is a part of the sea that is never stirred. When we dredge the bottom and bring up the

remains of animal and vegetable life we find that they give evidence of not having been disturbed in the least, for hundreds and thousands of years. The peace of God is that eternal calm which, like the cushion of the sea, lies far too deep down to be reached by any external trouble or disturbance; and he who enters into the presence of God becomes partaker of that undisturbed and undisturbable calm. Dr. A. T. Pierson

When winds are raging o'er the upper ocean,
And billows wild contend with angry roar,
'Tis said, far down beneath the wild commotion,
That peaceful stillness reigneth evermore.

Far, far beneath, the noise of tempest dieth,
And silver waves chime ever peacefully,
And no rude storm, how fierce soe'er it flieth,
Disturbs the Sabbath of that deeper sea.

So to the heart that knows Thy love, O Purest,
There is a temple sacred evermore,
And all the babble of life's angry voices
Dies in hushed silence at its peaceful door.

Far, far away, the roar of passion dieth,
And loving thoughts rise calm and peacefully,
And no rude storm, how fierce soe'er it flieth,
Disturbs the soul that dwells, O Lord, in Thee.
Harriet Beecher Stowe

"The Pilgrim they laid in a large upper chamber, facing the sunrising. The name of the chamber was Peace." From Bunyan's Pilgrim's Progress

October 21

For we know that if our earthly house of this tabernacle were dissolved, we have a building of God, an house not made with hands, eternal in the heavens (2 Cor. 5:1).

The owner of the tenement which I have occupied for many years has given notice that he will furnish but little or nothing more for repairs. I am advised to be ready to move.

At first this was not a very welcome notice. The surroundings here are in many respects very pleasant, and were it not for the evidence of decay, I should consider the house good enough. But even a light wind causes it to tremble and totter, and all the braces are not sufficient to make it secure. So I am getting ready to move.

It is strange how quickly one's interest is transferred to the prospective home. I have been consulting maps of the new country and reading descriptions of its inhabitants. One who visited it has returned, and from him I learn that it is beautiful beyond description; language breaks down in attempting to tell of what he heard while there. He says that, in order to make an investment there, he has suffered the loss of all things that he owned here, and even rejoices in what others would call making a sacrifice. Another, whose love to me has been proven by the greatest possible test, is not there. He has sent me several clusters of the most delicious fruits. After tasting them, all food here seems insipid.

Two or three times I have been down by the border of the river that forms the boundary, and have wished myself among the company of those who were singing praises to the King on the other side. Many of my friends have moved there. Before leaving they spoke of my coming later. I have seen the smile upon their faces as they passed out of sight. Often I am asked to make some new investments here, but my answer in every case is, "I am getting ready to move." Selected ☞

The words often on Jesus' lips in His last days express vividly the idea, "going to the Father." We, too, who are Christ's people, have vision of something beyond the difficulties and disappointments of this life. We are journeying toward fulfillment, completion, expansion of life. We, too, are "going to the Father." Much is dim concerning our home-country, but two things are clear. It is home, "the Father's house." It is the nearer presence of the Lord. We are all wayfarers, but the believer knows it and accepts it. He is a traveler, not a settler. R. C. Gillie ☞

The little birds trust God, for they go singing
From northern woods where autumn winds have blown,
With joyous faith their trackless pathway winging
To summer-lands of song, afar, unknown.

Let us go singing, then, and not go sighing:
Since we are sure our times are in His hand,
Why should we weep, and fear, and call it dying?
'Tis only flitting to a Summer-land.

Selected ☞

October 22

Now Moses kept the flock of Jethro his father-in-law, the priest of Midian: and he led the flock to the backside of the desert, and came to the mountain of God, even to Horeb. And the angel of the Lord appeared unto him in a flame of fire out of the midst of a bush (Exod. 3:1–2).

The vision came in the midst of common toil, and that is where the Lord delights to give His revelations. He seeks a man who is on the ordinary road, and the divine fire leaps out at his feet. The mystic ladder can rise from the marketplace to heaven. It can connect the realm of drudgery with the realms of grace.

My Father God, help me to expect Thee on the ordinary road. I do not ask for sensational happenings. Commune with me through ordinary work and duty. Be my Companion when I take the common journey. Let the humble life be transfigured by Thy presence.

Some Christians think they must be always up to mounts of extraordinary joy and revelation; this is not after God's method. Those spiritual visits to high places, and that wonderful intercourse with the unseen world, are *not* in the promises; the daily life of communion *is*. And it is enough. We shall have the exceptional revelation if it be right for us.

There were but three disciples allowed to see the Transfiguration, and those three entered the gloom of Gethsemane. No one can stay on the mount of privilege. There are duties in the valley. Christ found His life-work, not in the glory, but in the valley, and was there truly and fully the Messiah. The value of the vision and glory is but their gift of fitness for work and endurance. SELECTED

October 23

There hath not failed one word of all his good promise (1 Kings 8:56).

Someday we shall understand that God has a reason in every NO which He speaks through the slow movement of life. "Somehow God makes up to us." How often, when His people are worrying and perplexing themselves about their prayers not being answered, is God answering them in a far richer way! Glimpse of this we see occasionally, but the full revelation of it remains for the future.

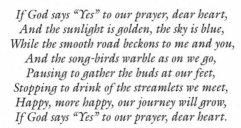

If God says "Yes" to our prayer, dear heart,
And the sunlight is golden, the sky is blue,
While the smooth road beckons to me and you,
And the song-birds warble as on we go,
Pausing to gather the buds at our feet,
Stopping to drink of the streamlets we meet,
Happy, more happy, our journey will grow,
If God says "Yes" to our prayer, dear heart.

If God says "No" to our prayer, dear heart,
And the clouds hang heavy and dull and gray;
If the rough rocks hinder and block the way,
While the sharp winds pierce us and sting with cold;
Ah, dear, there is home at the journey's end,
And these are the trials the Father doth send
To draw us as sheep to His Heavenly fold,
If God says "No" to our prayer, dear heart.

Oh, for the faith that does not make haste, but waits patiently for the Lord, waits for the explanation that shall come in the end, at the revelation of Jesus Christ! When did God take anything from a man without giving him manifold more in return? Suppose that the return had not been made immediately manifest, what then? Is today the limit of God's working time? Has He no provinces beyond this little world? Does the door of the grave open upon nothing but infinite darkness and eternal silence?

Yet, even confining the judgment within the hour of this life, it is true that God never touches the heart with a trial without intending to bring upon it some grander gift, some tenderer benediction. *He has attained to an eminent degree of Christian grace who knows how to wait.* SELECTED

When the frosts are in the valley,
And the mountain tops are grey,
And the choicest buds are blighted,
And the blossoms die away,
A loving Father whispers,
"This cometh from my hand";
Blessed are ye if ye trust
Where ye cannot understand.

If, after years of toiling,
Your wealth should fly away
And leave your hands all empty,
And your locks are turning grey,

Remember then your Father
Owns all the sea and land;
Blessed are ye if ye trust
Where ye cannot understand.

October 24

I will make thee a new sharp threshing instrument (Isa. 41:15).

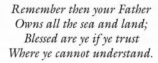

A bar of steel worth five dollars, when wrought into horseshoes, is worth ten dollars. If made into needles, it is worth three hundred and fifty dollars; if into penknife blades, it is worth thirty-two thousand dollars; if into springs for watches it is worth two hundred and fifty thousand dollars. What a drilling the poor bar must undergo to be worth this! But the more it is manipulated, the more it is hammered and passed through the fire, and beaten and pounded and polished, the greater the value.

May this parable help us to be silent, still, and longsuffering. Those who suffer most are capable of yielding most; and it is through pain that God is getting the most out of us, for His glory and the blessing of others. SELECTED

> *Oh, give Thy servant patience to be still,*
> *And bear Thy will;*
> *Courage to venture wholly on the arm*
> *That will not harm;*
> *The wisdom that will never let me stray*
> *Out of my way;*
> *The love that, now afflicting, knoweth best*
> *When I should rest.*

Life is very mysterious. Indeed it would be inexplicable unless we believed that God was preparing us for scenes and ministries that lie beyond the veil of sense in the eternal world, where highly tempered spirits will be required for special service.

> *The turning-lathe that has the sharpest knives*
> *produces the finest work.*

October 25

Hitherto have ye asked nothing in my name: ask and ye shall receive, that your joy may be full (John 16:24).

During the Civil War, a man had an only son who enlisted in the armies of the Union. The father was a banker and, although he consented to his son's going, it seemed as if it would break his heart to let him go.

He became deeply interested in the soldier boys, and whenever he saw a uniform, his heart went out as he thought of his own dear boy. He spent his time, neglected his business, gave his money to caring for the soldiers who came home invalid. His friends remonstrated with him, saying he had no right to neglect his business and spend so much thought upon the soldiers, so he fully decided to give it all up.

After he had come to this decision, there stepped into his bank one day a private soldier in a faded, worn uniform, who showed in his face and hands the marks of the hospital.

The poor fellow was fumbling in his pocket to get something or other, when the banker saw him and, perceiving his purpose, said to him: "My dear fellow, I cannot do anything for you today. I am extremely busy. You will have to go to your headquarters; the officers there will look after you."

Still the poor convalescent stood not seeming to fully understand what was said to him. Still he fumbled in his pockets and, by and by, drew out a scrap of dirty paper, on which there were a few lines written with a pencil, and laid this soiled sheet before the banker. On it he found these words: "Dear Father: This is one of my comrades who was wounded in the last fight and has been in the hospital. Please receive him as myself.—Charlie."

In a moment all the resolutions of indifference which this man made, flew away. He took the boy to his palatial home, put him in Charlie's room, gave him Charlie's seat at the table, kept him until food and rest and love had brought him back to health, and then sent him back again to imperil his life for the flag. SELECTED ☞

Now shalt thou SEE what I will do (Exod. 6:1).

October 26

He went up into a mountain apart to pray: and when the evening was come, he was there alone (Matt. 14:23).

The man Christ Jesus felt the need of perfect solitude—*Himself alone,* entirely by Himself, alone with Himself. We know how much intercourse with men draws us away from ourselves and exhausts our powers. The man Christ Jesus knew this, too, and felt the need of being by Himself again, of gathering all His powers, of realizing fully His high destiny, His human weakness, His entire dependence on the Father.

How much more does the child of God need this—*himself alone* with spiritual realities, *himself alone* with God the Father. If ever there were one who could dispense with special seasons for solitude and fellowship, it was our Lord. But He could not do His work or maintain His fellowship in full power without His quiet time.

Would God that every servant of His understood and practiced this blessed art, and that the church knew how to train its children into some sense of this high and holy privilege, that every believer may and must have his time when he is indeed himself alone with God. Oh, the thought to have God all alone to myself, and to know that God has me all alone to Himself! ANDREW MURRAY 🐝

Lamertine speaks in one of his books of a secluded walk in his garden where his mother always spent a certain hour of the day, upon which nobody ever dreamed for a moment of intruding. It was the holy garden of the Lord to her. Poor souls that have no such Beulah land! Seek thy private chamber, Jesus says. It is in the solitude that we catch the mystic notes that issue from the soul of things.

A Meditation

My soul, practice being alone with Christ! It is written that *when they were alone He expounded all things to His disciples.* Do not wonder at the saying; it is true to thine experience. If thou wouldst understand *thyself,* send the multitude away. Let them go out one by one till thou art left alone with Jesus.... Hast thou ever pictured thyself the one remaining creature in the earth, the one remaining creature in all the starry worlds?

In such a universe thine every thought would be "God and I! God and I!" And yet He is as near to thee as that—as near as if in the boundless spaces there throbbed no heart but His and thine. Practice that solitude, O my soul! Practice the expulsion of the crowd! Practice the stillness of thine own heart! Practice the solemn refrain "God and I! God and I!" Let none interpose between thee and thy wrestling angel! Thou shalt be both condemned and pardoned when thou shalt meet Jesus alone! GEORGE MATHESON 🐝

October 27

All thy waves and thy billows are gone over me (Ps. 42:7).

> They are HIS billows, whether they go o'er us,
> Hiding His face in smothering spray and foam;
> Or smooth and sparkling, spread a path before us,
> And to our haven bear us safely home.
>
> They are HIS billows, whether for our succor
> He walks across them, stilling all our fears;
> Or to our cry there comes no aid nor answer,
> And in the lonely silence none is near.
>
> They are HIS billows, whether we are toiling
> Through tempest-driven waves that never cease,
> While deep to deep with clamor loud is calling;
> Or at His word they hush themselves in peace.
>
> They are HIS billows, whether He divides them,
> Making us walk dryshod where seas had flowed;
> Or lets tumultuous breakers surge about us,
> Rushing unchecked across our only road.
>
> They are HIS billows, and He brings us through them;
> So He has promised, so His love will do.
> Keeping and leading, guiding and upholding,
> To His sure harbor, He will bring us through.

ANNIE JOHNSON FLINT

Stand up in the place where the dear Lord has put you, and there do your best. God gives us trial tests. He puts life before us as an antagonist face-to-face. Out of the buffeting of a serious conflict we are expected to grow strong. The tree that grows where tempests toss its boughs and bend its trunk often almost to breaking, is often more firmly rooted than the tree which grows in the sequestered valley where no storm ever brings stress or strain. The same is true of life. The grandest character is grown in hardship. SELECTED

October 28

But God, who is rich in mercy, for his great love wherewith he loved us, even when we were dead in sins, hath quickened us together with Christ ... and hath raised us up together, and made us sit together in heavenly places in Christ Jesus (Eph. 2:4–6).

This is our rightful place, to be "seated in heavenly places in Christ Jesus," and to "sit still" there. But how few there are who make it their actual experience! How few indeed think even that it is possible for them to "sit still" in these "heavenly places" in the everyday life of a world so full of turmoil as this.

We may believe perhaps that to pay a little visit to these heavenly places on Sundays, or now and then in times of spiritual exaltation, may be within the range of possibility; but to be actually "seated" there *every day and all day long* is altogether another matter; and yet it is very plain that it is for Sundays and weekdays as well.

A quiet spirit is of inestimable value in carrying on outward activities; and nothing so hinders the working of the hidden spiritual forces, upon which, after all, our success in everything really depends, as a spirit of unrest and anxiety.

There is immense power in stillness. A great saint once said, "All things come to him who knows how to trust and be silent." The words are pregnant with meaning. A knowledge of this fact would immensely change our ways of working. Instead of restless struggles, we would "sit down" inwardly before the Lord, and would let the divine forces of His Spirit work out in silence the ends to which we aspire. You may not see or feel the operations of this silent force, but be assured it is always working mightily, and will work for you, if you only get your spirit still enough to be carried along by the currents of its power. HANNAH WHITALL SMITH

There is a point of rest
At the great center of the cyclone's force,
A silence at its secret source;
A little child might slumber undisturbed,
Without the ruffle of one fair curl,
In that strange, central calm, amid the mighty whirl.

It is your business to learn to be peaceful and safe
in God in every situation.

318

October 29

He shall sit as a refiner and purifer of silver (Mal. 3:3).

Our Father, who seeks to perfect His saints in holiness, knows the value of the refiner's fire. It is with the most precious metals that the assayer takes the most pains, and subjects them to the hot fire, because such fires melt the metal, and only the molten mass releases its alloy or takes perfectly its new form in the mold. *The old refiner never leaves his crucible, but sits down by it,* lest there should be one excessive degree of heat to mar the metal. But as soon as he skims from the surface the last of the dross, and sees his own face reflected, he puts out the fire. ARTHUR T. PIERSON

He sat by a fire of seven-fold heat,
As He watched by the precious ore,
And closer He bent with a searching gaze
As He heated it more and more.
He knew He had ore that could stand the test,
And He wanted the finest gold
To mould as a crown for the King to wear,
Set with gems with a price untold.
So He laid our gold in the burning fire,
Tho' we fain would have said Him "Nay,"
And He watched the dross that we had not seen,
And it melted and passed away.
And the gold grew brighter and yet more bright,
But our eyes were so dim with tears,
We saw but the fire—not the Master's hand,
And questioned with anxious fears.
Yet our gold shone out with a richer glow,
As it mirrored a Form above,
That bent o'er the fire, tho' unseen by us,
With a look of ineffable love.
Can we think that it pleases His loving heart
To cause us a moment's pain?
Ah, no! but He saw through the present cross
The bliss of eternal gain.
So He waited there with a watchful eye,
With a love that is strong and sure,
And His gold did not suffer a bit more heat,
Than was needed to make it pure.

October 30

Let us run with patience (Heb. 12:1).

To *run* with patience is a very difficult thing. Running is apt to suggest the *absence* of patience, the eagerness to reach the goal. We commonly associate patience with lying down. We think of it as the angel that guards the couch of the invalid. Yet, I do not think the invalid's patience the hardest to achieve.

There is a patience which I believe to be harder—the patience that can run. To lie down in the time of grief, to be quiet under the stroke of adverse fortune, implies a great strength; but I know of something that implies a strength greater still: It is the power to *work* under a stroke; to have a great weight at your heart and still to run; to have a deep anguish in your spirit and still perform the daily task. It is a Christlike thing!

Many of us would nurse our grief without crying if we were *allowed* to nurse it. The hard thing is that most of us are called to exercise our patience, not in bed, but in the street. We are called to bury our sorrows not in lethargic quiescence, but in active service—in the exchange, in the workshop, in the hour of social intercourse, in the contribution to another's joy. There is no burial of sorrow so difficult as that; it is the "*running* with patience."

This was *Thy* patience, O Son of man! It was at once a waiting and a running—a waiting for the goal, and a doing of the lesser work meantime. I see Thee at Cana turning the water into wine lest the marriage feast should be clouded. I see Thee in the desert feeding a multitude with bread just to relieve a temporary want. All, all the time, Thou wert bearing a mighty grief, unshared, unspoken. Men ask for a rainbow in the cloud; but I would ask *more* from Thee. I would be, in my cloud, myself a rainbow— a minister to others' joy. My patience will be perfect when it can *work* in the vineyard. GEORGE MATHESON

> *When all our hopes are gone,*
> *'Tis well our hands must keep toiling on*
> *For others' sake:*
> *For strength to bear is found in duty done;*
> *And he is best indeed who learns to make*
> *The joy of others cure his own heartache.*

October 31

Likewise the Spirit also helpeth our infirmities; for we know not what we should pray for as we ought; but the Spirit itself maketh intercession for us with groanings which cannot be uttered. And he that searcheth the hearts knoweth what is the mind of the Spirit, because he maketh intercession for the saints according to the will of God (Rom. 8:26–27).

This is the deep mystery of prayer. This is the delicate divine mechanism which words cannot interpret, and which theology cannot explain, but which the humblest believer knows even when he does not understand.

Oh, the burdens that we love to bear and cannot understand! Oh, the inarticulate outreachings of our hearts for things we cannot comprehend! And yet we know they are an echo from the throne and a whisper from the heart of God. It is often a groan rather than a song, a burden rather than a buoyant wing. But it is a blessed burden, and it is a groan whose undertone is praise and unutterable joy. It is "a groaning which cannot be uttered." We could not ourselves express it always, and sometimes we do not understand any more than that God is praying in us, for something that needs His touch and that He understands.

And so we can just pour out the fullness of our heart, the burden of our spirit, the sorrow that crushes us, and know that He hears, He loves, He understands, He receives; and He separates from our prayer all that is imperfect, ignorant and wrong, and presents the rest, with the incense of the great High Priest, before the throne on high; and our prayer is heard, accepted, and answered in His name. A. B. SIMPSON

It is not necessary to be always speaking to God or always hearing from God, to have communion with Him; there is an inarticulate fellowship more sweet than words. The little child can sit all day long beside its busy mother and, although few words are spoken on either side, and both are busy, the one at his absorbing play, the other at her engrossing work, yet both are in perfect fellowship. He knows that she is there, and she knows that he is all right. So the saint and the Savior can go on for hours in the silent fellowship of love, and he be busy about the most common things, and yet conscious that every little thing he does is touched with the complexion of His presence, and the sense of His approval and blessing.

And then, when pressed with burdens and trouble too complicated to put into words and too mysterious to tell or understand, how sweet it is to fall back into His blessed arms, and just sob out the sorrow that we cannot speak! SELECTED

November 1

When the cloud tarried ... then the children of Israel ... jour-
neyed not (Num. 9:19).

This was the supreme test of obedience. It was comparatively easy to strike tents, when the fleecy folds of the cloud were slowly gathering from off the tabernacle, and it floated majestically before the host. Change is always delightful; and there was excitement and interest in the route, the scenery, and the locality of the next halting-place. But, ah, the tarrying.

Then, however uninviting and sultry the location, however trying to flesh and blood, however irksome to the impatient disposition, however perilously exposed to danger—there was no option but to remain encamped.

The psalmist says, *"I waited patiently for the Lord; and he inclined unto me, and heard my cry."* And what He did for the Old Testament saints He will do for believers throughout all ages.

Still God often keeps us waiting. Face to face with threatening foes, in the midst of alarms, encircled by perils, beneath the impending rock. May we not go? Is it not time to strike our tents? Have we not suffered to the point of utter collapse? May we not exchange the glare and heat for green pastures and still waters?

There is no answer. The cloud tarries, and we must remain, though sure of manna, rock-water, shelter, and defense. God never keeps us at post without assuring us of His presence and sending us daily supplies.

Wait, young man, do not be in a hurry to make a change! Minister, remain at your post! Until the cloud clearly moves, you must tarry. Wait, then, thy Lord's good pleasure! He will be in plenty of time! FROM DAILY DEVOTIONAL COMMENTARY

An hour of waiting!
Yet there seems such need
To reach that spot sublime!
I long to reach them—but I long far more
To trust HIS time!

"Sit still, my daughter"—
Yet the heathen die,
They perish while I stay!
I long to reach them—but I long far more
To trust HIS way!

> 'Tis good to get,
> 'Tis good indeed to give!
> Yet is it better still—
> O'er breadth, thro' length, down length, up height,
> To trust HIS will!

F. M. N.

November 2

But prayer ... (Acts 12:5).

But prayer is the link that connects us with God. This is the bridge that spans every gulf and bears me over every abyss of danger or of need.

How significant the picture of the apostolic church: Peter in prison, the Jews triumphant, Herod supreme, the arena of martyrdom awaiting the dawning of the morning to drink up the apostle's blood, and everything else against it. *"But prayer was made unto God without ceasing."* And what was the sequel? The prison open, the apostle free, the Jews baffled, the wicked king eaten of worms, a spectacle of hidden retribution, and the Word of God rolling on in greater victory.

Do we know the power of our supernatural weapon? Do we dare to use it with the authority of a faith that commands as well as asks? God baptizes us with holy audacity and divine confidence! He is not wanting great men, but He is wanting men who will dare to prove the greatness of their God. But God! But prayer! A. B. SIMPSON

Beware in your prayer, above everything, of limiting God, not only by unbelief, but by fancying that you know what He can do. Expect unexpected things, *above all* that we ask or think. Each time you intercede, be quiet first and worship God in His glory. Think of what He can do, of how He delights to hear Christ, of your place in Christ; and expect great things. ANDREW MURRAY

Our prayers are God's opportunities.

Are you in sorrow? Prayer can make your affliction sweet and strengthening. Are you in gladness? Prayer can add to your joy a celestial perfume. Are you in extreme danger from outward or inward enemies? Prayer can set at your right hand an angel whose touch could shatter a millstone into smaller dust than the flour it grinds, and whose glance could lay an army

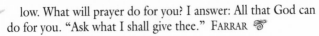

low. What will prayer do for you? I answer: All that God can do for you. "Ask what I shall give thee." FARRAR

Wrestling prayer can wonders do,
Bring relief in deepest straits;
Prayer can force a passage through
Iron bars and brazen gates.

November 3

On all bare heights shall be their pasture (Isa. 49:9 RV).

Toys and trinkets are easily won, but the greatest things are greatly bought. The topmost place of power is always bought with blood. You may have the pinnacles if you have enough blood to pay. That is the conquest condition of the holy heights everywhere. The story of real heroisms is the story of sacrificial blood. The chief values in life and character are not blown across our way by vagrant winds. Great souls have great sorrows.

Great truths are dearly bought, the common truths,
Such as men give and take from day to day,
Come in the common walk of easy life,
Blown by the careless wind across our way.

Great truths are greatly won, not found by chance,
Nor wafted on the breath of summer dream;
But grasped in the great struggle of the soul,
Hard buffeting with adverse wind and stream.

But in the day of conflict, fear and grief,
When the strong hand of God, put forth in might,
Plows up the subsoil of the stagnant heart,
And brings the imprisoned truth seed to the light.

Wrung from the troubled spirit, in hard hours
Of weakness, solitude, perchance of pain,
Truth springs like harvest from the well-plowed field,
And the soul feels it has not wept in vain.

The capacity for knowing God enlarges as we are brought by Him into circumstances which oblige us to exercise faith; so, when difficulties beset our path, let us thank God that He is taking trouble with us and lean hard upon Him.

November 4

As I was among the captives by the river of Chebar ... the heav-
ens were opened and I saw visions of God ... and the hand of
the Lord was there upon me (Ezek. 1:1, 3).

There is no commentator of the Scriptures half so valuable as a captivity. The old psalms have quavered for us with a new pathos as we sat by
our "Babel's stream," and have sounded for us with new joy as we found
our captivity turned as the streams in the south.

The man who has seen much affliction will not readily part with his
copy of the Word of God. Another book may seem to others to be identi-
cal with his own; but it is not the same to him, for over his old and
tearstained Bible he has written, in characters which are visible to no eyes
but his own, the record of his experiences, and ever and anon he comes
on Bethel pillars or Elim palms, which are to him the memorials of some
critical chapter in his history.

If we are to receive benefit from our captivity, we must accept the situation and turn it to the best possible account. Fretting over that from
which we have been removed or which has been taken away from us, will
not make things better, but it will prevent us from improving those which
remain. The bond is only tightened by our stretching it to the uttermost.

The impatient horse which will not quietly endure his halter only
strangles himself in his stall. The high-mettled animal that is restive in the
yoke only galls his shoulders; and everyone will understand the difference
between the restless starling of which Sterne has written, breaking its wings
against the bars of the cage, and crying, "I can't get out, I can't get out,"
and the docile canary that sits upon its perch and sings as if it would out-
rival the lark soaring to heaven's gate.

No calamity can be to us an unmixed evil if we carry it in direct and
fervent prayer to God, for even as one in taking shelter from the rain
beneath a tree may find on its branches fruit which he looked not for, so
we in fleeing for refuge beneath the shadow of God's wing, will always find
more in God than we had seen or known before.

It is thus through our trials and afflictions that God gives us fresh revelations of Himself; and the Jabbok ford leads to Peniel, where, as the result
of our wrestling, we "see God face-to-face," and our lives are preserved. Take
this to thyself, O captive, and He will give thee "songs in the night," and turn
for thee "the shadow of death into the morning." WILLIAM TAYLOR

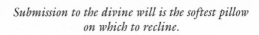

Submission to the divine will is the softest pillow
on which to recline.

It filled the room, and it filled my life,
With a glory of source unseen;
It made me calm in the midst of strife,
And in winter my heart was green.
And the birds of promise sang on the tree
When the storm was breaking on land and sea.

November 5

Is anything too hard for the Lord? (Gen. 18:14)

Here is God's loving challenge to you and to me today. He wants us to think of the deepest, highest, worthiest desire and longing of our hearts, something which perhaps was our desire for ourselves or for someone dear to us, yet which has been so long unfulfilled that we have looked upon it as only a lost desire, that which might have been but now cannot be, and so have given up hope of seeing it fulfilled in this life.

That thing, if it is in line with what we know to be His expressed will (as a son to Abraham and Sarah was), God intends to *do* for us, even if we know that it is of such utter impossibility that we only laugh at the absurdity of anyone's supposing it could ever now come to pass. *That thing* God intends to do for us, if we will let Him.

"Is anything too hard for the Lord?" Not when we believe in Him enough to go forward and do His will, and let Him do the impossible for us. Even Abraham and Sarah could have blocked God's plan if they had continued to disbelieve.

The only thing too hard for Jehovah is deliberate, continued disbelief in His love and power, and our final rejection of His plans for us. Nothing is too hard for Jehovah to do for them that trust Him. FROM MESSAGES FOR THE MORNING WATCH 🦑

November 6

As many as I love I rebuke and chasten (Rev. 3:19).

God takes the most eminent and choicest of His servants for the choicest and most eminent afflictions. They who have received most grace from God are able to bear most afflictions from God. Affliction does not hit the saint by chance, but by direction. God does not draw His bow at a venture. Every one of His arrows goes upon a special errand and touches no breast but his against whom it is sent. It is not only the grace, but the glory of a believer when he can stand and take affliction quietly. JOSEPH CARYL 🐚

If all my days were sunny, could I say,
"In His fair land He wipes all tears away"?

If I were never weary, could I keep
Close to my heart, "He gives His loved ones sleep"?

Where no graves mine, might I not come to deem
The Life Eternal but a baseless dream?

My winter, and my tears, and my weariness,
Even my graves, may be His way to bless.

I call them ills; yet that can surely be
Nothing but love that shows my Lord to me!

SELECTED 🐚

"The most deeply taught Christians are generally those who have been brought into the searching fires of deep soul-anguish. If you have been praying to know more of Christ, do not be surprised if He takes you aside into a desert place, or leads you into a furnace of pain.

"Do not punish me, Lord, by taking my cross from me, but comfort me by submitting me to Thy will, and by making me to love the cross. Give me that by which Thou shalt be best served . . . and let me hold it for the greatest of all Thy mercies, that Thou shouldst glorify Thy name in me, according to Thy will." A CAPTIVE'S PRAYER 🐚

November 7

But what things were gain to me, those I counted loss for Christ (Phil. 3:7).

⌒⌒

When they buried the blind preacher George Matheson, they lined his grave with red roses in memory of his love-life of sacrifice. And it was this man, so beautifully and significantly honored, who wrote,

O Love that wilt not let me go,
I rest my weary soul in Thee,
I give Thee back the life I owe,
That in thine ocean depths its flow
May richer, fuller be.

O Light that followest all my way,
I yield my flickering torch to Thee
My heart restores its borrowed ray,
That in Thy sunshine's blaze its day
May brighter, fairer be.

O Joy that seekest me through pain,
I cannot close my heart to Thee,
I trace the rainbow through the rain,
And feel the promise is not vain,
That morn shall tearless be.

O Cross that liftest up my head,
I dare not ask to fly from Thee,
I lay in dust life's glory dead,
And from the ground there blossoms red,
Life that shall endless be.

There is a legend of an artist who had found the secret of a wonderful red which no other artist could imitate. The secret of his color died with him. But after his death an old wound was discovered over his heart. This revealed the source of the matchless hue in his pictures. The legend teaches that no great achievement can be made, no lofty attainment reached, nothing of much value to the world done, save at the cost of heart's blood.

November 8

He took Peter and John and James, and went up into a mountain to pray. And as he prayed, the fashion of his countenance was altered, and his raiment was white and glistering ... they saw his glory (Luke 9:28–29, 32).
If I have found grace in thy sight, show me now thy way (Exod. 33:13).

When Jesus took these three disciples up into that high mountain apart, He brought them into close communion with Himself. They saw no man but Jesus only; and it was good to be there. Heaven is not far from those who tarry on the mount with their Lord.

Who has not in moments of meditation and prayer caught a glimpse of opening gates? Who has not in the secret place of holy communion felt the rush of some white surging wave of emotion—a foretaste of the joy of the blessed?

The Master had times and places for quiet converse with His disciples, once on the peak of Hermon, but oftener on the sacred slopes of Olivet. Every Christian should have his Olivet. Most of us, especially in the cities and towns, live at high pressure. From early morning until bedtime we are exposed to the whirl. Amid all this maelstrom how little chance for quiet thought, for God's Word, for prayer and heart fellowship!

Daniel needed to have an Olivet in his chamber amid Babylon's roar and idolatries. Peter found his on a housetop in Joppa; and Martin Luther found his in the "upper room" at Wittenberg, which is still held sacred.

Dr. Joseph Parker once said: "If we do not get back to visions, peeps into heaven, consciousness of the higher glory and the larger life, we shall lose our religion; our altar will become a bare stone, unblessed by visitant from Heaven." Here is the world 's need today—*men who have seen their Lord*. FROM THE LOST ART OF MEDITATION 🐦

Come close to Him! He may take you today up into the mountaintop, for where He took Peter with his blundering, and James and John, those sons of thunder who again and again so utterly misunderstood their Master and His mission, there is no reason why He should not take you. So don't shut yourself out of it and say, "Ah, these wonderful visions and revelations of the Lord are for choice spirits!" They may be for you! JOHN MCNEILL 🐦

November 9

They that dwell under his shadow shall return; they shall revive as the corn and grow as the vine (Hos. 14:7).

The day closed with heavy showers. The plants in my garden were beaten down before the pelting storm, and I saw one flower that I had admired for its beauty and loved for its fragrance exposed to the pitiless storm. The flower fell, shut up its petals, dropped its head; and I saw that all its glory was gone. "I must wait till next year," I said, "before I see that beautiful thing again."

That night passed, and morning came; the sun shone again, and the morning brought strength to the flower. The light looked at it, and the flower looked at the light. There was contact and communion, and power passed into the flower. It held up its head, opened its petals, regained its glory, and seemed fairer than before. I wonder how it took place—this feeble thing coming into contact with the strong thing, and gaining strength!

I cannot tell how it is that I should be able to receive into my being a power to do and to bear by communion with God, but I know it is a fact.

Are you in peril through some crushing, heavy trial? Seek this communion with Christ, and you will receive strength and be able to conquer. "I will strengthen thee."

Yesterday's Grief

The rain that fell a-yesterday is ruby on the roses,
Silver on the poplar leaf, and gold on willow stem;
The grief that chanced a-yesterday is silence that incloses
Holy loves when time and change shall never trouble them.

The rain that fell a-yesterday makes all the hillsides glisten,
Coral on the laurel and beryl on the grass;
The grief that chanced a-yesterday has taught the soul to listen
For whispers of eternity in all the winds that pass.

O faint-of-heart, storm-beaten, this rain will gleam tomorrow,
Flame within the columbine and jewels on the thorn,
Heaven in the forget-me-not; though sorrow now be sorrow,
Yet sorrow shall be beauty in the magic of the morn.

KATHERINE LEE BATES

November 10

Under hopeless circumstances he hopefully believed (Rom. 4:18 WEYMOUTH).

Abraham's faith seemed to be in a thorough correspondence with the power and constant faithfulness of Jehovah. In the outward circumstances in which he was placed, he had not the greatest cause to expect the fulfillment of the promise. Yet he believed the Word of the Lord and looked forward to the time when his seed should be as the stars of heaven for multitude.

O my soul, thou hast not one single promise only, like Abraham, *but a thousand promises,* and many patterns of faithful believers before thee: it behooves thee, therefore, to rely with confidence upon the Word of God. And though He delayeth His help, and the evil seemeth to grow worse and worse, be not weak, but rather strong, and rejoice, since the most glorious promises of God are generally fulfilled in such a wondrous manner that He steps forth to save us at a time when there is the least appearance of it.

He commonly brings His help in our greatest extremity, that His finger may plainly appear in our deliverance. And this method He chooses that we may not trust upon anything that we see or feel, as we are always apt to do, but only upon His bare Word, which we may depend upon in every state. C. H. Von Bogatzky

Remember it is the very time for faith to work when sight ceases. The greater the difficulties, the easier for faith; as long as there remain certain natural prospects, faith does not get on even as easily as where natural prospects fail. George Mueller

November 11

He shall come down like rain upon the mown grass (Ps. 72:6).

Amos speaks of the king's mowings. Our King has many scythes, and is perpetually mowing His lawns. The musical tinkle of the whetstone on the scythe portends the cutting down of myriads of green blades, daisies, and other flowers. Beautiful as they were in the morning, within an hour or two they lie in long, faded rows.

Thus in human life we make a brave show, before the scythe of pain, the shears of disappointment, the sickle of death.

There is no method of obtaining a velvety lawn but by repeated mowings: And there is no way of developing tenderness, evenness, sympathy, but by the passing of God's scythes. How constantly the Word of God compares man to grass, and His glory to its flower. But when the grass is mown, and all the tender shoots are bleeding, and desolation reigns where flowers were bursting, it is the most acceptable time for showers of rain falling soft and warm.

O soul, thou hast been mown! Time after time the King has come to thee with His sharp scythe. Do not dread the scythe—it is sure to be followed by the shower. F. B. Meyer

When across the heart deep waves of sorrow
Break, as on a dry and barren shore;
When hope glistens with no bright tomorrow,
And the storm seems sweeping evermore;

When the cup of every earthly gladness
Bears no taste of the life-giving stream;
And high hopes, as though to mock our sadness,
Fade and die as in some fitful dream,

Who shall hush the weary spirit's chiding?
Who the aching void within shall fill?
Who shall whisper of a peace abiding,
and each surging billow calmly still?

Only He whose wounded heart was broken
With the bitter cross and thorny crown;
Whose dear love glad words of joy had spoken,
Who His life for us laid meekly down.

Blessed Healer, all our burdens lighten;
Give us peace. Thine own sweet peace, we pray!
Keep us near Thee till the morn shall brighten,
And all the mists and shadows flee away!

November 12

These were the potters, and those that dwelt among plants and
hedges: there they dwelt with the king for his work (1 Chron. 4:23).

Anywhere and everywhere we may dwell "with the king for his work." We may be in a very unlikely and unfavorable place for this; it may be in a literal country life, with little enough to be seen of the "goings" of the King around us; it may be among the hedges of all sorts, hindrances in all directions; it may be furthermore, with our hands full of all manner of pottery for our daily task.

No matter! The King who placed us *"there"* will come and dwell there with us; the hedges are right, or He would soon do away with them. And it does not follow that what seems to hinder our way may not be for its very protection; and as for the pottery, why, that is just exactly what He has seen fit to put into our hands, and therefore it is, for the present, *"His work."*
FRANCES RIDLEY HAVERGAL 🐝

Go back to thy garden-plot, sweetheart!
Go back till the evening falls,
And bind thy lilies and train thy vines,
Till for thee the Master calls.

Go make thy garden fair as thou canst,
Thou workest never alone;
Perhaps he whose plot is next to thine
Will see it and mend his own.

The colored sunsets and starry heavens, the beautiful mountains and the shining seas, the fragrant woods and painted flowers, are not half so beautiful as a soul that is serving Jesus out of love, in the wear and tear of common, unpoetic life. FABER

The most saintly spirits are often existing in those who have never distinguished themselves as authors, or let any memorial of themselves to be the theme of the world's talk; but who have led an interior angelic life, having borne their sweet blossoms unseen like the young lily in a sequestered vale on the bank of a limpid stream. KENELM DIGBY

November 13

I know him, that he will command his children (Gen. 18:19).

God wants people that He can depend upon. He could say of Abraham, "I know him, that he will command his children . . . that the Lord may bring upon Abraham that which he hath spoken." God can be depended upon; He wants us to be just as decided, as reliable, as stable. This is just what faith means.

God is looking for men on whom He can put the weight of all His love and power and faithful promises. God's engines are strong enough to draw any weight we attach to them. Unfortunately the cable which we fasten to the engine is often too weak to hold the weight of our prayer; therefore God is drilling us, disciplining us to stability and certainty in the life of faith. Let us learn our lessons and stand fast. A. B. SIMPSON

God knows that you can stand that trial; He would not give it to you if you could not. It is His trust in you that explains the trials of life, however bitter they may be. God knows our strength, and He measures it to the last inch; and a trial was never given to any man that was greater than that man's strength, through God, to bear it.

November 14

Except a grain of corn fall into the ground and die, it abideth alone: but if it dies it bringeth forth much fruit (John 12:24).

❦

Go to the old burying ground of Northampton, Massachusetts, and look upon the early grave of David Brainerd, beside that of the fair Jerusha Edwards, whom he loved but did not live to wed.

What hopes, what expectations for Christ's cause went down to the grave with the wasted form of that young missionary of whose work nothing now remained but the dear memory, and a few score of swarthy Indian converts! But that majestic old Puritan saint, Jonathan Edwards, who had hoped to call him his son, gathered up the memorials of his life in a little book, and the little book took wings and flew beyond the sea, and alighted on the table of a Cambridge student, Henry Martyn.

Poor Martyn! Why should he throw himself away, with all his scholarship, his genius, his opportunities! What had he accomplished when he turned homeward from "India's coral strand," broken in health, and dragged himself northward as far as that dreary khan at Tocat by the Black Sea, where he crouched under the piled-up saddles, to cool his burning fever against the earth, and there died alone?

To what purpose was this waste? Out of that early grave of Brainerd, and the lonely grave of Martyn far away by the splashing of the Euxine Sea, has sprung the noble army of modern missionaries. LEONARD WOOLSEY BACON ❦

> Is there some desert, or some boundless sea,
> Where Thou, great God of angels, wilt send me?
> Some oak for me to rend,
> Some sod for me to break,
> Some handful of Thy corn to take
> And scatter far afield,
> Till it in turn shall yield
> Its hundredfold
> Of grains of gold
> To feed the happy children of my God?
>
> Show me the desert, Father, or the sea;
> Is it Thine enterprise? Great God, send me!
> And though this body lies where ocean rolls,
> Father, count me among all faithful souls.

November 15

Pressed out of measure (2 Cor. 1:8).
That the power of Christ may rest upon me (2 Cor. 12:9).

God allowed the crisis to close around Jacob on the night when he bowed at Peniel in supplication, to bring him to the place where he could take hold of God as he never would have done; and from that narrow pass of peril, Jacob became enlarged in his faith and knowledge of God, and in the power of a new and victorious life.

God had to compel David, by a long and painful discipline of years, to learn the almighty power and faithfulness of his God, and grow up into the established principles of faith and godliness, which were indispensable for his glorious career as the king of Israel.

Nothing but the extremities in which Paul was constantly placed could ever have taught him, and taught the church through him, the full meaning of the great promise he so learned to claim, "My grace is sufficient for thee."

And nothing but our trials and perils would ever have led some of us to know Him as we do, to trust Him as we have, and to draw from Him the measures of grace which our very extremities made indispensable.

Difficulties and obstacles are God's challenges to faith. When hindrances confront us in the path of duty, we are to recognize them as vessels for faith to fill with the fullness and all-sufficiency of Jesus; and as we go forward, simply and fully trusting Him, we may be tested, we may have to wait and let patience have her perfect work; but we shall surely find at last the stone rolled away, and the Lord waiting to render unto us double for our time of testing. A. B. SIMPSON

November 16

They overcame him by the blood of the Lamb. . . and they loved not their lives unto the death (Rev. 12:11).

When James and John came to Christ with their mother, asking Him to give them the best place in the kingdom, He did not refuse their request, but told them it would be given to them if they could do His work, drink His cup, and be baptized with His baptism.

Do we want the competition? The greatest things are always hedged about by the hardest things, and we, too, shall find mountains and forests and chariots of iron. Hardship is the price of coronation. Triumphal arches are not woven out of rose blossoms and silken cords, but of hard blows and bloody scars. The very hardships that you are enduring in your life today are given by the Master for the explicit purpose of enabling you to win your crown.

Do not wait for some ideal situation, some romantic difficulty, some far-away emergency; but rise to meet the actual conditions which the providence of God has placed around you today. Your crown of glory lies embedded in the very heart of these things—those hardships and trials that are pressing you this very hour, week, and month of your life. The hardest things are not those that the world knows of. Down in your secret soul unseen and unknown by any but Jesus, there is a little trial that you would not dare to mention, that is harder for you to bear than martyrdom.

There, beloved, lies your crown. God help you to overcome, and sometime wear it. SELECTED

It matters not how the battle goes,
The day how long;
Faint not! Fight on!
Tomorrow comes the song.

November 17

Hear what the unjust judge saith. And shall not God avenge his own elect which cry day and night unto him, though he bear long with them? I tell you that he will avenge them speedily (Luke 18:6–8).

God's seasons are not at your beck. If the first stroke of the flint doth not bring forth the fire, you must strike again. God will hear prayer, but He may not answer it at the time which we in our minds have appointed; He will reveal Himself to our seeking hearts, but not just when and where we have settled in our own expectations. Hence the need of perseverance and importunity in supplication.

In the days of flint and steel and brimstone matches we had to strike and strike again, dozens of times, before we could get a spark to live in the tinder; and we were thankful enough if we succeeded at last.

Shall we not be as persevering and hopeful as to heavenly things? We have more certainty of success in this business than we had with our flint and steel, for we have God's promises at our back.

Never let us despair. God's time for mercy will come; yea, it has come, if our time for believing has arrived. Ask in faith, nothing wavering; but never cease from petitioning because the King delays to reply. Strike the steel again. Make the sparks fly and have your tinder ready; you will get a light before long. C. H. SPURGEON 🕊

I do not believe that there is such a thing in the history of God's kingdom as a right prayer offered in a right spirit that is forever left unanswered. THEODORE L. CUYLER 🕊

November 18

Blessed is he, whosoever shall not be offended in me (Luke 7:23).

It is sometimes very difficult not to be offended in Jesus Christ. The offenses may be circumstantial. I find myself in a prison-house—a narrow sphere, a sick chamber, an unpopular position—when I had hoped for wide opportunities. Yes, but He knows what is best for me. My environment is of His determining. He means it to intensify my faith, to draw me into nearer communion with Himself, to ripen my power. In the dungeon my soul should prosper.

The offense may be mental. I am haunted by perplexities, questions, which I cannot solve. I had hoped that, when I gave myself to Him, my sky would always be clear; but often it is overspread by mist and cloud. Yet let me believe that, if difficulties remain, it is that I may learn to trust Him all the more implicitly—to trust and not be afraid. Yes, and by my intellectual conflicts, I am trained to be a tutor to other storm-driven men.

The offense may be spiritual. I had fancied that within His fold I should never feel the biting winds of temptation; but it is best as it is. His grace is magnified. My own character is matured. His heaven is sweeter at the close of the day. There I shall look back on the turnings and trials of the way, and shall sing the praises of my Guide. So, let come what will come, His will is welcome; and I shall refuse to be offended in my loving Lord. ALEXANDER SMELLIE 🕊

Blessed is he whose faith in not offended,
When all around his way

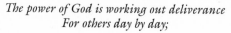

The power of God is working out deliverance
For others day by day;

Though in some prison drear his own soul languish,
Till life itself be spent,
Yet still can trust his Father's love and purpose,
And rest therein content.

Blessed is he, who through long years of suffering,
Cut off from active toil,
Still shares by prayer and praise the work of others,
And thus "divides the spoil."

Blessed are thou, O child of God, who sufferest,
And canst not understand
The reason for thy pain, yet gladly leavest
Thy life in His blest Hand.

Yea, blessed art thou whose faith is "not offended"
By trials unexplained,
By mysteries unsolved, past understanding,
Until the goal is gained.

FREDA HANBURY ALLEN 🐚

November 19

Thou, who hast showed us many and sore troubles, wilt quicken us again (Ps. 71:20 RV).

God *shows* us the troubles. Sometimes, as this part of our education is being carried forward, we have to descend into "the lower parts of the earth," pass through subterranean passages, lie buried amongst the dead, but never for a moment is the cord of fellowship and union between God and us strained to breaking; and from the depths God will bring us again.

Never doubt God! Never say that He has forsaken or forgotten. Never think that He is unsympathetic. He will *quicken* again. There is always a smooth piece of every skein, however tangled. The longest day at last rings out the evensong. The winter snow lies long, but it goes at last.

Be steadfast; your labor is not in vain. God turns again, and comforts. And when He does, the heart which had forgotten its psalmody breaks out in jubilant song, as does the psalmist: "I will thank thee, I will harp unto thee, my lips shall sing aloud." SELECTED 🐚

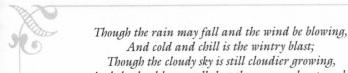

Though the rain may fall and the wind be blowing,
And cold and chill is the wintry blast;
Though the cloudy sky is still cloudier growing,
And the dead leaves tell that the summer has passed;
My face I hold to the stormy heaven,
My heart is as calm as the summer sea,
Glad to receive what my God has given,
Whate'er it be.
When I feel the cold, I can say, "He sends it,"
And His winds blow blessing, I surely know;
For I've never a want but that He attends it;
And my heart beats warm, though the winds may blow.

November 20

Blessed is he that waiteth (Dan. 12:12).

It may seem an easy thing to *wait,* but it is one of the postures which a Christian soldier learns not without years of teaching. Marching and quick-marching are much easier to God's warriors than standing still.

There are hours of perplexity when the most willing spirit, anxiously desirous to serve the Lord, knows not what part to take. Then what shall it do? Vex itself by despair? Fly back in cowardice, turn to the right hand in fear, or rush forward in presumption?

No, but simply wait. *Wait in prayer,* however. Call upon God and spread the case before Him; tell Him your difficulty, and plead His promise of aid.

Wait in faith. Express your unstaggering confidence in Him. Believe that if He keeps you tarrying even till midnight, yet He will come at the right time; the vision shall come, and shall not tarry.

Wait in quiet patience. Never murmur against the second cause, as the children of Israel did against Moses. Accept the case as it is, and put it as it stands, simply and with your whole heart, without any self-will, into the hand of your covenant God, saying, "Now, Lord, not my will, but Thine be done. I know not what to do; I am brought to extremities; but I will wait until Thou shalt cleave the floods, or drive back my foes. I will wait, if Thou keep me many a day, for my heart is fixed upon Thee alone, O God, and my spirit waiteth for Thee in full conviction that Thou wilt yet be my joy and my salvation, my refuge and my strong tower." FROM MORNING BY MORNING

Wait, patiently wait,
God never is late;
Thy budding plans are in Thy Father's holding,
And only wait His grand divine unfolding.
Then wait, wait,
Patiently wait.

Trust, hopefully trust,
That God will adjust
Thy tangled life; and from its dark concealings,
Will bring His will, in all its bright revealings.
Then trust, trust,
Hopefully trust.

Rest, peacefully rest
On thy Saviour's breast;
Breathe in His ear thy sacred high ambition,
And He will bring it forth in blest fruition.
Then rest, rest,
Peacefully rest!

MERCY A. GLADWIN

November 21

Roll on Jehovah thy way (Ps. 37:6, margin).

Whatever it is that presses thee, go tell the Father; put the whole matter over into His hand, and so shalt thou be freed from that dividing, perplexing care that the world is full of. When thou art either to do or suffer anything, when thou art about any purpose or business, go tell God of it, and acquaint Him with it; yes, *burden Him with it,* and thou hast done for matter of caring; no more care, but quiet, sweet diligence in thy duty, and dependence on Him for the carriage of thy matters. Roll thy cares, and thyself with them, as one burden, all on thy God. R. LEIGHTON

Build a little fence of trust
Around today;
Fill the space with loving work
And therein stay.
Look not through the sheltering bars
Upon tomorrow;
God will help thee bear what comes
Of joy or sorrow.

MARY BUTTS

We shall find it impossible to commit our way unto the Lord, unless it be a way that He approves. It is only by faith that a man can commit his way unto the Lord; if there be the slightest doubt in the heart that "our way" is not a good one, faith will refuse to have anything to do with it. This committing of our way must be continuous, not a single act. However extraordinary and unexpected may seem to be His guidance, however near the precipice He may take you, you are not to snatch the guiding reins out of His hands. Are we willing to have all our ways submitted to God, for Him to pronounce judgment on them? There is nothing a Christian needs to be more scrutinizing about than about his confirmed habits and views. He is too apt to take for granted the divine approbation of them. Why are some Christians so anxious, so fearful? Evidently because they have not *left their way with the Lord*. They took it to Him, but brought it away with them again. SELECTED

November 22

Believe ye that I am able to do this? (Matt. 9:28).

God deals with impossibilities. It is never too late for Him to do so, when the impossible is brought to Him, in full faith, by the one in whose life and circumstances the impossible must be accomplished if God is to be glorified. If in our own life there have been rebellion, unbelief, sin, and disaster, it is never too late for God to deal triumphantly with these tragic facts if brought to Him in full surrender and trust. It has often been said, and with truth, that Christianity is the only religion that can deal with man's past. God can "restore ... the years that the locust hath eaten" (Joel 2:25); and He will do this when we put the whole situation and ourselves unreservedly and believingly into His hands. Not because of what we are but because of what He is. God forgives and heals and restores. He is "the God of all grace." Let us praise Him and trust Him. FROM SUNDAY SCHOOL TIMES

> *Nothing is too hard for Jesus*
> *No man can work like Him.*

"We have a God who delights in impossibilities." Nothing too hard for Me.
ANDREW MURRAY

November 23

Thou hast shewed thy people hard things (Ps. 60:3).

I have always been glad that the psalmist said to God that some things were *hard*. There is no mistake about it; there are hard things in life. Some beautiful pink flowers were given me this summer, and as I took them I said, "What are they?" And the answer came, "They are rock flowers; they grow and bloom only on rocks where you can see no soil." Then I thought of God's flowers growing in hard places; and I feel, somehow, that He may have a peculiar tenderness for His "rock flowers" that He may not have for His lilies and roses. MARGARET BOTTOME

The tests of life are to make, not break us. Trouble may demolish a man's business but build up his character. The blow at the outward man may be the greatest blessing to the inner man. If God, then, puts or permits anything hard in our lives, be sure that the real peril, the real trouble, is what we shall lose if we flinch or rebel. MALTBIE D. BABCOCK

> *Heroes are forged on anvils hot with pain,*
> *And splendid courage comes but with the test.*
> *Some natures ripen and some natures bloom*
> *Only on blood-wet soil, some souls prove great*
> *Only in moments dark with death or doom.*

God gets His best soldiers out of the highlands of affliction.

November 24

Be still, and know that I am God (Ps. 46:10).

Is there any note of music in all the chorus as mighty as the emphatic pause? Is there any word in all the Psalter more eloquent than that one word, Selah (Pause)? Is there anything more thrilling and awful than the hush that comes before the bursting of the tempest and the strange quiet that seems to fall upon all nature before some preternatural phenomenon or convulsion? Is there anything that can touch our hearts as the *power of stillness*?

There is for the heart that will cease from itself, "the peace of God that passeth all understanding," a "quietness and confidence" which is the source of all strength, a sweet peace "which nothing can offend," a deep rest which the world can neither give nor take away. There is in the deepest center of the soul a chamber of peace where God dwells, and where, if we will only enter in and hush every other sound, we can hear His still, small voice.

There is in the swiftest wheel that revolves upon its axis a place in the very center, where there is no movement at all; and so in the busiest life there may be a place where we dwell alone with God, in eternal stillness. There is only one way to know God. "Be still, and know." "God is in His holy temple; let all the earth keep silence before him." SELECTED ☞

"All-loving Father, sometimes we have walked under starless skies that dripped darkness like drenching rain. We despaired of starshine or moonlight or sunrise. The sullen blackness gloomed above us as if it would last forever. And out of the dark there spoke no soothing voice to mend our broken hearts. We would gladly have welcomed some wild thunderpeal to break the torturing stillness of that over-brooding night.

"But Thy winsome whisper of eternal love spoke more sweetly to our bruised and bleeding souls than any winds that breathe across aeolian harps. It was Thy 'still small voice' that spoke to us. We were listening and we heard. We looked and saw Thy face radiant with the light of love. And when we heard Thy voice and saw Thy face, new life came back to us as life comes back to withered blooms that drink the summer rain."

November 25

Take the arrows. . . . Smite upon the ground. And he smote thrice and stayed. And the man of God was wroth with him, and said, Thou shouldest have smitten five or six times (2 Kings 13:18–19).

How striking and eloquent the message of these words! Jehoash thought he had done very well when he duplicated and triplicated what to him was certainly an extraordinary act of faith. But the Lord and the prophet were bitterly disappointed *because he had stopped halfway*.

He got something. He got much. He got exactly what he believed for in the final test, but he did not get all that the prophet meant and the Lord wanted to bestow. He missed much of the meaning of the promise and the fullness of the blessing. He got something better than the human, but he did not get God's best.

Beloved, how solemn is the application! How heartsearching the message of God to us! How important that we should learn to pray through! Shall we claim all the fullness of the promise and all the possibilities of believing prayer? A. B. SIMPSON

Unto him that is able to do exceeding abundantly above all that we ask or think (Eph. 3:20).

There is no other such piling up of words in Paul's writings as these, "exceeding abundantly above all," and each word is packed with infinite love and power to "do" for His praying saints. There is one limitation, "according to the power that worketh in us." He will do just as much *for* us as we let Him do *in* us. The power that saved us, washed us with His own blood, filled us with might by His Spirit, kept us in manifold temptations, will work for us, meeting every emergency, every crisis, every circumstance, and every adversary. THE ALLIANCE

November 26

And Caleb said unto her, What wouldest thou? Who answered, Give me a blessing; for thou hast given me a south land; give me also springs of water. And he gave her the upper springs, and the nether springs (Josh. 15:18–19).

There are both upper and nether springs. They are *springs,* not stagnant pools. There are joys and blessings that flow from above through the hottest summer and the most desert land of sorrow and trial. The lands of Achsah were "south lands," lying under a burning sun and often parched with burning heat. But from the hills came the unfailing springs that cooled, refreshed, and fertilized all the land.

There are springs that flow in the low places of life, in the hard places, in the desert places, in the lone places, in the *common places,* and no matter what may be our situation, we can always find these upper springs.

Abraham found them amid the hills of Canaan. Moses found them among the rocks of Midian. David found them among the ashes of Ziklag when his property was gone, his family captives and his people talked of stoning him, but "David encouraged himself in the Lord."

Habakkuk found them when the fig tree was withered and the fields were brown, but as he drank from them, he could sing: "Yet will I rejoice in the Lord and joy in the God of my salvation."

Isaiah found them in the awful days of Sennacherib's invasion, when the mountains seemed hurled into the midst of the sea, but faith could sing: "There is a river whose streams make glad the city of God. God is in the midst of her: she shall not be moved."

The martyrs found them amid the flames, and reformers amid their foes and conflicts, and we can find them all the year if we have the Comforter in our hearts and have learned to say with David: *"All my springs are in thee."*

How many and how precious these springs, and how much more there is to be possessed of God's own fullness! A. B. SIMPSON

I said: "The desert is so wide!"
I said: "The desert is so bare!"
What springs to quench my thirst are there?
Whence shall I from the tempest hide?"

I said: "The desert is so lone!
Nor gentle voice, nor loving face
Will brighten any smallest space."
I paused or ere my moan was done!

I heard a flow of hidden springs;
Before me palms rose green and fair;
The birds were singing; all the air
Did shine and stir with angels' wings!

And One said mildly: "Why, indeed,
Take over-anxious thought for that
The morrow bringeth! See you not
The Father knoweth what you need?"

SELECTED

November 27

For with God nothing shall be impossible (Luke 1:37).

Far up in the alpine hollows, year by year God works one of His marvels. The snow patches lie there, frozen with ice at their edge from the strife of sunny days and frosty nights; and through that ice-crust come, unscathed, flowers that bloom.

Back in the days of the bygone summer, the little soldanelle plant spread its leaves wide and flat on the ground, to drink in the sun rays, and it kept them stored in the root through the winter. Then spring came, and stirred the pulses even below the snow-shroud, and as it sprouted, warmth was given out in such strange measure that it thawed a little dome in the snow above its head.

Higher and higher it grew and always above it rose the bell of air, till the flower-bud formed safely within it: and at last the icy covering of the air-bell gave way and let the blossom through into the sunshine, the crystalline texture of its mauve petals sparkling like snow itself as if it bore the traces of the flight through which it had come.

And the fragile thing rings an echo in our hearts that none of the jewel-like flowers nestled in the warm turf on the slopes below could waken. We love to see the impossible done. And so does God.

Face it out to the end, cast away every shadow of hope on the human side as an absolute hindrance to the divine, heap up all the difficulties together recklessly, and pile as many more on as you can find; you cannot get beyond the blessed climax of impossibility. Let faith swing out to Him. He is the God of the impossible. SELECTED

November 28

Thou makest the outgoings of the morning and evening to rejoice (Ps. 65:8).

Get up early and go to the mountain and watch God make a morning. The dull gray will give way as God pushes the sun toward the horizon, and there will be tints and hues of every shade that will blend into one perfect light as the full-orbed sun bursts into view. As the King of day moves forth majestically, flooding the earth and every lowly vale, listen to the music of heaven's choir as it sings of the majesty of God and the glory of the morning.

> *In the holy hush of the early dawn*
> *I hear a Voice—*
> *"I am with you all the day,*
> *Rejoice! Rejoice!"*

The clear, pure light of the morning made me long for the truth in my heart, which alone could make me pure and clear as the morning, tune me up to the concert-pitch of the nature around me. And the wind that blew from the sunrise made me hope in the God who had first breathed into my nostrils the breath of life; that He would at length so fill me with His breath, His mind, His Spirit, that I should think only His thoughts, and live His life, finding therein my own life, only glorified infinitely. What should we poor humans do without our God's nights and mornings? GEORGE MACDONALD

In the early morning hours,
'Twixt the night and day,
While from earth the darkness passes
Silently away;

Then 'tis sweet to talk with Jesus
In thy chamber still—
For the coming day and duties
Ask to know His will.

Then He'll lead the way before you,
Mountains laying low;
Making desert places blossom,
Sweet'ning Marah's flow.

Would you know this life of triumph,
Victory all the way?
Then put God in the beginning
Of each coming day.

November 29

Nevertheless afterward (Heb. 12:11).

There is a legend that tells of a German baron who at his castle on the Rhine, stretched wires from tower to tower, that the winds might convert them into an aeolian harp. And the soft breezes played about the castle, but no music was born.

But one night there arose a great tempest, and hill and castle were smitten by the fury of the mighty winds. The baron went to the threshold to look out upon the terror of the storm, and the aeolian harp was filling the air with strains that rang out even above the clamor of the tempest. It needed the tempest to bring out the music!

And have we not known men whose lives have not given out any entrancing music in the day of a calm prosperity, but who, when the tempest drove against them have astonished their fellows by the power and strength of their music?

Rain, rain
Beating against the pane!
How endlessly it pours
Out of doors
From the blackened sky—
I wonder why!

Flowers, flowers,
Upspringing after showers,
Blossoming fresh and fair,
Everywhere!
Ah, God has explained
Why it rained!

You can always count on God to make the "afterward" of difficulties, if rightly overcome, a thousand times richer and fairer than the forward. "No chastening ... seemeth joyous ... nevertheless afterward...." What a yield!

November 30

And seekest thou great things for thyself? seek them not: for, behold, I will bring evil upon all flesh, saith the Lord: but thy life will I give unto thee for a prey in all places whither thou goest (Jer. 45:5).

A promise given for hard places, and a promise of safety and life in the midst of tremendous pressure, a life "for a prey." It may well adjust itself to our own times, which are growing harder as we near the end of the age, and the tribulation times.

What is the meaning of "a life for a prey"? It means a life snatched out of the jaws of the destroyer, as David snatched the lamb from the lion. It means not removal from the noise of the battle and the presence of our foes; but it means a table in the midst of our enemies, a shelter from the storm, a fortress amid the foe, a life preserved in the face of continual pressure: Paul's healing when pressed out of measure so that he despaired of life; Paul's divine help when the thorn remained, but the power of Christ rested upon him and the grace of Christ was sufficient. Lord, give me my life for a prey, and in the hardest places help me today to be victorious. FROM DAYS OF HEAVEN UPON EARTH

We often pray to be delivered from calamities; we even trust that we shall be; but we do not pray to be made what we should be, in the very presence of the calamities; to live amid them, as long as they last, in the consciousness that we are held and sheltered by the Lord, and can therefore remain in the midst of them, so long as they continue, without any hurt. For forty days and nights, the Savior was kept in the presence of Satan in the wilderness, and that, under circumstances of special trial, His human nature being weakened by want of food and rest. The furnace was heated seven times more than it was wont to be heated, but the three Hebrew children were kept a season amid its flames as calm and composed in the presence of the tyrant's last appliances of torture as they were in the presence of himself before their time of deliverance came. And the livelong night did Daniel sit among the lions, and when he was taken up out of the den, "no manner of hurt was found upon him, because he believed in his God." They dwelt in the presence of the enemy because they dwelt in the presence of God.

December 1

There remaineth, therefore, a rest to the people of God (Heb. 4:9).
The rest includes victory, "And the Lord gave them rest round about; . . . the Lord delivered all their enemies into their hand" (Josh. 21:44).
He will beautify the meek with victory (Ps. 149:4, Rotherham, margin).

An eminent Christian worker tells of his mother who was a very anxious and troubled Christian. He would talk with her by the hour trying to convince her of the sinfulness of fretting, but to no avail. She was like the old lady who once said she had suffered so much, especially from the troubles that never came.

But one morning the mother came down to breakfast wreathed in smiles. He asked her what had happened, and she told him that in the night she had a dream.

She was walking along a highway with a great crowd of people who seemed so tired and burdened. They were nearly all carrying little black bundles, and she noticed that there were numerous repulsive looking beings which she thought were demons dropping these black bundles for the people to pick up and carry.

Like the rest, she too had her needless load and was weighed down with the Devil's bundles. Looking up, after a while, she saw a Man with a bright and loving face, passing hither and thither through the crowd and comforting the people.

At last He came near her, and she saw that it was her Savior. She looked up and told Him how tired she was, and He smiled sadly and said:

"My dear child, I did not give you these loads; you have no need of them. They are the Devil's burdens and they are wearing out your life. Just drop them; refuse to touch them with one of your fingers and you will find the path easy and you will be as if borne on eagle's wings."

He touched her hand, and lo, peace and joy thrilled her frame and, flinging down her burden, she was about to throw herself at His feet in joyful thanksgiving, when suddenly she awoke and found that all her cares were gone. From that day to the close of her life she was the most cheerful and happy member of the household.

> *And the night shall be filled with music,*
> *And the cares that infest the day,*
> *Shall fold their tents like the Arabs,*
> *And as silently steal away.*
>
> LONGFELLOW

December 2

Perfect through sufferings (Heb. 2:10).

Steel is iron *plus* fire. Soil is rock, *plus* heat, or glacier crushing. Linen is flax *plus* the bath that cleans, the comb that separates, and the flail that pounds, and the shuttle that weaves. Human character must have a *plus* attached to it. The world does not forget great characters. But great characters are not made of luxuries, they are made by suffering.

I heard of a mother who brought into her home as a companion to her own son, a crippled boy who was also a hunchback. She had warned her boy to be very careful in his relations to him, and not to touch the sensitive part of his life but go right on playing with him as if he were an ordinary boy. She listened to her son as they were playing; and after a few minutes he said to his companion: "Do you know what you have got on your back?" The little hunchback was embarrassed, and he hesitated a moment. The boy said:

"It is the box in which your wings are; and someday God is going to cut it open, and then you will fly away and be an angel."

Someday, God is going to reveal the fact to every Christian, that the very principles they now rebel against have been the instruments which He used in perfecting their characters and molding them into perfection, polished stones for His great building yonder. CORTLAND MYERS 🕊

Suffering is a wonderful fertilizer to the roots of character. The great object of this life is character. This is the only thing we can carry with us into eternity. . . . To gain the most of it and the best of it is the object of probation. AUSTIN PHELPS 🕊

By the thorn road and no other is the mount of vision won.

December 3

Is it well with thy husband? Is it well with the child? And she answered, It is well (2 Kings 4:26).

Be strong, my soul!
Thy loved ones go
Within the veil. God's thine, e'en so;
Be strong.

Be strong, my soul!
Death looms in view.
Lo, hear thy God! He'll bear thee through;
Be strong.

For sixty-two years and five months I had a beloved wife, and now, in my ninety-second year I am left alone. But I turn to the ever-present Jesus, as I walk up and down in my room, and say, "Lord Jesus, I am alone, and yet not alone—Thou art with me, Thou art my Friend. Now, Lord, comfort me, strengthen me, give to Thy poor servant everything Thou seest he needs." And we should not be satisfied till we are brought to this, that we know the Lord Jesus Christ experimentally, habitually to be our Friend: at all times, and under all circumstances, ready to prove Himself to be our Friend. GEORGE MUELLER 🕊

Afflictions cannot injure when blended with submission.

Ice breaks many a branch, and so I see a great many persons bowed down and crushed by their afflictions. But now and then I meet one that sings in affliction, and then I thank God for my own sake as well as his. There is no such sweet singing as a song in the night. You recollect the story of the woman who, when her only child died, in rapture looking up, as with the face of an angel, said, "I give you joy, my darling." That single sentence has gone with me years and years down through my life, quickening and comforting me. HENRY WARD BEECHER

E'en for the dead I will not bind my soul to grief;
Death cannot long divide.
For is it not as though the rose that climbed my garden wall
Has blossomed on the other side?
Death doth hide,
But not divide;
Thou art but on Christ's other side!
Thou art with Christ, and Christ with me;
In Christ united still are we.

December 4

He went up into a mountain apart (Matt. 14:23).

One of the blessings of the old-time Sabbath was its calm, its restfulness, its holy peace. There is a strange strength conceived in solitude. Crows go in flocks and wolves in packs, but the lion and the eagle are solitaires.

Strength is not in bluster and noise. Strength is in quietness. The lake must be calm if the heavens are to be reflected on its surface. Our Lord loved the people, but how often we read of His going away from them for a brief season. He tried every little while to withdraw from the crowd. He was always stealing away at evening to the hills. Most of His ministry was carried on in the towns and cities by the seashore, but He loved the hills the best, and oftentimes when night fell He would plunge into their peaceful depths.

The one thing needed above all others today is that we shall go apart with our Lord, and sit at His feet in the sacred privacy of His blessed presence. Oh, for the lost art of meditation! Oh, for the culture of the secret place! Oh, for the tonic of waiting upon God! SELECTED

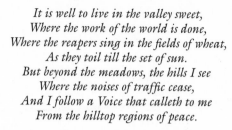

It is well to live in the valley sweet,
Where the work of the world is done,
Where the reapers sing in the fields of wheat,
As they toil till the set of sun.
But beyond the meadows, the hills I see
Where the noises of traffic cease,
And I follow a Voice that calleth to me
From the hilltop regions of peace.

Aye, to live is sweet in the valley fair,
And to toil till the set of sun;
But my spirit yearns for the hilltop's air
When the day and its work are done.
For a Presence breathes o'er the silent hills,
And its sweetness is living yet;
The same deep calm all the hillside fills,
As breathed over Olivet.

Every life that would be strong must have its Holy of Holies
into which only God enters.

December 5

O Lord, I know that the way of man is not in himself: it is not in
man that walketh to direct his steps (Jer. 10:23).
Lead me in a plain path (Ps. 27:11).

Many people want to direct God instead of resigning themselves to be directed by Him; to show Him a way instead of passively following where He leads. MADAME GUYON

I said: "Let me walk in the field";
God said: "Nay, walk in the town";
I said: "There are no flowers there";
He said: "No flowers, but a crown."

I said: "But the sky is black,
There is nothing but noise and din";
But He wept as He sent me back,
"There is more," He said, "there is sin."

I said: "But the air is thick,
And fogs are veiling the sun";
He answered: "Yet souls are sick,
And souls in the dark undone."

I said: "I shall miss the light,
And friends will miss me, they say";
He answered me, "Choose tonight,
If I am to miss you, or they."

I pleaded for time to be given;
He said: "Is it hard to decide?
It will not seem hard in Heaven
To have followed the steps of your Guide."

I cast one look at the field,
Then set my face to the town;
He said: "My child, do you yield?
Will you leave the flowers for the crown?"

Then into His hand went mine,
And into my heart came He;
And I walk in a light Divine,
The path I had feared to see.

GEORGE MacDONALD

December 6

Behold, I come quickly: hold that fast which thou hast, that no man take thy crown (Rev. 3:11).

George Mueller bears this testimony, "When it pleased God in July, 1829, to reveal to my heart the truth of the personal return of the Lord Jesus, and to show me that I had made a great mistake in looking for the conversion of the world, the effect that it produced upon me was this: From my *inmost soul* I was stirred up to feel compassion for perishing sinners, and for the slumbering world around me lying in the wicked one, and considered, 'Ought I not to do what I can for the Lord Jesus while He tarries, and to rouse a slumbering church?'"

There may be many hard years of hard work before the consummation, but the signs are to me so encouraging that I would not be unbelieving if I saw the wing of the apocalyptic angel spread for its last triumphal flight in this day's sunset; or if tomorrow morning the ocean cables should thrill us with the news that Christ the Lord had alighted on Mount Olivet or Mount Calvary to proclaim universal dominion. O you dead churches, wake up! O Christ, descend! Scarred temple, take the crown! Bruised hand, take the sceptre! Wounded foot, step the throne! Thine is the kingdom. REV. T. DeWITT TALMAGE, D.D.

It may be in the evening,
When the work of the day is done,
And you have time to sit in the twilight,
And watch the sinking sun,
While the long bright day dies slowly
Over the sea,
And the hours grow quiet and holy
With thoughts of Me;
While you hear the village children
Passing along the street—
Among those passing footsteps
May come the sound of My Feet.
Therefore I tell you, Watch!
By the Light of the evening star
When the room is growing dusky
As the clouds afar,
Let the door be on the latch
In your home,
For it may be through the gloaming
I will come.

December 7

Ye shall not see wind, neither shall ye see rain; yet that valley shall be filled with water, that ye may drink, both ye, and your cattle, and your beasts. And this is but a light thing in the sight of the Lord: He will deliver the Moabites also into your hand (2 Kings 3:16–18).

To human thinking it was simply impossible, but nothing is hard for God.

Without a sound or sign, from sources invisible and apparently impossible, the floods came stealing in all night long; and when the morning dawned, those ditches were flooded with the crystal waters and reflecting the rays of the morning sun from the red hills of Edom.

Our unbelief is always wanting some *outward sign*. The religion of many is largely sensational, and they are not satisfied of its genuineness without manifestations, etc.; but the greatest triumph of faith is to be still and know that He is God.

The great victory of faith is to stand before some impassable Red Sea, and hear the Master say, *"Stand still, and see the salvation of the Lord,"* and *"Go forward!"* As we step out without any sign or sound—not a wave-splash—and wetting our very feet as we take the first step into the waters, still marching on we shall see the sea divide and the pathway open through the very midst of the waters.

If we have seen the miraculous workings of God in some marvelous case of healing or some extraordinary providential deliverance, I am sure the thing that has impressed us most has been the quietness with which it was all done, the absence of everything spectacular and sensational, and the utter sense of nothingness which came to us as we stood in the presence of this mighty God and felt how easy it was for Him to do it all without the faintest effort on His part or the slightest help on ours.

It is not the part of faith to *question*, but to *obey*. The ditches were made, and the water came pouring in from some supernatural source. What a lesson for our faith!

Are you craving a spiritual blessing? Open the trenches, and God will fill them. And this, too, in the most unexpected *places* and in the most unexpected *ways*.

Oh, for that faith that can act by faith and not by sight, and expect God to work although we see no wind or rain. A. B. SIMPSON

December 8

Put on ... as the elect of God, ... kindness (Col. 3:12).

There is a story of an old man who carried a little can of oil with him everywhere he went, and if he passed through a door that squeaked, he poured a little oil on the hinges. If a gate was hard to open, he oiled the latch. And thus he passed through life lubricating all hard places and making it easier for those who came after him.

People called him eccentric, queer, and cranky; but the old man went steadily on refilling his can of oil when it became empty, and oiled the hard places he found.

There are many lives that creak and grate harshly as they live day by day. Nothing goes right with them. They need lubricating with the oil of gladness, gentleness, or thoughtfulness. Have you your own can of oil with you? Be ready with your oil of helpfulness in the early morning to the one nearest you. It may lubricate the whole day for him. The oil of good cheer to the downhearted one—Oh, how much it may mean! The word of courage to the despairing. Speak it.

Our lives touch others but once, perhaps, on the road of life; and then, mayhap, our ways diverge, never to meet again. The oil of kindness has worn the sharp, hard edges off of many a sin-hardened life and left it soft and pliable and ready for the redeeming grace of the Savior.

A word spoken pleasantly is a large spot of sunshine on a sad heart. Therefore, "Give others the sunshine; tell Jesus the rest."

We cannot know the grief
That men may borrow;
We cannot see the souls
Storm-swept by sorrow;
But love can shine upon the way
Today, tomorrow;
Let us be kind.
Upon the wheel of pain so many weary lives are broken,
We live in vain who give no tender token.
Let us be kind.

"Be kindly affectioned one to another with brotherly love" (Rom. 12:10).

December 9

For this our light and transitory burden of suffering is achieving for us a weight of glory (2 Cor. 4:17 WEYMOUTH).

"Is achieving for us. . . ." The question is repeatedly asked—Why is the life of man drenched with so much blood and blistered with so many tears? The answer is to be found in the word "achieving"; these things are achieving for us something precious. They are teaching us not only the way to victory, but better still the laws of victory. There is a compensation in every sorrow, and the sorrow is working out the compensation. It is the cry of the dear old hymn:

> *Nearer my God to Thee, nearer to Thee,*
> *E'en tho' it be a cross that raiseth me.*

Joy sometimes needs pain to give it birth. Fanny Crosby could never have written her beautiful hymn, "I shall see Him face-to-face," were it not for the fact that she had never looked upon the green fields nor the evening sunset nor the kindly twinkle in her mother's eye. It was the loss of her own vision that helped her to gain her remarkable spiritual discernment.

It is the tree that suffers that is capable of polish. When the woodman wants some curved lines of beauty in the grain he cuts down some maple that has been gashed by the ax and twisted by the storm. In this way he secures the knots and the hardness that take the gloss.

It is comforting to know that sorrow tarries only for the night; it takes its leave in the morning. A thunderstorm is very brief when put alongside the long summer day. "Weeping may endure for the night, but joy cometh in the morning." FROM SONGS IN THE NIGHT

> *There is a peace that cometh after sorrow,*
> *Of hope surrendered, not of hope fulfilled;*
> *A peace that looketh not upon tomorrow,*
> *But calmly on a tempest that it stilled.*
>
> *A peace that lives not now in joy's excesses,*
> *Nor in the happy life of love secure;*
> *But in the unerring strength the heart possesses,*
> *Of conflicts won while learning to endure.*
>
> *A peace there is, in sacrifice secluded,*
> *A life subdued, from will and passion free;*
> *'Tis not the peace that over Eden brooded,*
> *But that which triumphed in Gethsemane.*

December 10

If I am in distress, it is in the interests of your comfort, which is effective as it nerves you to endure the same sufferings as I suffered myself. Hence my hope for you is well-founded, since I know that as you share the sufferings you share the comfort also (2 Cor. 1:6–7).

Are there not some in your circle to whom you naturally betake yourself in times of trial and sorrow? They always seem to speak the right word, to give the very counsel you are longing for; you do not realize, however, the cost which they had to pay ere they became so skillful in binding up the gaping wounds and drying tears. But if you were to investigate their past history you would find that they have suffered more than most. They have watched the slow untwisting of some silver cord on which the lamp of life hung. They have seen the golden bowl of joy dashed to their feet, and its contents spilt. They have stood by ebbing tides, and drooping gourds, and noon sunsets; but all this has been necessary to make them the nurses, the physicians, the priests of men. The boxes that come from foreign climes are clumsy enough; but they contain spices which scent the air with the fragrance of the Orient. So suffering is rough and hard to bear; but it hides beneath it discipline, education, possibilities, which not only leave us nobler, but perfect us to help others. Do not fret, or set your teeth, or wait doggedly for the suffering to pass; but get out of it all you can, both for yourself and for your service to your generation, according to the will of God. SELECTED

Once I heard a song of sweetness,
As it cleft the morning air,
Sounding in its blest completeness,
Like a tender, pleading prayer;
And I sought to find the singer,
Whence the wondrous song was borne;
And I found a bird, sore wounded,
Pinioned by a cruel thorn.

I have seen a soul in sadness,
While its wings with pain were furl'd,
Giving hope, and cheer and gladness
That should bless a weeping world
And I knew that life of sweetness,
Was of pain and sorrow borne,
And a stricken soul was singing,
With its heart against a thorn.

Ye are told of One who loved you,
Of a Saviour crucified,
Ye are told of nails that pinioned,
And a spear that pierced His side;
Ye are told of cruel scourging,

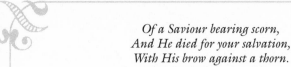

Of a Saviour bearing scorn,
And He died for your salvation,
With His brow against a thorn.

Ye "are not above the Master."
Will you breathe a sweet refrain?
And His grace will be sufficient,
When your heart is pierced with pain.
Will you live to bless His loved ones,
Tho' your life be bruised and torn,
Like the bird that sang so sweetly,
With its heart against a thorn?

Selected

December 11

Ye servants of the Lord, which by night stand in the house of the Lord. The Lord that made heaven and earth bless thee out of Zion (Ps. 134:1, 3).

Strange time for adoration, you say, to stand in God's house by night, to worship in the depth of sorrow—it is indeed an arduous thing. Yes, and therein lies the blessing; it is the test of perfect faith. If I would know the love of my friend I must see what it can do in the winter. So with divine love. It is easy for me to worship in the summer sunshine when the melodies of life are in the air and the fruits of life are on the tree. But let the song of the bird cease and the fruit of the tree fall, and will my heart still go on to sing? Will I stand in God's house by night? Will I love Him in His own right? Will I watch with Him even one hour in His Gethsemane? Will I help to bear His cross up the dolorous way? Will I stand beside Him in His dying moments with Mary and the beloved disciple? Will I be able with Nicodemus to take up the dead Christ? Then is my worship complete and my blessing glorious. My love has come to Him in His humiliation. My faith has found Him in His lowliness. My heart has recognized His majesty through His mean disguise, and I know at last that I desire not the gift but the Giver. When I can stand in His house by night I have accepted Him for Himself alone. George Matheson

My goal is God Himself, not joy, nor peace,
Nor even blessing, but Himself, my God;

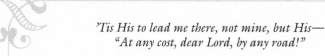

'Tis His to lead me there, not mine, but His—
"At any cost, dear Lord, by any road!"

So faith bounds forward to its goal in God,
And love can trust her Lord to lead her there;
Upheld by Him, my soul is following hard
Till God hath full fulfilled my deepest prayer.

No matter if the way be sometimes dark,
No matter though the cost be ofttimes great,
He knoweth how I best shall reach the mark,
The way that leads to Him must needs be straight.

One thing I know, I cannot say Him nay;
One thing I do, I press towards my Lord;
My God my glory here, from day to day,
And in the glory there my Great Reward.

December 12

The last drops of my sacrifice are falling; my time to go has come. I
have fought in the good fight; I have kept the faith (2 Tim. 4:6–7).

As soldiers show their scars and talk of battles when they come at last to spend their old age in the country at home, so shall we in the dear land to which we are hastening, speak of the goodness and faithfulness of God who brought us through all the trials of the way. I would not like to stand in the white-robed host and hear it said, "These are they that came out of great tribulation, *all except one*."

Would *you* like to be there and see yourself pointed at as the one saint who never knew sorrow? Oh, no! for you would be an alien in the midst of the sacred brotherhood. We will be content to share the battle, for we shall soon wear the crown and wave the palm. C. H. SPURGEON

"Where were you wounded?" asked the surgeon of a soldier on Lookout Mountain. *"Almost at the top,"* he answered. He forgot even his gaping wound—he only remembered that he had won the heights. So let us go forth to higher endeavors for Christ and never rest till we can shout from the very top, "I have fought a good fight, I have finished my course, I have kept the faith."

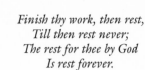

Finish thy work, then rest,
Till then rest never;
The rest for thee by God
Is rest forever.

God will not look you over for medals, degrees or diplomas,
but for scars.

Of an old hero the minstrel sang—

With his Yemen sword for aid;
Ornament it carried none,
But the notches on the blade.

What nobler decoration of honor can any godly man seek after than his scars of service, his losses for the crown, his reproaches for Christ's sake, his being worn out in his Master's service!

December 13

I will give thee the treasures of darkness (Isa. 45:3).

In the famous lace shops of Brussels, there are certain rooms devoted to the spinning of the finest and most delicate patterns. These rooms are altogether darkened, save for a light from one very small window, which falls directly upon the pattern. There is only one spinner in the room, and he sits where the narrow stream of light falls upon the threads of his weaving. "Thus," we are told by the guide, "do we secure our choicest products. Lace is always more delicately and beautifully woven when the worker himself is in the dark and only his pattern is in the light."

May it not be the same with us in our weaving? Sometimes it is very dark. We cannot understand what we are doing. We do not see the web we are weaving. We are not able to discover any beauty, any possible good in our experience. Yet if we are faithful and fail not *and faint not,* we shall some day know that the most exquisite work of all our life was done in those days when it was so dark.

If you are in the deep shadows because of some strange, mysterious providence, do not be afraid. Simply go on in faith and love, never doubting. God is watching, and He will bring good and beauty out of all your pain and tears. J. R. MILLER

The shuttles of His purpose move
To carry out His own design;
Seek not too soon to disapprove
His work, nor yet assign
Dark motives, when, with silent tread,
You view some sombre fold;
For lo, within each darker thread
There twines a thread of gold.

Spin cheerfully,
Not tearfully,
He knows the way you plod;
Spin carefully,
Spin prayerfully,
But leave the thread with God.

FROM THE CANADIAN HOME JOURNAL

December 14

His disciples said unto him, Lord, teach us to pray ... and he said
unto them, When ye pray, say ... Thy kingdom come (Luke
11:1–2).

When they said, "Teach us to pray," the Master lifted His eyes and swept the far horizon of God. He gathered up the ultimate dream of the eternal, and, rounding the sum of everything God intends to do in the life of man, He packed it all into these three terse pregnant phrases and said, "When you pray, pray after this manner."

What a contrast between this and much praying we have heard. When we follow the devices of our own hearts, how runs it? "O Lord bless *me*, then my family, my church, my city, my country," and away on the far fringe as we close up, there is a prayer for the extension of His kingdom throughout the wide parish of the world.

The Master begins where we leave off. The world *first*, my personal needs second, is the order of this prayer. Only after my prayer has crossed every continent and every far-flung island of the sea, after it has taken in the last man in the last backward race, after it has covered the entire wish and purpose of God for the world, only then am I taught to ask for a piece of bread for myself.

When Jesus gave His all, Himself for us and to us in the holy extravagance of the cross, is it too much if He asks us to do the same thing? No man or woman amounts to anything in the kingdom, no soul ever touches even the edge of the zone of power, until this lesson is learned that Christ's business is the supreme concern of life and that all personal considerations, however dear or important, are tributary thereto. DR. FRANCIS

When Robert Moffat, the veteran African missionary and explorer, was asked once to write in a young lady's album, he penned these lines:

> *My album is a savage breast,*
> *Where tempests brood and shadows rest,*
> *Without one ray of light;*
> *To write the name of Jesus there,*
> *And see that savage bow in prayer,*
> *And point to worlds more bright and fair,*
> *This is my soul's delight.*

And His Kingdom shall have no frontier (Luke 1:33, old Moravian version).

> *The missionary enterprise is not the church's afterthought;*
> *it is Christ's forethought.*
>
> HENRY VAN DYKE

December 15

Trust also in him (Ps. 37:5).

The word *trust* is the heart word of faith. It is the Old Testament word, the word given to the early and infant stage of faith. The word *faith* expresses more the act of the will, the word *belief* the act of the mind or intellect, but trust is the language of the heart. The other has reference more to a truth believed or a thing expected.

Trust implies more than this, it sees and feels, and leans upon a person, a great, true, living heart of love. So let us "trust also in him," through all the delays, in spite of all the difficulties, in the face of all the denials, notwithstanding all the seemings, even when we cannot understand the way, and know not the issue; still "trust also in him, and he will bring it to pass." The way will open, the right issue will come, the end will be peace, the cloud will be lifted, and the light of eternal noonday shall shine at last.

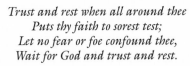

Trust and rest when all around thee
Puts thy faith to sorest test;
Let no fear or foe confound thee,
Wait for God and trust and rest.

Trust and rest with heart abiding,
Like a birdling in its nest,
Underneath His feathers hiding,
Fold thy wings and trust and rest.

December 16

And there was Anna, a prophetess ... which departed not from the temple, but served God with fastings and prayers night and day (Luke 2:36–37).

No doubt by praying we learn to pray, and the more we pray the oftener we can pray, and the better we can pray. He who prays in fits and starts is never likely to attain to that effectual, fervent prayer which availeth much.

Great power in prayer is within our reach, but we must go to work to obtain it. Let us never imagine that Abraham could have interceded so successfully for Sodom if he had not been all his lifetime in the practice of communion with God.

Jacob's all-night at Peniel was not the first occasion upon which he had met his God. We may even look upon our Lord's most choice and wonderful prayer with his disciples before His Passion as the flower and fruit of His many nights of devotion, and of His often rising up a great while before day to pray.

If a man dreams that he can become mighty in prayer just as he pleases, he labors under a great mistake. The prayer of Elias which shut up heaven and afterwards opened its floodgates, was one of a long series of mighty prevailings with God. Oh, that Christian men would remember this! Perseverance in prayer is necessary to prevalence in prayer.

Those great intercessors, who are not so often mentioned as they ought to be in connection with confessors and martyrs, were nevertheless the grandest benefactors of the church; but it was only by abiding at the mercy-seat that they attained to be such channels of mercy to men. We must pray to pray, and continue in prayer that our prayers may continue.
C. H. Spurgeon

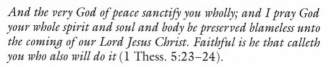

*And the very God of peace sanctify you wholly; and I pray God
your whole spirit and soul and body be preserved blameless unto
the coming of our Lord Jesus Christ. Faithful is he that calleth
you who also will do it* (1 Thess. 5:23–24).

Many years since I saw that "without holiness no man shall see the
Lord," I began by following after it and inciting all with whom I had intercourse to do the same. Ten years after, God gave me a clearer view than I ever
had before of the way to obtain it; namely, by faith in the Son of God. And
immediately I declared to all, "We are saved from sin, we are made holy by
faith." This I testified in private, in public, and in print, and God confirmed
it by a thousand witnesses. I have continued to declare this for above thirty
years, and God has continued to confirm my work. JOHN WESLEY (1771)

"I knew Jesus, and He was very precious to my soul; but I found
something in me that would not keep sweet and patient and kind. I did
what I could to keep it down, but it was there. I besought Jesus to do
something for me, and, when I gave Him my will, He came to my heart
and took out all that would not be sweet, all that would not be kind, all
that would not be patient, and then HE shut the door." GEORGE FOX

My whole heart has not one single grain, this moment, of thirst after
approbation. I feel alone with God; He fills the void; I have not one wish,
one will, one desire, but in Him; He hath set my feet in a large room. I
have wondered and stood amazed that God should make a conquest of all
within me by love. LADY HUNTINGTON

"All at once I felt as though a hand—not feeble, but omnipotent; not
of wrath, but of love—was laid on my brow. I felt it not outwardly but
inwardly. It seemed to press upon my whole being, and to diffuse all
through me a holy, sin-consuming energy. As it passed downward, my heart
as well as my head was conscious of the presence of this soul-cleansing
energy, under the influence of which I fell to the floor, and in the joyful surprise of the moment, cried out in a loud voice. Still the hand of power
wrought without and within; and wherever it moved, it seemed to leave the
glorious influence of the Savior's image. For a few minutes the deep ocean
of God's love swallowed me up; all its waves and billows rolled over me."
BISHOP HAMLINE

Holiness—as I then wrote down some of my contemplations on it—
appeared to me to be of a sweet, calm, pleasant, charming, serene nature,

which brought an inexpressible purity, brightness, peaceful-
ness, ravishment to the soul; in other words, that holiness made the
soul like a field or garden of God, with all manner of pleasant fruits and
flowers, all delightful and undisturbed, enjoying a sweet calm and the gentle vivifying beams of the sun. JONATHAN EDWARDS

Love's resistless current sweeping
All the regions deep within;
Thought and wish and senses keeping
Now, and every instant clean:
Full salvation! Full salvation!
From the guilt and power of sin.

December 18

In all these things we are more than conquerors through him that
loved us (Rom. 8:37).

The gospel is so arranged and the gift of God so great that you may
take the very enemies that fight you and the forces that are arrayed against
you and make them steps up to the very gates of heaven and into the presence of God.

Like the eagle, who sits on a crag and watches the sky as it is filling
with blackness, and the forked lightnings are playing up and down, and
he is sitting perfectly still, turning one eye and then the other toward the
storm. But he never moves until he begins to feel the burst of the breeze
and knows that the hurricane has struck him; with a scream, he swings his
breast to the storm and uses the storm to go up to the sky; away he goes,
borne upward upon it.

That is what God wants of every one of His children, to be more than
conqueror, turning the storm-cloud into a chariot. You know when one
army is more than conqueror it is likely to drive the other from the field,
to get all the ammunition, the food and supplies, and to take possession
of the whole. That is just what our text means. There are spoils to be taken!

Beloved, have you got them? When you went into the terrible valley of
suffering did you come out of it with spoils? When that injury struck you and
you thought everything was gone, did you so trust in God that you came out
richer than you went in? To be more than conqueror is to take the spoils from
the enemy and appropriate them to yourself. What he had arranged for your
overthrow, take and appropriate for yourself.

When Dr. Moon, of Brighton, England, was stricken with blindness, he said: "Lord, I accept this talent of blindness from Thee. Help me to use it for Thy glory that at Thy coming Thou mayest receive Thine own with usury." Then God enabled him to invent the Moon Alphabet for the blind, by which thousands of blind people were enabled to read the Word of God, and many of them were gloriously saved. SELECTED

God did not take away Paul's thorn; He did better—He mastered that thorn and made it Paul's servant. The ministry of *thorns* has often been a greater ministry to man than the ministry of *thrones*. SELECTED

December 19

It shall turn to you for a testimony (Luke 21:13).

Life is a steep climb, and it does the heart good to have somebody "call back" and cheerily beckon us on up the high hill. We are all climbers together, and we must help one another. This mountain climbing is serious business, but glorious. It takes strength and steady step to find the summits. The outlook widens with the altitude. If anyone among us has found anything worthwhile, we ought to "call back."

If you have gone a little way ahead of me, call back—
'Twill cheer my heart and help my feet along the stony track;
And if, perchance, Faith's light is dim, because the oil is low,
Your call will guide my lagging course as wearily I go.

Call back, and tell me that He went with you into the storm;
Call back, and say He kept you when the forest's roots were torn;
That, when the heavens thunder and the earthquake shook the hill,
He bore you up and held you where the very air was still.

Oh, friend, call back, and tell me for I cannot see your face;
They say it glows with triumph, and your feet bound in the race;
But there are mists between us and my spirit eyes are dim,
And I cannot see the glory, though I long for word of Him.

But if you'll say He heard you when your prayer was but a cry,
And if you'll say He saw you through the night's sin-darkened sky—
If you have gone a little way ahead, oh, friend, call back—
'Twill cheer my heart and help my feet along the stony track.

SELECTED

December 20

Yet I am not alone, because the Father is with me (John 16:32).

It need not be said that to carry out conviction into action is a costly sacrifice. It may make necessary renunciations and separations which leave one to feel a strange sense both of deprivation and loneliness. But he who will fly, as an eagle does, into the higher levels where cloudless day abides, and live in the sunshine of God, must be content to live a comparatively lonely life.

No bird is so solitary as the eagle. Eagles never fly in flocks; one, or at most two, ever being seen at once. But the life that is lived unto God, however it forfeits human companionships, *knows divine fellowship.*

God seeks eagle-men. No man ever comes into a realization of the best things of God, who does not, upon the Godward side of his life, learn to walk alone with God. We find Abraham alone in Horeb upon the heights, but Lot, dwelling in Sodom. Moses, skilled in all the wisdom of Egypt must go forty years into the desert alone with God. Paul, who was filled with Greek learning and had also sat at the feet of Gamaliel, must go into Arabia and learn the desert life with God. Let God isolate us. I do not mean the isolation of a monastery. In this isolating experience He develops an independence of faith and life so that the soul needs no longer the constant help, prayer, faith, or attention of his neighbor. Such assistance and inspiration from the other members are necessary and have their place in the Christian's development, but there comes a time when they act as a direct hindrance to the individual's faith and welfare. God knows how to change the circumstances in order to give us an isolating experience. We yield to God and He takes us through something, and when it is over, those about us, who are no less loved than before, are no longer depended upon. We realize that He has wrought some things in us, and that the wings of our souls have learned to beat the upper air.

We must dare to be alone. Jacob must be left alone if the angel of God is to whisper in his ear the mystic name of Shiloh; Daniel must be left alone if he is to see celestial visions; John must be banished to Patmos if he is deeply to take and firmly to keep "the print of heaven."

He trod the winepress alone. Are we prepared
for a "splendid isolation" rather than fail Him?

December 21

To him will I give the land that he hath trodden upon ... because he hath wholly followed the Lord (Deut. 1:36).

Every hard duty that lies in your path, that you would rather not do, that it will cost you pain and struggle or sore effort to do, has a blessing in it. Not to do it, at whatever cost, is to miss the blessing.

Every hard piece of road on which you see the Master's shoe-prints and along which He bids you follow Him, surely leads to blessing, which you cannot get if you cannot go over the steep, thorny path.

Every point of battle to which you come, where you must draw your sword and fight the enemy, has a possible victory which will prove a rich blessing to your life. Every heavy load that you are called to lift hides in itself some strange secret of strength. J. R. MILLER

I cannot do it alone;
The waves run fast and high,
And the fogs close all around,
The light goes out in the sky;
But I know that we two
Shall win in the end,
Jesus and I.

Coward and wayward and weak,
I change with the changing sky;
Today so eager and bright,
Tomorrow too weak to try;
But He never gives in,
So we two shall win,
Jesus and I.

I could not guide it myself,
My boat on life's wild sea;
There's One who sits by my side,
Who pulls and steers with me.
And I know that we two
Shall safe enter port,
Jesus and I.

December 22

Lo, an horror of great darkness fell upon him (Gen. 15:12).

The sun at last went down, and the swift, eastern night cast its heavy veil over the scene. Worn out with the mental conflict, the watchings, and the exertions of the day, Abraham fell into a deep sleep, and in that sleep his soul was oppressed with a dense and dreadful darkness, such as almost stifled him, and lay like a nightmare upon his heart. Do you understand something of the horror of that darkness? When some terrible sorrow which seems so hard to reconcile with perfect love, crushes down upon the soul, wringing from it all its peaceful rest in the pitifulness of God, and launching it on a sea unlit by a ray of hope; when unkindness and cruelty maltreat the trusting heart, till it begins to doubt whether there be a God overhead who can see and still permit—these know something of the "horror of great darkness." It is thus that human life is made up; brightness and gloom; shadow and sun; long tracks of cloud, succeeded by brilliant glints of light, and amid all divine justice is working out its own schemes, affecting others equally with the individual soul which seems the subject of special discipline. O ye who are filled with the horror of great darkness because of God's dealings with mankind, learn to trust that infallible wisdom, which is co-assessor with immutable justice; and know that He who passed through the horror of the darkness of Calvary, with the cry of forsakenness, is ready to bear you company through the valley of the shadow of death till you see the sun shining upon its farther side. Let us, by our Forerunner, send forward our anchor. Hope, within the veil that parts us from the unseen; where it will grapple in ground and will not yield, but hold until the day dawns, and we follow it into the haven guaranteed to us by God's immutable counsel. F. B. MEYER

The disciples thought that that angry sea separated them from Jesus. Nay, some of them thought worse than that; they thought that the trouble that had come upon them was a sign that Jesus had forgotten all about them and did not care for them. Oh, dear friend, that is when troubles have a sting, when the Devil whispers, "God has forgotten you; God has forsaken you"; when your unbelieving heart cries as Gideon cried, "If the Lord be with us, why then is all this befallen us?" The evil has come upon you to bring the Lord nearer to you. The evil has not come upon you to separate you from Jesus, but to make you cling to Him more faithfully, more tenaciously, more simply. F. S. WEBSTER, M.A.

Never should we so abandon ourselves to God as when He seems to have abandoned us. Let us enjoy light and consolation when it is His pleasure to give it to us, but let us not attach ourselves to His gifts, but to Himself; and when He plunges us into the night of *pure faith,* let us still press on through the agonizing darkness.

> *Oh, for faith that brings the triumph*
> *When defeat seems strangely near!*
> *Oh, for faith that brings the triumph*
> *Into victory's ringing cheer—*
> *Faith triumphant; knowing not defeat or fear.*
>
> HERBERT BOOTH

December 23

The journey is too great for thee (1 Kings 19:7).

And what did God do with His tired servant? Gave him something good to eat and put him to sleep. Elijah had done splendid work and had run alongside of the chariot in his excitement, and it had been too much for his physical strength, and the reaction had come on, and he was *depressed.* The physical needed to be cared for. What many people want is sleep and the physical ailment attended to. There are grand men and women who get where Elijah was—under the juniper tree! and it comes very soothingly to such to hear the words of the Master: "The journey is too great for thee, and I am going to refresh you." Let us not confound physical weariness with spiritual weakness.

> *I'm too tired to trust and too tired to pray,*
> *Said one, as the over-taxed strength gave way.*
> *The one conscious thought by my mind possessed,*
> *Is, oh, could I just drop it all and rest.*
>
> *Will God forgive me, do you suppose,*
> *If I go right to sleep as a baby goes,*
> *Without an asking if I may,*
> *Without ever trying to trust and pray?*
>
> *Will God forgive you? why think, dear heart,*
> *When language to you was an unknown art,*
> *Did a mother deny you needed rest,*
> *Or refuse to pillow your head on her breast?*

Did she let you want when you could not ask?
Did she set her child an unequal task?
Or did she cradle you in her arms,
And then guard your slumber against alarms?

Ah, how quick was her mother love to see,
The unconscious yearnings of infancy.
When you've grown too tired to trust and pray,
When over-wrought nature has quite given way:

Then just drop it all, and give up to rest,
As you used to do on a mother's breast,
He knows all about it—the dear Lord knows,
So just go to sleep as a baby goes;

Without even asking if you may,
God knows when His child is too tired to pray.
He judges not solely by uttered prayer,
He knows when the yearnings of love are there.

He knows you do pray, He knows you do trust,
And He knows, too, the limits of poor weak dust.
Oh, the wonderful sympathy of Christ,
For His chosen ones in that midnight tryst,

When He bade them sleep and take their rest,
While on Him the guilt of the whole world pressed—
You've given your life up to Him to keep,
Then don't be afraid to go right to sleep.

ELLA CONRAD COWHERD

December 24

And Isaac went out to meditate in the field at the eventide (Gen. 24:63).

We should be better Christians if we were more alone; we should do more if we attempted less and spent more time in retirement and quiet waiting upon God. The world is too much with us; we are afflicted with the idea that we are doing nothing unless we are fussily running to and fro; we do not believe in "the calm retreat, the silent shade." As a people, we are of a very practical turn of mind; "we believe," as someone has said, "in having all our irons in the fire, and consider the time not spent between the anvil and the fire as lost, or much the same as lost." Yet no time is more profitably spent than that which is set apart for quiet musing, for talking with God, for looking up to heaven. We cannot have too many of these open spaces in life, hours in which the soul is left accessible to any sweet thought or influence it may please God to send.

"Reverie," it has been said, "is the Sunday of the mind." Let us often in these days give our mind a "Sunday," in which it will do no manner of work but simply lie still, and look upward, and spread itself out before the Lord like Gideon's fleece, to be soaked and moistened with the dews of heaven. Let there be intervals when we shall do nothing, think nothing, plan nothing, but just lay ourselves on the green lap of nature and "rest awhile."

Time so spent is not lost time. The fisherman cannot be said to be losing time when he is mending his nets, nor the mower when he takes a few minutes to sharpen his scythe at the top of the ridge. City men cannot do better than follow the example of Isaac, and, as often as they can, get away from the fret and fever of life into fields. Wearied with the heat and din, the noise and bustle, communion with nature is very grateful; it will have a calming, healing influence. A walk through the fields, a saunter by the seashore or across the daisy-sprinkled meadows, will purge your life from sordidness and make the heart beat with new joy and hope.

The little cares that fretted me,
I lost them yesterday,
Out in the fields with God.

Christmas Eve

Bells Across the Snow

O Christmas, merry Christmas,
Is it really come again,
With its memories and greetings,
With its joy and with its pain!
There's a minor in the carol
And a shadow in the light,
And a spray of cypress twining
With the holly wreath tonight.
And the hush is never broken
By laughter light and low,
As we listen in the starlight
To the "bells across the snow."

O Christmas, merry Christmas,
'Tis not so very long
Since other voices blended
With the carol and the song!
If we could but hear them singing,
As they are singing now,
If we could but see the radiance
Of the crown on each dear brow,
There would be no sigh to smother,
No hidden tear to flow,
As we listen in the starlight
To the "bells across the snow."

O Christmas, merry Christmas,
This never more can be;
We cannot bring again the days
Of our unshadowed glee,
But Christmas, happy Christmas,
Sweet herald of good will,
With holy songs of glory
Brings holy gladness still.
For peace and hope may brighten,
And patient love may glow,
As we listen in the starlight
To the "bells across the snow."

FRANCES RIDLEY HAVERGAL

December 25

His name shall be called Emmanuel. . . . God with us (Matt. 1:23 RSV).
The Prince of Peace (Isa. 9:6).

There's a song in the air!
There's a star in the sky!
There's a mother's deep prayer,
And a baby's low cry!
And the star rains its fire
While the beautiful sing,
For the manger of Bethlehem cradles a King.

A few years ago a striking Christmas card was published, with the title, "If Christ had not come." It was founded upon our Savior's words, "If I had not come." The card represented a clergyman falling into a short sleep in his study on Christmas morning and dreaming of a world into which Jesus had never come.

In his dream he found himself looking through his home, but there were no little stockings in the chimney corner, no Christmas bells or wreaths of holly, and no Christ to comfort, gladden, and save. He walked out on the public street, but there was no church with its spire pointing to heaven. He came back and sat down in his library, but every book about the Savior had disappeared.

A ring at the doorbell, and a messenger asked him to visit a poor dying mother. He hastened with the weeping child and as he reached the home, he sat down and said, "I have something here that will comfort you." He opened his Bible to look for a familiar promise, but it ended at Malachi, and there was no gospel and no promise of hope and salvation, and he could only bow his head and weep with her in bitter despair.

Two days afterward he stood beside her coffin and conducted the funeral service, but there was no message of consolation, no word of a glorious resurrection, no open heaven, but only "dust to dust, ashes to ashes," and one long eternal farewell. He realized at length that "He had not come" and burst into tears and bitter weeping in his sorrowful dream.

Suddenly he woke with a start, and a great shout of joy and praise burst from his lips as he heard his choir singing in his church close by:

> O come, all ye faithful, joyful and triumphant,
> O come ye, O come ye to Bethlehem;
> Come and behold Him, born the King of Angels,
> O come let us adore Him, Christ, the Lord.

Let us be glad and rejoice today, because "He *has* come." And let us remember the annunciation of the angel, "Behold I bring you good tidings of great joy, *which shall be to all people,* for unto you is born this day in the city of David a Savior, which is Christ the Lord" (Luke 2:10–11).

> He comes to make His blessing flow,
> Far as the curse is found.

May our hearts go out to the people in heathen lands who have no blessed Christmas day. "Go your way, eat the fat, drink the sweet, and send portions unto them for whom nothing is prepared" (Neh. 8:10).

December 26

Sit ye here while I go and pray yonder (Matt. 26:36).

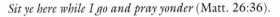

It is a hard thing to be kept in the background at a time of crisis. In the Garden of Gethsemane eight of the eleven disciples were left to do nothing. Jesus went to the front to pray; Peter, James, and John went to the middle to watch; the rest sat down in the rear to wait. Methinks that party in the rear must have murmured. They were *in* the garden, but that was all; they had no share in the cultivation of its flowers. It was a time of crisis, a time of storm and stress; and yet they were not suffered to work.

You and I have often felt that experience, that disappointment. There has arisen, mayhap, a great opportunity for Christian service. Some are sent to the front; some are sent to the middle. But *we* are made to lie down in the rear. Perhaps sickness has come; perhaps poverty has come; perhaps obloquy has come; in any case we are hindered and we feel sore. We do not see why we should be excluded from a part in the Christian life. It seems like an unjust thing that, seeing we have been allowed to enter the garden, no path should be assigned to us there.

Be still, my soul, it is not as thou deemest! Thou are *not* excluded from a part of the Christian life. Thinkest thou that the garden of the Lord has only a place for those who walk and for those who stand! Nay, it has a spot consecrated to those who are compelled to *sit*. There are three voices in a verb—active, passive, and neuter. So, too, there are three voices in Christ's verb "to live." There are the active, watching souls, who go to the front and struggle till the breaking of day. There are the passive, watching souls, who stand in the middle and report to others the progress of the fight. But there are also the neuter souls—those who can neither fight nor be spectators of the fight, but have simply to lie down.

When that experience comes to thee, remember, thou are not shunted. Remember it is *Christ* that says, "Sit ye here." *Thy* spot in the garden has *also* been consecrated. It has a special name. It is not "the place of wrestling," nor "the place of watching," but "the place of waiting." There are lives that come into this world neither to do great work nor to bear great burdens, but simply to be; they are the neuter verbs. They are the flowers of the garden which have had no active mission. They have wreathed no chaplet; they have graced no table; they have escaped the eye of Peter and James and John. But they have gladdened the sight of *Jesus*. By their mere perfume, by their mere beauty, they have brought Him joy;

by the very preservation of their loveliness in the valley they have lifted the Master's heart. Thou needst not murmur shouldst thou be one of these flowers! SELECTED

December 27

His soul entered into iron (Ps. 105:18).

Turn that about and render it in our language, and it reads thus, *"Iron entered his soul."* Is there not a truth in this? That sorrow and privation, the yoke borne in the youth, the soul's enforced restraint, are all conducive to an iron tenacity and strength of purpose, and endurance or fortitude, which are the indispensable foundation and framework of a noble character.

Do not flinch from suffering; bear it silently, patiently, resignedly; and be sure that it is God's way of infusing iron into your spiritual life. The world wants iron dukes, iron battalions, iron sinews, and thews of steel. *God wants iron saints;* and since there is no way of imparting iron to the moral nature but by letting people suffer, He lets them suffer.

Are the best years of your life slipping away in enforced monotony? Are you beset by opposition, misunderstanding, and scorn, as the thick undergrowth besets the passage of the woodsman pioneer? Then take heart; the time is not wasted; God is only putting you through the iron regimen. The iron crown of suffering precedes the golden crown of glory. And iron is entering into your soul to make it strong and brave. F. B. MEYER

> *But you will not mind the roughness nor the steepness of the way,*
> *Nor the chill, unrested morning, nor the searness of the day;*
> *And you will not take a turning to the left or the right,*
> *But go straight ahead, nor tremble at the coming of the night,*
> *For the road leads home.*

December 28

Rejoice in the Lord alway: and again I say, Rejoice (Phil. 4:4).

> *Sing a little song of trust,*
> *O my heart!*
> *Sing it just because you must,*

As leaves start;
As flowers push their way through dust;
Sing, my heart, because you must.

Wait not for an eager throng—
Bird on bird;
'Tis the solitary song
That is heard.
Every voice at dawn will start,
Be a nightingale, my heart!

Sing across the winter snow,
Pierce the cloud;
Sing when mists are drooping low—
Clear and loud;
But sing sweetest in the dark;
He who slumbers not will hark.

"An' when He hears yo' sing, He bends down wid a smile on His kin' face an' listens mighty keerful, an' He says, 'Sing on, chile, I hears, an' I's comin' down to deliber yo': I'll tote dat load fer yo'; jest lean hawd on Me and de road will get smoother bime by.'"

December 29

Arise ... for we have seen the land, and behold, it is very good; and are ye still? be not slothful to go, and enter to possess the land ... for God hath given it into your hands; a place where there is no want of anything that is in the earth (Judg. 18:9–10).

Arise! Then there is something definite for us to do. Nothing is ours unless we take it. "The children of Joseph, Manasseh and Ephraim, *took their inheritance*" (Josh. 16:4). "The house of Jacob shall *possess their possessions*" (Obad. 17). "The upright shall have good things *in possession.*"

We need to have appropriating faith in regard to God's promises. We must make God's Word our own personal possession. A child was asked once what appropriating faith was, and the answer was, "It is taking a pencil and underscoring all the me's and mine's and my's in the Bible."

Take any word you please that He has spoken and say, "That word is my word." Put your finger on this promise and say, *"It is mine."* How much of the Word has been endorsed and receipted and said, "It is done"? How many promises can you subscribe and say, "Fulfilled to me"?

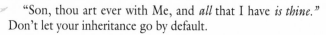

"Son, thou art ever with Me, and *all* that I have *is thine.*"
Don't let your inheritance go by default.

"When faith goes to market it always takes a basket."

December 30

Peter was kept in prison: but prayer [instant and earnest prayer] was made for him (Acts 12:5, margin).

Peter was in prison awaiting his execution. The church had neither human power nor influence to save him. There was no earthly help, but there was help to be obtained by the way of heaven. They gave themselves to fervent, importunate prayer. God sent His angel, who aroused Peter from sleep and led him out through the first and second wards of the prison; and when they came to the iron gate, it opened to them of its own accord, and Peter was free.

There may be some iron gate in your life that has blocked your way. Like a caged bird you have often beaten against the bars, but instead of helping, you have only had to fall back tired, exhausted, and sore at heart. There is a secret for you to learn, and that is *believing* prayer; and when you come to the iron gate, it will open of its own accord. How much wasted energy and sore disappointment will be saved if you will learn to pray as did the church in the upper room! Insurmountable difficulties will disappear; adverse circumstances will prove favorable if you *learn to pray,* not with your own faith but with the faith of God (Mark 11:22, margin). Souls in prison have been waiting for years for the gate to open; loved ones out of Christ, bound by Satan, will be set free when you pray till you definitely believe God. C. H. P.

Emergencies call for intense prayer. *When the man becomes the prayer* nothing can resist its touch. Elijah on Carmel, bowed down on the ground, with his face between his knees, that was prayer—the man himself. No words are mentioned. Prayer can be too tense for words. The man's whole being was in touch with God and was set with God against the powers of evil. They couldn't withstand such praying. There's more of this embodied praying needed. FROM THE BENT-KNEE TIME

"Groanings which cannot be uttered are often prayers which cannot be refused." C. H. SPURGEON

December 31

Hitherto hath the Lord helped us (1 Sam. 7:12).

The word "hitherto" seems like a hand pointing in the direction of the *past*. Twenty years or seventy, and yet "hitherto hath the Lord helped us!" Through poverty, through wealth, through sickness, through health; at home, abroad, on the land, on the sea; in honor, in dishonor, in perplexity, in joy, in trial, in triumph, in prayer, in temptation—"hitherto hath the Lord helped!"

We delight to look down a long avenue of trees. It is delightful to gaze from one end of the long vista, a sort of verdant temple, with its branching pillars and its arches of leaves. Even so look down the long aisles of your years, at the green boughs of mercy overhead and the strong pillars of lovingkindness and faithfulness which bear up your joys.

Are there no birds in yonder branches singing? Surely, there must be many, and they all sing of mercy received "hitherto."

But the word also points *forward*. For when a man gets up to a certain mark and writes "hitherto," he is not yet at the end; there are still distances to be traversed. More trials, more joys; more temptations, more triumphs; more prayers, more answers; more toils, more strength; more fights, more victories; and then come sickness, old age, disease, death.

Is it over now? No! there is more yet—awakening in Jesus' likeness, thrones, harps, songs, psalms, white raiment, the face of Jesus, the society of saints, the glory of God, the fullness of eternity, the infinity of bliss. Oh, be of good courage, believer, and with grateful confidence raise thy "Ebenezer," for,

> *He who hath helped thee hitherto*
> *Will help thee all thy journey through.*

When read in heaven's light, how glorious and marvelous a prospect will thy "hitherto" unfold to thy grateful eye. C. H. SPURGEON

The alpine shepherds have a beautiful custom of ending the day by singing to one another an evening farewell. The air is so crystalline that the song will carry long distances. As the dusk begins to fall, they gather their flocks and begin to lead them down the mountain paths, singing, "Hitherto hath the Lord helped us. Let us praise His name!"

And at last with the sweet courtesy, they sing to one another the friendly farewell: "Goodnight! Goodnight!" The words are taken up by the echoes, and from side to side the song goes reverberating sweetly and softly until the music dies away in the distance.

So let us call out to one another through the darkness, till the gloom becomes vocal with many voices, encouraging the pilgrim host. Let the echoes gather till a very storm of Hallelujahs breaks in thundering waves around the sapphire throne, and then as the morning breaks we shall find ourselves at the margin of the sea of glass, crying, with the redeemed host, "Blessing and honor and glory be unto him that sitteth on the throne and to the Lamb forever and ever!"

This my song through endless ages,
Jesus led me all the way.

AND AGAIN THEY SAID, HALLELUJAH! (Rev. 19:3 RV).

Acknowledgments

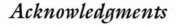

The compiler takes pleasure in acknowledging the kindness of authors and publishers who, very generously, have granted permission to use extracts from their copyrighted publications.

Among those to whom such acknowledgments are due are the following: to Fleming H. Revell Company for selections from the books of F. B. Meyer and Andrew Murray; to Dr. C. G. Trumbull for extracts from *Messages for the Morning Watch* and the *Sunday School Times;* to the Christian Alliance Publishing Company for quotations from *Days of Heaven upon Earth* and other publications, also excerpts from sermons and tracts by Dr. A. B. Simpson; and to Miss Annie Johnson Flint for her poems.

Indulgence is begged in case of failure to reach any other author or holder of copyrighted selections.

We want to hear from you. Please send your comments about this
book to us in care of the address below. Thank you.

ZondervanPublishingHouse
Grand Rapids, Michigan 49530
http://www.zondervan.com